ENGLISH HISTORIANS
ON THE
FRENCH REVOLUTION

ENGLISH HISTORIANS
ON THE
FRENCH REVOLUTION

BY

HEDVA BEN-ISRAEL

Senior Lecturer in Modern History at the
Hebrew University, Jerusalem

CAMBRIDGE
AT THE UNIVERSITY PRESS
1968

PUBLISHED BY
THE SYNDICS OF THE CAMBRIDGE UNIVERSITY PRESS

Bentley House, P.O. Box 92, 200 Euston Road, London, N.W.1
American Branch: 32 East 57th Street, New York, N.Y. 10022

© CAMBRIDGE UNIVERSITY PRESS 1968

Library of Congress Catalogue Card Number: 67-12259

Standard Book Number: 521 05389 7

Printed in Great Britain by
Spottiswoode, Ballantyne and Co. Ltd.
London and Colchester

IN MEMORY OF MY FATHER

CONTENTS

CONTENTS

PREFACE

It needs to be shown that the English historians of the French Revolution in the nineteenth century can legitimately be grouped together to form a school and to be studied as a connected group of writings. The study of historiography is by now an accepted field of inquiry and yet historians professing it often find it necessary to justify their interest. These apologies indicate the different approaches to the subject. Some study historiography as part of the history of ideas, that is, they examine historical writings for their *weltanschauung* or the general interpretation of history which they expound or betray. From this point of view the actual subject matter of the historical work examined is of subordinate importance. It is natural that many of the writings on the French Revolution lend themselves to this kind of inquiry since the Revolution was a focal point for many currents of thought and fertile ground for the growth of new ones.

There are also historians who follow the very process of the accumulation of knowledge and the appearance of new information, the growth of criticism and the changing historical versions, the discoveries and the contributions of documents and of scholars. This kind of study if applied to the whole of Revolutionary historiography would also reveal the expansion of interpretation. It would show how this historiography changed from a political debate to an ideological struggle. It would show how the Revolution, at first regarded as a flash of lightning, now born now dead, later appeared as the visible aspect of an invisible historical process which has no beginning and no ending. The notion of the Revolution expanded until it became identified with the whole process of history.

The method of studying the English historians cannot be the same as that which would be used in surveys of French Revolutionary historiography in its entirety. In studying the English historians of the French Revolution it is the historians and not their subject matter which must stand in the foreground, though at a further stage this very procedure enables us to get behind the historians and closer to the effect which the Revolution had on England. The English historians do not bring out the development of Revolutionary studies as a whole but they have a story of their own to tell.

It is a commonplace to talk of the last century as having been shaped by the French Revolution, but the greatest effects of the Revolution have been wrought through the power of words on paper. The assumption on which an investigation like this rests is that writing history is not a purely 'academic' activity detached from the course of 'real' history.

ix

It creates concepts which in themselves take part in the conscious life of societies. They are both a product of and an influence on the society of which they form a part. No historical description is complete without an account of the modes of historical thinking prevalent in a people or in a period concerning its own past or other historical phenomena. On this assumption it is often necessary to take into account 'bad' as well as good history writing, false as well as true, the poets and the novelists as well as the historians, publicists and politicians who have so often made new history out of their understanding of the old.

There were many direct ways in which the Revolution affected its posterity. Social and economic changes, legal and constitutional innovations survived 1815 and generated further change. There were also the less tangible influences, the results of personal experiences and impressions, of individual and national life, of suffering and elation, memories and traumas. They all affected history through the agency of a generation of men who lived through them. But the most far reaching effects of the Revolution down to our own day were surely wrought through historical consciousness and interpretation. The concrete and the psychological aftermath cannot explain the universal repercussions reverberating from the Revolution. Even in the actual period of upheaval it was the self consciousness and volubility of the Revolution that impressed the world, contributing much to the production of the events in the years after 1789, and determining the means by which those years were to acquire so great an influence over after-history, when the Revolution itself was supposed to have ceased to exist as an active force. To contemporaries, and still more to later generations, it has been through the historical medium that the Revolution could be felt and seen.

Reporters, spies, agents and diplomats may help to communicate some impressions of a Revolution that is taking place on the other side of the channel. Between these reports, however, and the mind of the great mass of people who stay at home, there were other intermediaries who really created the image of the Revolution that came to prevail in this country. By that same effect they helped indirectly to shape the course of British politics in the nineteenth century. The importance of public opinion in England, the existence of parties and religious sects, the resulting awareness of the relation between ideas and politics, between principles and life, made the English impression of the Revolution particularly significant from the very first. It seems that a larger part of the public was earlier interested in the Revolution and in its implications than was the case in other countries. The mass of learned and unlearned pamphlets on the subject support this impression.

No study connected with the French Revolution can claim to have exhausted relevant materials. The course of this historiography was interwoven with other streams of life and thought in England and in

Europe. It was affected by events no less than by writings, by historical as well as by political theory, by currents of thought, literary fashions, social and economic progress, moral and spiritual aspirations. No study can forge all the links; indeed it could go wrong in attempting. But it is possible to draw some attention to a continuous historical activity and to focal points in its course.

Since this study deals with writings produced over a century, the great variety of materials often imposes different approaches. The chapter on the Revolutionary decade, for instance, on which much has been written before, and the chapters analysing the historical minds of Croker or Acton may seem hardly to belong to the same book. But it is one of the objects of this study, though it treats different periods and writers in different ways, to bring out the continuity and connections in this large body of historical literature.

This study is based mainly on its direct sources, i.e. the English writings on the French Revolution. These are listed in the chronological bibliography (pp. 284–99) and in the special bibliographies for Smyth (p. 299), Carlyle (p. 300), Croker (p. 300) and Acton (p. 302). The fact that it covers a long period and a wide range of materials, and has had to take into account all sorts of historical influences as well as biographical data, made it necessary to consult a large number of books on nineteenth-century history, politics, literature, biography, of which only a fraction are mentioned in the footnotes. These sources include the writings on England and the French Revolution (e.g. by Brown, Cobban, Halévy, Laprade, Brinton) and the writings on general historiography (e.g. by Woodward, Gooch, Acton, Feuter, Geyl, Aulard, and others), though they do not as a rule cover the English historiography. A Russian work on this subject, by Kareiev, which was considered (by Brinton) the best of its kind, is typical in containing only a few and conventional remarks on Burke, Mackintosh and Carlyle.

JERUSALEM
1964
                                        H. B.-I.

Acknowledgements

This study was begun while I was a research student at Girton College, Cambridge, enjoying scholarships from the British Council and from Girton College. It was continued on periods of leave from the Hebrew University, Jerusalem. To all these my sincere thanks are due.

I am most deeply grateful to Professor Butterfield for his interest and encouragement, and for constant guidance, advice and criticism.

Parts of Chapters 5, 7 and 8 have appeared in similar form in 'Carlyle and the French Revolution', *The Historical Journal* (1958), vol. I, p. 115; 'Smyth on the French Revolution', *Journal of the History of Ideas* (1960), vol. XXI, p. 571; 'French Revolution and Romanticism in Historiography', *Iyyun* (1962), vol. 13, p. 91.

                                        H. B.-I.

ABBREVIATIONS

A.H.R.	*American Historical Review.*
Aulard, 'Carlyle'	A. Aulard, 'Carlyle Historien de la Révolution Française', *La Révolution française* (1912), LXII.
B.F.R.	*British and Foreign Review.*
Blackwood's	*Blackwood's Magazine.*
B.M.	British Museum.
B.Q.R.	*British Quarterly Review.*
C.M.H.	*Cambridge Modern History.*
C.R.	*Contemporary Review.*
C.U.L.	Cambridge University Library.
D.N.B.	*Dictionary of National Biography.*
D.R.	*Dublin Review.*
E.B.	*Encyclopaedia Britannica.*
E.C.S.	Acton, *Essays on Church and State.*
E.H.R.	*English Historical Review.*
E.R.	*Edinburgh Review.*
Fortnightly	*Fortnightly Review.*
F.Q.R.	*Foreign Quarterly Review.*
F.R.	*French Revolution.*
G.M.	*Gentleman's Magazine.*
Harrold	C. F. Harrold, 'Carlyle's General Method in *The French Revolution*', in *Publications of the Modern Language Association of America* (1928), XLIII, 1150–69.
H.E.S.	Acton, *Historical Essays and Studies.*
H.F.E.	Acton, *History of Freedom and Other Essays.*
H.F.R.	*Home and Foreign Review.*
H.Z.	*Historische Zeitschrift.*
Jennings	L. J. Jennings, *Croker Papers* (1884–5).
L.Q.R.	*London Quarterly Review.*
M.R.	*Monthly Review.*
N.B.R.	*North British Review.*
N.C.	*Nineteenth Century.*
Q.R.	*Quarterly Review.*
R.2.M.	*Revue des deux Mondes.*
Rév. fr.	*La Révolution française.*
R.H.	*Revue Historique.*
R.P.	Roscoe Papers.
R.Q.H.	*Revue des Questions Historiques.*
T.L.S.	*Times Literary Supplement.*

PART I

THE FORMATION OF A VIEW

CHAPTER I

THE FIRST DECADE

CURRENT HISTORY

In England, even more than in France, the history of the French Revolution was being written before the story of it was completed; more writings on the subject were produced in this country before 1800 than in any decade of the nineteenth century. Attempts at judgment and interpretation were made before the Revolution had shown the course it was to take, and only the *Annual Register*, at first, urged that it would be a better service to future historians to collect the facts. The first decade of writings is therefore a period of chaos when anything connected with the French Revolution—propaganda or imaginative literature in prose and verse— went under the name of history. The diversity of the early writings is due to the nature of the Revolution itself whose many aspects called forth journalistic, political, biographical and sentimental reactions.

The practical effect of the Revolution on the political attitudes and activities of English government and society has proved a fascinating subject to many historians. The voluntary reaction of a relatively free and disinterested country to the Revolution seemed a useful vantage point from which to view that eventful period. The study of English political history under the effect of the Revolution also provides an abundance of data on the questions so many historians posed concerning England's apparently traditional dislike of revolution. Again, in the course of the contemporary debate on the Revolution Burke, Paine, Mackintosh, Godwin, and later Malthus and Coleridge produced writings which remained classics in English political theory. The period moreover provided the literary historians with some prominent examples of political literature as well as literary politics.

All this makes the history of England in the last decade of the eighteenth century a fruitful field of study. The actual history of the period has been reconstructed with attention to foreign and theoretical influences, and the philosophy and literature produced during these years have been studied in relation to political and literary history. The one aspect of the period relatively neglected is the early growth of the historical study of the Revolution. The place of Burke or Paine in political theory has so transcended the actual events of the early 1790s that it seemed perhaps trivial to examine their great writings in relation to the precise stage in revolutionary history in which they were produced; and yet we know how strong and decisive the immediate effect of certain revolutionary

moments was on observers. In later generations historians of political
theory could conveniently treat the political writings of the whole decade
of revolution as if they all existed simultaneously as complete entities
each presenting a separate and complete attitude to the whole Revolution.
But the attitudes of contemporaries were formed under the daily influence
of news, fears, historical and journalistic accounts. The theoretic disquisi-
tions could only affect people in conjunction with concrete notions about
day-to-day events in France and in England. This is where the neglect
of the contemporary historical activity as distinguished from the political
theory has left a certain gap in our understanding of the period.

The historical self-consciousness of the Revolution—its loud acclama-
tions of its own importance and of its projected consequences—hurried
on the process by which the Revolution was to be transformed from
politics into history. The revolutionaries had strong though not consistent
feelings about their place in history. The idea recurs among them that the
Revolution would wipe out the past and inaugurate a new era in the story
of humanity. The revolutionaries, by their supreme confidence in their
power to turn history where they will, supplied their later enemies with
their strongest weapon against the heritage of the Revolutionary ideas.
The view of Condorcet, that history provided warning rather than
guidance, raised in the course of the Revolution efforts to abolish the
study of the past and to burn libraries and archives. It was, significantly,
the greatest enemy of the Revolution who rose to the challenge of this
historical self-consciousness; in accordance, as it were, with the Revolution's own wishes, he raised early, clearly and provocatively the question
of the connection between the Revolution and history. This was Burke's
contribution to historiography. He thus brought to the fore at once a
fundamentally historical, almost academic approach which historians
normally awaken to long after the event. The introspection of the Revolution and the philosophy of Burke together geared the contemporary
debate to the great historical questions of whether the Revolution was
a normal development or a catastrophe, a stage in political progress or
the release of infernal forces.

There were other causes which combined to produce an early appearance of historically minded writings on the French Revolution in
England and perhaps a more professional approach. The uneven
quality of works produced before 1800 is evident from any comparison
of Burke's *Reflections* with the sermon which provoked them or with
most of the replies which they in turn provoked. Apart from the political
debate in writings of which some remained classics of politics, there were
also writings like Young's *Travels* and Moore's *Journal* which contained
authentic information, and also descriptions and accounts which constitute early attempts at historical narratives, like the anonymous
Impartial History, Adolphus's *Biographical Memoirs* or the accounts in

4

the *Annual Register*.[1] This was not at all due to greater political objectivity. The connection between politics and history which had long been significant in this country was accentuated at this time, and in its way advanced the writing of history. In England knowledge of the events could not be so readily assumed as in France. The story, therefore, had to be told. Even for political purposes the actual narrative method was useful, and criticism of historical inaccuracies was useful propaganda.[2] A suitable version of revolutionary history did half the political work. Although professions of impartiality and pretensions to the use of original materials were lip service paid to historical conventions of long standing, the importance of the early writings is precisely in the extent to which proper history and criticism were attempted in spite of political controversy, distorted perspective and defective methods. As outsiders the English had to write from written sources rather than from memory, so that from the start they had to look for authorities and establish their trustworthiness. This was one of the reasons why, for example, the *Annual Register* for 1791 was delayed until 1795. Having 'copied from the best English channels of information', the letter which Louis XVI left in Paris on 20 June 1791, the editors realized that the document had been mutilated 'for the worst purposes of fraud'. They then found the original, made a new translation and printed both texts. They ascribed much importance to the affair and wrote that fabrications of this kind 'are more injurious to truth than volumes of misrepresentations and partial narratives, for it is by the test of documents that the merits of discordant accounts must be ultimately tried'. The editors add 'Introductory Remarks on the Falsities of the Common Translations', in which they analyse the motives of the falsifiers. It is alleged that they have omitted accounts of actions which are 'not altogether congenial to the old fashioned prejudices of Englishmen'. On the whole a comparison of the texts shows that the editors read perhaps too much into the alterations, but it is significant how strongly they felt the need to warn the public against 'a treacherous and malignant warfare by poisoning the springs of history'.[3]

Politicians soon became aware that the Revolution had created a wider reading public for political affairs and that there was a need to control the subject. The revolutionary generation itself had no doubt concerning the much debated question of the theoretic causes of the Revolution. The extraordinary outburst of political theory as well as the immediate reaction of the government and all parties attest to the widespread recognition of the great power of words over politics, and

---

[1] Probably written by R. Laurence. Also histories by Wollstonecraft, Gifford, Playfair, etc.

[2] 'To judge the information of those who have undertaken to guide and enlighten us' is the declared purpose of Burke's translation of Brissot's *Letter* (Brissot, *Letter*, p. xxxi). 'Realizing the truth will induce loyalty to England's rulers' (p. xxxiii).

[3] The *Annual Register* for 1791 (London, 1795), pp. v–vi, 131–5, 220, 217–20, 221–32.

of the nature of the Revolution as a 'philosophical' event. The government ran papers (like *The Sun* and *The Briton*) which offered suitable interpretations of events in France and went to great expense to procure news and maps.[1] Both sides knew the value of mere authoritative news. *Hog's Wash* (so named to remind people of Burke's contempt for the 'swinish multitude') wrote that a war against French principles would be useless without a law against 'the importation of News into Great Britain'.[2] The government also employed writers to explain, for instance, that the Revolution was a movement against religion, and it is well known that the most vigorous anti-Jacobin action was taken against booksellers and publications, i.e. against the bearers of revolutionary ideas.

BEFORE THE 'REFLECTIONS'

The writings which appeared before Burke's *Reflections* show that his influence on the historical understanding of the outbreak was not in proportion to his influence on the political attitude.[3] The reaction to the Revolution did not begin, like most accounts of it, in the summer of 1789, but in the previous year. The assumption that Englishmen were taken by surprise has to be modified by the evidence of the year 1788. The press reported French events regularly, sometimes complaining of the difficulty of procuring information. They quoted documents concerning the constitutional struggles in France and thought that these struggles would lead to a constitution like that of England. They wrote for instance that if, in assembling the States General the King of France succeeded in substituting for the silence of the old documents, the 'general opinion of his subjects', then the 'envied constitution of Great Britain will be transferred to France'. One of the comments of the *Gentleman's Magazine* was that a constitutional attitude had become prevalent in France, and it had given rise to hopes that could never again be vanquished. The reports in the periodicals of 1788 clearly detect an aristocratic revolt against the reforming measures of the King; they speak of insurrections produced by 'revolutionary writings', and of rumours of a bankruptcy, insidiously and 'industriously circulated'.[4] We thus have, before 1789, a scheme of the immediate causes of the outbreak in which the role of the reactionary *parlements* is not unjustly assessed.

The natural calamities of that year figure largely in the news and show that the element of 'fatality' in them, made much of later, was not entirely an afterthought. The *Annual Register* for 1790 wrote that the eclipse and hurricane of 1788 changed the character of the French nation; and again

---

[1] E.g. *The Sun*, 6 July 1792. [2] *Hog's Wash*, No. 2, 14 Sept. 1793.
[3] It is commonly accepted that Burke 'turned the tide' (Gooch, *C.M.H.*, VIII, 755).
[4] E.g. *G.M.* (July–Dec. 1788), LVIII, 448, 646, 736, 749, 1016, 1020, 1111.

that the severity of the winter hardened the people and made them cruel. Lecky, much later writes, 'Another agency, more terrible and more powerful than . . . political propagandism, was . . . hastening the Revolution . . . A great famine . . . a long drought . . . and a hailstorm . . . It would be difficult to exaggerate the importance of this famine among the causes of the French Revolution. It gave the movement its army . . . and savage earnestness.'[1]

The fact that 1788 was the centenary year of the Glorious Revolution had a lasting effect on the English attitude to the events in France after 1789. But preoccupation with 1688 was in itself the effect of a state of mind in England on the subject of reform. Most of those taking part in the debate on the French Revolution, on both sides, were reformers. Though the term radical was unused or used in abuse, Pitt had held radical principles on the subject of reform. On the other hand Cartwright and even Horne Tooke were conservative in the sense that they believed either that they were following the dictates of English history, or that they were restoring the constitution. It was thanks to the campaign for Parliamentary reform that societies for the commemoration of 1688 were formed mainly by Dissenters whose political and religious education and their roots in seventeenth-century political theory prepared them for the ideas, especially those of popular sovereignty and natural rights, proclaimed by the French. While the principles of a just Revolution were foremost in men's minds, events in France were easily and happily accepted. It was the entrance of the organized mob factor which later caused some reconsideration of the attitude in many people.

At first the general agreement about the Revolution existed which was to emerge again when the storm was over. The press of 1788 and 1789 on the whole accepted the need for changes in France and welcomed the attempts at reform, thus dissociating itself from the extreme anti-revolutionary view. The *Monthly Review* praises Calonne's proposal of reform which 'from its extraordinary spirit a Briton or American might be proud to own'. Some periodicals consistently supported the innovations proposed in the constitution of the States General, and some showed an enthusiasm which one would not have expected to find before the fall of the Bastille.[2] The numerous orations and sermons which celebrated the English Revolution mostly expressed political contentment. One, at the London Tavern, is notable for wishing success to France 'for the recovery of their liberty', and for its hope for an alliance in the interests of world freedom.

The account of the year 1789 in the *Annual Register*, written while Burke was still connected with it, presents a moderate view, and one

---

[1] Lecky, *A History of England* (new ed. 1892), VI, 344–6.

[2] E.g. *M.R.* (Jan.–June 1789), Appendix. 'May success attend the friends of freedom in every part of the globe.'

similar to that which emerges from the press of 1788. The struggles of the *parlements* appears as a revolt of the nobility against the King's innovations which, it is said, instead of strengthening his position, weakened his defences. The story of 1789 is the one which was to recur endlessly, a story of fatal concessions, the Orleanist faction, Necker's inactivity, the violent temper of Paris, the clumsy handling of 23 June, the folly of the court in attempting to use force. This basic pattern, and the more or less equal distribution of blame, did not undergo violent changes for some time. It was the contemporary English view of events in France. It is only when we reach the period of republican agitation in England that the nation seems split from top to bottom over French history. For there was a deep rift over practical political affairs, and the Revolution brought the views of irreconcilable extremes to the surface. Contemporaries described the dispute between Burke and Fox as a 'public schism, involving public principles of the first magnitude'.[1] But extremism remained an exception in political theory as it was in political life.[2] Most people's initial reactions to the French Revolution were mainly affected by the English reform movement which preceded the Revolution and by the French liberal presentations of their revolutionary aims in 1789. The violent voices soon to be heard were fierce reactions to two strong and new influences—the excesses in France and the awareness of a new situation for England in her foreign relations. They did not represent the beginnings of basically antagonistic historical schools. As long as the Revolution in France lasted the English view was still in the making.

The debate on the French Revolution took place on many different levels, as is clearly shown in Cobban's selection, and the Parliamentary debates contain as much historical thought as is to be found outside Parliament. The great and well-known speeches of Burke, Fox and Sheridan crystallize attitudes to be met with again and again.[3] It was mainly Fox's attitude which was to become common in England. It grew from pre-revolutionary English principles and not from the Revolution itself, and it was unhistorical in denying anything new in the principles of the French Revolution. When Burke spoke of anarchy in France Fox replied by balancing the crimes against past sufferings and future benefits. Sheridan claimed that the principles of the French Revolution were those of 1688 and that there had been no French constitution to overthrow. Some days later Burke spoke against the notion that the French were having an 'English' Revolution, Fox disclaimed any wish for a purely democratic government, Sheridan defended

[1] *Annual Register* (1791), pp. iv–v.
[2] 'They who do not dread it, love it', Burke wrote of the Revolution in his introduction to Brissot's *Letter*.
[3] E.g. *Parl. Hist.* XXVIII, 353–67, 367–70; XXIX, 366–88.

the *Assemblée* against Burke, and Pitt concluded the debate with hope for liberty and order in France.

The counter-revolutionary views in England did not all start in Burke's mind[1] and American alienation—it is interesting to note—had started even earlier. Franklin was alarmed by the news of July 1789; Washington, Jefferson and Morris thought the Revolution had gone far enough about the same time. Opinion in England was also changing in several ways. Burke himself, according to Lord Holland, turned against the Revolution after the suppression of the ecclesiastical revenues. Romilly left Paris in September 1789 already disappointed, though his final conversion was caused by the September massacres of 1792. On the other hand, the Birmingham mobs were activated by a fear of revolution in England which was widely considered excessive. The bulk of the people, including Pitt, had confidence in England's security and still judged France by the reports, more or less favourable, which most of the travellers brought back.

It was after the Parliamentary debates of February 1790, and against a background of still wide sympathy for the Revolution, that the *Reflections* came out in November 1790, and the heated war of writings burst forth in 1791.

BURKE AND THE CONTEMPORARY INTERPRETATIONS

It is necessary to distinguish between Burke's influence on politics and that on historiography. In the contemporary debate the political differences are much more striking than those on points of historical interpretation.[2] (Though in fundamental political views too, Burke's opponents did not consciously cross the lines which separated liberal reform from social revolution. Not even Paine, as later English socialists realized.) The one important historical point which was deeply controversial was that of the degree of novelty in the French Revolution and the corollary question of the degree of similarity between the French and English revolutions. Both questions were connected with that of the interpretation of the Glorious Revolution. No other differences in historical opinion—whether France had a constitution, whether its priests were God-fearing, whether the Queen was a modest woman or the court extravagant—none of these could raise a national storm of

---

[1] Brown shows that in Manchester, e.g., anti-revolutionary activities were organized before revolutionary ones.

[2] An anonymous contemporary in 1793 compiled *A Comparative Display of . . . British Writers on . . . the French Revolution.* His chapter headings are those of the *Vindiciae Gallicae* and Burke's opponents are given the last word. He quotes mainly from Burke, Mackintosh, Christie, Boothby, Belsham, Lofft, Priestley, Paine. There is no attention to chronology. Opinions are grouped on topics like: I. The State of France previous to the Revolution; II. The Excesses; III. The National Assembly; IV. The New Constitution, etc.

controversy in England. But the comparison with England—this was not an academic question but a vital problem involving a practical policy toward reform and change. It was a worthy cause for a thorough-going inquiry which was only ostensibly a debate on the French Revolution. It explains why the English debate started so early, so heatedly and, in a sense, so theoretically, on the signal given by Price's innocent provocation, 'Behold the light you have struck out, before setting America free, reflected in France, and then kindled into a blaze that lays despotism in ashes.'

To defend the French Revolution on the ground of its similarity to the English Revolution was to adopt a revolutionary interpretation of 1688. The implications are well known. In 1688 Parliament deposed one king and chose another and yet attempted to minimize whatever revolutionary notions the deed implied. The novel pattern was woven into the old fabric. The conservative interpretation said that the extraordinary measure had no precedent and was no model; it was forced by unique circumstances unlikely to be repeated; it did not mean that a right of deposition existed in the constitution. In this spirit Burke attacked Price's interpretation. In later editions of his *Discourse*, Price elaborated his claim that the Act of Settlement had laid down safeguards against future tyrants. Price interpreted the Act as a constitutional change giving new powers to Parliament. 'First; The right to liberty of conscience. . . . Secondly; The right to resist power when abused. And, Thirdly; The right to choose our own governors; to cashier them for misconduct; and to frame a government for ourselves.'[1]

On this interpretation the French seemed worthy though mild pupils of England. Burke's point of departure was his insistence on the absolute novelty of French principles. This question of novelty seemed the great problem in practical politics as well as in historical evaluation. Throughout a century of historical thinking the comparison between France and England penetrated English thought. It is posed again and again in increasingly complicated ways, dictated by new circumstances and new social theories, but always as a vital point of interpretation. The habit of thinking simultaneously on three distinct problems, the French Revolution, the Glorious Revolution, and the current question of reform, could never be dislodged. It is in this sense that Burke had the most far-reaching influence on the historiography of the Revolution. He 'set the terms of the whole subsequent discussion', as Cobban says, but he did not prescribe the English view.

The contemporary English writers on the Revolution prove the hopelessness of generalizing on any logical connection between practical attitudes to the Revolution and the philosophies behind those attitudes. There is no logical pattern in the way philosophical and historical ideas

[1] Price, *A Discourse* (5th ed. 1790), p. 34; Cobban, *Debate* (2nd ed. 1960), p. 61.

affected political views. More went into the making of individual attitudes than can be logically analysed. From the beginning there were not two opposite and consistent constructions, and theoretic confusion reigned in all political camps. At the root of Burke's anti-Revolutionism was what he hated as the intellectual presumption of the revolutionaries, their confidence that their wills and brains can direct world history. This went of course with Burke's deep reverence for the mysterious and accumulating wisdom of past ages, manifesting itself in the hallowed present, the ripe and natural fruit of history as designed by Providence. This is a common systematization of Burke's philosophy, but it is not because of it that men followed his banner. Educated men had been brought up on the enlightened belief in the beneficient powers of reason and philosophy. The words liberal and philosophical have almost synonymous connotations in the popular writings of the period. Most intelligent people shared Burke's belief that philosophy had its share in causing the Revolution, but where he saw a conspiracy of socially up-rooted intellectuals allied to soulless financiers, they saw philosophy, reason, and moral principle brought to bear on politics. And this to them was a great thing. 'The genius of philosophy is walking abroad', people said with Mrs Barbauld, and the motif is often repeated. Both Mackintosh and Mary Wollstonecraft stressed the attempts of the Revolution to redress real grievances but they also celebrated the happy union of politics and philosophy. Arthur Young, who had no love for visionary ideas, admitted that the existence of the grievances would not alone have brought about their redressing. The English revolutionaries living in France, toasting the Revolution and addressing the Convention, often said, 'You have taken up arms solely to make reason and truth triumph.' Miss Williams wrote with admiration of the revolutionaries that they were putting theory to practice and shaping the future on the principle that 'nothing which is morally wrong can be politically right'. This rationalist principle recurs endlessly in the writings of the period and is acclaimed by all sides as the greatest philosophical lesson of history. It is found in writers as late as Smyth and Alison. It is the essence of the belief in the power of reason to enthrone on earth the rule of moral good.

The same writers, however, also abandoned themselves to the impact of other sentiments. Even such a revolutionary as Miss Williams praised the French for what appear like Burkian qualities, such as distrusting reason alone and building on the sound foundations of men's habits.[1] The charges of 'political atheism' and cold rationalism, which later

---

[1] In 1792 she writes that living in France is living in a romance, that the age of chivalry has returned. She praises the French for wallowing in enthusiasm whereas the English are ashamed to weep during the performance of a tragedy (Williams, *Letters* (1792), pp. 4–5).

became the rallying point for Burke's converts, were scorned at the time. Both sides appealed to both reason and emotion, as did the revolutionaries in France. Miss Williams is a particularly apt example for this confused, romantic and rationalist revolutionism.

Miss Williams was like the popular image of a Girondin, without the violence and without the pessimism. Hers was the poetic brand of revolutionary sympathy, and she always stressed its emotional more than its rational basis. It is in the name of stark nature that others too, like Mary Wollstonecraft, Boothby, Parr, Paine, rebuke Burke in endless variations of Paine's deathless phrase: 'He pities the plumage, but forgets the dying bird.' In early revolutionary writings romanticism, which was to gain force from the anti-revolutionary sentiment, was at first favourable to the Revolution. It is amusing to trace the commonplaces of the time change hands between the pro- and anti-revolutionaries. The romantic notion, for instance, as Miss Williams put it in 1790 ('beauty rising out of confusion'), William Blake in 1791 ('to plant beauty in the desert craving abyss') and Hannah More in 1793 ('from the ruins of tyranny, and rubbish of popery a beautiful and finely framed edifice would in time have been constructed'), of good coming out of evil, was used for the defence of doubtful revolutionary phenomena.[1] The opposite view can be found, for instance, in Burke's preface to his son's translation of Brissot's *Letter to his Constituents*. It is the classical notion that beauty is achieved through orderly means. Another current coin was the phrase that, 'nothing which is morally wrong can be politically right'. The revolutionaries often quoted it at the idealistic outbreak of the Revolution. Their enemies later felt it had more appropriately become their weapon when the period of violence and terror set in. The sides changed ground and the revolutionaries were now defending the need for coercion and even for the shedding of blood. Miss Williams was credulous and muddled, but she exhibited prevalent feelings, and she shared the self-importance of the revolutionaries. Having spent much time in France she is an English example of that revolutionary mentality which various and incompatible ideals were firing with a restless and muddled enthusiasm during the early years of the Revolution. There was hero-worship for the King or Necker or the members of the States General; there was on the other hand the assertion of the common individual; there were horror and elation intensifying each other; there was the fascination with all that was 'new', and, at the same time, the idyllic belief in the restoration of man's ancient paradise. Miss Williams also represents the warring emotions of love for 'humanity' and hatred for its enemies, creating an inner tension which sometimes made for cruel fanaticism and sometimes, as with Miss Williams and other

[1] H. M. Williams describes a ceremony in which a twisted tree was burned and a tall straight one was made to rise from the ashes.

English observers, for self delusions. They often muse that, with no more blood, 'liberty would be bought cheaply'.

Burke's immediate effect was also practically emotional rather than the effect of a psychological theory of emotions. His patriotic panic for England won him adherents who cared little about his theories of human or of social development. Burke's emotional reaction to the personal tragedies was of the same sentimental quality as that of Miss Williams, even if it fed on different victims. Helped by the presence of the émigrés, it also had the more specific effect of early starting in England the sentimental approach to the personal stories of the victims which is usually associated with French Restoration writings. Those who refused to be swept by emotions and did care for theory and 'philosophy', like Mackintosh, reasoned against Burke and only became converted to him by the rational argument of experience. When they came round to his politics they at first distrusted his philosophy and always his history. Mackintosh, for instance, came to believe that the error of the revolutionaries was not that they had speculated but that they had speculated badly. ·

It is true that an antithetical philosophy to Burke's, a cold rationalistic creed, was preached by Godwin. And his wife, Mary Wollstonecraft, claimed that shuddering at crimes would distort our judgment of the Revolution. But Godwin's three-guinea book on *Political Justice*, though it exercised a profound influence on intellectual people for a short period, never became a best-seller; he disclaimed any wish for violence, and his eccentric disciples left him as soon as they reached the bottom of his thought. Coleridge, who in 1795 was still writing a sonnet to Godwin, 'O formed t'illume a sunless world forlorn', wrote the following year, 'I consider Mr Godwin's principles as vicious, and his book as a pander to sensuality. Once I thought otherwise.'[1]

Godwin's abstract theories were not formed by the Revolution; nor, like the abstract theories of Owen, were they likely to inspire revolution. He was, as Stephen called him, 'a quiet and amiable dreamer'.[2] Mary Wollstonecraft, on the other hand, was carried away by the event itself, but her idea that violence and crime were not organic to the Revolution, though crudely expressed by her, was shared by Mackintosh and in a more moderate form appears in the traditional outlook later to be held by Mill, Macaulay and Morley. This outlook insists on separate treatment for the various aspects of the Revolution; it allows praise for reforms and moral indignation at crimes. Mackintosh and Romilly

---

[1] *Morning Chronicle* (10 Jan. 1795); *The Watchman* (2 Apr. 1796); 'Forgive me, Freedom! O forgive those dreams', Coleridge sang in 1798.

[2] L. Stephen, *History of English Thought in the Eighteenth Century*, 2 vols. (London, 1881). Godwin, who was also called 'a casuist and a fanatic; a Jesuit and a Jacobin', recanted in 1801, through feeling and not thought as he explained, became religious and, in his words, 'John Bullish'.

practised Madame de Staël's injunction, to speak of the Revolutionary age 'as if it were already remote' more than twenty years before even she thought this possible. They separated the Revolution from the revolutionaries, the reforms from the excesses. This was to become the corner-stone of the English attitude to the French Revolution and it was this that Burke refused to accept.

The philosophical anarchy which reigned in the contemporary debate shows that political theory did not move parallel to political history. Surely Burke was right at least on this. The first decade of English writings on the Revolution brings out, on the one hand, the emergence of certain, almost 'pure', political systems. It demonstrates, on the other hand, the inconsistency of most of the writers who expounded these systems in great confusion while drawing on historical examples out of a quickly shifting scene which they misunderstood. It is useful to remember that, for instance, the belief in the novelty of the French principles was shared by the extreme defenders of the Revolution like Paine, and its extreme haters like Burke; that both Burke and Bentham, the authors of the truly polar traditions in nineteenth-century England, detested the French Revolution, that they both approached it as political empiricists equally repulsed by the philosophy of man's natural rights. According to Bentham, man possessed only legal rights. Burke, more metaphysically, said that man possessed only social and inherited rights. Bentham's devastating analysis of the Declaration of Rights as Anarchical Fallacies is no less condemnatory than Burke's attack. Nor did it prevent Bentham from unloading on revolutionary France a multitude of plans, legal and constitutional advice, frankly hoping that in an innovating régime they would have the chance of a trial.

Even before Bentham had written (and carefully concealed) his critique of the Declaration of the Rights of Man, Dumont, before any other Benthamite, expounded Bentham's criticism of that Declaration and of the Revolutionary spirit in general in the *Groenvelt Letters* of 1792 which were generally attributed to Romilly, another disciple of Bentham.[1] But Dumont had himself, as collaborator to Mirabeau, helped in the composition of a draft Declaration! And Dumont was later to write memoirs so moderate and conservative that in 1832 they supplied both reformists and anti-reformists with supports for their views. Dumont early contributed to the later comprehensiveness of the English view of the Revolution, as Madame de Staël was also to do. He signified the later combination of utilitarianism and the theory of rights which Bentham's theory rejected but which practical politics dictated and which in the hands of Bentham's disciples turned utilitarianism from a philo-

[1] Romilly wrote a few of the letters. Those by Dumont were translated by James Scarlett, later Lord Abinger. After Romilly's disappointment in the Revolution, he burned the *Letters*.

sophic system to a political force in English Radicalism round 1830. The Radicals of 1830 admired both Bentham and the sentimentalities of the Girondins which he abhorred. In a review of Brissot's *Memoirs* (1830) in the *Westminster*, the Girondins are extolled as pure and consistent while Marat and Robespierre are dismissed as monstrous and contemptible. Brissot's view is quoted that 'Bentham beheld the breaking forth of our Revolution with pleasure'.[1] The philosophic inconsistencies were as irrelevant to practical politics as they were to historical interpretation. It is almost true to say that the more confused the philosophy, the more effective the history. Those contemporaries who, like Mackintosh (or Priestley), expressed the Whig reaction to the Revolution, expounded their approval by referring both to the theory of utility and to that of natural rights. 'When I assert that a man has a right to life, liberty etc. I only mean to enunciate a *moral maxim*, founded on *general interest*, which prohibits any attack on these possessions . . . all rights, natural as well as civil, arise from expediency'.[2] This was philosophically muddled, but historically it was important in several ways. It reflected the multitude of theories affecting revolutionary France itself as well as the ambiguous and empiricist nature of the general English reaction. It is significant that Mackintosh, who like Bentham erred in imagining the French to be amenable to English guidance and tuition, unlike Bentham hotly defended the Revolution. A poor philosopher, he realized the many-sided and lasting effects of events in France, invited his readers to 'place the scene of the French Revolution in a remote age' for the correction of 'moral optics',[3] and did in fact anticipate the view of the Revolution which was to last Englishmen for generations to come.

Burke's contribution to the historiography of the event was that he treated the Revolution in its widest historical context. He detected underlying tendencies which others did not see. His historical insight was not an unmixed blessing. We know now how closely he was connected with the counter-revolution. Practically it can be claimed that his influence served as a more subtle kind of Brunswick manifesto to push the Revolution to excesses and to guide it (through warnings and prophecies) into the condemned channels it might have missed.[4] Arthur Young wisely wrote in 1792 of the abuse of France in the English press,

---

[1] *Westminster* (Apr. 1831), XIV, 332.

[2] Mackintosh, *Vindiciae*, 216–17.

[3] Mackintosh, *Vindiciae*, 195. Mme de Staël, in *Considerations* (London, 1818), I, 2, proposed to speak of the revolutionary age 'as if it were already remote'.

[4] 'If ever a foreign prince enters into France, he must enter it as into a country of assassins. The mode of civilized war will not be practised: nor are the French, who act on the present system entitled to expect it' (Burke, *A Letter to a Member of the National Assembly* (1791), p. 37).

that it was both unfair and imprudent to enrage the French people who were in a position to act against 'contumely'.

In the interpretation of the Revolution Burke, through his long-sightedness, started the tendency to interchange meaning with cause and result with motive, which gave rise to two common errors. One was to exaggerate the influence of philosophy on the outbreak of the Revolution and to charge that philosophy with political objectives of which it was innocent; the other was to misjudge actors and thinkers in the light of results they did not seek. It is nevertheless Burke's achievement that, by broadening the field, he made such errors possible.

The teaching of Burke was not immediately heeded and the proportion of writings against him is overwhelming. In France too, as A. Young observed to his surprise, most writings were for the Revolution and none against.[1] In the course of 1792, in connection with events in France and with policy in England, the change occurred. The massacres of September did what 10 August had not done: completed Romilly's alienation from the Revolution.[2] The French decree of November, which called nations to revolt, finally made Pitt panic and also enhanced the literary campaign against revolution. Sir William Maxwell, who had sympathized with the Revolution, now employed writers to show that it was bent on the destruction of Christianity.

When the war and the Terror came, the fulfilment of Burke's prophecies heightened his reputation as an historian. It was characteristic of the early defenders of the Revolution that they defended it on grounds that they could not maintain for long. They said, for instance, that it was not anti-religious, that it did not follow a purely rationalistic code of morals, that there was no violence on a large scale, that there was no aggressiveness towards other countries. The temporary advantages which Burke's opponents derived from his exaggerations soon turned against them. It now seemed less important if Burke had claimed that France had a perfect constitution before 1789, or if he imagined the Revolution to be the result of a conspiracy on the part of the *philosophes*. What mattered was that he had foreseen the aggression, tyranny, violence and denial of liberty. Burke's opponents, after having derived some effect by 'proving' that Burke was chastising the Jacobins as 'regicides' when 'the King is alive and chooses his ministers from among them', or seeing irreligion in a régime which had granted toleration to Protestants, often had, in subsequent editions or even before their replies reached the press, to eat their words, and insert feeble excuses for events whose existence

[1] A. Young, *Travels* (ed. 1900), p. 153.

[2] In May 1792 Romilly wrote that his conviction that the Revolution was a glorious event was unshaken by the excesses (Romilly, I, 349). On Sept. 1792 he wrote to Dumont, 'How could we ever be so deceived in the character of the French nation as to think them capable of liberty?' It is then that he speaks of the 'republic of tigers'.

they had emphatically denied.[1] As Mr Fox was reputed to have said, 'Burke is often right, only he is right too soon'.[2]

The dramatic events of 1792, the war, 10 August, the September Massacres, the establishment of the Republic, the November decree, the threat to England, prompted narratives and discussions, but towards the end of the year the point of the debate was changing; it was no longer the academic question of how one should judge the Revolution but whether one should make war on it. The political rather than the historical issue now came to the fore. Later, with regicide, war and the growing influence of Burke, writings on the Revolution tended again to become moral treatises. The diminution of contact with France, and the reversal of the Revolution's policy of a free press, made it more easy for writers to take this course. Paris was cut off even for official information between 1793 and 1794, and the internal history of France in those years was less known than that of previous revolutionary years.

England was frightened of French history. The Whigs had dreaded the execution of the French King as the ruin of their party. The 'respectable classes' were afraid of appearing disloyal. Paine's writings were at the height of their popularity and liberals refused to read them. Sympathy with the Revolution wandered to the half-educated whose motives were not the same as in the case of the philanthropists and the reformers who had espoused 1789; it lost in breadth and became dogmatic. Moderate sympathy was silent and extreme revolutionism was not represented in historical writings. The embittered émigrés now supplanted the liberal travellers as channels of information and 'authority' passed to those who knew émigrés and shared their feelings. Isolated works now reflected a decided anti-revolutionism.

The year 1794 was important in the story of the English reaction. The state trials, anti-Jacobinism, violent Republicanism and passions in general were at their height. It was naturally the year for dramatic recantations. It was also a year rich in histories. A vituperative anonymous history of Robespierre came out, probably by Gifford the anti-Jacobin. But this was also a favourable moment for sympathizers with

---

[1] T. Cooper, *A Reply to Mr Burke's Invective* . . . (1792). (On 30 April 1792 Burke had referred in Parliament to men who entered 'into an alliance with a set in France of the worst traitors and regicides . . . the Jacobins . . . the names he alluded to were Thomas Cooper and James Watt' (*Parl. Hist.* XXIX, 1322–3); see also XXX, 552: 'Mr Cooper and Mr Watt . . . kissed the bloody cheek of Marat.') A footnote in Cooper's second edition adds that since his reply had been written, the king's treachery had compelled the nation to depose him.

J. Courtenay's *Philosophical Reflections* (1790) is a satirical work pretending to preach submission. It 'proves' from history that to preserve life and property one should submit them cheerfully and that the French abolished Christianity by tolerating Protestants.

Miss Williams, in addition, insisted at first that the revolutionaries retained their urbanity, politeness and culture and were not, as was said in England, 'barbarous levellers'.

[2] Quoted by Cobban, *Debate*, p. 100 from *Diaries and Letters of Madame d'Arblay*, ed. C. Barrett (1904), V, 91–3.

the early revolution, who had been bewildered and stupified by the Terror, to catch their breath and derive new hope for revolutionism from the fall of Robespierre. This is the theme of Coleridge's *Fall of Robespierre*. Arthur Young was rewriting in a new spirit and Mary Wollstonecraft came out with a *History*.[1] There was a collection of State Papers, Richard Burke's translation of Brissot's *Letter*, a very influential anonymous *Impartial History* and an almost identical account in the *New Annual Register*. It declared its politics as Whig, its aim as impartiality, and its historical method to be guided by utility rather than by ornament.

THE RUNNING COMMENTATORS

Of special interest are those writings which, like the *Deux Amis* in France, presented, over a number of years, a changing reaction. The writings of Miss Williams, Arthur Young, and the *Annual Register* are of this kind. Miss Williams's letters written between 1790 and 1796[2] show how she who was enthusiastic about the Revolution grew to hate the Jacobins who imprisoned her and almost executed her, without renouncing the Revolution, or confessing to any error of judgment. Had she been challenged on the point, she could even, like Arthur Young, have pointed to the apprehensions which the first outbursts of violence had aroused in her.[3] The main interest of her letters is in their mixed and overflowing sentiments, but some of her descriptions are the accounts of an observant eye-witness. We get, for instance, a full and intimate description of the Federation; the preparations, decorations, order of procession, the King's oath, Lafayette's refusal to order the performance to be repeated, the wet weather; and she hopefully repeats the phrase then coined, 'la révolution Françoise est cimentée avec de l'eau, au lieu de sang'.[4]

Arthur Young is of incomparably higher value. His *Travels* are an important document (though much garbled in editions and translations), and the essays which he continued to write, though less known, are the best informed and thoughtful contemporary study of the events, as well as an expert's economic commentary. Morley wrote that Young's writings were worth more than Burke, Paine and Mackintosh put together.[5] Young is sometimes thought of as one of the extreme converts, mainly because of his pamphlet, *The Example*. But even in 1789 when

[1] In *Four New Letters of M. Wollstonecraft and H. M. Williams* (Berkeley, 1937), there is a request from M.W. to her American friend John Barlow for revolutionary materials. Her thesis is that the Revolution is a 'natural consequence of intellectual movement'. The violence she traces to previous cruelty in quelling riots.

[2] Miss Williams went to France in 1788 to stay with a sister married to a French Protestant minister Athanes Coquerel. Her nephew was in possession of her manuscripts in 1830.

[3] 'For the first time, I lamented the Revolution', she wrote in 1790, at the sight of the 'lanterne' (Williams, *Letters* (1790), p. 81).

[4] *Ibid.* p. 15. On Miss Williams see also above, pp. 11–12.

[5] Morley, *Burke*, 162.

he described a grim picture of the condition of the French peasantry he had also warned that the people would make ill use of freedom. In an essay probably written over several months from 1791 to 1792,[1] a fair and thorough study of the Revolution, he approved of some political aspects of the Revolution and exposed professionally the economic measures. He did not see enough protection to property and disliked the *assignats*. Young studied a collection of Revolutionary materials made by Liancourt and was the first serious student of the *cahiers*, a source of great importance which was long-after neglected. He claimed that the *cahiers* clearly demanded that the Assembly should assume power and undertake widespread attack on abuses. This he wrote against the arguments of both Burke and Calonne, but Young, like Burke, stressed the great danger to property from those who have political power without having property. He defined the problem of modern politics as that of making both freedom and property secure.[2] Young saw with prophetic assurance that the Revolution would spread to Europe and be more harmful there. The mischief and anarchy, he foresaw, would be in proportion to the lack of preparedness on the part of governments. In April 1792 he added a note that if the Germans won in Europe, England would be endangered. England, he felt, should support France for it held the balance of the world. Young's prognostications stood far above the common level of writings. 'The revolution and anti-revolution parties of England have', he felt ,'exhausted themselves on the French question.' When the war broke out he foresaw that neither the lack of discipline nor the financial derangement would matter to France because every man, woman and child would be fighting.[3] In this he proved a better prophet than Burke, whose reputation suffered temporarily from the success of French arms.

Arthur Young was in the main stream of English Revolutionary studies though much ahead of his time in his method. He claimed, as others did, that it was those who remained sympathetic towards the French Revolution, after it had changed its principles, who were guilty of inconsistency. He saw the necessity for changes and yet saw them go too far, and he always traced the excesses partly to past oppression and partly to the nature of all mobs. Young gives a grim picture of the state of the peasantry, based on acute observation. He could never go back on his clear verdict that anyone studying the old régime cannot deny the absolute necessity of revolution, especially since he made that verdict

[1] In different places in the essay we find 'the present moment 1791' and 'this moment March 1792'.

[2] Young insists on the distinction between France and America in this respect. In America all property is safe, in France none and in England only half as proved by the Birmingham riots. Only those intent on spreading revolution confuse the French and American systems. But Young wonders whether America will stay virtuous after it amasses riches.

[3] Young wrote this on 26 April 1792 after hearing of the war.

when already fully aware of the dangers of the Revolution. He was not at all sure that 'Experiment' was altogether unnecessary in politics although he speaks in June 1789 of the strange appeal to 'ideal and visionary rights of nature'. He knew that grievances alone could not have started the Revolution. He wanted Europe to meet the Revolution half-way and he early said that the merit of the Revolution was that of destruction, words so often repeated in England, e.g. by Macaulay in 1832. Another typically Whig principle in Young is that governments which reject 'all innovations lest they should lead to greater', will be swept away. Above all he saw clearly the predominance, the danger, and the failure of the principle of equality in the Revolution. He early argued with Frenchmen that the overwhelming power of the *Tiers Etat* which they declared might result in a bad constitution and he was always answered that the people must have the power to do good whatever use they make of it. Young's *Travels* were printed by order of the Convention and distributed among the communes. It is said that they had a practical influence.

The *Annual Register* for the revolutionay years is important as a conscious contemporary history written for posterity, as the nearest approach to an official attitude, as widely read then, and extensively used later. Its writers realized the importance of the events and showed something like a sense of historical responsibility. They took care in compiling documents and investigating facts, bearing in mind future historians. They claimed to have used 'immediate and original authorities' wherever possible, otherwise, the best 'authenticated accounts'.[1] They also had private information from persons 'actively engaged in the scenes'. The French Revolution made writers aware of the difficulties of writing contemporary history. The *Monthly Review* also wrote that, 'even in tranquil times it is difficult to obtain the strict historical truth', for politicians see to it that history is falsified before it reaches the public; that only an impartial mind can detect deception in newspapers and pamphlets; that posterity will understand better 'the sources and springs of that movement which subverted the French monarchy'. The *Annual Register* even earlier discusses the problem at some length, suggesting that since the duty of writing contemporary history is so delicate when there is no implicit evidence and no cool reader, perhaps it should not be considered amiss in a contemporary historian not to have a 'view' at all but laboriously to collect all ascertained facts, 'compare all, collect from all, but surrender his judgment to none'. The future historian will then be able to use these collections and 'dispose them in harmonious

[1] The regular chapter on French history was left out of the volume for 1791 in order that it might not be hastily compiled.

The *Annual Register* for 1792 claimed to have used about 200 publications connected with the Revolution, 'occasionally referring in the notes to the various sources, from whence our information was derived'.

masses'. Contemporaries cannot value the importance of events since new information will bring new light, as is daily happening. One of its guiding principles, that 'the best testimony is that which witnesses furnish against themselves', was later, by means of private papers, used to refute most of the *Annual Register*'s sources, as for instance, the memoirs of Bouillé and Dumouriez. Another principle, that of accepting only such documents or statements as are 'admitted or at least uncontradicted' by those whose interest is to refute them, also shows the awareness of criticism and yet the insufficiency of the tests. When we analyse sections in the *Annual Register* we see the futility of its historical aspirations; it appears to have been produced largely by putting together whole passages from recent publications, especially the memoirs, published in England, of Bouillé, Dumouriez, Dr Moore, Bertrand and others.[1] But its aspirations for a detached and critical treatment of facts had a sobering effect in the midst of violent partisanship. The pattern of the history told in the *Annual Register* is influenced by one of its chief sources, the *Deux Amis* of the earlier years which is generally of bourgeois tone, pro-king, anti-court, against violence (even though violence was due to oppression), anti-clerical without being anti-religious, anti-extremist and hopeful, in the spirit of 1789.

ADOLPHUS

The first writer to try to reassemble the story retrospectively in the way the historian does was Adolphus, whose *Biographical Memoirs* came out in 1799 and his *History* in 1803. Adolphus received much praise, e.g. from Windham, Croker, and Malmesbury.[2] His real merit was that in his work the suspicion of news and writings, which had already existed since the beginning of the Revolution, and the constant effort of party writers on both sides to discredit each other's narratives, had matured into a critical method. His incentive for writing, according to his own account, was his dissatisfaction with the prevailing system of misrepresentation, abuse and recrimination, and with the self-eulogy of the memoir-writers. He tested memoirs against other narratives, and he claimed that defenders of the Revolution had used the memoirs indiscriminately, and they had imposed on a public which had neither the leisure nor the disposition to check their authorities. Adolphus proposed to do precisely this, to compare discordant accounts and draw results 'warranted by circumstances and authorities'. In order to avoid the imputations of 'intended error' he will advance no unauthenticated assertion, thus

---

[1] The section on the flight to Varennes, when analysed, proves to have been made up of large extracts out of Bouillé, Bertrand, Moore, J[eudi] D[u] G[our] Limon.

[2] E. Henderson, *Recollections of John Adolphus* (London, 1871), p. 96 ; Malmesbury, *Recollections*, p. 101; Croker, 'Robespierre'.

giving his work a claim over the 'political romances' appearing daily.

In Adolphus we have an early example of the tendency to criticize books and judge between them in an attempt to verify fact. Adolphus writes as one would expect a later generation to write, he believes himself far enough removed from the event, and he claims that the springs of action are disclosed. 'What has usually formed the researches of subsequent generations, and been slowly produced under the name of secret history, now stands unveiled.' The diligent inquirer now has before him private motive as well as public conduct. If Adolphus seems over satisfied with scanty and sometimes worthless materials, it is not because he had no notion of the use of sources. He actually limited the scope of his work by the nature of his materials and he knew that information depended on historical circumstances. The discovery he made, and which gave him such confidence in his sources, was that 'secret history' was brought into the open by the struggles for life between the revolutionary factions. In the course of violent recriminations facts were revealed which in temperate discussions 'would have been studiously secreted'. Burke had written in 1794 that with Brissot's manifesto 'the whole mystery of the French Revolution was laid open in all its parts'.[1] But Adolphus saw that it is by collating conflicting evidence that something new may be extracted from them. After Robespierre's fall, wrote Adolphus in 1799, conditions changed and it would take another revolution to throw that period into the light and to reveal the mysteries which baffle research. Adolphus was thus the first to understand the peculiar value as sources of the ephemeral publications. The fact that hints on motives of individuals and parties could be derived from their apologies and recriminations, was later to make Croker's collections so important.

Among early English students of the Revolution, the best researchers were its haters. They seem to have had a more urgent need to fall back, through detailed research, on facts, perhaps because the appeal of the opposite school was denied them. Burkianism did not yet have the makings of a popular creed. Educated people had been brought up on liberal principles and did not easily renounce them. They disbelieved some of the horrors and overrated royalist distortion. Minute criticism such as that of Adolphus was effective, and some historians later marvelled how many of the horrible and disbelieved accounts proved in the end to have been correct.

Adolphus had of course a strong political bias. In the *Memoirs* he said that his object was to expose tyranny and hypocrisy, to trace the effect of individuals and of principles which together under the pretence of improving the conditions of mankind subverted the social order. In the *History* his aim was 'to collect facts, to arrange them clearly and place

[1] Brissot, *Address*, p. xxx.

22

them in such a view that the observations to which they give rise may seem rather to originate in the mind of the reader than to flow from the author', but his practice was not quite as deceitful as his theory might suggest.

Adolphus makes a curious distinction between history and biography when he says that to trace the influence of the economists and philosophers is the task of an historian, and not of a biographer like himself. In dealing with the causes of the Revolution Adolphus did not therefore choose to go into economic calculations or, as he put it, to speculate whether the abuse of monastic vows provoked the excesses of the revolutionaries. He said that the principal causes were the American war, the King's reforms and the ambitions of Mirabeau, Necker and Orleans. The last named remained for Adolphus the villain of the piece. He blamed the philosophers only for a turbulent state of mind but thought they could have been restrained. He held that a strong government could have restrained the disruptive influences.

Adolphus supported his statements by many references to most of the French (especially Bertrand's) and English writings known at the time. He had some oral information from émigrés (he later met Dumouriez and, oddly, entertained Garat). Much of his effort is directed at the refutation of English Whig versions, such as that of the *Impartial History*, by discrediting their sources (e.g. Rabaut). Adolphus did not become a proper student of the Revolution, as Croker was to be, and he did not continue to study it systematically or to bring his work up to date. He visited France in 1820 and the journal he kept then, and which is partly published in his *Recollections*, shows that he was emotionally fascinated by the French Revolution. He revived scenes and collected anecdotes but rewrote nothing. His best historical efforts were devoted to English history where he had more influence with subsequent historians. His judiciousness and fairness in English history have caused his French writings to be dismissed as biased. But the best in Adolphus, the care for fact, the explanation of motive and character, are as evident in his work on France. He was the first to show that the Revolution must be carefully studied and not merely argued about. In 1799 he said that the memoirs are not to be trusted as sources, and he began the critical examination of historians. Perhaps his greatest contribution lay in his confessions of ignorance. As Croker—who was stimulated by Adolphus— said, Adolphus at least identified problems. Driven by a political bias he prepared the separation between politics and history.

CHAPTER 2

HISTORY IN TIME OF WAR

The Napoleonic period is often left out of historiographical accounts. It is a sterile period in history-writing in general, the dead silence which followed the battle over the practical interpretation of the course of history, and preceded the outburst of historical consciousness and activity after the Restoration. In France the Imperial régime censored writings, greatly limited the activities of historians and encouraged those who wrote about recent history to represent the Revolution as an intermediate phase of anarchy which was happily brought to an end by the First Consul.

England had the advantage of freer inquiry and a somewhat calming political temper. The events of the French Revolution suffered a recess in historians' (and most peoples') minds at a time when Napoleon's conquests and meteoric rise were astounding contemporaries. The great European changes imparted to pre-Napoleonic history the character of outdated news. All previous history shrank to parish importance as Burke had said of an earlier period. The Revolution was generally referred to as 'the origins of the war' and its internal history was given negligible space in the chiefly military histories of the period. The darkness which shrouded the inner workings of the Revolutionary machine during the dictatorships preceding Napoleon's was now even less penetrable. Although English historians were wary of Napoleon's 'court historiographers' they had little authentic information of their own on anything except military history, which therefore flourished at the time and remained a favourite subject afterwards.

The interest in the military campaigns occasionally led to a wider interest in the relations of the Revolution with Europe in general. J. Bigland's voluminous writings, constantly revised, re-edited and translated, are an example of this new tendency to present the Revolution in its European context. In his *Sketch* Bigland's view is clearly European. His analysis of the climate of opinion before the Revolution, of a social structure drained of its social reality, of the twofold influence which the American Revolution had on France (the financial burden and the Republican example), was probably read by future historians. Bigland's main efforts in military history make him a remote ancestor of historians like Fyffe and Holland Rose. The absence of party spirit, of moralizing, the concise intelligent arrangement of material, also make his book the first English textbook for the history of the period, of the kind which became more common later and reached its best standard in Morse

Stephens. The pattern laid by Bigland for the progression of the Revolution itself was also to become fairly common: the *philosophes* disseminated but did not create the new spirit; the *parlements* were rebellious, the middle classes inexperienced and the people inflamed; when he humbled England in America Louis XVI was digging his own grave; the States General ushered in the crisis it was meant to prevent; the nation on the whole wanted constitutional monarchy but the rivalry between the executive and legislature made for greater reliance on the mob; mutual fear banished wisdom, and in times of peril the middle course proved the most dangerous policy; the King's flight from the Civil Constitution justified distrust in him and created the republican opportunity. As for French relations with Europe, Bigland realized that there were mysteries, e.g. about the Mantua affair, and he condemned the Brunswick manifesto. The European powers, instead of supporting the constitutionalists inside France, united France against them and by their military successes caused the massacres and the republic. France submitted to ferocious tyranny because of the invasion, and under military pressure made long strides in science and tactics. Bigland, like other liberals, protested against the confusion of reformers and revolutionaries in England, claimed that the danger to England was exaggerated and that the unnecessary war was provoked by England.

Apart from such general work the period is more significantly characterized by some inquiries into the diplomatic origins of the war; by the historical criticism which was applied to new works on the Revolution; and above all by the emergence of the typical English attitude to the Revolution.

DIPLOMATIC STUDIES

The study of the origins of the war emerged through the endless debate in parliament, in pamphlets, in histories and in poems on whether England should fight France. Since 1792, two features of British views on France had been significant. With regard to the Revolution there was a variety of shades of criticism and a vague but growing consensus of opinion on some basic issues. On the practical issue of war or peace, however, little ambiguity was possible, and opinion was more clearly divided, though the line of division did not always coincide with the line dividing the political parties. As time went on the attitude to the war embraced more and more factors which had nothing to do with the initial causes of the war or with the principles of the French Revolution. Economic factors and Napoleon's territorial ambitions loomed large, and the war had become a vested interest and a motive force in itself. People debating war or peace after 1800 did not always argue from the French Revolution. The debate was influenced by an intricate set of motives, opinions and calculations. English opinions about Napoleon form a large subject in themselves.[1] The personal estimates of Napoleon; the old sympathies or hatreds of the Revolution; the views held on the connection between Napoleon and the Revolution; the patriotism fanned by the war; the new nationalist feelings raised by the war; the old and new activities of the 'Jacobins' and the friends of Napoleon in Britain; the speculations about his world-wide plans of conquest; these and many more factors constantly acted on each other in the most inconsistent combinations to produce a multitude of reactions all coloured by prejudice, ignorance, interest, imagination and monetary passions. English opinions on Napoleon can therefore hardly be reduced to any hard lines and even on the favourite question of whether he was the heir or the destroyer of the Revolution the party writers were hopelessly muddled, changing their ambiguous views under the influence of the latest news or the current political debate.

On the one aspect of this subject which interests us here, on the influences which now affected the interpretations of the early French Revolution, it is possible to make some general remarks. To many, Napoleon was 'a clever desperate Jacobin, even Terrorist', as Malmesbury called him in 1796,[2] and 'a successful Jacobin', in 1803. The *anti-Jacobin*, the fiercest of Jacobin-baiters in England, turned against Napoleon with violence, while some revolutionary societies turned to him with hope. To the extreme revolutionaries, therefore, as well as to the extreme Tories, Napoleon often (but not always) embodied the spirit of the Revolution. Most groups held more complicated views. The important debates of 1800 in Parliament bring out the fact that his haters were on the whole less inaccurate in their estimates of his intentions. Lord Holland, Fox and Hazlitt were always making wrong guesses about his love of peace. Pitt at first hoped for anti-revolutionary gains in England from Napoleon's undisguised absolutist tendencies, and Canning hoped that Napoleon would lead to the restoration of the monarchy in France. Coleridge in 1800 disliked the *coup d'état* but liked the resulting absolute power, and Southey declared that Napoleon made him anti-Gallican. Fox, Sheridan and Mackintosh admitted the act of usurpation but claimed that France, because she was steeped in anarchy, needed and wanted it. Tory opinion was more united concerning Napoleon than Whig opinion. Tories now stressed the necessary identity of Revolution and Despotism, and hated both in Napoleon. Whigs sometimes defended him as a stabilizing influence, sometimes condemned him as a king, but on the whole were silent in the interest of patriotism. Many of them detested his dictatorial régime and it helped many former friends of France and antagonists of the war to resolve their painful conflict of loyalties to both liberty and patriotism by enabling them to view Napoleon as the

[1] See F. J. Maccunn, *The Contemporary English View of Napoleon* (London, 1914).
[2] Malmesbury, *Diaries* (London, 1944), IV, 233.

destroyer and not as the heir to the liberal Revolution. They dissociated Napoleon from the liberal Revolution and denounced his tyranny. They could assume a patriotic position without losing face and without renouncing liberty. Anyone could wish England to defeat its national enemy, more especially when that enemy was an absolute ruler, without condemning the early French Revolution outright and even without justifying the early coalitions' wars. When Napoleon's Empire appeared as a violation of the principles of the early Revolution the latter gained by comparison. The more tyrannical Napoleon became at home and the more aggressive abroad, the easier it became for English liberals to de-nounce his régime and his aggression and yet to extol the early Revolution and the Anglophile reformers who were believed to have started it. One could question the justness of the original war against France whether one wanted to decide present-day issues by that argument or, on the contrary, wished to stress the complete novelty of the present war against Napoleon.

We know that the conflict concerning Napoleon was a very real one for certain Whigs. The Cambridge historian Smyth, who had been steadily moving away from revolutionary enthusiasm since 1789, reached a point after 1800 when his inner conflict between his love of peace and his patriotism became so painful that he begged his friend Roscoe, the historian and the politician who retained both his extreme reformist opinions and also his pro-French sympathies, to spare him any talk about the war because Roscoe's abuse of England made him (Smyth) 'quite wretched'.[1] It shows the conflict and confusion in the historian's mind that in a letter on the subject he both rebukes Roscoe's belief in Napoleon's 'disposition to be at peace' and at the same time supplies him with an argument for his forthcoming pamphlet for peace, that 'Mr Fox always contended that Buonaparte would suppose that he [Buonaparte] should never be considered as a regular sovereign till he had remained so some time in a state of peace'.[2]

This complicated set of feelings and debates on Napoleon, war and Revolution was the occasion for an early attempt to study from the records the outbreak of war, made by Herbert Marsh, a theologian, politician, Bishop and Cambridge Professor. He was one of the foremost men in Cambridge in his time and a formidable divine. He was 'accus-tomed to laborious and accurate investigations' through his writings on theology and his training in the new German methods in biblical criti-cism, and he used his qualities in a political work written in Germany which was meant to exculpate England in the eyes of Germany from the charge of having started the war. His thesis was simply that Pitt was naturally anxious to preserve neutrality but the French needed war and resolved on having one while their emissaries were negotiating peace.

[1] R.P. 4576, 1 Jan. 1806.   [2] R.P. 4597, 15, 16 July 1810.

The proof ranges over two volumes which constitute a brief more than a history, but which for that reason employ detailed documentary criticism. Marsh is able to show that the French themselves believed in England's sincere wish for neutrality. Bouillé's evidence is quoted to show that the French were fully aware of the emptiness of the Pilnitz threat because the condition for action—England's connivance—was known to be non-existent. The King of Sweden wrote to Bouillé that he feared English opposition. Even Brissot said on 20 October 1791 that England was trying to calm the 'Diet against France'. Marsh shows that it is only after 10 August 1792 that charges against England were made in France. Brissot himself admits as much. He shows that not even the English proclamations made in May 1792 were regarded by the French as intended against themselves. Even when Gower left Paris on the King's deposition, Le Brun still hoped for the continuation of English neutrality. Marsh is less convincing when he claims that the Bills which followed the French Declaration of 19 November were of a strictly internal character, even though he can quote Kersaint as saying as late as 1 January 1793 that Pitt did not want war.

In his second volume Marsh is mainly concerned with exposing the falsity of French diplomatic interpretations of the decree of 19 November offering help to rebellious peoples, and that of 15 December 1792 declaring as enemies of France all unrevolutionary countries. The latter decree Marsh held to be a formal declaration of war. With great zeal, but less dexterity, Marsh exposes the hypocrisy of Chauvelin in his correspondence with Pitt in which he tried to explain away the offensive decrees. For this he has recourse to a letter of Le Brun rejoicing at insurrections in Germany (caused by the decree), to public speeches, and to the argument that Chauvelin had in any case proved faithless in Holland and Belgium. Marsh thus reveals his scarcity of direct documentary evidence on this point as well as his own indiscriminate use of public statements as evidence of foreign policy. Both his bias and his ignorance of the internal history of the Revolution come out in his analysis of the French motives in seeking war (hatred of kings as kings, belief that revolutionary principles are already triumphant in other countries) and in his account of the French parties. The Jacobins, he says, were illiterate anarchists whereas the Girondins were men of talent and education. Marsh was far more successful in diplomatic reconstruction than in political analysis, though he made the generalization that in a shuffle between two unprincipled parties the one which goes to greater lengths wins through its appearance of consistency. He thought that both French parties wanted war but later accused each other of having provoked it.

Apart from English pamphlets (e.g. by Belsham, Erskine and Bowles), Marsh's work resulted from a controversy in some German papers. Marsh apparently converted his German opponents to his view. His work was later translated into English, had great success, gained Marsh a pension from Pitt and a proscription from Napoleon. It launched him on a prolonged duel of 'refutations' and 'vindications' against the Foxite Whig Belsham, who had little of Marsh's critical ability. Marsh's work, though obviously biased in its political motive, remained for long the authoritative contemporary defence of England's part in the war.[1] Marsh also presents an example of pure conservatism in church and state. Though influenced by German methods of research and though obviously intending to arouse nations to war there was not a whiff of German romanticism or metaphysics about him. His minute work was later used by eminent historians—like Lecky, for instance—to the end of the century, and some of his conclusions were later supported by the archives. In England it was important as having begun early the detailed study of the diplomatic relations of the Revolution with Europe.

There was another sense in which the relations of the Revolution with Europe as a whole were beginning to be understood. A French work by Hauterive tried to justify France on a wider historical deduction than had been done so far.[2] He claimed that the European system which had been impaired by Russia and Prussia (e.g. in Poland), and the extension of the colonial system mainly by Britain, was now corrected. By means of the federal system France could now protect a united Europe against England. This work called forth a reply from Friedrich Gentz, who was the pupil and translator of Burke, the most influential of anti-French writers of the period. In his *De l'État de l'Europe*,[3] Gentz attempted in vain to defend Britain's policy and to call for another coalition. He wrote that the Revolution did not correct, but rather created, European disorder at a time when the old system was advancing towards greater security. Gentz went further than his master Burke in saying that French power was to be feared under any form of government. He was alone in his view in Prussia, where the censor repressed his work. After Pitt went out of office he also lost the support—both moral and material —of the British government. In his later work *Fragments about the Balance of Power* of 1806, Gentz is even more extreme in his demand for war at all costs. He had, he claimed, two objects, to guard Germany against French influences and to save France from self-annihilation.

---

[1] E.g. *M.R.* (Feb.–Mar. 1800), xxxi, 165, describes Marsh's *History* as 'the ablest work on the subject which has yet appeared'. Griffith, the editor, was a Whig and a Dissenter but he had a reputation for impartiality. The review was, according to B. C. Nangle, *The Monthly Review*, 2nd series, 1790–1815 (Oxford, 1955), written by G. Butler, D.D., who was, like Marsh, a Cambridge Divinity professor.

[2] A. M. B. de L. Comte d'Hauterive, *De l'état de la France* . . . (Paris, 1800). Translated by L. Goldsmith as *State of the French Republic at the end of the year VIII* (London, 1801). Hauterive's work was violently anti-British and very effective in Germany.

[3] F. von Gentz, *On the State of Europe before and after the French Revolution* . . . Translated by J. C. Herries. 4th ed. (London, 1803).

He rebukes not only France but the big nations who shared the plunder with her at the expense of the smaller states of Europe.

It is interesting to note Gentz's reception in England, especially in view of his admiration for England and of his influence in spreading Burkian ideas abroad. He was in London in 1802, received and complimented by the King and Queen.[1] In Whig circles this great admirer of England was not enthusiastically received. His first *Edinburgh* reviewer, Jeffrey, was in no position to answer Gentz's argument based on his notion of the development of the European system, but he was vaguely inimical to Gentz's partisan and 'alarmist' writing, and to his consuming fear of French power which had replaced the fear of French principles. There is not a statement in Jeffrey's review which is based on a concrete reading of the international situation, or its past history. He often answers Gentz simply by saying that the principle of Balance is immortal, and could not therefore have been impaired by France. Gentz's second volume was given to Brougham who was something like the *Edinburgh*'s specialist on Europe. He attacks Gentz's notion of saving France from herself as the same hypocritical pretext which had been used for the partition of Poland, which was the real beginning of the breakdown of the European system. He charges Gentz with overrating the coalition's chance of victory and underrating the evil of war. Brougham frankly wished to see England out of the war.

LIVE HISTORICAL DEBATES

The same preoccupation with the war which gave rise to military histories, diplomatic studies, and to a renewed interest in the European system, also determined the manner in which memoirs and documents of Revolutionary history were received. This manner is illustrated by controversies including historians and politicians in which historical facts, documents or narratives figure in political discussion. Few histories of the Revolution were written in France at the time, but in England there were the émigrés, who were still deeply engrossed in revolutionary history and free to start early the personal quarrels, *apologiae*, and violent recriminations which in France characterized the writings of the Restoration. English translators, printers and friends centred round these émigrés, interpreting their points of view to the English public.

In this category of writings, the publication of Bertrand de Moleville's *Annals of the French Revolution* (the English translation was published before the French original) at the beginning of 1800 was important. Though his work was in a sense, as Thompson says, an anti-revolutionary pamphlet, he had both documents and first-hand information at his

[1] G. Mann, *Secretary of Europe* (Yale, 1946), chapter VI.

disposal. It was again the preoccupation with the war that determined the reception of the new book. Fox could not have read it through when on 4 February 1800 he said in Parliament that there was now documentary proof that Louis XVI 'entered negotiations with foreign powers, not to partition France but to dictate by force of arms and to compel them to depart from the system which they thought necessary to their own internal happiness'. Fox was speaking in the House against the war and it seems that he fancied that the case against war in 1800 could be enforced by a discovery concerning the origins of the war, by proof that Louis XVI brought the war on by negotiating with his country's enemies. Fox was prompted by exactly the same sort of political motivation as Herbert Marsh. Perhaps he knew better than to believe that the blunders of a French King long dead should affect the foreign policy of England in 1800, but he did not resist the temptation to revive the old battle when new weapons were thrown into his hands. He was relying on Bertrand's *Annals*. When the latter read the report of the speech in the *Morning Chronicle* the following day, he wrote to Fox to correct his misreading of the appropriate passage, denied that he (Bertrand) had written that Louis XVI wanted a coalition against France, invited Fox to read the chapter where he explained that the plan advised by Montmorin, proposed by the King, discussed by the Emperor and Artois, and adopted at Mantua on 20 May 1791, was to have a *feigned* coalition between Austria, Prussia, Russia, Spain, Naples and Sardinia in order 'to declare but not to make actual war against France'.[1] Fox replied at once that 'they who threaten do, in my apprehension, attempt to dictate by force'. He meant to show, he said, that France had good cause to declare war on Austria. When Bertrand replied that Louis had no other way, and, later, that the Mantua project in any case came to nothing and moreover remained utterly secret until he (Bertrand) published it, and could not therefore have influenced France's decision to go to war, Fox only said that in any case it proved that there was a just cause for war, that the French suspicions were correct. Bertrand later referred Fox to another chapter of his work in which Brissot is quoted as saying that the Jacobins wanted war in order to pin treachery on the King because 'the scrupulous exactness with which the King, faithful to his oath, adhered to the constitution, had hitherto disconcerted the projects of the Jacobins'.[2]

We know now that Fox was attacking, and Bertrand was defending, Louis XVI's loyalty to France, on the ground of a forged document. Bertrand himself had already urged the production of this paper in a letter to the Convention during the King's trial. Two years later, in 1795, Dr Moore mysteriously got hold of it and printed in his book what seems

[1] Bertrand, *Annals* (1800), IV, 8–9.
[2] Correspondence between M. Bertrand de Moleville and the Hon. C. J. Fox (London, 1800).

to be a shortened version of Bertrand's text.[1] Dr Moore inadvertently hit on the truth, discovered only a century later, when he attributed the plan to Calonne, who, as we know now, was the author of the forged document.

The correspondence between Fox and Bertrand started another debate, between Bertrand and Mallet-du-Pan, who in his *Mercure Britannique*[2] declared the whole Mantua project to be a fiction, and Bertrand's extract therefore worthless. Bertrand replied that the MS. existed with the Emperor's notes and that he, Bertrand, had a copy of it. Mallet-du-Pan knew what he was talking about but he allowed the controversy to die out and to be summed up in a later edition of Bertrand in a conciliatory manner, probably by Dallas, friend and translator to émigrés. To this English friend of émigrés, defender of French royalists and scourge of revolutionaries, the distinctions between the liberal Mallet who had tried to save the constitutional monarchy and the counter-revolutionary Bertrand (who accused Siéyès of being in the King's pay), was unimportant. One was either a revolutionary or a counter-revolutionary. 'You could not be just by halves to Louis XVI', Bertrand, characteristically, wrote to Fox. But this was just what Fox could be. Not being obliged to declare for a complete policy or party in matters of French history, he could well afford to blame Louis XVI's secret foreign policy while lamenting the faults that ruined him. As foreigners, even the most partisan English politicians could occasionally assume the role of future historians.

The Fox–Bertrand–Mallet controversies show how, in the course of a political debate on the war in 1800, a mysterious but significant moment in the history of the Revolution is not indeed unravelled, but at least identified, held up as important, discussed, guessed at. Another case, similarly exposing the Whig preoccupation with discrediting the war through references to its treacherous origins, produced results of a lower order. It forms another illustration of politics misusing history and of the defective methods with which one of the earliest of forged collections of royal letters was met.

When Helen Maria Williams, of Revolutionary renown, published a collection of eighty letters of Louis XVI[3] they were widely believed to be genuine in spite of Bertrand's attempt to discredit them.[4] Francis Horner the Whig reviewer[5] tackled the publication for exactly same purpose

[1] Bertrand, *Annals*, IV, 70–6. See below, pp. 252–3
[2] *Mercure Britannique* (London, 1798–1800), no. 34, p. 94.
[3] *The Political and Confidential Correspondence of Lewis XVI with Observations on each Letter* by H. M. Williams. 3 vols. (London, 1803). Miss Williams claimed that some of the letters were in her possession.
[4] [A. Fr. L. Bertrand de Moleville], *A Refutation of the Libel on the Memory of the late King of France* (London, 1804).
[5] *E.R.* (Oct. 1803), III, 211.

that Fox tackled Bertrand, that is, in the service of the anti-war campaign. In both cases the bases of argument were forged papers, the aim political warfare, and the conclusions were nevertheless historically correct. Horner, too, extracts from the false letters the fact that Breteuil was negotiating with foreign powers with the King's sanction. But Horner, though he saw no external evidence for their authenticity, made a case for the genuineness of the letters on what then went as 'internal evidence', namely, the manner and sentiment, as well as the consideration that the revolutionary Miss Williams would hardly promote a forgery so creditable to the late King. (Horner apologizes for his ungallant presumption against Miss Williams by saying that in an offence against humane feelings sex cannot soften the punishment.) For the purposes of the anti-war campaign it was necessary to stress the treacherous nature of the negotiations, but, in the spirit of the time which courageously lamented the French King, Horner described Louis as consistent, sincere, benevolent, popular and revolutionary. The King, says Horner, belongs to that 'memorable list of enthusiasts' of 'a benevolence too sanguine' who acted at the beginning of the Revolution with incautious haste. But he added that it would have been dishonourable in Louis XVI not to attempt to restore order even through treachery. Some Whigs at that time wanted to eat their cake and have it.

THE ROLE OF THE 'EDINBURGH'

The foundation of the *Edinburgh Review* in 1802 was an important event in the English historiography of the Revolution. The reviews in those days contained articles by the leaders in politics and literature. The *Edinburgh* occupies a special place both intellectually and politically. It was mainly through writings in reviews, prompted by reactions to various works on the Revolution and connected subjects, that the English writers were arriving at a moderate political attitude to the Revolution which long survived those years' writings. An historical interpretation was being formed in spite of the fact that writings were strongly prompted by the great concern of the Whigs over English politics. The complex attitude to Napoleon, the practical question of peace and war, and the disappointment over reform in England all coloured their interpretation but paradoxically also contributed to the formation of their historical outlook.

The fixed pattern for debates over reform in the first decade is commonly represented by sayings like the Whig phrase, 'Enemies to revolutions are friends to timely reform', which would normally be answered by something like Windham's: 'Would you repair your house in the hurricane season?' or Pitt's, 'This is not a time to make hazardous experiments.' During the wars the only reforms still strongly agitated for were the abolition of the slave trade and the repeal of the Test Acts. As far as parliamentary reform was concerned the Whigs admitted solemnly that the greatest harm the French Revolution had done to England was to throw her reform back by discrediting the cause of liberty. The historical efforts of the politically-minded Whigs were therefore frankly and purposefully directed to saving the ravished reputation of liberty from those who confounded the salutary and the pernicious in the French Revolution. This primary concern with making distinctions, with analysis and with discrimination, could be useful to the history of the French Revolution at that stage of its development.

The attitude of the Revolution emerging from a multitude of book-reviews in the early years of the century is the most important aspect of this period for us here. In a sense the *Edinburgh* stands between Burke and Carlyle. Acton said that Carlyle's volumes 'delivered our fathers from thraldom to Burke'.[1] It was, however, by the Whig and Radical reviewers of this period that we can watch the English view of the Revolution emancipate itself from Burke. It was, incidentally, under the influence of Jeffrey and Mill, the Whig and Radical editors and reviewers, both known authorities on the French Revolution, that Carlyle began to study the subject. If his work effected a political emancipation (and this was true, as we shall see, only in a peculiar sense), this was the result of a tendency which, in England in any case, was as old as the Revolution of 1789 and not, as is sometimes said, of 1830. The *Edinburgh* was pleading for a more discriminating attitude to the Revolution before the wars were over and before many people were ready to listen; but it was the general view expressed then, by Jeffrey, Sidney Smith, Horner, Mackintosh and others, that gradually became the traditional liberal view.[2]

The early English studies of the Revolution were shaped by two main influences. The wider sympathies of the Whigs, with their conflicting loyalties to liberty, to social order, to country and constitution, made for an anti-extremism, for self-contradiction, for muddled and dishonest thinking which often distorted the facts of history, but in the long run it also made for greater historical fairness. The *Edinburgh* had to find its way among a perplexing number of views on the Revolution, and it gradually began to show a certain consistency in rejecting the extreme and generalizing anti-revolutionary writings which opposed even the constitutional movement in the French Revolution and to accept views as those of Mounier and Malouet who defended that movement while exposing its errors. The Tories, on the other hand, with more narrow and

[1] Acton, *F.R.* p. 358.
[2] The *E.R.* (1803), II, I, explains that the destruction of Jacobinism has calmed political controversy and restored general agreement on basic principles. It is in questions of foreign policy that partiality and exaggeration now reign.

clearly pronounced views, contributed to the study of the Revolution (as Adolphus and Marsh had already conspicuously done) through acuter criticism and a more determined search for facts. Only in this sense did political standpoints at first vaguely coincide with different historical methods. Both tendencies were represented in the early *Edinburgh* which reflected the indecision characterizing party politics in this era of transition. Anti-Jacobin policy was relaxed at the time when the nation was united against Napoleon. Reform was still unpopular and revolution anathema, but even Southey still wrote in 1808, 'I wish for reform, because I cannot but see that all things are tending toward revolution, and nothing but reform can by any possibility prevent it.' Even the *Monthly Review* spoke of 'revolutionary despotism'. The *Edinburgh* and other reviews also reflected the sentimental feelings for the sufferings of the royal family and other victims of the Revolution, the horror at the indiscriminate violence of the Terror shared by Whigs and Tories, and for ever colouring English reactions to the Revolution.

The formation of a widely held liberal view on the Revolution at that time was, paradoxically, partly due to the gradual return of Burke into the philosophy of the party he seemed to have betrayed and which his attitude to the Revolution had certainly split. A peculiar way of digesting Burke's ideas is apparent in some early English writings on the French Revolution especially in the *Edinburgh*, where Revolutionary works were often reviewed. The earliest French writings on the Revolution were not so much personal memoirs as attempts at evaluating the event. Although Lacretelle, Toulongeon and Beaulieu clearly wrote from a political standpoint, these earliest French contemporary writers wrote from a more impersonal if not more impartial point of view than many Restoration authors of intensely personal and bitterly calumnious memoirs. Bailly's work too, as contemporary as any could be—for he was guillotined in 1793—though it appeared under the name *Mémoires d'un Temoin* (1804), is to this day considered a fair historical appraisal of the events. Bailly and Lacretelle remained favourite authorities in England and works written from a moderate royalist point of view. Lacretelle was so like a proper narrative history that English reviewers, not yet ready for 'pictorial' history, criticized its lack of interpretation. Mounier and Mallet du Pan, on the other hand, discussed the intellectual causes of the Revolution, a question previously raised by Dr Robison and the Abbé Barruel.

It is with Mounier's discussion of the causes of the Revolution that the *Edinburgh*, significantly, began its life just as the *Cambridge Modern History* was to begin its volume on the French Revolution with an account of this discussion, a hundred years later. Mallet du Pan had accused the philosophers in his *Mercure* of having weakened the defences of the old régime. Mounier in reply denied the influence of the philosophers. He said that the desire for liberty was born of the envy of England and America and that the crimes of the Revolution were not due to principles but to unprincipled men. Jeffrey, in an *Edinburgh* article which was described half a century later by Brougham as 'one of the most remarkable pieces that ever adorned the periodical literature of any country', took up the subject, and he again asserted the influence of the philosophers. Mounier argued as he did not because he wished to 'clear' the philosophers of blame. As a practical parliamentarian he even claims that Rousseau, Mably and Condorcet, far from being influential, were ridiculed. Jeffrey, on the other hand, though he admitted the concrete causes of the Revolution (especially the American example, economic grievances and the growth of the middle classes), made the point that grievances appeared intolerable only because philosophy held them up to detestation. On the other hand he held that the exact share of the writers could never be measured and unlike Mounier he did seek to 'clear' some of them (though not Rousseau or Mably) of the guilt of having inspired Robespierre. One of Mounier's weak arguments is that the same ideas could not possibly have influenced such different men as, for example, Lafayette, Robespierre and Napoleon. Jeffrey let it stand. It was not yet seen at the time even by Jeffrey, the champion of a discriminating attitude to the Revolution, that different mentors could have inspired different stages or actors of the Revolution and thus influenced its changing course. It is in connection with the *philosophes* that we also find in the *Edinburgh* the connection of democracy with irreligion which was to remain a recurring view in England. Deism was shaken off as completely as Jacobinism by the repentant Whigs.

A more profound thinker among the Whigs was Mackintosh whose development since he entered the debate on the Revolution with his *Vindiciae Gallicae* is of great significance. Mackintosh's case was the model for the process by which many moderate and liberal reformers came to be alienated from the French Revolution having at first accepted it with enthusiasm. Already in 1797, perhaps under the influence which the invasion of Switzerland had on him, Mackintosh reviewed Burke's *Regicide Peace* in the *Monthly Review* in a way which made Burke forgive and respect him. Mackintosh then professed discipleship to Burke and was warmly received. Reading Mackintosh's glowing letter, Burke nevertheless discerned in it, what he only put privately to Dr Laurence, that Mackintosh's 'supposed conversion' was only for home affairs and in regard to France he remained as Jacobin as ever.[1]

The distinction which Burke made goes to the heart of many 'moderate'

---

[1] *Memoirs* of Mackintosh (London, 1835), I, 86–98. Mackintosh did not begin writing for the *E.R.* until 1813. He had written several reviews in the *M.R.* including one on Burke's *Letter to a Noble Lord*, *M.R.* (1796), XIX, 314 and one on 'Two Letters' and 'Thoughts on the Prospect of a Regicide Peace', *ibid.* XXI, 306, 403.

conversions, and, more important, it illustrates perfectly the peculiar influence which Burke had on his Whig disciples. They were cases in which men did not, like Southey or Coleridge or Windham, for instance, pass from one extreme to the other, or change their principles in politics—they merely changed their attitude to current affairs in France and in England. At home they rallied to save their country and its constitution, more especially when the foreign enemy was an absolute ruler. We find people like Mackintosh who had written against Burke now writing under the influence of Burke and occasionally in the language of Burke.

In 1803, Mackintosh defended Peltier, an English printer charged with libel against Napoleon during the period of peace which followed the treaty of Amiens, when it was felt that the English and French newspapers both reflected and augmented the threat of war. The virulent *Times* and Coleridge's attacks in the *Morning Post* (for which he was nearly arrested by Napoleon) seemed grave dangers to peace. The trial of Peltier took place on 21 February 1803[1] and in his memorable defence Mackintosh had occasion to condemn the course which the French Revolution had taken and to show, in his defence of English liberty and especially liberty of speech, the Burkian influence which had developed his thought since 1791. Amidst Europe's ruins he saw Britain alone stand, 'that ancient fabric, which has been gradually reared by the noble wisdom and virtue of our fathers'.

Mackintosh's 'ingenious sophistry', however, did not convince all the Whigs that Peltier was unjustly condemned.[2] In his speech Mackintosh imagined that Napoleon would fall through a violent internal Revolution, but he showed better foresight in perceiving, at a time when at least the social Revolution was supposed to be dead, the survival of a spirit of revolutionism in a huge underground body of desperate, rootless men, unorganized but with 'a principle of fidelity stronger than any that ever held together a society'.

Although the early reviewers demand more fairness in judging the Revolution, less comprehensive condemnation, more distinction between errors and crimes; although they are anxious that justice should be done to the early reformers and the liberal philosophers, we find Jeffrey, in reviewing Bailly's *Memoirs*, also repeating Burke-like criticisms of the early leaders of the Revolution, though he prefers to quote the authority of Hume for some of them. They should have known, he says, that popularity with mobs as well as violence must inevitably lead to military despotism; that legislation cannot be passed rashly 'like toasts in an

---

[1] The proceedings were published as *On the Trial of John Peltier, Esq. for a Libel against Napoleon Bonaparte . . . and Mackintosh's Defence*, Taken in shorthand by Mr Adams (1803).

[2] *E.R.* (July 1803), II, 476.

election dinner'; that government must be manned by the natural aristocracy of rank and wealth for institutions alone do not confer authority on individuals. In England, he boasts, influence is not borrowed from office and men submit to rulers who could have enforced their measures through their social standing even without Parliament. The French Revolution failed because the deputies had no natural authority save that of hired advocates and because they failed to join forces with the liberal nobility. The unpardonable sin of the revolutionaries was their intellectual presumption, and Jeffrey also speaks of society as having to grow like an organism and not to be constructed like a machine.

Herbert Spencer begins his essay on the 'Social Organism' with the words, 'Sir James Mackintosh got great credit for the saying that "constitutions are not made but grow".' This, he continues, proves the age's ignorance of social science. 'Universally in Mackintosh's day, things were explained on the hypothesis of manufacture rather than that of growth.'[1] The fact that people like Jeffrey and Mackintosh were arriving at organic notions of society and of historical development through thought about the Revolution, brings out a continuity of some importance. Their ideas grew out of eighteenth-century English thought through the direct influence of Burke. The Burkian influence is here harnessed in the interests of a liberty. The notion of organic social development was in Whig thought an indigenous growth not shaped by Germany even as Coleridge and Wordsworth were undergoing foreign romantic influences. Most important, it grew without a conscious philosophical revolt against the eighteenth century. Jeffrey never read a German work then or later without disliking it. Mackintosh was more widely read and more 'metaphysical'. He was an historian, lawyer and political theorist but he was no consistent philosopher. This is what makes him so important for us. He had early expressed the Whig attitude to the French Revolution on the ground of the theory of natural rights combined with utilitarianism and he thought nothing now of adding to this mixture Burkian theories of continuity and organicism. He early symbolized the comprehensiveness, *ad hoc* empiricism of English historiography. As in the case of the political attitude to the Revolution, therefore, so in that of the philosophical interpretation, we find the Whig contributors to the *Edinburgh* and to the *Monthly Review* standing between Burke and Carlyle. Carlyle did not derive entirely from Germany. It seems, curiously, that both the emancipation from Burke and the Burkian influence grew in him in the course of his apprenticeship with Whiggism, when 'Burkianism' itself was being transformed.

The Whigs were now willing to learn continuity, gradualness and organicism from Burke but not to accept his historical diagnosis of the essence of the Revolution, nor his rejection on principle of any revolution.

[1] H. Spencer, *Essays*, 2nd series (London, 1863).

The liberal attitude to the Revolution remained empirical, based on the distinction between 'good' and 'bad' elements, between just principles and excesses, between sacrifices and perverse crimes. Whereas Burke had rejected the whole of the Revolution as a disease in the body politic of Europe which can only be removed by a severe and drastic amputation, the English historiography from its clumsy beginnings attempted a more complicated and subtle operation of making distinctions within the large body of ideas and deeds comprising the Revolution. This attitude adopted by the early publicists and would be historians, formulated in review articles, was to be even more accentuated after the Restoration when on the continent reaction against the Revolution would reach its height.

In its practical judgments on the Revolution, however, the *Edinburgh* as a whole began with a cautious spirit. It hoped for a juster verdict on the Revolution but often hesitated to pronounce it. Jeffrey demands more fairness, especially for the maligned philosophers and the moderate and erring actors. But in specific statements he condemns errors no less harshly than crimes. When the *Review* met extreme views on its own side, as those of Belsham the Foxite Whig who pronounced Burke mad, or those of Stephens who in his *History of the Wars* sympathized too zealously with the Girondins, it criticized them sharply. Belsham was the party historian *par excellence*, in English as well as in French history. He wrote voluminously against the war and against clericalism, clashing with Marsh and Adolphus who were far superior to him as historians. On the French Revolution he held the orthodox but extreme Whig view, approving of the early stages but, after 1795, unable to see right on any side, French or English. It seems as if the reviewer of Belsham was dissociating himself from views he might have accepted in a more decent garb. It is Belsham's party spirit which he criticizes rather than his party views. The fear for the fate of a young review to which Tories were still contributing and subscribing must also have weighed with the editor.

The strong objection to the party spirit of Belsham as unhistorical and the exposure of the historical inadequacy of Stephens also show how far in advance of historical writing, criticism was at the time. Stephens, for instance, claimed that he had access to all the fountain-heads of information, and Murray ridiculed this claim. He knew that 'important and authentic materials seldom appear for a long time after the period' since those best acquainted with events do not hasten to write. And he exposed Stephens's method of 'manufacturing' books as merely cutting up newspapers and memoirs and compiling the extracts. Murray claims to expose a whole brand of ignorant historians who acquire a philosophy and then compile a history 'from the most ordinary materials'. Murray is somewhat unfair to Stephens who has interesting characterizations and he ridicules a paragraph which lists a series of poignant and almost Carlylean epithets.

THE WHIG SPLIT AND THE TORY 'QUARTERLY'

The change to the left which came over the *Edinburgh* about 1808 was connected with the question of the war. In 1808 a wave of nationalism determined the Spanish people to reject a liberal but alien rule in a national rising. It was on the issue of England's policy in Spain, and on the implications for the government's policy at home, that controversy flared up. An article in the *Edinburgh* written jointly by Jeffrey and Brougham caused the *Edinburgh* to split and the Tory contributors (like Murray, Southey and Scott) to withdraw and to found the rival *Quarterly Review*. The tone of the *Edinburgh* now became more radical. The 'Don Cevallos' article which raised this political tempest is interesting in bringing out the complex of new social and political notions emerging in Europe and affecting both practical politics and historical thinking. The writers' theme is that the Spanish nationalist rising, because it was so obviously a rising of 'the people . . . above all the lower orders', deserted by the treacherous aristocracy, and aimed against the 'enemy of both national independence and civil liberty', was a victory for liberalism, 'a lesson to all governments—a warning to all oligarchies'. 'We can once more utter the words of *liberty* and *people*, without starting at the echo of our own voices, or looking around the chamber for some spy or officer of the government.' The Spanish rising, they say, rehabilitated 'salutary, just and necessary revolution' and reawakened 'liberty and patriotism which many have supposed were extinguished since the French Revolution'. The most offending passage was that professing expectant joy at a revolution in England which would raise 'the power of real talent and worth, the true nobility of a country', and exalt the masses under the guidance of 'that virtual aristocracy, to direct the councils of England' in accordance, of course, with the spirit of the constitution. The article provoked something like anti-Jacobin feelings not only outside but also inside Whiggism. The fundamental theme was not confined to radicals and it was expressed in almost the same words by Coleridge in the *Courier*,' It was the noble efforts of Spanish patriotism that first restored us, without distinction of party, to our characteristic enthusiasm for *liberty*.' Just as Napoleon's despotism had enabled some liberals to accept the anti-French war, so the popular rising in Spain infused some of the ex-revolutionaries with their old enthusiasm. But Brougham's elaboration of the practical inferences went far in its democratic spirit. The split in the *Edinburgh* signified a deeper rift inside the Whig party. The end of the first decade of the century brought to a head the inner tensions within the liberal ranks. The Whigs who had for long rallied to themselves a variety of people who either retained their belief in reform, or opposed the policy of the government, or preferred peace to war, began to feel the impact of views too divergent to be any longer compatible. While Burkian influences were, in a modified form, finding their way back into many Whig hearts, new Benthamite and radical theories and temperaments were winning away some of the liberals. The left had for some time been called the Mountain. Bentham, who was no democrat, had kept outside the political parties of Tories, Whigs or Jacobins. Now when Jacobinism had disappeared, Radicalism could grow as a political party. In 1809 Bentham's *Catechism of Parliamentary Reform* appeared. The force of Utilitarianism so far indifferent to parliamentary reform was brought to bear on the constitution. The combination of Bentham, Mill, Romilly, Place, each with his particular sphere of activity, was the real beginning of Philosophical Radicalism as a political factor. The Whigs were now constantly debating amongst themselves gradual reform, as against more extreme demands, in series of letters and pamphlets printed or exchanged between Brougham, Roscoe, Shepherd and others. In spite of the comparatively smooth transition in England to nineteenth-century modes of thought, in spite of the almost imperceptible transformation of rationalist liberalism into a more historical, more imaginative conception of man and society, a choice was nevertheless forced on those who prided themselves on being true lovers of freedom, whether progress was to be continued along the slow, traditional Whig lines or dictated by the new Radicalism, by economic theories and thorough-going social reforms. The conflict was real and resulted in new political alignments. Part of the former Whigs became indistinguishable from Tories, in their concern for the Preservation of a basically aristocratic social order. The other part became radical. New Benthamite Radicalism served history at first only as a challenge and a provocation. We can watch the influence of its appearance, at this political turning point, on the historian Smyth who had been an antagonist of Burke's ideas in the 1790s, but, like his prototype Mackintosh, had moved closer to them by now. Smyth's lifelong friend Roscoe, historian, reformer and politician, had remained an active radical reformer and was now in the thick of the Whig controversy about the rate of reform. In 1810 Roscoe opposed a pamphlet of Brougham in favour of gradual reform in a *Letter* demanding more drastic measures, 'because much will be obtained as well as little'. Smyth wrote to Roscoe that such a policy was unstatesmanlike and that he agreed with Burke that 'step by step is the proper and only Mode for getting things done quietly and securely'. Incidentally we hear that Roscoe's *Letter* was also shown to Bentham who liked it.[1]

[1] R.P. 4597, 15, 16 July 1810. Some of the relevant publications are Roscoe, *Letter to Henry Brougham* (Apr. 1810); Brougham, *E.R.* (Apr. 1810); Brougham, *E.R.* (July 1812), xx, 127; *Q.R.* (June 1812), vii, 265–81.

Smyth's opposition to the new radicalism is interesting because it was connected with his thought on the French Revolution, and he later repeated it in his lectures. There Smyth was glibly to list the Benthamites, Owenites and other groups of reformers and social innovators as visionaries and dreamers who endangered their own age as the French and English revolutionaries ('the Paines and the Godwins') had endangered England at the time of the French Revolution. At this early stage Smyth was vaguely dissociating himself from these rising radical influences, which he judged in the light of the French Revolution.

The political storm over Spain is significant also as being symptomatic of the emergence of new historical notions. In a sense the *Edinburgh* split on the question of a romantic nationalism against international liberalism. The *Edinburgh*, though it wished the Spaniards well, was pessimistic about their prospects. Will England insist on constitutional government in Spain as a condition for rendering help? Is the reactionary Spanish nobility to be supported against the foreign enemy as well as against the popular rising? Are the people of Spain to be robbed of the fruits of their rising for freedom? The general stand for nationalism *and* liberalism taken both by Brougham in the *Edinburgh* and by Coleridge, is the alternative offered to the alliance of nationalism with reaction which was soon to set in all over Europe. In the course of the wars the appearance of the principle of nationalism in English history had already been perceptible. There had been examples of an exclusive and Imperialistic spirit, for instance, in Macfarlane's *History* of 1796. After the beginning of the Peninsular war histories appear which are frankly chauvinistic and stress national characteristics in a fatalistic spirit. But we do not find that nationalist histories are invariably illiberal. The extreme spirit of blind and mystic devotion to nationalism found in Wordsworth's pamphlet on the *Convention of Cintra*, though it is a measure of the intensity of the nationalist feeling, and though it may have had practical effect on the national attitude to the war, is not commonly found in historical and political writings.[1] The *Convention of Cintra* is the English document on nationalism as Burke's *Reflections* are on conservatism. Coleridge, moreover, took over against Napoleon the role Burke had filled against the French Revolution. With a similar mixture of prophetic insight and single-minded hatred, he indulged in the kind of journalism which embarrassed the Generals fighting against Napoleon. Coleridge and Wordsworth were more ferocious nationalists than the soldiers, politicians or historians. Southey's writings, as, for example, his *Nelson*, were a more typical product of the kind of romantic nationalism appearing in England. Southey early saw that even dry antiquarianism like that of Turner could serve to arouse nationalist consciousness. Consistent in the glorification of England, Southey was

---

[1] E.g. Napier's *Peninsular War*, Macfarlane, Hewson, Clarke, Bisset.

as averse to mysticism in patriotism as to enthusiasm in religion. The restrained temper of early English romanticism in history, together with the liberal tone of nationalist sentiments which even Coleridge shared with Brougham, explains the apparently incongruous fact that, from the beginning of the century, liberalism, romanticism and nationalism, all repressed by Napoleon and all united against him, grew and spread together.

If the *Edinburgh* view on the French Revolution was moving nearer to Burkian ideas, the new Tory *Quarterly* was also meeting it half-way. In view of the specific differences from which the Tory review sprang it is interesting to see whether it also provided a different view of the French Revolution. The *Quarterly* produced its first comprehensive article on the subject in a review of the *Biographie Moderne* in 1813. This work had first appeared in 1800, was suppressed presumably for exposing the inconsistency of ex-republicans, and suppressed again after a subsequent attempt in 1806. It had already been reviewed by the *Edinburgh* in 1809. Its treatment by the *Quarterly* is typical of the more detailed and factual interest in the Revolution which characterized the Tory writers and which the *Quarterly* was to maintain. If we compare the articles in both reviews we find the *Quarterly* making corrections of facts while the *Edinburgh* is preoccupied with the cause of liberty. The Revolution, we read in the latter *Review*, was not all fanaticism and liberty need not have been dishonoured; England had so far learnt only half the lesson; the crimes were partly due to the rulers' neglect to make timely concessions. Apart from these commonplaces of Whiggism there is a sentimental admiration for the victims of the Revolution. The author realizes also the difficulty of writing on the Revolution at a time when talent, materials and liberty of the press were still wanting. A Tacitus would be needed to do justice to a period which gave the abridged experience of centuries. The leading events of the Revolution, writes the reviewer, were affected by pamphlets and public debates and consummated by battles and treaties. The *Edinburgh* article was general and uninspired. Southey was the Tory most knowledgeable about the Revolution, but if he wrote the *Quarterly* review of the same work, he would be badly chosen to present an anti-revolutionary diatribe, for in historiography imaginative qualities placed him above party-boundaries. William Gifford was the proper anti-Jacobin historian, and when the *Quarterly* had considered to let Gifford loose against the Jacobins, Southey threatened to withdraw 'being of any party rather than the anti-Jacobin'. The story of the Revolution as told by Southey in that review is not unusual but the judgments on the successive groups of revolutionaries and especially on the individuals show signs of the old romantic enthusiasm. He moves from one group to another with historical and psychological sympathy. They all meant well though they erred in judgment, and from the King downward they all contributed to the outbreak. Mounier, Lally, Barnave were succeeded by inferior men but the writer admired Desmoulins and refused to believe the worst about him. Of Danton he wrote that he had saved his country and that he would almost have atoned for his crimes if his educational scheme had been carried out. Robespierre, though his description is dominated by the colour of blood, is held up as one whom the Revolution found good and made wicked.

Southey adopts from the *Biographie* an idea which Croker was fully to develop later, that Robespierre was made a scapegoat, and he believed that Robespierre meant to stop the Terror. Southey also generalized the notion that the Revolution corrupted the revolutionaries. He quoted Saint Just's saying, 'on ne peut point régner innocement', said that any unbridled authority was moral poison and illustrated this from history. Acton did not of course invent the notion that absolute power corrupts; nor did Southey, or St. Just, but it is interesting that at an early date, by widening the meaning of St Just's pronouncement on kings (which St Just may have learnt from Montesquieu), and by actually attempting to explain characters and phases of the Revolution by the corruption induced by power, Southey was contributing a point of interpretation to the history of the Revolution. Southey himself, and after him Brougham,[1] applied this point to St Just himself who, wrote Brougham, had been virtuous and enthusiastic but 'corrupted by absolute power'. By saying that the Revolution corrupted the revolutionaries Southey implies that in a revolution there is a force at work which is stronger than the men of the revolution themselves. The Revolution, as it were, acquired a motive force of its own which drove and directed its erstwhile makers. These notions were fully developed later in the century when the concept of independent motive forces in history gained vogue on the continent and disrepute in England. Here the notion of the inevitable course of revolution adopted perhaps from Hume or from Burke makes an early appearance in England before the argument about it blazed forth from the 1820s onwards.

Southey also showed a profound interest, unusual at the time, in the conspiracy of Babeuf, which he examined for its avowed connection with the ideas of Robespierre, its economic ideals and political plans. It later became the sport of Radicals to compare with deadly effect Southey's early and late political pronouncements to the permanent disparagement of his reputation. For his writings on the Revolution it is of greater interest to discern, behind the change of front, his persistent admiration for real courage, greatness and originality as shown in Desmoulin, Danton and Babeuf. Southey had admired Babeuf in 1797 when he was beginning to cool towards France and it was then as later the revolutionary's originality and sincerity as well as the thorough-going attack

[1] Brougham, *Historical Sketches*, IV, 116.

on social and economic evil which had a grip on Southey. Southey's and Coleridge's rebellion against economic exploitation and for state control was as genuine a residue of their own 'spirit of the French Revolution' as the belated efforts for parliamentary reform of the loyal Whigs were of theirs. It was a sharper and more imaginative insight into the historical significance of events taking place before their eyes which made it possible for people like Southey and Mackintosh, from different political camps, to discern before the Restoration what most people began to see only after 1830, that the revolution had become a living force, even when there was no party upholding it, and that as a 'religion without a church' it had come to stay in European History.

CHAPTER 3

ENGLISH HISTORY *VIS-À-VIS*
THE BOURBONS (1815–1830)

THE RESTORATION

The restoration of the Bourbons did not seem certain before Waterloo and the vicissitudes of the moment brought forth some telling expressions of opinion. English opinion was on the whole, for selfish reasons, in favour of a restoration and Tories like the young Macaulay rejoiced in 'peace with a Bourbon . . . bound to us by ties of gratitude'. Political reaction reached its high-water mark when final victory vindicated the war party though reaction never became as extreme in England as it did on the continent. England had not suffered the violent imposition of an alien revolution through conquest, nor did she have a bitter sense of guilt at revolutionary excesses to push her reaction to extremes. Neither her own suffering from the Revolution nor her enthusiasm for it had been so great as to cause an outburst of profound hatred for all revolutions.

The liberals were uncertain whether to welcome the restoration of national institutions in Europe or to deplore reinstated despotism. To Hazlitt, Byron and Shelley it was of course liberty which was defeated at Waterloo. In any case the economic burdens continued to remind many that the war had perhaps been avoidable after all. The despotic suppression of Spanish constitutionalism by Ferdinand VII with the help of British gold and blood, and later the intolerant policy of the Bourbons in France, helped to crystallize liberal antagonism to the restored powers, and to confirm many a liberal in his old views on the French Revolution. This attitude is perhaps indicated in the immediate reactions towards an old revolutionary brought forward by the events of the Restoration. Carnot, who had always fared better in England than other revolutionaries, thanks to his military talent and republican integrity, now gained in reputation through his struggles with the French government. His banishment in 1797 and his refusal to serve Napoleon had made his good name, and opinion was not reversed when he finally joined the Emperor in his hour of need. Carnot wrote a famous *Memoir to the King* in defence of the old revolutionaries which was naturally banned for its forceful condemnation of the royalists who had deserted Louis XVI. 'Vous le laissez seul à la merci de ceux que vous aviez irrités contre lui', he wrote. 'Vous exigez des autres une vertue plus qu'humaine, tandis que vous donnez l'exemple de la désertion et de la felonie.' The French government filled the papers with replies to the forbidden work, thus spreading its fame. The introduction of the *Mémoire* to England was not auspicious. Goldsmith, the Englishman who translated it, was notorious for having in turn served the Revolution, Napoleon and Louis XVIII as well as plotted against each of them. Brougham's review of the *Memoir* is little short of a eulogy of Carnot. He repeated from Carnot what was to become the unanswerable nationalist argument of the school of Thiers, that the saviours of France were accused of treachery by men who had fought against their country. Brougham regretted that Carnot had not dissociated himself from Robespierre as he did later from Napoleon but he goes so far as to defend the act of regicide on the ground of the war and the will of the nation. Like Fox in 1793 he claimed it was not for England to condemn France for regicide. Eleven months later when Carnot shared the disgrace of Napoleon's adventure, and found himself proscribed by the decree of 24 July, the *Edinburgh* still defended and admired him, stressing in his defence the new danger of absolutism.[1] Brougham remained a friend and admirer of Carnot. He devoted to him one of his historical sketches comparing Carnot's 'solid genius' and 'intellectual excellence' to the brilliant but worthless Mirabeau. In his efforts to dissociate Carnot from the Terror he even tried to minimize the responsibility of the Committee of Public Safety as a whole.

The more general immediate effect of the Restoration on English historical studies was to make the French Revolution suddenly cease to be outdated news and become a legitimate subject for historical investigation. One product of this were the textbooks on the history of the Revolution. Bigland continued as a versatile writer on history and theories of history. The most successful of school textbooks was Mrs Markham's history of France (omitting cruelty and party politics), continuously re-edited to shape children's notions of the French Revolution to the end of the century.[2]

THE SPIRIT OF REVOLUTIONISM

The renewal of historical interest came at first with the simple assumption that it was all over. 'The volcano is now extinguished; and we may approach the crater with perfect security,' wrote the *Quarterly* in 1814. Whether they considered Napoleon to have been the executor or the executioner of the Revolution, most people saw his fall as the final decease of the Revolutionary period. The shock of his return immediately brought forth declarations that France had gone too far for a restoration. Shaken out of their initial complacency, some writers became so cautious that for years they doubted the stability of the Restoration government.

---

[1] *E.R.* (Oct. 1815), xxv, 442–55.
[2] Mrs Markham was Elisabeth Penrose (1780–1837), the daughter of the inventor Cartwright. Her history of France is said to have sold 100,000 copies.

Also, people began to think seriously on the problem of the survival of the Revolution. Some writers had already foreseen that certain effects of the Revolution could never be undone and that its lingering spirit was destined to remain a live factor in European history. People thought seriously on the period they had lived through and on its aftermath. To understand history rightly suddenly seemed a matter of vital importance. They studied the Revolution in order to arrive at some universal truth beyond it and in order to train for a correct reading of their own times. Life seemed to depend on correct historical understanding.

The realization that the spirit of revolution was alive and possibly spreading helped to make the time auspicious for revolutionary studies. The educated classes were too alarmed by economic unrest, by the seething masses and by signs of the growing power of organized labour, to indulge in vain revolutionary sympathies. They sought inspiration and protection in principles which made for stability. The Restoration made England acquire a deeper sense of national virtue, a consciousness of political and historical well-being, a feeling fostered by the new romantic admiration for England abroad. On the other hand, the signs of unrest which followed the coming of peace also brought a certain revival of the anxieties of the 1790s when it seemed necessary to wield the power of history in order to discredit revolution and ensure political and social safety. The Jacobin and anti-Jacobin activities of 1816 and 1817 were reminiscent of Revolutionary times. There were a Committee of Public Safety, tricolors, riots and republicanism.[1]

The letters of Southey and of Smyth show how the Restoration turned their minds again and again to the subject of the French Revolution. The peace clearly introduced a new element of fear into Smyth's thoughts. Economic depression had shaken his confidence in the political and social stability of the country.[2] Unemployment and agitation gave him the fear of the organized poor which he had not known during the French Revolution and which he denied existed then in England to any dangerous degree. Above all, he said clearly, the present conditions impressed on him the duty of lecturing to Cambridge students on the French Revolution in order to ward off revolution. The present conditions also helped to shape or rather to distort his understanding of certain aspects of the event. He kept his eyes on the new industrial districts and drew on their examples when he wanted to illustrate popular agitation in the French Revolution.

A remarkable incident concerning Southey illustrates the prevailing state of mind among people of his kind with regard to the French Revolution after the Restoration, when political feeling ran high. Southey's

[1] The *Parl. Deb.* for 1817 contain many references to the 1790s, e.g. in connection with bills for the suspension of the Habeas Corpus Act.
[2] R.P. 4620, 13 May 1817.

extreme 'conversion' from enthusiastic revolutionism despised by many liberals (especially since his advantages from it were so evident) was widely discussed in 1817 as a result of a surreptitious publication of his revolutionary drama *Wat Tyler*, written in 1794. Southey had celebrated the Revolution in 1792, was slightly chilled by the execution of the Girondins in 1793, but remained a violent revolutionary for many years, until Napoleon turned him against France. The painful question of reconciling revolutionary sympathies and present-day politics was again raised and it was raised also in Parliament. William Smith, Member for Norwich, went to Parliament armed with a copy of the drama and with a number of the *Quarterly* which contained a new article ascribed to the Poet Laureate. During the debate he found occasion to compare the texts and denounce the arch Tory as a renegade. Brougham of course joined in the hue and cry.[1] Southey replied in an indignant and rather fine *Letter*[2] in which he claimed mainly that he had outgrown the errors of *Wat Tyler*, but was not ashamed of its spirit. He said it was mischievous, but not seditious. It had been written at a time when Republicanism was dangerous to hold and anti-Jacobinism was as intolerant as Jacobinism was now (1817). This was a stock line of defence with Southey. He wrote in almost the same words to his brother and to others. To Lord Liverpool he wrote that the spirit of Jacobinism had sunk to the rabble who in 1793 would have torn him to pieces for Jacobinism as they would now for anti-Jacobinism. He had discarded, he said, his belief in revolution but retained a zealous love for liberty.

The incident caused much searching of heart, especially among mild liberals who had defended the Revolution in its time. Many felt that Southey was speaking for them when he said that he did not transfer his sympathies from the French people fighting for liberty to the French military oppressor. The Whig politicians like Brougham, Roscoe and Smith, who were practically involved in the matter, waged war against Southey for his offensive references to themselves, to the *Edinburgh Review* and to the old anti-war party. (Southey had spoken of people who opposed their country's cause, Ultra-Whigs and Anarchists, from Mr Brougham downward.) Others, however, like Smyth in Cambridge, more detached from present-day politics and from the battle of the reviews, felt sympathy for Southey's position and considered the moral problem involved. Smyth, significantly, refused to condemn Southey outright on the ground that the Revolution was 'such an event that ... the general rules of moral criticism ... ought to be suspended as in the case of Burke, for instance, and the alarmists of the period'.

The reference to Burke in this context is telling, for it is since the Restoration that the Whigs have found it possible at last fully to forgive

[1] *Parl. Deb.* xxxv (Jan.–Apr. 1817), 14 March 1817, cols. 1088–1100.
[2] A letter to William Smith, M.P., from Robert Southey Esq. (London, 1817).

Burke his 'extravagances' as they called them, and to re-establish him as the sage of their party, essentially a protagonist of the cause of political liberty as they understood it. It would almost seem possible to reconstruct much of the Whig–Tory debates of the period as a struggle over the heritage of Burke and over the correct assessment of his essential teaching. We know that Tory opinion regretted the absence, in the service of their party's propaganda, of a name like Burke's. The reconciliation of the liberal-minded with Burke had already started earlier, but the acceptance of Burke as the prophet of the new European order by the concert of learned opinion abroad enhanced this revival of a rival Burkianism. Again, as in the first wave of enthusiasm for Burke, his ideas were balanced by another work of a more moderate character.

MADAME DE STAËL'S INFLUENCE

At the height of the anti-revolutionary political reaction which swept Europe after the Restoration, Madame de Staël's *Considerations* on the French Revolution exercised a great influence on England in reviving serious interest in the Revolution and in shaping English views on the subject. Madame de Staël's work performed a similar task to that which Mackintosh's *Vindiciae Gallicae* had done earlier. It served as an antidote to extreme anti-revolutionism on the one hand and to Jacobinism on the other. It showed Englishmen that the extreme political doctrines of Romantic reaction were not essential to the historiography of the Revolution. In Madame de Staël members of both the great political parties in England found a writer to their heart. An enthusiastic Romantic in literature, a student of the organic connection between national life and national literature, a true lover of political liberty, an admirer of England and English institutions, a pupil of Burke, and withal a moderate and sane defender of the principles of the early French Revolution.

Madame de Staël expressed with clarity the idea that the great political dividing line passed outside Whig and Tory. This implied that there were two opposing streams within Whiggism, as was indeed clearly brought out by Philosophical Radicalism. It is significant therefore that her critics in England were the radicals who considered her Tory because they said policy meant to her more than principle. Bentham refused to meet her, and the youthful Mill wrote fiercely against her, calling her 'the most questionable of witnesses except on facts within her immediate observation'. Her English Whig friends were Mackintosh and Horner, and Lord Brougham wrote a highly eulogistic article on her in his *Historical Sketches*. She herself had been both a republican and a constitutional monarchist but felt no loyalty either to the Bourbons or to the Republic. Smyth in his lectures describes her as 'the most beautiful of all, Madame de Staël, one who from the liveliness of her imagination and the quickness of her feeling, could sympathize with whatever was reasonable or affecting in . . . every party in turn; but who was in truth most deeply and most honourably attached to the principles of civil and religious liberty'.[1]

Madame de Staël's view of the Revolution rested on ground common to Whigs and Tories though her bias in treating the role of her father was discerned and rejected by all. Writing under the combined influences of Necker's attempt to establish an English constitution in France, of the teaching of Burke and of a romantic admiration for English institutions, she formed her view of the Revolution with English elements and as an outsider found it easier to amalgamate them. She thus gave an impetus to the formation of an English interpretation of the Revolution. She described the outbreak of the Revolution not as a distortion of the healthy process of history, but rather as the result of material and spiritual causes as well as circumstances. One of her most important contributions was to trace and make respectable a tradition of revolution in French history in the same way that 1688 was accepted by the Whigs. Liberty is ancient, she said, and French history is a story of conflicts all tending towards greater freedom.[2] Her notion that the Revolution began to go wrong in 1791 and that its negation of liberty was not an inevitable process, but rather the result of crimes and errors, was congenial to English opinion. Those who had welcomed the Revolution in its early stages and later turned away from it believing it to have degenerated and to have betrayed its initial ideal of liberty were now confirmed in their view by a great authority and grateful for being helped to remain consistent. Like Constant they felt that it was not necessary to dishonour twenty-seven years. Like Madame de Staël the English historians always stressed the crucial importance of the early stages.

HISTORY AND POLITICS

In England the history of the French Revolution worked to a fundamentally different effect in politics than it did in France and the development of the historical literature itself presents a different process. In France the period of the Restoration is distinguished mainly by writings against the Revolution (though it is not true, as is often said, that until 1823 no one wrote about the Revolution except with repugnance, remembering only the tyranny and the blood), by the flow of memoirs and the emphasis on personal roles in the events. During this period history-writing played an extraordinary role in the politics of the time. It is widely recognized that Mignet and Thiers through their histories prepared the way for the Revolution of 1830 and the constitutional monarchy. They became important examples of the long-lasting association between

[1] Smyth, *F.R.* I, 171.   [2] Staël, *Considerations*, 16–17.

historical interpretations of the Revolution and the political parties of the day. The Revolution continued to be a live issue of party politics through historical consciousness and historical writings, affecting the events of the nineteenth century, the new revolutions, the making and unmaking of kings and dynasties. The French royalists like Bouillé and Bertrand had already prepared and partly presented their versions of Revolutionary history in exile. After the Restoration their efforts were rivalled by those of the liberals who dared to oppose the government. There was not even pretence at detachment by the writers of memoirs, or even the collectors of materials. Even before Buchez, editors of documents explained in their prefaces the political causes which they wished to arm, 'de souvenirs, d'exemples et d'inspiration'. Historians fought practical battles over the reconstruction of society. The political role of historiography in France of the Restoration was so obvious that to some students of the period it has obscured all other causes for the extraordinary revival of history. A profound revolution in European modes of thought is sometimes reduced to the practical needs of party politics, or even to the prudent desire of publicists to stay out of prison by using weapons drawn from the apparently innocuous arsenal of history. Though this over-simplifies the case, it is nevertheless true that in France the divisions between historical interpretations followed the party lines and seemed to grow even deeper as the century progressed. It was not so in England.

For historians writing on the Revolution in England, there was, of course, much less at stake, politically, than for their French counterparts. If contemporary interests felt themselves to be touched by any bias in the historical interpretation, the interplay between the history and the politics was of a peculiar kind. At first, there had been an urgent contest between the parties and within the parties concerning the acceptance or rejection of the French Revolution. Later, when war broke out, it was necessary to foster the spirit of loyalty and this showed itself in the historiography of the time. From the start, controversy sharpened the critical faculties, and the result was a growing fairness and impartiality from all sides. The tendency had been towards the construction of a unified view. The war and the approximation of Tory and Whig political principles were general factors connected with this. More specifically, this approximation was helped by the growing influence of Burke on liberal thinkers and by the popularity of Madame de Staël's liberal interpretation. At a later stage, the appearance in England of more extreme parties—and of movements like Social Toryism, which cut across the old party lines—was also unfavourable to the formation of clear-cut party lines in Revolutionary historiography.

There were, of course, those who believed in an intrinsic correspondence between the political parties in England and the antagonistic groups in the French Revolution. Each of the political parties could, in any case, find convenient analogies to make political warfare and abuse more pointed and forceful. But the conflicting ways in which the Revolution was put to political use might suggest a divergence much greater than really existed on the subject of the historical interpretation of the Revolution. For in England politicians felt quite free to use the episodes of the Revolution for purposes of momentary effect in political debate, often without consistency, and always without committing themselves (as they did in France) to the full logical and practical consequences of their analogies. In England one did not defend Robespierre simply because one was a Republican or a believer in terror. The liberals were often fiercer in their writings against the Jacobins than the Tories, perhaps because they felt more sharply the need to dissociate themselves from revolutionaries; the Tories were more severe in criticizing the reforming nobility. Croker, for instance, thought that Robespierre fell because he intended to go back to a system based on religion and moral principle, and Macaulay, similarly, said that Danton was a victim in the cause of mercy and order.

A UNIFIED VIEW EMERGES

In the 1820s the English historical view of the French Revolution seems to be emerging. It is only at a superficial glance that there seem to be Whig and Tory interpretations corresponding to the violent antagonisms in current politics. Whigs and Tories were fully aware that the battle between them would decide the direction of English politics on important issues for a long time; the party journals and reviews fought hard over every aspect of life and thought, relating everything to political issues. We therefore turn to the *Edinburgh* and *Quarterly*, the great party organs, voicing their party's views on politics, literature and history, expecting to find in them two streams of thought, a constantly recurring debate on the French Revolution along the lines laid down by Burke and his opponents; two schools of history to go with two schools of politics.

If we compare the writings on the Revolution in the *Edinburgh* and *Quarterly* we find that the rival periodicals afford, in fact, striking evidence for the view that the two parties do not have two basically different historical interpretations of the Revolution. We have already seen the reconciliation of the Whigs with Burkianism through articles in the *Edinburgh*. The Tory *Quarterly*, too, contained from its outset a series of unexpected pronouncements on the Revolution: that it was caused by the profligacy and misconduct of previous governments; that it would have occurred even if Voltaire and Rousseau had never lived;[1] that 'with all its errors, faults and crimes', it was the inevitable result of all past French history; that the disordered finances resulted from breaches of faith by previous governments; that the revolutionary persecution of

[1] 'Lacretelle's 18th century', *Q.R.* (Apr. 1814), XI, 138.

religion was the progeny of St Bartholomew.[1] This, surely, was not the history Burke had taught. Though he talked of defects in the French character, the Revolution was to him the child of the mind of a recent generation, of upstart talent united with monied interest. It was usually the defenders of the Revolution who would show its crimes to have been modelled on the crimes of the *ancien régime*. In England the example of St Bartholomew's day was often on people's minds. Pitt himself quoted it in connection with Louis XVI's death. In Catholic France such ardent defenders of the Revolution as Berville, Buchez or Louis Blanc quoted the example of St Bartholomew in this way.

Tory opinion was changing on the effect as well as on the causes of the Revolution. The *Quarterly* in 1826 reached a point when it felt the need for an apology for Burke's total condemnation of the French Revolution. It claimed that, 'because the French Revolution has, in the ultimate issue of events, proved beneficial to France', and to the world in the extension of liberty, it must not be assumed that Burke loved despotism and hated freedom. Should he have been indifferent to present evil because ultimate good may come out of it? This apology rests mainly on Burke's concern for English liberties, and these are admitted to have been very imperfect at the time.[2] The interesting thing is that in the eyes of some of his followers Burke had lost the title for far reaching prophecy, though his predictions for the period before 1815 were still quoted in his favour. This amounts in fact to a Tory acceptance of the Revolution as an event in the course of history and not against its grain, for the benefit, and not to the damage of mankind. It is perhaps interesting to note that this Tory apology for Burke in the *Quarterly* comes a year after the *Edinburgh* published Macaulay's political apology for Milton the revolutionary, and a clear cut condemnation of Charles I which readers were led to apply to Louis XVI.

The *Quarterly*, having criticized Burke, having apologized for his erroneous judgment on the causes and consequences of the French Revolution, also found it difficult to differ from the Whigs on points of fact. If we compare the parallel reviews in the *Edinburgh* and *Quarterly* of a rather important publication, *The Royal Memoirs*, of 1823, we see in what sense it is true to say that though the reviews were strongly aware of their duty to conduct political warfare over history, they do basically offer the same history in fact if not in tone. The *Royal Memoirs* were translated and annotated by Croker, who also reviewed his own edition in the *Quarterly*. This work marks an important step in Croker's own contribution as a historian and as such will be treated later. What is of interest here is the Whig–Tory exchange about the Revolution which it occasioned. The Whig reviewer abuses the ultra-royalism of Croker, who,

[1] 'Lacretelle's Constitutent Assembly', *Q.R.* (Jan. 1823), XXVIII, 271.
[2] 'Prior's Life of Burke', *Q.R.* (Sept. 1826), XXXIV, 457.

he says, 'is romantic about the subject to enthusiasm'. He tries unsuccessfully to discredit the political fairness of the annotations, but has to admit that the notes deserve praise 'for their fullness and apparent accuracy'. One of the royal memoirs was by Louis XVIII and Croker criticized it severely both as to style and as to sentiments. The *Edinburgh* thought this an unexpected attitude in a Tory towards a reigning monarch and alleged therefore that it was due to Louis XVIII's early revolutionary sympathies.

The Whig reviewer is determined to disapprove even when he cannot entirely disagree, but he differs only slightly from Croker in his judgments. He certainly disagrees on Lafayette and objects to the irrelevant attacks on Napoleon; but he condemns, as hotly as Croker, the barbaric treatment of the royal prisoners, adding vaguely, however, that the narratives of these latter are not without their falsity. When the Whig reviewer declares the King's timidity the cause of the failure of the flight to Varennes, he can quote the 'ultra-royalist editor' himself as saying that no one had a right to command except Louis, and Louis's only orders were to do nothing. The Whig reviewer criticizes Croker not for his historical annotations but rather in spite of them. The best tribute to Croker, and incidentally the best indication of the non-political trend in historiography, is the Whig charge that there was more inconsistency in him than was ever found in a party paper. We gain a view not only of the approximation of Whig and Tory views but also of the lingering differences between them at the time, through another Whig charge, that 'the heavy pages of the mere plodding anecdote-monger, the collector of names, the rectifier of dates, and collater of parallel accounts of passages almost all devoid of real importance', will not convert any one to the bigoted Bourbons. We see the Whigs in the old-fashioned role which their historians regularly followed. Without advancing a fundamentally different presentation or interpretation of historical fact, they offer a slightly modified view, a scorn for research and detail, a love of general principles, and the assumption that history is meant for political persuasion. The concrete work is carried forward by the plodding Tory.

In this sense certainly, but perhaps in this sense only, can it be said of such cold-blooded historians as Croker that they were 'Romantic' while their Whig opponents, warm lovers of humanity as they considered themselves, were heirs of the abstract rationalist creed. If 'Romantic' to many meant sentimentality about the royal family and the nobility of France, then the Tories could claim a bigger share of this feeling. If 'Romantic' in history meant having a greater interest in the details and 'particular truths' of history, the Tory claim at this stage would also be much stronger. The eighteenth-century notion that 'bad' periods in history were not worth studying was inherited from rationalist historiography mainly by Whigs and Radicals. Hallam considered the period before the twelfth century as useless to history. Smyth taught his students that some 'profligate periods' (as for example the reign of Louis XV) were not worth studying, and Mill, when under the influence of the utilitarian approach to history at its worst, held the Napoleonic period to be useless to history and no challenge to an historian. Its 'ordinary characters and ordinary events', he said, its 'obvious causes' and the 'lowest impulses' to action, demand but inferior historical qualities; even historical inaccuracies, he held, do not matter in a period so unimportant 'for any purpose of utility or instruction'.

SCOTT AND MILL

The tendency towards a basically unified and non-political view is shown in the party reviews (including the *Westminster*) in Smyth's academic work and in the histories of Hazlitt, Scott and Alison. Croker's absorption in detailed investigation and Carlyle's scorn for political dissertations in history later put both these writers within the scope of this tradition, though both would have scorned the idea of being 'moderates'. It is this charge of moderateness, of having an 'original liberality' and indifference to political opinion, which Mill brings against Scott's *History of Napoleon*. Held against Hazlitt's *Napoleon*, Scott's work appeared to Carlyle (possibly before he read it) to belong to an opposite school, as he wrote to Goethe. But the differences between Scott and Hazlitt are in fact greater concerning Napoleon than concerning the history of the Revolution. *Blackwood's Magazine*, in reviewing the *Génie de Christianisme* in 1832, wrote that it was to the glory of Conservatism that the two greatest writers of the age, Scott and Chateaubriand, devoted their talents to its support.[1] That Scott was considered the English champion of Conservatism proves both the mildness of English conservatism and its dearth of ideologists. Mill also traces Scott's 'liberality' to his desire to please everybody. Scott, in fact, pleased nobody. Writing his history anonymously at first, he could not seek information and meant to use only ordinary materials. When he discarded his anonymity he made use of some original materials. In 1826 he went to Paris; through Canning he obtained access to Foreign Office documents about St Helena; he had information from Macdonald, Napoleon's Scottish Marshal, a bundle of notes about Spain from Wellington. He wrote nine volumes in twelve months and his proof reader had to struggle with inaccuracies five hours per sheet. One of the men researching for Scott sent him a letter full of anecdotes by Captain Usher of the *Undaunted* which had been given to the *Quarterly* and left unused by Croker. When Scott's book came out he received numerous corrections and all but fought a duel with Gourgaud over his alleged treachery to

[1] *Blackwood's* (Aug. 1832), XXXII, 217.

Napoleon. (Scott's soldier-son then suggested that the family be divided into the writing and fighting departments.)

Two important points seem to emerge from Scott's history. The fact that Scott, who had great influence on Romantic history, did not himself write romantic but rather reflective history; and the fact that this militant Tory did not produce a bigoted anti-Revolutionary work.[1] The first two volumes of Scott's *History of Napoleon* are a history of the French Revolution, the one beginning with the question of the causes, the other ending with the fall of Robespierre. Scott described the Revolution as resulting from long preparation and widespread causes: 'A great force was prepared to level institutions which were crumbling to pieces by themselves.'[2] This became a stock phrase in revolutionary historiography, shared by Whigs and Tories alike, by Jeffrey, Scott, Alison, Carlyle, and others. Brougham wrote in similar words, that no financial disorder or statesmen's errors could have 'dislocated . . . a system which had not been prepared to crumble in pieces by the ravages of time, or the undermining of public opinion, or the ferment of popular discontent'. Mathiez much later was to compare the collapse of the old order to 'the sudden collapse of a ruined crumbling building'. This stock phrase implies a judgment on the *ancien régime* which could not be held by its defenders.

As Mill put it, Scott treated 'democratic principles' with respect, thus pleasantly surprising a part of his reading public which was more used to abuse. A Tory, says Mill, must read Scott with 'some mitigation of his prejudices'. Mill, however, thought that Scott's impartiality was really due to an indifference to opinions. Scott's historical comments form an uneven series of judgments. In some he naïvely judges France on the basis of the English model, arguing that France could have borrowed institutions of freedom from England. In others he thinks more profoundly. Scott, before historical materialism, understood the theory later to appear on Mathiez's as well as Acton's pages, that it was the power and wealth of the middle classes which drove them to revolution.

It was not in the nature of man, that the bold, the talented, the ambitious, of a rank which felt its own power and consequence, should be long contented to remain acquiescent in political regulations, which depressed them in the state of society beneath men to whom they felt themselves equal in all respects, excepting the factitious circumstances of birth, or of church orders;

and later,

Thus, a body, opulent and important . . . were arranged in formidable array against the privileges of the nobles and clergy, and bound to further the approaching changes by the strongest of human ties, emulation and self interest.[3]

[1] See D. Forbes, 'The Rationalism of Sir Walter Scott', *The Cambridge Journal* (Oct. 1953), VII, 20.
[2] Scott, *Napoleon*, I, 46.   [3] Scott, *Napoleon*, I, 44.

Mill, oddly, felt that Scott was exaggerating the role of envy. Did the peasants then rise so that the merchants' sons could get commissions in the army? asks Mill. Scott does not, on the whole, ascribe as much influence to social and economic grievances as to philosophy and irreligion. In the spirit of the enlightenment he remarks on the harm done to the public mind through censorship. Because practical criticism was forbidden, political speculation tended to become more and more abstract and divergent from political practice.

John Stuart Mill belonged with Southey, Croker and Brougham to that small band of Englishmen who in the 1820s were fired by the ambition to write the English history of the French Revolution, who made themselves experts on the subject, but were destined to see the prizes carried off in the 'thirties by two others of their number, Alison and Carlyle. As early as his review of Mignet in 1826, Mill began his endless complaints concerning the ignorance prevailing in England on the Revolution. The English view, he said quite wrongly, was entirely dominated by the 'indiscriminate invective' of the anti-reform campaign. He often stated his intention of dealing more fully with the subject. It was not until he handed over to Carlyle his collection of materials that Mill gave up the idea. When in 1828 he reviewed Scott's *Life of Napoleon* he included in it some of his own findings.

It is not always remembered how far Mill's mind was, in the midst of his early philosophical training, occupied with problems of history writing. He early formulated views about the aims and methods of history. The reviews of Mignet and Scott include sketches of the nature and the history of historical studies. History, says Mill for instance, started as a mere narrative, but became in modern times a study in which facts are subservient to philosophy. Between these two styles stand historians like Hume and Mignet who combine dramatic interest with philosophical instruction, though their popularity proves the shallowness of their thought. Good history, in Mill's opinion, should turn facts to use by subordinating them to principles. A historian must be, 'in short, a philosopher', and also practised in weighing testimony, 'in one word, a judge'. Because Mill was looking to history for philosophical instruction, he chose to ignore the Napoleonic period as unimportant. On the study of Revolutionary history he held more interesting views. Its extraordinary events, complicated causes, breathless rapidity and moving forces require a technique as yet unknown to conventional historical writing. Since the novelty of the French Revolution lay in the part played by a whole people, its understanding required familiarity with the nature of popular enthusiasm. Party, class and individual interests influence the current but cannot withstand it. The future historian of the French Revolution would have to draw from 'the primaeval fountain of human nature itself'; to understand how a *people* acts we also need to know how its civilization, morals, modes of thought and social relations were shaped; the historian of the Revolution would have to know the science of government and legislation, the theory and practice of politics. It is odd to find in the young Mill such modern historical aspirations as the study of human motivation and mob psychology side by side with such notions as the barrenness of the Napoleonic period and the sub-servience of fact to philosophy. It is equally typical of the haphazard penetration of new ideas about history in England that Mill, the Philo-sophical Radical, is able to criticize Scott, the Romantic Tory, for Scott's basic mis-comprehension of the French Revolution which, according to Mill, resulted from the narrow axiom that whatever is English is best for all. Scott, claimed Mill, simply judged other nations by English practice without social and political considerations. He is ignorant of the peculiar structure, development, circumstances and spirit of France.[1] That this was not a chance remark, and that Mill understood its implications for history, is shown in another place where he says that to condemn even the constitutional monarchists as theorists because they did not adopt 'tried' English forms, is as visionary and theoretical as the revolutionary ideas themselves. The same charge of not allowing for basic differences between nations and periods is also implied when Mill discusses Scott's treatment of certain revolutionaries, like Madame Roland, whose writ-ings are read by Scott out of the context of the moral and stylistic standards of her time.

In his concrete statements on the Revolution, Mill stressed economic grievances making much of Arthur Young's evidence. Feelings are not excited by abstractions, he says. He defends most of the philosophers from the charge of irreligion, and all of them from that of a conspiracy. During the Revolution, he holds, a multitude of factions arose which the historians usually lump together as having started simultaneously with the Revolution and as sharing in the guilt of the Terrorists. He holds that there was at the beginning no Republican party, only republican theory. It was with Orleanism and not with Republicanism that the King's enemies were charged. The Girondins were not 'reckless en-thusiasts', but admirable men for whom Mill demands justice. Mill shows great familiarity with Revolutionary sources, other historians' inaccuracies, and is skilful in collecting evidence from different memoirs to prove for instance that the King provoked the action of 14 July.

THE REACTION AGAINST FATALISM

One of the features which united English historical opinion on the Revolution, especially in this period of formation, was a peculiar

[1] Scott did occasionally deserve such criticism. See, e.g., Scott, *Napoleon*, II, 140-1.

reaction against the first important French histories of the Revolution. Mignet and Thiers were the first to give a complete narrative and basic interpretations. They distinguished between 1789 and 1793. The first period expressed the good spirit of the Revolution, that of the *bourgeois* aiming at control and efficiency. It was therefore French and traditional, its inspiration was Montesquieu rather than Rousseau. The period beginning in 1793 is explained by the necessities of war. Mignet and Thiers were commonly understood to have evolved three interconnected theories, that of the inevitability of the Revolution and of each of its stages; that of the justification of the Terror through a theory of necessity as well as the practical necessity of the war; and that of the action of impersonal forces in history stronger than man. Mignet wrote, 'Les hommes font les choses profondes avec ignorance. Dieu, dont ils sont les instrumens, dépose moins souvent des desseins dans leur esprit que dans leur situation. Il se sert de leurs passions pour les accomplir.' Mignet conveys his interpretation more often by tone than explicitly. Hundreds of statements are given in the passive voice or in an impersonal way. Measures were adopted; approval was received; confusion reigned; parties were deprived of power; effects were produced; 'death became the sole means of governments, and the republic was abandoned to daily and systematic executions'.[1] The cumulative effect of this tone is to suggest an impersonal agency as the actor behind the scenes. Sometimes the 'laws of progress' are more explicitly stated. 'Napoleon represented for France, as Cromwell did for England, the government of the army which is always established when a revolution is contested; it then changes its nature little by little and instead of being civil as it had been at first, becomes military.' Or, 'in a revolution everything depends upon a final refusal and a first struggle'.[2] Above all the impression of 'necessity' and inner justification is obtained through lack of moral judgment and through the presentation of the Terror as the action of a war government against enemies. Mignet presents the execution of the Queen as meant against Europe; that of Bailly, against the Constitutionalists. There is no mention of the guillotine in Mignet, nor of 'the lantern' in Thiers. Thiers wrote in his introduction, 'If we have to uphold the same cause, we have not to defend their conduct, for we can separate liberty from those who have rendered it service or disservice.' But Thiers's practice is in fact better represented by statements like, 'In war nothing but the possibility of success can justify cruel enterprises.'[3] Thiers explained and justified all that had happened and never condemned the French nation. Both historians moved from Lafayette to Brissot, to Danton and to Napoleon, describing a natural process not always moral

---

[1] Mignet, *History of the French Revolution from 1789–1814* (1826), p. 290.
[2] Mignet, *F.R.* 480, 290.
[3] Thiers, *F.R.* pp. xv, 99.

but always reasonable, accepting it in the same way that the French people had done at the time.

It was acceptable to Tories, Whigs and Radicals that the political point of view of Mignet and Thiers was that of constitutional monarchists, and that they made the distinction between the early Revolution and the Terror. Mill received Mignet favourably, though he deplored his all-to-easy generalizations and his straining after sententiousness. This, by the way, Mill considered a French vice, prominent in Madame de Staël. Mill quoted from Mignet a list of epigrammatic generalizations in order to analyse and refute them. It was not, however, so much the Philosophical Radical who was himself searching for laws in history, as Whig and Tory opinion which was roused by Mignet's and Thiers's implications of inevitability. The impersonal attitude to the historical development of the Revolution and to its moral problems raised against it English opinion and left an indelible mark on English historiography. The historical quality of Thiers and Mignet, especially the latter, was greatly admired and use was made of the authority of these writers. But both were widely and violently attacked for their interpretation which was named 'fatality'. Mignet and Thiers did introduce into the history of the Revolution a new notion, historical determinism with a romantic aura. They pity all, reproach all, and mourn all. They patriotically stress the military glory, always thinking of France as a whole. Against this interpretation the English historians rose to a man, always insisting on the predominant part played by 'crime and error'. Here again the influence of Madame de Staël on English historians was great. It was her evidence and interpretation which they quoted against Mignet. The conservative romanticists had contributed before Thiers and Mignet to the theory of inevitability rejected by England. De Maistre had written in his *Considér-ations* (2nd ed. 1797), p. 31, 'les crimes des tyrans de la France devenoient les instrumens de la Providence', and also, 'ce ne sont point les hommes qui mènent la révolution, c'est la révolution qui emploie les hommes'. 'Elle va toute seule.'

Because it is common in discussions of French Revolutionary historio-graphy simply to class Madame de Staël and Mignet together as liberals, constitutionalists, and moderate admirers of the early Revolution, it is particularly interesting to note how early some English historians noted the deep chasm which was opening between the French historians' inter-pretations, leading on the one side to historical empiricism and on the other to determinism. Long before Michelet, Mignet's work struck many as preaching both the acceptance of the whole Revolution and the acceptance of the *necessity* for the whole Revolution. Smyth wrote about Mignet and Thiers that they 'destroy their moral sensibilities and escape from responsibility by notions of necessity'. Croker wrote, 'the un-happy necessity [of the crimes] is deplored but asserted.' Thiers, he writes, assumed a 'mask of impartiality and moderation'. Carlyle wrote in a letter that Thiers's wonderful system of ethics was that every hero turns out to be justified in whatever he did. Thackeray, in reviewing Carlyle, stressed his superiority to Thiers, whose immoral impartiality meant excusing all sides out of moral indifference. More than sixty years after Mignet's and Thiers's histories were published, after a period in which some of the greatest interpretations of the Revolution had appeared, the *English Historical Review* welcomed the fact that Morse Stephens (in 1886!) did not adopt Mignet's interpretation of fatality. Earlier Lamartine gained popularity in England because he was believed to have written against Mignet's theory of necessity; and John Morley had cause to complain that anyone who showed cause and effect in history was in England called a Fatalist.

CHAPTER 4

THE MEMOIRS

In France the Restoration started a flood of royalist memoirs which both excited and satisfied the prevalent sentiments. England took part in the production of memoirs and similar literature in various ways. Accounts of residence in France had preceded the Restoration. Some of them written as letters have some value as immediate reactions. New memoirs reached the English public as soon as they appeared. There were French editions published in England, English translations and English accounts based on the published memoirs. The reviews in the journals found so much that was new that their pages often consist mainly of quotations.

In France the survivors of the revolutionary generation were still alive, passionately concerned with their past experiences and present reputations. Books took part in personal quarrels over facts and honours, and duels were fought in the cause of history. Some important French memoirs had already been published in England before the Restoration. The writers living in England as émigrés were sensitive about their English reputations and their public modified their tone. Bouillé and Bertrand, Dumouriez and Mallet du Pan occasionally expressed curiously English sentiments and they were trusted and liked in wide circles in England. Bouillé said that he wrote his memoirs in order to correct some English misrepresentations of his actions, and Bertrand engaged in public controversy with Fox, Mallet du Pan, Miss Williams and others. Of the English writers associated with the émigrés, translating and expounding their writings, a prominent figure was Dallas. He wrote anti-revolutionary poems and novels and, in his own words, 'fought in the armour of Mallet du Pan', in bringing out the English edition of the *Mercure Britannique*. He translated from manuscript Bertrand de Moleville's works. When his two patrons engaged in controversy over facts in Bertrand's history, it was probably Dallas who attempted to reconcile their views and thus maintain the appearance of a uniform anti-revolutionary front. French Revolutionary materials also got into many English memoirs of the reign of George III. The links between English and French intellectuals before and during the Revolution, and the connections with the emissaries of France and with the émigrés, make some of these English memoirs sources for French Revolutionary history. The flood of Restoration material showed historians that the subject of the Revolution grew more difficult with the accumulation of materials. Some critics still hoped that all would be revealed with the posthumous memoirs of Siéyès or Lafayette, just as others had previously hoped that the unravelling of the Orleans conspiracy held the key to all the secrets.

Other historians realized with frantic exasperation, just when direct evidence was becoming available and important, how fast the witnesses were dying out, taking vital secrets with them, how much evidence was being wilfully or accidentally destroyed and how fast the scene was changing. While a constant effort was being made for private or for disinterested purposes to unravel the facts, a counter effort was deliberately made to obliterate from record and from memory certain important facts. These activities were quite real in those days. They gave rise on the one hand to authentic publications, and on the other, to the destruction of papers, to forgeries and (as in the case of Madame Campan for instance) the adaptation of accounts to the changing régimes. There were masses of spurious memoirs: memoirs of Lamballe written by Guénard,[1] those of Levasseur by Roche, those of Barras by Rousselin, those of Fleury by Lafitte,[2] those of Fouché by Beauchamp,[3] those of Robespierre by Reybaud, and those of Weber, the foster-brother of Marie Antoinette, by Lally Tollendal. Though the journal of Cléry was genuine, his memoirs were apocryphal.

Another tendency of the time was to extract from the lips of the dying, reminiscences and confessions which might make a historian immortal. Both Thiers and Lamartine were still able to use such sources to a large extent. In England, Carlyle was the most anxious to do this, but it was Croker who, in fact, had the easiest access to revolutionary figures. The amount of falseness which came forth from contemporaries was prodigious.[4] Lies and errors sowed the seeds of numerous weeds which had to be laboriously uprooted much later when they had multiplied, by historians whose time and talent were wasted in this destructive task. At its most effective the weeding was to be done late in the century and outside England. The memoirs were exposed mainly with the help of the private letters of the writers. Flammermont showed that Madame Campan wrote a panegyric of the Queen to recommend herself to the new powers that be; Aulard showed that Talleyrand explained his conduct while seeking office under the Restoration; Sybel showed that Dumouriez lied to justify defeat and defection; Lenz showed that Bouillé accommodated facts to his personal purposes, especially with regard to the preparations for the flight to Varennes. One English example of spurious writing was the memoirs which Catherine Marchioness Solari, an

[1] *Mémoires de la princesse de Lamballe* [par Mme Guénard], 4 vols.
[2] *Mémoires de Fleury de la Comédie-française.* 6 vols. (1835–7) [by J. B. Lafitte].
[3] *Mémoires de Fouché, duc d'Otrante,* 2 vols. (Paris, 1824). It was generally believed at the time (see *Biographie Universelle* ix, VIII, 474, and *Biographie Générale*) that Beauchamp worked with authentic papers of Fouché. The Duke of Wellington assured Alison that the negotiations of 1809 are accurately described and that the memoirs contained facts which no one but Fouché knew. Alison used this information.
[4] Revellière-Lepeaux wrote in his *Memoirs,* 'not a single warrant for arrest was issued after 19th Fructidor'. V. Pierre, in *La Déportation Ecclésiastique sous le Directoire* (1895), produces 231 signed by Revellière-Lepeaux himself.

adventuress and a liar, brought out in 1826, pretending that they were based on the authentic papers of Princess Lamballe. It is so worthless a fiction that one is surprised to find a new edition as late as 1895 and, even more, to find it cut to pieces in the *English Historical Review* by Pollard. Pollard must also have been the 'deadly specialist' who exposed C. R. L. Fletcher's 'splendid piece of spoof', a piece of work supposedly by R.Hesdin, *The Journal of a Spy in Paris During the Reign of Terror, Jan.– July 1794* (London, 1895). It was published as a genuine document and, as Sir Charles Oman wrote in his *Memoirs*, it was welcomed as a most valuable contribution to the history of the French Revolution, until Pollard declared it a forgery, and was puzzled by its lack of motive !ial[1] The appearance of such a work, as well as its treatment in numerous reviews, reflects the widespread though ineffectual interest in new documents, questions of authenticity and forgeries.

Although the early memoirs were sometimes taken for history, and their complete overthrow as a reliable source could only take place in the second half of the century after the beginning of the publication of the contemporary letters and the opening of other sources, there is not really a period when it can be said that there was no criticism of memoirs or that their unreliability was not realized. Historians were, of course, more credulous and the critical apparatus had not yet been built up, but there were numerous beginnings of useful tests and there was a questioning attitude. Alison wrote in 1833 that 'the most interesting record of those times is to be found in the contemporary memoirs by the principal sufferers'.[2] But the *Monthly Review*, in reviewing Adolphus as early as 1799, had already said that the memoirs (except the royal ones) were written by men black with crime.[3] Macaulay, in his article on Barère almost half a century later, tried, among other things, to expose Barère's own lies in his memoirs. But in producing proof he limited himself to well-known facts easily established by reference to the *Moniteur*, showing, for instance, Barère's part (in spite of his denials) in the death of the Queen and of the Girondins. A critical attitude to the memoirs appeared early among English historians, although they were later to be left far behind when the French and German historians systematically destroyed all the favourite authorities.

CROKER'S TECHNIQUE

The most assiduous English critic of the memoirs was Croker, who learnt his trade as a historian in the critical examination of other writers' facts. Croker's treatment of French Revolutionary memoirs is as

---

[1] See Sir Charles Oman, *Memories of Victorian Oxford* (London, 1941), p. 125; H. M. Stephens in *A.H.R.* (1895–6), I, 755; *E.R.* (1896); A. F. Pollard in *E.H.R.* (1896), XI, 594–7; *Athenaeum* (16 May 1896), p. 650.
[2] Alison, *History* (1833), vi.   [3] C. L. Moody, *M.R.* (1799), XXXI, 67.

ambiguous as his whole position as a historian. It is surprising that the weight of his powerful criticism was not turned on this, now so obvious, target. He realized the unreliability of memoirs as a source, and he criticized and discredited some of them. But his achievement in this respect is not comparable to that which he had in criticizing historians. Madame Campan gets away with a great deal more than M. Thiers, and the narrative of Madame d'Angoulême as a child is declared the most valuable document on Varennes. The preferences are not really political, but result partly from the nature of Croker's tools. He knew well the working of the political mind but had little insight into human nature as a whole. The personal element which pervades the subjective narrative of a memoir, Croker was unable to approach close enough even for destructive criticism. With historians he was at home. They collected, selected, presented and misrepresented facts, and Croker could do the same against them. The practical political motive, as in the case of Thiers, Croker was specially qualified to dissect.

Croker cannot be said to have dealt the mortal blow to the memoirs though he did something in that direction. He mainly discredited them indirectly by using better material. At a time when many people knew only memoirs, and others complained about the vast amount of materials, Croker alone cried out for more and knew what was wanted. He knew that it would be through additional contemporary materials that the memoirs could be checked and refuted. One other writer curiously appears to share this ground with Croker. Mill seems to combine the lessons of romanticism and studiousness when he writes:

The documents which breathe the living spirit of the time, the only monument of really contemporary history (which is the most different thing imaginable from history written by contemporaries after they had undergone a thousand changes of opinion and feeling, and when the genuine impression of the present events has faded from their recollections) are the decrees of the national assemblies, the speeches of their members, the papers laid before them, and the immensely numerous books, pamphlets, and periodicals of the day.

But for Mill the writing of history was to remain a theoretical prescription. Croker tried to follow out in practice very similar ideas.

In criticizing particular memoirs, however, Croker's standards were often conventional. Madame Campan's case is notorious. Her authority was later overthrown on grounds which Croker suspected but rejected.[1] He chose to establish her reliability through reasoning. He said that she had opportunity, honesty and an 'air of sincerity'; her family's republicanism made her own defence of the Queen convincing; she had nothing to gain by falsely extenuating the Queen's conduct, for nothing could please Napoleon less. The attacks she received from both sides

---

[1] See Flammermont, 'Études Critiques sur les Sources de l'Histoire du XVIIIme Siècle', *Bulletin de la Faculté des lettres de Poitiers* (1885).

prove that she disappointed all partisan expectations. Croker, nevertheless, accepts what he likes of Campan's evidence, and rejects, for instance, her assertion that the Queen suspected a 'plot' by Pitt.[1] He does not reconcile this with his assertion that Campan was absolutely reliable for anything concerning the Queen. A more glaring example is connected with Croker's inveterate hatred for Napoleon. Napoleon claimed Campan's authority for his statement that on the night of 5 October 1789 the Queen received Fersen. The question of the 'conjugal fidelity' of Marie Antoinette had always been very much on the minds of anti-Revolutionary writers in England. It was widely discussed when Lord Holland's *Memoirs* revived the 'calumnies' against the Queen. Croker's elaborate refutation of Napoleon's statement is highly deceptive. He claims, on the one hand, that Campan could not have said this because she (Campan) gives a different version of the events of that night, in her memoirs, and on the other hand, that she could not have told Napoleon anything, since she was not in Versailles that night. Croker either does not realize, or hopes others will not do, that if Campan was away from Versailles her evidence is equally invalid for or against the Queen. Croker, at this point, is simply using Campan to defend the reputation of the Queen.

Although detecting forgeries and spurious memoirs was his favourite activity, Croker made few major discoveries and often burst into open doors. He declared, for instance, that Lauzun's memoirs were an infamous forgery, having ascertained this 'by a comparison of dates as well as of circumstances', but he fairly credits Salgue with the exposure and he need not have gone further for proof than the open correspondence on the subject.[2]

In one case Croker claims undeserved credit and handles a review badly. When Le Vasseur's *Memoirs* came out in 1829, a court of law judged that the author was Achilles Roche. It came out that Le Vasseur, in infirm old age, gave some notes and instructions to his son, who with the help of the *Moniteur* produced a volume which Rapilly accepted. Rapilly employed Roche to expand it. He claimed it was a mere skeleton, while young Le Vasseur claimed it to have been a proper volume. Neither of them asserted that it was written by old Le Vasseur.[3] The *Quarterly*

[1] J. M. Thompson quotes Croker's evidence on this point (J. M. Thompson, *The French Revolution* (Oxford, 1951), 4th ed., p. 450). Croker questioned survivors of Pitt's administration before he concluded that up to the war Pitt observed pedantic neutrality ('Madame Campan's Memoirs', *Q.R.* (1823), XXVIII, 463). He claims also to have consulted 'public and private correspondence of ministers and ambassadors' especially at Paris. In 1855 Croker added a note specifying the names of people individually consulted on the point (Croker, *Essays*, p. 104).

[2] The MS. was acquired during the Empire by the Duc de Rovigo, Minister of the Police. When it was published in 1818, Rovigo was asked by Salgue why he had let it go and answered that he, Rovigo, had not had private possession of it.

[3] Le Vasseur was a medical man who held office under the Convention and voted for the death of the King. Exiled during the Restoration, he came back in 1830. The transcripts of the trial appear in *Mémoires de René Levasseur* (de la Sarthe) (Paris, 1829–31), IV, 291–377.

reviewer declares that his suspicions had anticipated the legal decision, but that this latter saved him the trouble of a critical examination. He adds that the work would not have been reviewed except to expose a fabrication. These statements appear to be mere journalistic tricks. Having promised an exposition, the reviewer simply goes on to say that he will now treat the work *as if genuine*, because, as he says, it had been sanctioned by Le Vasseur and because it expressed the sentiments of a party now in power under Thiers. The rest of the review, in a manner unlike Croker's, simply rebukes Le Vasseur for exonerating crime. The discrepancy between the two parts of the review and the flimsiness of the arguments bridging them is explained by a manuscript note in a bound collection of Croker's articles, which reads: 'This review was written (by F. E. [Francis Ellis?]) in the supposition that the book was *genuine*. Mr Croker was asked to fit it to the true state of the case—namely that the work was a mere forgery—He could do so but imperfectly.' It does not explain why the review was not rewritten, but clarifies the double authorship,[1] exposes the patched-up excuses for treating the work as if genuine, contradicts the statement that it would not have been reviewed if genuine, and shows that Croker, far from discovering the forgery, was asked to rewrite the article with due attention to the discovery of the forgery.

One other case of Croker's criticism of memoirs is interesting as bringing out more clearly than any other Croker's handling of his sharpest weapon: his knowledge of the sources. He could approach a writer confidently, search him at a glance and put his hands on the stolen goods. The case is that of the so called Memoirs of Louis XVIII.[2] 'Mentiris impudentissime', he exclaims, 'these Memoirs are not only not written by the king, but they are not compiled by any one who could ever have approached his Majesty in his private or even in his public character.'[3] His impressive display of evidence consists partly of a set of 'technical marks of fabrication', discrepancies in dates and tone (partly spotted by a comparison with Monsieur's authentic account of his flight to Brussels),[4] errors in names, in forms of address and etiquette. More powerful proof shows how the work had been concocted from other works, by comparing passages, words, topics, style and even mistakes with those of the sources used. He shows that hundreds of anecdotes were simply copied from

---

[1] The article is listed as Croker's in Brightfield's bibliography.

[2] *Mémoires de Louis XVIII, receuillis et mis en ordre* par M. le duc de D ×××.6 vols. (Paris, 1832–3). *The Memoirs of Louis XVIII*. Written by himself, 2 vols. (London, 1832), seem to be an abridged translation of the former. Croker reviewed the French publication in *Q.R.* (Dec. 1832), XLVIII, 455–80. See also *Q.R.* (1837), LVIII, 406–13.

[3] These spurious memoirs were in fact (though Croker learnt this only later) written by E. L. de Lamotte Houndancourt, afterwards Lamotte Langon.

[4] Croker had translated and edited this account in his *Royal Memoirs* (1823).

Bachaumont[1] with obvious and incriminating carelessness. One of many examples is the sixty pages of lists and anecdotes about the Assembly of the Notables copied from Bachaumont. One list, which in Bachaumont is headed 'seven bishops' and includes seven names, has in the *Memoirs*, eight names, under the same heading. Croker spots the error of the copyist who wrote instead of 'of Rhodez, seignelay—Colbert de Castle hill', 'of Rhodez, seignelay—Colbert; of Gast, le Tria', thus inventing a M. Le Tria, Bishop of Gast. Whether correct or not, the point illustrates the sort of treatment Croker subjected his materials to. He is often carried away by zeal, but, even in doing so, he perfected a method which was not sharper than was needed for French Revolutionary materials. He exposes the sources of the *Memoirs*, and he shows that what is said of the King's private life includes nothing which is not in the public journals. Incidentally he explains that the *Memoirs* are a fabrication not only because they were not written by the King, but because even the information which is stolen is false. By now he knows that Bachaumont, Georgel, Bezenval, Ferrières and even Mesdames Dessand and Campan are often fallacious through ignorance, prejudice or malice.[2]

The merit of this exposure is Croker's own even if his suspicion was aided by hints from Paris. He was not offended when a literary friend in Paris wrote to express his amazement that he should have troubled to expose an imposture which 'tout le monde avait déjà apprécié'. Croker denied this on behalf of the London 'monde', and claimed that Talleyrand had been taken in until he read Croker's article. The real importance of the review lies not in whether it killed a worthless book, but in its display, at an early period, of an example of 'textual criticism' applied to French Revolutionary *mémoires*.

The criticism of memoirs was not, as we have seen, the most important development in English historiography at the time and Croker was as yet definitely unique in sharpening his tools for it. The most typical historical treatment of the French Revolution in the years between 1789 and 1832 was the lectures first delivered by the Regius Professor at Cambridge in the late 'twenties. They faithfully embody so many of the ambiguous and evanescent attitudes in history and in politics in those years of transition. Politics was the keynote of the teaching of history at the universities and was to remain so for a long time. Smyth was the first academic scholar in England to take up the subject of the Revolution as a whole. 'We are all more indebted to him than we know', writes a reviewer in the *Westminster* in 1856, suggesting that Macaulay had

---

[1] A literary journal abounding in court gossip. Thirty-six volumes appeared between 1762 and 1787 (*Mémoires secrets pour servir à l'histoire de la république des lettres en France, depuis 1762 jusqua'à nos jours* [1787] . . . par M. de Bachaumont).

[2] *Q.R.* (Jan. 1823), XXVIII, 449–64.

probably been introduced to history by Smyth and comparing Smyth (in some respects, favourably) with Macaulay. Smyth, he says, treats history with diffidence and not, like Macaulay, with over-confidence. Whereas Macaulay exhausts his subject, Smyth shows it to be inexhaustible. He trained two generations of the political intellect of the University and his lectures, as fresh in 1856 as they had been forty years earlier, explain why Cambridge had produced so many illustrious thinkers. His early judgment on the Revolution was that which all arrived at later.[1] This extraordinary tribute written as late as 1856 was of course exaggerated, but Smyth has an important place in English Revolutionary historiography. With prominent political and educational objectives he inaugurated a period of disinterested study. He elevated what had been a weapon of politics to a level where it was to depend on a wide and fair reading of the sources. Had Smyth published his lectures when he finished writing them in the early 1830s, he would not have missed the fame which was justly his as a pioneer.

[1] *Westminster* (1856), LXV, 611.

CHAPTER 5

WILLIAM SMYTH

THE PROFESSOR

William Smyth was the first Englishman to write on the French Revolution as a historian. He combined some of the qualities which other contemporaries had, but his work surpassed theirs in quality through his conscious application to it of an academic spirit and mind. He was twenty-four when the Revolution broke out, a poet, an enthusiastic liberal and reformer. In his uneventful life, Eton and Cambridge are the main landmarks. Except for three years between 1793 and 1795, when he was tutor to Sheridan's son, Smyth was in Cambridge from 1783 to 1847, as Pensioner at Peterhouse at first, fellow from 1787, tutor from 1797, and Regius Professor of Modern History from 1807 to his retirement in 1847. The years he spent with the Sheridans constituted his chief experience of life outside a university. The sixty years in Cambridge, he devoted to poetry and study, to history, to teaching and entertaining students, and to the social and musical pleasures of the place. During the vacations he visited his relations and friends, went up to London to attend a debate or to meet his political friends of the Holland House circle.

Smyth was generally liked and widely admired.[1] His striking old-fashioned appearance, his grave principles and amusing conversation, his real vocation for teaching and love for the arts, impressed all who passed through Cambridge, so that anecdotes about him are scattered over many memoirs. His intellectual attainments are reflected mainly in his lectures on the French Revolution which in old age he came to regard as the sum total of his life's efforts.[2]

Smyth had been a mathematician and a classicist, and while attending the historical lectures of his predecessor, Symonds, he wrote that he was not doing much for his own intellect.[3] His qualification for the Chair, was a lively interest in politics, and the appointment was a political one, obtained through his Whig friends. James Mackintosh, who heard of it in India, expressed his delight and offered Smyth a plan for his lectures.[4] Smyth, however, had one of his own, and in 1809 began to deliver his

---

[1] Harriet Martineau spoke disparagingly of Smyth in her biographical sketch of the Marquis of Lansdowne, and Gooch, half-heartedly, defends Smyth against her 'sharp tongue' in his study of the Cambridge Chair of Modern History.
[2] R.P. 4663, 20 May 1840. See below, p. 299, for a bibliographical note on Smyth.
[3] R.P. 4561, 18 March 1798.
[4] *Memoirs of the Life of Sir James Mackintosh* (London, 1835), I, 412 *et seq.*

two-year course on modern history covering the medieval and modern period down to the American Revolution.[1]

The course on the French Revolution belongs properly to the period of the 1820s and 1830s when it was conceived, written, delivered and repeated. Smyth's letters show that his interest in the Revolution, like that of other people, was reawakened after the end of the wars, when the Revolution had become a subject of historical enquiry. It was then that Smyth first visited Paris ('better late than never', he wrote[2]). The references to the Revolution, now abounding in his letters, show that two of the main influences drawing him to the study of the Revolution, were that of Burke and that of Madame de Staël. Smyth had already been reconsidering Burke in connection with contemporary politics. Madame de Staël he had always admired, but the appearance of her *Considerations* in 1817 was an event in his life. He devoted the summer of 1818 to her 'very beautiful and very sensible' book and wrote to various friends how much he admired it.[3] He read it slowly, stopping to muse over 'the happy hours and fierce debates' of the Revolutionary period. While his interest in the Revolution was deepening, Smyth was also beginning to tire of his 'easy annual duty' of repeating his old lectures, and he felt that his studies were at a deadlock. He was saying nothing new about the period he treated, and he dared not descend to a period nearer his own.[4] Finally, in 1821, the wish was born 'to attempt something with reference to the commencement of the French Revolution'.[5] To attempt, however, as will be seen, in a very cautious manner.

In 1823 Smyth was deep in study, 'sinking down for more than two years into inertness and despair, from the apparent magnitude and importance of the subject'.[6] In 1826 he was drawing up some lectures,[7] and, that summer, books accompanied him on his visits to friends.[8] It was then, too, that he acquired the invaluable help and constant encouragement of Mr Mallet, the son of Mallet du Pan, who acted for Smyth as a Revolutionary expert.[9] In the Michaelmas Term 1826, Smyth delivered the first part of the course. The announcements Smyth made in 1830 to his audience and to his friends,[10] that he had decided to write

[1] This course was in 1823 abridged and the lectures on Louis XIV and XV were later attached to the course on the French Revolution.

[2] R.P. 4619, 14 July 1816. Smyth announces that he is going to Paris on the 20th. K. T. B. Butler writes that, 'as far as can be discovered he never once left these shores' (K. T. B. Butler, 'A Petty Professor of Modern History: William Smyth (1765–1849)', *Cambridge Historical Journal* (1948), IX, 220). There is one indication that he might have been in Paris. Speaking of St Croix's account of 10 August, Smyth said in his lectures that having looked for it in vain in Paris, he found it in the Lansdowne Collection in London (Smyth, *F.R.* II, 335).

[3] R.P. 4621, 29 July 1817; R.P. 4626, 26 Sept. 1818. Thomson Correspondence. B.M. Add. MS. 35, 265, 27 Aug. 1818; R.P. 4626, 26 Sept. 1818.

[4] R.P. 4626, 26 Sept. 1818.   [5] R.P. 4638, 23 Dec. 1821.

[6] Smyth, *F.R.* III, 245.   [7] R.P. 4644, 22 Feb. 1826.

[8] R.P. 4645, 26 Aug. 1826.   [9] R.P. 4646, 22 Apr. 1827.

[10] R.P. 4654, 19 Feb. 1830; *F.R.* III, 244.

no more new lectures, indicate that he had at first intended to carry the lectures forward in time. The only lectures he wrote after 1830 were introductions and conclusions which apply the lessons of the Revolution to the present times, examine the Republican example afforded by America, and summarize the whole of history in order to show how the present state of Europe resulted from past events.[1]

Why did Smyth resolve to stop writing when he did? To Roscoe he writes that when Mr Mallet was so satisfied with the lectures on the Terror, 'it immediately occurred to me that I had better stop when I was considered as having done well'. The reason he gave to his audience was that he had traced the 'Rise Progress and Termination' of the new opinions, and that under Napoleon the old opinions won, and the question only remained who was to reign. The audience begged him to proceed, assuring him of 'the Vigour' of his faculties, but he refused, he says, as 'mere Prudence dictated'.[2] This had been conjectured to refer to his determination not to meddle in contemporary politics.[3] It seems rather that it was the decision to stop at a high-water mark which prudence dictated. Smyth really considered the battle between the old and new opinions far from terminated.[4] If he was anxious to avoid direct references to contemporary politics, this need not have stopped him from lecturing on Napoleon. It was the Revolutionary, rather than the Napoleonic, era which lent itself to comparisons with the politics of 1830, and yet Smyth lectured on it, adding remarks and lectures which point out these very comparisons. Smyth stopped short of the Napoleonic period because he rightly felt his inadequacy for treating it. Napoleon always baffled him, and he was in agreement neither with himself, nor with his friends about him. It needed more than 'proper principles' to understand the Napoleonic period.

POLITICAL TRANSFORMATION

The history of Smyth's political development between the Revolution and the Reform Bill is the history of an old Whig who did not come to

[1] There were forty-four regular lectures (of which the first four were transferred from the course on Modern History), and six supplementary ones. Of the latter, three are preliminary lectures for the courses of 1832, 1833 and 1835, and they apply the lessons of the Revolution. Two lectures delivered at the end of the course of 1836 are on America, and one, of 1837, summarizes European history. One other lecture, on the causes of the Revolution, was found among Smyth's papers and was first published in the 1855 edition of his lectures.

[2] 'Many agreeable things were said to me and some Regret was expressed that I did not proceed as I was still, it was said, in the Vigour of my Faculties; but be this point as it may, in a Question of this kind more than Faculties are concerned and I have done only what Prudence dictated' (R.P. 4654, 19 Feb. 1830). Miss Butler reads this passage slightly differently (Smyth's handwriting is almost illegible). Butler, *op. cit.* p. 231.

[3] Butler, *op. cit.* pp. 231–2.

[4] In 1826 Smyth told his students that it was the daily growing importance of the Revolution which made him lecture on it (*F.R.* I, 94; see also III, 324; II, 415).

terms with the nineteenth century. It is the story of his changing attitude to Burke and to the debate on Burke, to the Revolution and to English politics. The letters Smyth wrote to Roscoe all his life, contain the most direct information we have on his intellectual and political development.

When Smyth met him, Roscoe, a self-educated man of talent and good works, was well known in Liverpool. He had an interest in Italian literature, was a great collector of books, prints and *objets d'art*, and, when in business, an able and generous banker. His politics were liberal and reforming. He fought slavery and Catholic disabilities in verse,[1] in prose[2] and in parliamentary speeches during his short tenure of a seat in 1806–7. His more lasting fame he made with historical works on Lorenzo de Medici[3] and Leo X,[4] for which Lord Holland and others collected materials in Italy. Roscoe welcomed the Revolution with odes,[5] wrote against Burke and the war, and supported parliamentary reform.

To Roscoe, and his friends Currie[6] and Shepherd, who represented the reforming interest of Liverpool, Smyth always remained indebted. He shared their aspirations in the 1780s. At Eton he had been devoted to poetry,[7] but at Peterhouse he talked politics to the small hours of the morning.[8] He was there in 1789. Though he was ever writing lyrics, Smyth never wrote a political verse in his life. He was free from the poetic enthusiasm which characterized a familiar class of undergraduates of the time. Though never carried away, Smyth indicated later that he had welcomed the Revolution. In his lectures, without explicitly referring to himself, he often contrasts the wisdom with which men (or 'we') can judge the Revolution now, with the vain hopes that had been entertained at the time. Enthusiasm, he often says, was in proportion to intelligence. There are endless allusions to the blind sympathy which lovers of liberty had felt.[9] Smyth at one time shared the attitude which his heroes Fox, Sheridan, and Mackintosh advocated in and outside Parliament. It survived the massacres of September; and this fact was to become a point of wonder and shame to him.[10] The Terror, though it made him miserable, did not unwhig him and when the war broke out he was bitterly against it. The years of war 1793–9 Smyth spent under Sheridan's roof.

---

[1] E.g. *The Wrongs of Africa* (1787).

[2] E.g. *A General View of the African Slave Trade* (1788).

[3] *The Life of Lorenzo de Medici, called the Magnificent*, 2 vols. (Liverpool, 1795).

[4] *The Life and Pontificate of Leo the Tenth*, 4 vols. (Liverpool, 1805).

[5] 'O'er the vine-cover'd hills and gay regions of France' was popular for some time.

[6] James Currie, M.D. (1756–1806). In 1793 he wrote (as Jaspar Wilson) *A Letter to Pitt* against war, which went into many editions and ruined his practice.

[7] 'Autobiographical Sketch' written in 1847 and the preface by Smyth's brother to the 5th ed. of Smyth's *English Lyrics* (1850).

[8] *Memoir of Mr Sheridan* (Leeds, 1840), 9–10. The Parliamentary debates, he writes, were mild compared to those in the College cells.

[9] E.g. *F.R.* I, 198–9.   [10] E.g. *F.R.* II, 91–3.

The *Memoir* he wrote on Sheridan touches but lightly on politics, but conveys Smyth's admiration for the man. With a mixture of gravity and humour, without glossing over faults or minimizing any of Sheridan's moral defects, Smyth brings out the genius, charm and force as well as the irresponsibility of Sheridan's character. Sheridan, who insisted on inspecting Smyth before engaging him as tutor for the son on whom he doted, would not have employed a man whose politics differed from his own.[1] He used to enlighten Smyth on politics, and, when in 1806 the Whigs came in, he wished to know whether he could be of any assistance to Smyth or his family.[2]

Another influence on Smyth was that of Mackintosh. Mackintosh's alienation from the French Revolution was the model for many Whigs. It was certainly the model for Smyth though with him the process was slower. He was never wholly anti-Burke or pro-Burke. Despising Burke in his youthful letters and venerating him in his mature lectures, he was always with Burke in the sense in which Burke was always with himself, in the primary concern for the preservation of the British Constitution and social order. Smyth started, as Mackintosh did, in a different direction, but gradually inclined towards Burke. But this is anticipating, for as late as 1797 Smyth wrote, 'I have long since given up Burke and having now no suspicion that he can be right have no patience to wait till he is shown to be wrong. He is with his readers either God or the Devil.'[3]

His contemporary reaction to the Revolution and the wars was only one of the elements which made up the political views Smyth expounded as a historian thirty years later. Though it is to a certain extent true, as he and his family were anxious to assert, that he was a consistent 'Whig of the old school, whom . . . Burke would have been happy to have acknowledged',[4] and that he had 'settled political and moral principles', there was in the process from politics to history, through which Smyth passed, a great deal which affected and shaped his political attitude to the Revolution, as well as his principles in general. This can only be gathered from hints on his reactions to political events, references to Burke, and the gradual alienation from the 'New Whiggism' of his friend Roscoe.

Up to his appointment to the Regius Professorship in 1807, Smyth was, politically speaking, with his friends. His interest in politics was keen and in 1800 he contemplated writing a pamphlet 'in favour of

---

[1] 'The last finish to Sheridan's perfections in my eyes . . . he was a Whig' (*Sheridan*, 9). His talents and politics 'were the great object of my constant idolatry' (*ibid.* 10).

[2] *Ibid.* 66. Smyth contributed anecdotes to Th. Moore, *Memoirs of Sheridan.* See Moore, *Sheridan*, 3rd ed. (1825), 11, 180, 249–50, 488; Smyth, *Sheridan*, 44.

[3] R.P. 4560, 13 Jan. 1797.

[4] W. Smyth, *English Lyrics*, 5th ed. (1850), xxiv. The preface is by Smyth's brother who edits the volume.

Forestallers'.[1] In Cambridge he opposed the erection of a statue to Pitt.[2] His great concern was for Catholic emancipation and he cried alas when a majority in the Senate carried the Vice-Chancellor's proposal of a petition against Lord Howick's Act, for the admission of Catholics into the army and navy.[3] When Roscoe stood for Parliament, Smyth had little hope that a 'Foe to the Slave Trade and Dissenter' would be elected by the Captains and Tradespeople of Liverpool, 'the Church and King Firebrands and all the stupid ignorant People'.[4] When Roscoe was elected, he urged him to raise his voice against the 'Servility and Bigotry' in the House and in the nation.[5]

The conservative influence of historical study, and of the Regius Professorship which he regarded as office under the government,[6] began to operate in 1807. It was then that Smyth offered to test Roscoe's political arguments, as one who is fit to raise objections.[7] Soon after, Smyth secured Roscoe's advice on some of his lectures,[8] but took care to retain his own views. In 1813, Smyth was criticized in the University for not stating the 'marked difference between Papists and Protestants on Tolerance'. His critic thought that this left 'an inference to be drawn . . . against all Religions', and Smyth promised to reconsider his views. He wrote to Roscoe, making clear that he wanted help with references and was not asking for views. He knew that Roscoe's views would be too extreme.[9]

In the course on modern history written round 1810, the lecture best calculated to reveal Smyth's political views at the time is the one on 1688, which he partly treats in terms of the controversy between Burke and Price in 1791. He rejects Price's view that 1688 established the right of Englishmen to cashier their kings, and also Burke's view that it denied such a right for ever. He rules rather that the Bill, without explicitly stating the fact, effected a renovation of the constitution; it restored the right of the people in emergencies, to depart from the regular line of the succession.[10] In other lectures Smyth showed his admiration for Burke's stand on America but ridiculed his blindness in regard to forces operating in pre-revolutionary France.[11]

Round the year 1810, when Benthamite influences began to affect part of the Whig party, Smyth became more conservative and opposed

---

[1] R.P. 4562, 30 Nov. 1800. This probably refers to Lord Kenyon's proposal to fight scarcity by reviving the obsolete laws against regrating and forestalling.

[2] R.P. 4582, 26 Apr. 1806.   [3] R.P. 4588, 22 Mar. 1807.

[4] R.P. 4584, 17 Nov. 1806. I.e. the slave Captains who stood to lose from Roscoe's anti-slavery interest.

[5] R.P. 4589, Apr. 1807.

[6] 'Autobiographical Sketch' in *English Lyrics* (1850).

[7] R.P. 4593, 20 Jan. 1808; R.P. 4597, 15, 16 July 1810.

[8] R.P. 4596, 10 Dec. 1809; R.P. 4589, Apr. 1807; R.P. 4595, 24 July 1808.

[9] R.P. 4605, 13 Mar. 1813.   [10] Smyth, *Modern History* (1840).

[11] *F.R.* I, 79–80.

demands for radical reforms. In 1810 he still encouraged Roscoe to write for peace and reform and predicted success.[1] But in 1813, when Roscoe was writing against Canning, Smyth thought his pamphlet, 'loose, declamatory and sometimes unfair', and predicted that what Canning would write in reply, in the *Quarterly*, would be effective and fair.[2] The *Quarterly* had been founded to combat the tendency towards the left which the *Edinburgh* was showing. Smyth, it seems, was finding more things to like in the new review than he had expected. We know, in any case, that he took both reviews regularly[3] and that he was to become more and more critical of the *Edinburgh*.

As regards Napoleon it must be said that Smyth had no interesting views. In 1800 Smyth knew that Roscoe would not agree with him in the view that Napoleon could have given peace to Europe had he been magnanimous.[4] Later he refused to discuss the war with Roscoe altogether. Roscoe's pamphlets show that his views were not so extreme; and in 1808, when warlike feelings became widely popular due to the Spanish rising, he wrote to Smyth, 'I execrate the rapacity and ambition of Buonaparte and should be truly glad to see his projects defeated'.[5] Later Smyth repeated more calmly that he had always found Roscoe too favourable to Napoleon.[6] Smyth never resolved his inner conflicts with regard to Napoleon and characteristically never attempted to lecture where he could not judge.

The Restoration and the economic unrest which followed it impressed on Smyth the duty of lecturing on the French Revolution. The fears of social disorder strongly coloured his views on the subject. He read French Revolutionary events in the light of industrial disorder in England. But it was, above all, the influence of Madame de Staël which turned Smyth to Revolutionary studies and affected his political attitude, though he was aware of her filial prejudices. Whatever Necker or Madame de Staël say, he wrote, 'the minister was unfit for his situation'. Madame de Staël kept alive his sympathy with the early Revolution, and affected his understanding of the course of revolutionary events. Like Madame de Staël, Smyth always stressed the importance of the early stages, and when later he arrived at his chief interpretative idea, that there was nothing inevitable about the Revolution, and that every one of its stages was due to folly and crime, it was Madame de Staël he quoted to support his position.

[1] R.P. 4597, 15, 17 July 1810. See above, pp. 41–2.
[2] R.P. 4610, 17 Jan. 1813.
[3] M. A. Kelty, *Reminiscences of Thought and Feeling*, p. 148.
[4] R.P. 4562, 30 Nov. 1800.
[5] R.P. 4595, 24 July 1808. Roscoe's letter is interesting in view of the debates on Spain that year. He writes that if the result of Napoleon's defeat would be a relapse of the Spaniards 'into the same intellectual and moral imbecility', there is nothing for liberty to rejoice at. Still he wishes them well, since they are fighting, if not for liberty, at least for independence.
[6] R.P. 4597, 15, 16 July 1810.

The interaction between politics and history appears to be almost over-simplified in Smyth's case. If contemporary conditions drove him to the study of the Revolution, it is even more obvious how much this study helped to formulate his political opinions and to intensify the process of his growing conservatism. Witnessing the event did little to shape Smyth's overall views before the need arose to think back historically on the Revolution as a whole. As soon as he began reading Revolutionary materials in 1819, he told Roscoe that for fifty years the time would not be ripe for such pamphlets on political reform as he was writing; and he said this not on the common ground that the Revolution had put English reform back, but on the general grounds, that society was not prepared, that the seed must be sown long before any effect is even sought.[1] He urged patience in reforms and quoted history for the slow progress of common sense among the masses.[2]

When Smyth began to write his lectures on the French Revolution in 1826, his tone was fixed. 'I preach moderation', he announced, and, for once, he expressed some doubt as to the effect of his teaching. His studies brought forth a political statement at last. 'I see nothing for this country and never did but an Aristocracy with popular feelings, everything else seems to me to lead to Servility . . . and Republicanism.'[3] As a result of this new independence he did not consult Roscoe when he was preparing the French Revolutionary course, but told him that an excellent judge, both of facts and opinions, the son of Mallet du Pan, was approving of his work, and that he (Smyth) knew he could not satisfy 'the more modern school of our youthful politicians the followers of Bentham'.[4] Roscoe was influenced by that school. In the letters of 1826 and 1827 Smyth wrote with excitement on practical affairs. To Roscoe, he wrote of the 'old Tory doctrines' as fatal to the constitution,[5] and in a letter to Thomson, the composer, he severely criticized the government.[6] These letters, written at the moment when Smyth was drawing up his lectures, show the outmoded notions of political conflicts with which he approached history. In 1837, amidst political agitation he feared and hated, Smyth wrote that 400 years earlier social struggles were to be expected, 'but why there should *now* be a contest . . . between "the people and their masters" . . . seems no longer very intelligible'.[7] Though study helped to formulate his opinions, the formula reflected his essentially anomalous position. Later, in 1840 Smyth wrote that his lectures had

---

[1] R.P. 4629, 27 May 1819. [2] R.P. 4643, 5 Dec. 1824.
[3] R.P. 4646, 22 Apr. 1827. [4] R.P. 4650, 4 Apr. 1828.
[5] R.P. 4646, 22 Apr. 1827. This is said in connection with Croker's management of the Tory press. 'The old Tory doctrines . . . can only leave no difference between a king of England and of France.'
[6] Thomson Corresp. 27 Mar. 1826 B.M. Add. MS. 35, 265, f. 162. 'They have filled the land with Wretchedness and Poverty.'
[7] *F.R.* III, 429.

been written in the spirit of 1688, 'but they go no further; nor do I at all admire the popular Party of the Present Period'.[1] The flag of Old Whiggism which Smyth flourished in a changed world could have only a theoretic meaning. It emphasized in him the quality of an armchair historian, a type which was so prevalent and so greatly criticized at the time.

The theoretic air of the lectures resulted also from the fact that Smyth's studies severed his connections with practical politics. There are few political letters after 1828, and none in the same tone. Writing his lectures in old age and half-blindness, Smyth's eyes were turned back to memories, and he soon began to speak of the world as if he no longer belonged to it.[2] This helps to explain the philosophic and the moral tone, the generous comprehensiveness in regard to opinions, the unhistorical application of his conclusions to the world around him, and the unchanging form in which the lectures were repeated. New works were read only to confirm old theories.[3]

In this growing detachment, Smyth's practical interest in Catholic emancipation was brought to a climax in 1829, when he listened to the debates and rejoiced over the victory though he wished it had been achieved by a more direct influence of principle. He had lived to see, he wrote, 'the Cause of Civil and Religious Liberty so asserted in both Islands and High Church Politics at an End'.[4] With the revolutions of 1830, however, Smyth could have had no sympathy, and it is unlikely that he received well the congratulations Roscoe thought fit to send him, on the revolutions, 'especially in France and Poland', or that he shared his friend's anxiety for the result of the 'present struggle between despotism and liberty'. Smyth was mildly favourable to the Reform Bill. It was after the Reform Bill that his terror of democracy grew. At a time when the Whigs sighed with relief because of the moderateness of 1832, and Croker resigned from Office under a government he believed to be rushing towards revolution, Smyth adopted Tory fears. These he expressed in his new introductory lectures. They show his great alarm at the popular political literature of the time, attack the idea of equality and call the rule of a majority, the rule of physical force. They also show the influence of Tocqueville's book on America which seemed to Smyth to call for a warning.[5] He thought Tocqueville's notions too democratic, especially his view that since ancient times everything 'has tended to establish the

---

[1] Smyth to Mallet, 1840. B.M. Add. MS. 39, 809.

[2] E.g. R.P. 4646, 22 Apr. 1827; R.P. 4654, 19 Feb. 1830; R.P. 4655, 3 May 1830; R.P. 4650, 4 Apr. 1828. In the last mentioned letter Smyth says that writing his lectures is a blessing, like any occupation, 'when life is hastening to its close . . . one seems no longer to belong to the world or its concerns'.

[3] E.g. I, 198, 303, 304, 372.

[4] R.P. 4652, 14 Apr. 1829; Thomson Corresp. B.M. Add. MS. 35, 265.

[5] *F.R.* III, 389, 352–402 contains two lectures devoted to America. Tocqueville taught Smyth that democracy is 'a principle perfectly intolerant, perfectly merciless to every other' (*F.R.* III, 360).

equality of mankind', but he welcomed the implications of Tocqueville's criticisms of America. The introductory lecture Smyth wrote in 1833 differed markedly from that of 1832, which had favoured reform. It is a warm defence of the English nobility and of aristocracy in general. Smyth now held that it was not the French nobility but the 'démocratie royale' which had ruined Louis XVI. In his new mood of political alarm, Smyth considered his lectures an urgent duty and in 1834 abridged his course on modern history, from his impatience to return to the Revolution.[1] His attacks in the new lectures were directed against the exclusive rule of the middle classes and of public opinion, and mainly against unconstitutional and visionary theories concerning institutions[2] and property.[3] His fierceness against Owen,[4] the Saint Simonians, the Chartists and the 'workers as they call themselves in America'[5] was due to their belief in perfectibility, Godwin's doctrine, as he thought of it, 'revived to disgrace the human understanding'.[6] Smyth's religion and common sense combined to reject this belief which he saw as the seat of the eighteenth-century malady, and the cause of all revolutions. On the other hand, Smyth had a more concrete fear based on his reading of radical political literature. He feared that a social revolution, and a redistribution of property, would follow the increase in the political power of the lower classes.

I wage war only with exclusive systems, with this democratic doctrine, which first appeared in the arrogant pages of Paine, that no government can be lawful which rests not on the will of the majority, told by the head, that aristocracies of every kind, of birth, of rank, and of property, are mere usurpation and tyranny and with the gradual civilization of the world, must necessarily disappear. I look to no such revolutions in the world, or rather in human nature.[7]

One of Smyth's friends, who admired his lectures on the Revolution, read with pain the supplementary ones 'written under the influence of panic since the passing of the Reform Bill' and grieved that he had been 'seared out of his old Whig principles', and that he held up to England 'the frenzied acts of French slaves'.[8] Another admirer wrote that, though the Professor had been 'a Whig of the old school', his later talk is of the 'Whigs having lost their wits and of the Tories beginning to come to their senses'.[9] Smyth's latest conservatism does not affect his actual history

---

[1] *F.R.* III, 309, 323, 324.   [2] *F.R.* III, 323, 393.

[3] Smyth opposed the idea that 'property is no legal heir to respect' (*F.R.* III, 310–11) 'The natural rulers of mankind must be found in the aristocracies of birth, knowledge and affluence' (*F.R.* III, 359–60).

[4] Smyth met Owen who discussed with him an idealized world (*F.R.* III, 297–8).

[5] *F.R.* III, 298, 52.

[6] Smyth describes Godwin as an early Saint-Simonian (*F.R.* III, 299).

[7] *F.R.* III, 383, 401. Smyth objected to the 'vulgarization' of life through democratic principles (*F.R.* III, 418).

[8] Lucy Aiken, 7 Feb. 1841, *The Correspondence of W. E. Channing 1826–1842* (1874), p. 380.

[9] *Christian Examiner* (1841), XXIX, 366.

of the Revolution, but it completes the picture of his mind's development. The fears of the 'thirties gradually abated, and in 1840 it seemed 'perfectly clear' to Smyth 'that the Radicals cannot succeed in their Republican notions in Church and State', and the less he had to fear from them, the less indignant he was about them.[1] Like many liberals of the 1840s, Smyth believed democracy dead.

With age and growing conservatism Smyth also became more religious. From hostile references to the 'government in Church and State' he had moved to a spirit of resignation and religious sentiment.[2] When he had said all he had to say in the lectures, he wrote a book on the *Evidences of Christianity*, which is based on his experiences at the time of the Revolution when all established beliefs had been questioned. It seems to be intended mainly to fight the Deists on their own ground.

THE INFLUENCE OF BURKE

Burke was the central figure in Smyth's intellectual development and in his attitude to the Revolution. 'I read it [Burke's *Reflections*] over and over, and as the events of the world come changing and crowding upon me, every year with more and more admiration at the profound philosophy which it contains.'[3] His basic principles did not change when they developed from their position behind Fox to that behind Burke. He always allowed moral considerations to outweigh all others, so that he could never follow any one party. The aim, he announced in the first lecture, was to show 'how revolutions are to be avoided while reforms are accomplished'.[4] In the end, he left the 'parting legacy' that 'the friends of freedom are not to identify themselves with the French Revolutionists'. His theme is clearly ordered liberty, moderation and moral politics. Smyth applies these general principles to individual events even if this produces a historically impossible situation. He was not primarily concerned with a credible picture, but with judging human actions. He based his view not on a narrow condemnation of the Revolution, but on a wide sympathy which had been qualified by the influence of Burke and of events. It is as if later writers passed through the same stages between enthusiasm and disappointment as contemporaries of the Revolution had done. They sympathized with the beginning of the Revolution and at some point renounced it. Smyth was both a contemporary and a later historian, and as a historian he disapproved of the Revolution at an earlier stage during its course, than he had actually done as an observer.

[1] Letter to Mallet, B.M. Add. MS. 39.809; see also R.P. 4663, 20 May 1840.
[2] In 1836 he speaks of 'our glorious constitution in church and state' (*F.R.* III, 354).
[3] *F.R.* III, 290. Smyth also said it would satisfy his hopes to have taught students to read Burke properly, to distinguish the philosophy from the declamation, the reason from the imagination.
[4] *F.R.* I, 96.

81

He disapproved now on new grounds, based on a new understanding of Burke.

Smyth also had to come to terms with what had been his enthusiastic reaction to the Revolution. He thought, like Southey, that benevolent and intelligent lovers of liberty naturally fell into such errors of judgment. Using Madame de Staël's story of her own initial enthusiasm and of Madame de Montmorin's portentous feelings at the opening of the States General,[1] Smyth said that worldly people often judge practical affairs more accurately than persons of genius. Burke alone was an exception. Though Smyth made much of Burke's insight he did not recommend his actual judgments. Smyth always considered the *ancien régime* corrupt and badly in need of reform. He had little respect for the French constitution, the nobility or the *parlements*. He saw the Revolution as a result of bad government, and not of a conspiracy of upstarts. Smyth thought Burke too severe on the Constituent Assembly, and he differed from him in his judgment on the Girondins. Nowhere is Smyth more favourable to the Revolution than in the lecture on the causes which, in 1840, possibly for this very reason, he left unprinted.[2] It seems to belong to the end of what Smyth regarded as the first phase of the Revolution, that is, after 14 July 1789, and it represents a summary of that period which Smyth always considered the crucial period. It shows that Smyth clearly saw the Revolution as having been started by the *parlements* through their prolonged resistance to pecuniary reforms and their adoption of revolutionary means. In allocating blame, he always insisted that the 'first criminality' belonged to the privileged.[3] On the crucial point of the Bastille, he declared for the people. He thought that the court meant to use coercion,[4] and that this attempt and the insincerity of the court justified the rising. The rising of 14 July 'was an impulse in itself virtuous, and a measure in itself necessary'. The court was insincere, the 'triumph of the Assembly was desirable, the insurrection of the city was defensive'. Smyth is not usually so outspoken. In most of his statements he reached an equilibrium between his love of liberty, and his hatred of violence. Smyth fell easily into the error of assuming the Revolution to have been an unsuccessful attempt to imitate Britain. He always distinguished the reformers from the men of violence, but he thought that even men like Mounier and Lally, though virtuous, were erring.

Smyth learnt from Burke the lesson that the Revolution was an event in moral history. His frequent discussions of the moral aspect of the Revolution occur mostly in the context of the English debate on the

---

[1] *F.R.* I, 171–2. Alison and Acton also describe this incident.

[2] It was found among his papers and first published in the 1855 edition.

[3] Smyth's favourite quotation from Burke is that 'early revolutions are amicable arrangements with a friend in power'.

[4] Smyth was pleased with Ferrières's unexpected confirmation of a royalist plot (*F.R.* I, 295).

event, which remained all important in Smyth's thought. The writings of the Revolutionary period represented, or even constituted, for Smyth the Revolution in its most terrifying aspect, namely in its theory. He believed that this aspect of the case had been neglected by the English who dislike theoretical morality. In this story the hero is Burke, and Godwin is the villain, whose design was to make man 'a creature of reason only'. Burke's glory was that he discerned the tendency to pervert man's spiritual life and his innate sense of moral duty. As an antidote to the danger, Burke brought an insistence on the authority of habits, feelings, instincts, and prejudices. But the man who actually overthrew Godwin's system was, in Smyth's opinion, Malthus.

If it were possible to systematize Smyth's thought, his theory would seem to be, that at the root of the moral evils of the Revolution there were two doctrines, utility and perfectibility. The doctrine of utility, admissible only as a general guide, the Revolutionaries and their advocates applied to individual cases. They used it to authorize unnatural acts and an inhuman moral code. Smyth was vehement on the subject of the use of the doctrine of utility for the justification of the Terror, as a means to an end. 'The great rule of morality', he said, 'is that we are not to do evil that good may come.' The greatest Revolutionary crime was that they sought an ultimate good through evil and presented outrages against humanity as sacrifices for it.[1]

Smyth distinguished between the moral and political debate on the Revolution. He studied the latter in connection with the English publications, the societies and the parliamentary debates. He believed that Paine and some of the societies meant to bring about revolution in England,[2] and that their activities had a real effect on France, and caused the French offer of assistance to revolutionary nations.[3] In this connection Smyth went through the works of Paine, Mrs Barbauld, Mackintosh, Romilly and others, outlined their arguments, and analysed Burke's role as a political prophet. He pointed out, however, the point neglected by admirers of Burke's foresight, that Burke had not foreseen the obedience and the success of the French armies. In discussing the literature of the period, Smyth often dealt with the general and the specific indiscriminately, as contemporaries themselves had done. Godwin's moral theories are in his discussion mixed up with practical affairs, on which they had no influence.

Smyth's attitude to the question of the war is revealing in its ambiguities. His prevailing view is that England's security made war unnecessary.

---

[1] *F.R.* III, 252, 256, 350–1.

[2] He believed that the Constitutional Society hoped for a Convention (III, 137); that some societies grew violent in proportion to French violence (III, 36); that Fox never favoured Grey's Friends of the People (III, 37–8), that 'sober-minded' members of some societies were ashamed of the resolutions passed (III, 36).

[3] *F.R.* III, 37.

But he also said that the King's execution had made war inevitable and that England had in fact already become part of the Revolution and a field for the battle between old and new. He was hesitant about the justice of the war and reaches opposite conclusions when arguing on historical or on moral grounds. Studying the state of England, he concluded there was no need for war. Even after admitting that Marsh, for instance, had made a 'weighty argument' on the basis of the diplomatic documents, Smyth waived the finality of this proof and maintained that the main issue was not who had started the war, but whether it was a war against Jacobinism.[1] Smyth held that to talk of the Scheldt or the mutinies was to make it a war of underhand dealings. He also said that, though opinion had supported Pitt, the historian could judge against Pitt, now that the issues complicating the matter were cleared. When, however, Smyth was discussing the nature of revolutionary ideas and their proselyting spirit, he claimed that the danger of the French generals and commissioners, the menace of irresistible military science and of the doctrines of equality, had to be fought, if civilization was to be saved.

Smyth distinguished between the French war against Europe and that against England. The former he considered provoked by the Austrian ultimatum. In the documents of the allies he saw an 'objectionable tone of interference' which put 'international law' on the side of the Revolution. The allies also brought the worst out in the Revolution. It is on England's role that there was an ambiguity in Smyth's opinion, but his prevailing view was against the war.

AS HISTORIAN

Smyth's theory and practice as a historian can be derived from his own historical writings, and his discussions of his own and other historians' methods. The first lecture he ever wrote, the introductory lecture to the course on modern history, is on the study of history. In this lecture he had been assisted by Roscoe and Whishaw,[2] but there is yet another source for the most interesting part of his lecture, the description of a rejected plan for a series of lectures on 'universal history'. By this term Smyth understood the history of modern Europe, the progress of the mind, society and happiness, 'of the intellectual character of the species'. The narrative was to exclude details, temporary things and 'peculiar events that do not concern the general interest of mankind'. It would not tell the individual histories of nations, but only their histories in conjunction, indicating only those changes which left permanent effects on the history of Europe as a whole.

[1] *F.R.* III, 40.
[2] Whishaw won a prize at Cambridge in 1790 for a dissertation showing that the French Revolution would be beneficial to England. Romilly to Mme Gautier, 20 Aug. 1790 (Romilly, *Memoirs* (1840), I, 404).

Of the two main ideas in this plan, the first, namely the idea that history should record the progress of civilization, was one which Smyth learnt from Voltaire, whom elsewhere he praised for having directed history to its proper subjects, 'the arts, manners, and laws of every country, the progress of society, the history of human happiness'.[1] The source of the second idea, that universal history should rise above the peculiarities of national histories, is found in a private letter Smyth received from James Mackintosh. On hearing of Smyth's appointment, Mackintosh offered him a plan for a series of lectures on universal history.[2] By that, he wrote, 'I do not mean the collection of the histories of separate nations', though English compilers had used the term in this sense. He explained that the histories of France and Germany remained separate, even if put in one volume. Universal history recorded events which altered the relative positions of the nations or 'materially affected the whole of them when considered as one society'. All temporary or local events with no permanent effect on the civilization of the European community, must be excluded.[3] 'It will probably be information to you', wrote Mackintosh, 'that the compendiums of Universal History published in Germany will furnish most useful models and materials.'

There is no reason to suppose that Smyth read German or looked up the universal histories. Mackintosh's letter explains how an echo of the latest foreign theories on universal history appears in the opening lecture of the most conventional teacher of history, who treated with suspicion all new theories. Smyth adopted neither Mackintosh's nor any other plan for a regular history. He chose instead, for both his courses, a method best suited to his own mind and aims.

Smyth must be considered in relation to the rationalist tradition. He admired Hume, Robertson and Gibbon, as perfect models for historians. The discovery that history should include all aspects of civilization he considered the last word in historical theory, though he did not follow it in practice. He held the rationalist view that history was a teacher of morals and politics, and that it taught through analogies and methods of abstraction. Smyth differed from the historians he admired in his neglect of literary form. He sacrificed form for the sake of the historical aim, and the aim was the search for universal truths. 'I repeat my sentiment again and again, totally regardless of what may be the rules of taste or propriety of composition', he confessed in his lectures. His didactic aim was strengthened by the fact that the Regius Professorship had been established to provide a practical training for statesmen. His

---

[1] *F.R.* I, 18.

[2] *Memoirs of the Life of Sir James Mackintosh* (London, 1835), I, 412–13. Mackintosh hoped that Smyth as Professor would improve on Gray, who was an artist, and 'born 30 years too soon for the philosophy and criticism of modern history'.

[3] Smyth used the same phrase.

method was shaped by his educational task.[1] Instruction to him meant the drawing of lessons. Because he distrusted prescription and wished his students to judge independently, he adopted the method of presenting every subject from different points of view. This led to repetitions and to a diffuse manner which has been called 'circumambulatory'. It subordinated the structure of the lectures to an extraneous object[2] and made Smyth impatient with detail and reluctant to follow up points or construct a narrative. His piecemeal analysis of events, and the search for 'philosophy teaching by experience', displayed the evils of 'speculative history' which the romantics deplored. Atmosphere is absent, even concrete material seems transformed and unreal, single actions are tested by moral, philosophical and political criteria totally outside themselves, and the background which makes action credible is ignored.[3]

Smyth defended the idea that historical facts can be used as the basis for analogies with other ages, when many people were already protesting against it. Some of the reformers of the 1830s, for instance, refused to be instructed and warned by the French Revolution of 1789, and claimed that peoples and conditions were different. Smyth, just like Croker, replied that human nature, as well as the great moral and political principles, do not change.[4]

In the 1820s the whole of Smyth's thought converged on the Revolution and in his lectures he tried to achieve the synthesis of his entire mind. He himself later summed up his subject matter.

No lecturer had ever such a subject presented to him before; for my subject embraced whatever could concern the vices and virtues, the passions and the genius of mankind; whatever could affect the right of property, the domestic charities; the claim of mercy and justice among men; the love of peace, the love of freedom, a sense of duty, of piety, of religion; all that is owing to our fellow creatures on earth, all that is due to Heaven; all these were to be explained, adjusted and exemplified.[5]

His lectures were a series of moral and political reflections, for which his mentality was especially suited. The fundamental question for Smyth was which was the best form of government, and he had no doubt that there was one answer. He steered through political views, upheld moderation, denounced violence with the ease of a man who had grown up in an age saturated with political discussion. Smyth may also have

[1] Smyth distinguished between the task of the lecturer and that of the historian, partly as an excuse for avoiding detail.

[2] Smyth treated the Revolution in two courses of twenty-four lectures each. The first was supposed to bring out the guilt of the privileged orders, the second—that of the popular party. To meet the danger that some of the students may only learn half the lesson, there was offered every year a lecture of conclusions drawn from the whole story (*F.R.* III, 325–6).

[3] The discursive quality in Smyth's lectures is brought out forcibly if we compare them with those delivered at the same time (1829) by Niebuhr. The latter form a straight narrative with no discussion of sources or problems of historical knowledge.

[4] Lecture of 1837 (*F.R.* III, 520).

[5] *F.R.* III, 263. See also III, 325.

felt an unfulfilled hankering after practical politics in an age when many men combined politics and literature.[1] He made the study of history a compensation—a realm which he created and ruled. It was a realm based on a few principles which seemed to Smyth to emerge from history. Smyth saw, for instance, as a lesson of the Revolution, the principle that executive powers must never be made too weak. The principle that nothing which is morally wrong can be politically safe, seemed to Smyth to be the one consistent law in history, and he often attached it to stories of crime and punishment in history, as that of the rise and fall of Napoleon. France treated Corsica treacherously in 1769 with the result that from Corsica came the rod which chastised the Bourbons. Smyth first pointed this out in 1810. When Napoleon himself fell, Smyth considered his moral doubly confirmed and added a remark to this effect. Sometimes the historian and the moralist were not in harmony and Smyth had to admit that Louis XVI's virtues were of no use to him and that positive vices might have saved him.[2]

Smyth believed that his method served the needs of impartiality and often repeated with pride the praise he had received of being the most impartial historian of the Revolution.[3] His impartiality consisted partly of following no one view and shunning the appearance of finality. Smyth was in 1856 favourably compared to Macaulay for his diffidence in stating opinions. But Smyth's impartiality was also based on the belief that 'good and bad are everywhere mixed' and on a genuine political independence. He was impatient with partisanship in history, and complained that historians now pronounced on the characters of the past as if they were personally involved with them. There was also a scholarly basis to his impartiality. The only important academic treatment of the Revolution before Smyth had been the diplomatic study of the origins of the war by Herbert Marsh.[4] But Marsh had written for the specific purpose of defending England in the eyes of Germany. Although Smyth shared something of the publicist-like nature of the early historiography of the Revolution, there was a basic honesty in his approach which his political object of inculcating moderation could do little to bias. Long before he wrote his lectures, he had sought to elevate even political pamphlets by what he recommended as a 'philosophic method', of

---

[1] This is illustrated by Smyth's bitter reaction to Roscoe's election to Parliament, when Smyth accurately prophesied that Roscoe would be 'hooted from the Hustings where he was huzzad' (R.P. 4584, 17 Nov. 1806; 4586, 12 Feb. 1806). Smyth expressed great contempt for worldly success, even for literary fame (R.P. 650, 10 May 1806; 4559, 6 Dec. 1796).

[2] *F.R.* I, 72.

[3] E.g. R.P. 4646, 22 Apr. 1827.

[4] Marsh was Professor of Divinity while Smyth was Professor of Modern History. 'At an immense distance below Marsh, but undoubtedly the second in the University, is Smyth' ('Struggles of a Poor Student through Cambridge', *London Magazine* (1 Apr. 1825), N.S.1., 503–4). This article was written by Solomon Atkinson. See J. A. Venn, *Alumni Cantabrigienses*, Pt. II, Vol. I.

'drawing from the whole a result, whatever that result might be'.[1] When he applied this method to his own work on the Revolution, it amounted to a new open-minded approach, based on wide materials and following their evidence as he understood it.

AS CRITIC OF HISTORIANS

The preoccupation with books and the use of Revolutionary materials is, next to the teaching aim, the most conspicuous quality of the lectures. It accentuated the tendency already prevalent in England, of treating the Revolution indirectly, through the criticism of published books. In the course of modern history, Smyth had explained that his time permitted him only to discuss what and how the students should read. For the lectures on the Revolution he adopted the same method, for an additional reason. His letters show that he considered it a safe course to take on a controversial subject.[2] This method made the lectures what a contemporary called 'a history of histories'. Apart from histories, he brought together, to bear on the Revolution, the philosophical, political, economic and moral literature of the period. He tried to see the period in all its aspects and he gained another dimension by reflecting on historians' works. His treatment of the Revolution was therefore conducted on different levels. Smyth read widely in the sources available to him. He read, for instance, all except one of the early histories mentioned by Aulard.[3] He did not, however, merit the praise which Acton put down in a manuscript note and possibly read to his audience, that 'we shall be fortunate if we ever obtain as complete a mastery of existing information as he had in his time'.[4] One tends at first to overrate the unexpected scholarly merit of Smyth. The list of books he used is impressive, but, by 1840, more material was available than Smyth could master. Acton also overlooks the fact that, of the books which appeared between 1828 and 1840, few were included[5] and none led to any revision of the text.[6] Smyth had asserted that he was keeping pace with the literature and all his critics but one took his word for it.[7] In fact he looked at some new

---

[1] R.P. 4597, 15, 16 July 1810. This advice was offered for a political pamphlet. In a lecture of 1832 Smyth expected political as well as historical writers to act like judges and not advocates (*F.R.* III, 288).

[2] R.P. 4638, 23 Dec. 1821.

[3] A. Aulard, 'Les Premiers historiens de la Révolution', *Études et Leçons*, 6th series (1910). The exception is a Latin work by Lorenz.

[4] 'One of those whom I have the honour to succeed.' 'A modest and upright endeavour to explain what was known for certain before the great epoch of revolutionary studies began.' 'It is not a work of genius like Carlyle's, but we shall be fortunate...' (C.U.L. Add. MS. 5649).

[5] Dumont's *Mirabeau* (1832); Jefferson's *Memoirs* (1830); A. Lameth's *Constitutional Assembly* (1828); Tocqueville's *America* (1835).

[6] E.g. *F.R.* III, 275.

[7] The one who did not was an American critic who in 1841 showed how shockingly out of date Smyth was in American history (*Christian Examiner* (1841), XXIX, 366–73).

publications but only to be confirmed in some old opinion,[1] and he neglected many important works. He claimed later that he had always continued to look for new individual characteristics,[2] but he added not a word of character delineation. Macaulay said that Dumont had created for the first time a credible human Mirabeau,[3] but Smyth saw nothing new in Dumont. Nor did Smyth sum up 'established fact' as Acton said, or 'sift the authorities', as Alison said.[4] He was too wary of being entangled in a thorough study of detail, for his knowledge ever to become mastery.

Smyth used mainly histories and memoirs. He read some periodical publications of the Revolutionary and the following period,[5] and he used some original manuscript material, which was lent him out of the papers of Mallet du Pan. There are also the many philosophical works which he considered as bearing directly on the problems raised by the Revolution. He used his sources indiscriminately. His general method was to state the circumstances of an event and then quote a variety of sources to illustrate it from different sides.[6] Quotations largely make up his lectures, but Smyth is always there manipulating his materials to convey his ideas. He is saved from a biased use of materials because he is true to his further aim of presenting all sides for the reader's judgment especially on controversial points.[7]

Smyth valued facts highly, but was timid in handling them. He later claimed that it was to avoid theories that he had diligently searched the sources for facts.[8] But while he was writing the lectures he seems to have seen all facts as established. He was uncritical, and treated with respect unworthy material, which he styled 'the documents of the case'. In dealing with disputed facts, he exclaimed, impatiently, that it did not matter, for instance, when, how, or with whom the Queen left the Tuileries as long as we know that she came out. He said that the contradictions in memoirs had as little to do with the truth of history, as those in the gospels had with the truth of religion. He could never disprove statements of facts, though he often scolded others who were too sure of

---

[1] The lecture on Dumont illustrates this. Smyth was also pleased to read that Jefferson had advised the patriots to accept 'the proposals of the court' on 23 June (*F.R.* I, 198).

[2] *F.R.* III, 275.

[3] Macaulay, 'Dumont', *E.R.* (1832), LV, 552.

[4] Alison also said that Smyth reviewed the memoirs with 'the acuteness of a critic and the spirit of a philosopher'.

[5] Smyth procured the *Mercure* for the University through his connection with the Mallet family (*F.R.* I, 331).

[6] These may be memoirs, letters or even street placards. See, e.g., *F.R.* I, 82.

[7] The story of the plans preceding 14 July 1789 is told twice through royalist and popular writers respectively. There are many examples of the same story told from different sides. For the account of 4 August Smyth quotes many writers, including Burke and Mackintosh, speeches from Bailly's notes, the *Mercure*, Mirabeau's *Speeches*, Ferrieres, etc. (*F.R.* I, 323–41).

[8] *F.R.* III, 275.

them. When the *Edinburgh* reviewer wrote that the royal flight could have been saved if anybody had been able to ride for help at 6 m.p.h., Smyth scolded 'lively and able' journalists who, 'in their closets or over their wine', jump to conclusions which ruin men's reputations.

Sometimes Smyth shirked the responsibility of determining fact and sometimes he did even less. When 'overpowered to weariness and despair' by the vast amount of contradictory material about the outbreak of the war, Smyth fell back from the histories and the memoirs to the state papers. By these, he said, 'nations and parties must be tried', but he did not base a narrative on them, nor list them. He simply recommended this material for the students' perusal. He considered sources as supports for arguments; there is enough, he says, to prove either that France was aggressive or that she was fighting in self defence. Having spent months on the documents, he left the story they tell, for the one (to him) important revelation, the 'objectionable tone of interference' on the part of the allies.

Smyth betrayed a vain desire for the raw materials of history in cases when he attempted to study them directly. He found his documents as selected by other historians or in proper collections.[1] He once tried to reconstruct a lost manuscript from available materials.[2] He also checked the authenticity of an early letter by Burke, by applying to the descendant of the recipient,[3] and he followed the stories of the notorious forgeries of the time. He recommended the double test of internal and external evidence for historical authenticity.[4] He suspected the *Memoirs of Louis XVIII* because they lacked external evidence, although he thought that internal evidence pronounced for them. When Croker exposed this work, Smyth was pleased to recall his own suspicions but he ignored the fact that it was mainly on internal evidence that Croker tore it to pieces.[5]

Smyth envied French historians their resources in oral and manuscript material.[6] Whatever first hand information he had from the son of Mallet du Pan, in reminiscences, advice, criticism and documents, he appreciated deeply and used extensively.[7] Smyth printed for the first time Mallet du Pan's draft of the letter he wrote under the King's instructions and took to the allies, and which resulted in the Brunswick manifesto.[8] It was a document of some importance as Mallet's own version of his mission

---

[1] He often ignores the mediation of historians (e.g. II, 101), or dissociates himself from their view (e.g. I, 133). He used Mirabeau's *Speeches* and the *Debates* of the Convention. But he looked for speeches in the *Mercure* though he knew them to be imperfectly reported there.

[2] Necker's proposed constitution of 23 June.

[3] The letter to Lord Charlemont dated August 1789. It contains the phrase, 'The spirit it is impossible not to admire' (referring to the Revolution).

[4] R.P. 4583, 18 June 1806.   [5] *F.R.* III, 277–8. See above, pp. 68–9

[6] *F.R.* I, 54.

[7] He announced the news of having acquired Mallet's help three times to the same person (R.P. 4645, 26 Aug. 1826; 4646, 22 Apr. 1827; 4650, 4 Apr. 1828. See also *F.R.* I, 10).

[8] Mallet du Pan, *Memoirs* (1851), p. 290.

differs from that given by Bertrand. Smyth did not use this isolated document well. Unable to tell a story except along lines laid down by previous historians, he followed Bertrand, and even analysed the inaccurate text which Bertrand printed, before he revealed that 'materials even more ample than these exist', and produced Mallet's paper. Smyth's independence consisted of drawing his own conclusions from the document. He picked from Bertrand's argument (designed to prove the King's hostility to war), the very points which defeat it; and in using Mallet du Pan's papers he condemned the action in which Mallet acted as adviser and agent.

Smyth used, for the episode of 10 August, three manuscript accounts, written for Mallet du Pan by three Swiss officers who had taken part in the fighting. From these, and some published accounts, he compiled a narrative of the event, and he also printed extracts from one of the manuscript accounts, that of Forestier. Another of these, that of Durler, was, after some wanderings, acquired by the British Museum in 1882, used and printed by Morse Stephens. Stephens valued the document highly and said, 'for whom it was drawn up there is no trace'. We know that it was drawn up for Mallet du Pan in preparation for a history, and that Smyth had used it years before Stephens, with a similar appreciation of its value and a superior knowledge of its history.[1] Smyth also used for 10 August a book which Stephens, sixty years later, declared to be the only book dealing exclusively with the part of the Swiss.[2]

In examining Smyth's method we have so far seen him as a teacher who reflects on history, and as a historian who reads sources. Neither as a philosopher nor as a technical historian were Smyth's achievements great. His philosophy alone was neither original nor profound and his critical method was deficient, though he introduced a truly historical spirit into English writings on the Revolution. Smyth's importance is connected with his predominant interest in assessing and criticizing historical writings. Without this interest his ideas would be too abstract, and with it, his deficiencies in criticism do not appear to result from any contempt of fact. Through other historians' writings, Smyth is linked to both reflective and historical literature. It is this combination which lends him importance. Neither a philosopher like Burke, nor a researcher like Croker, he was more of a historian than either.

Having learnt from Voltaire and Burke to view the Revolution in its widest aspect, Smyth took a further step alone when he brought out the wider significance of the event, through its history and literature. He

---

[1] 'I have been furnished, by the kindness of Mr Mallet with some narratives that were sent his father by three of the different Swiss officers who survived.' They agree, he adds, with Weber's officer who was with Durler, Mallet's correspondent, in the great court (Smyth, *F.R.* II, 266). See below, pp. 236–7.

[2] P. d'Altishofen, *Recit de la Conduite des Gardes Suisses* (Geneva, 1824). Smyth apparently used an earlier edition.

was able to show Burke's ideas against a more recent background, and he treated the writings of the 1790s as part of the Revolution. His conversion to Burke was partly due to the realization that Burke's opinion was not merely a political view, but a historical force. Smyth had learnt to see history as affected by ideas in the course of studying pre-revolutionary writings. Like Lacretelle and, long after, Acton, he ascribed great importance to Fénelon.[1]

Because Smyth became a historian by looking through historians, there is some interest in his treatment of books as such. He noted their interplay,[2] and related them to the conditions under which they were written. He studied, for instance, the effect of political changes on the successive editions of Saint Simon's *Memoirs*.[3] He thought that Lacretelle on the Revolution had 'a chance of impartiality' through writing under Napoleon, for he could praise neither the *ancien régime* nor republican anarchy, and he knew that Lacretelle's opinions on England were inspired by Napoleon.[4] Occasionally we find in Smyth a well-rounded criticism of a historian. Voltaire, for instance, is studied separately as thinker and as historian. His principles, his views of history, his care with sources and his tone of presentation, the influence of his times and background, all are included.[5] To a similar effect, through scattered remarks, Smyth examined Lacretelle's conscious and unconscious prejudices, and his historical qualities. Some writers, however, like Necker, are treated argumentatively as if they were contemporary opponents.[6]

Smyth made little distinction between histories and memoirs and classed both as exoteric history. He thought that reading memoirs distinguished historians from the general readers, but he also considered such reading more entertaining than instructive, and useless in forming great principles, which are the object of history. He objected to memoirs mainly as to a bad influence. He was more aware of political than of personal prejudices, and doubted the truth of interpretations more than of facts. He says, however, that Bertrand's facts 'are one thing, and his opinions another', and that the former may be influenced by the latter. He detected national prejudices and advised that French histories should be balanced by English ones.[7] Some of Smyth's contemporaries were treating memoirs more critically. Smyth was bad at detection,[8] but in a sense he was in advance of his time, when he regarded all the memoirs and the histories written before Thiers and Mignet, as evidence, above all,

---

[1] *F.R.* I, 22–7; 83–4. Smyth points out the revolutionary nature of Fénelon's ideas.

[2] E.g. *F.R.* I, 39.

[3] *F.R.* I, 13–14. He notes that only after the Revolution could they be published in full.

[4] *F.R.* I, 21, 54, 55, 83.

[5] *F.R.* I, 18–20, 53, 55. 'This most amusing of writers has authorities for his facts and proper foundations on which to rest the liveliness of his sallies.'

[6] E.g. *F.R.* I, 145, 151, 152, 155, 156.   [7] *F.R.* I, 11, 52.

[8] A wrong guess was that 'Groenvelt' was an Englishman. He later inserted a footnote correcting this, but did not change the text (*F.R.* I, 241, 246).

of contemporary opinion. He often illustrates a case by a passage from a memoir, adding that 'such opinions form part of the case'.[1] So distinctly did Smyth see memoirs in this light, that he overlooked the fact that they were written after the events and contained modified opinions.

AS PHILOSOPHER OF HISTORY

Of all Smyth's criticisms of historians, the most important is his denunciation of Thiers and Mignet and the modern French school which they represented to him. He was offended by the 'doctrine of necessity' in their interpretation because it disposed of moral responsibility and deprived 'good politics' of its efficacy.[2] Smyth was one of the earliest English thinkers whose morals and politics were outraged by these new logical accounts of the Revolution. Carlyle, Bulwer, Thackeray and many others noted the 'immorality' in Mignet's and Thiers's interpretations. There had been excuses of inevitability since the days when the Terror had been justified by the theory of necessity. The novelty in Thiers and Mignet was their merit and influence as historians and their attempt to give more than partial justification. It seemed to Smyth that by 'resolving everything into a sort of concatenated series of events . . . that . . . could not have happened otherwise', they caused a theory of historical inevitability to emerge from their account of the development of the Revolution.

Smyth was so strongly affected because his historical view of the Revolution was part of his religious, political and philosophical ideas, and these were firmly based on free will and the power of moral and wise politics. Smyth, after all, only taught history because he considered individual decisions important. The historians he criticized, sinned against the same moral rules as the revolutionaries themselves. 'I accuse the French historians . . . of deserting the cause of humanity . . . for the miserable reason of making a case for their country.' The absolute moral standard which Smyth applied to the Revolution itself he extended to its historians and this gives a higher meaning to his moral criterion for evaluating historians. He shows a sense of the moral responsibility of historiography on a deeper level than that required merely for sound political instruction. 'He who justifies a crime is little to be distinguished from the criminal',[3] writes Smyth with Acton-like severity, and it is this judgment on historians, which raises Smyth above the crowd of half-Whig half-Tory historians whose moderation lacked the positive moral principle.

---

[1] E.g. *F.R.* I, 137–8, 165, 234–5. Even Arthur Young is quoted more as an opinion than as a source (*F.R.* I, 216).

[2] E.g. *F.R.* I, 96, 139; II, 46; III, 248. Necessity destroys 'the province of the reflecting historians' (*F.R.* I, 96). The French historians 'betray the cause of humanity and violate the truth of history' (*F.R.* III, 238). See above, pp. 61–2.

[3] *F.R.* I, 96, 313.

The denunciation of the theory of inevitability was mostly, at that time, a denunciation of democracy, because to justify the whole Revolutionary chain was connected with the acceptance of the Revolution. But Smyth showed deeper insight into the powers latent in nineteenth-century philosophies of history, when he wrote that the same theory of inevitability could be used both for 'democratic' violence and for the denial of liberty. These 'doctrines of despair', as he called them, because they left nothing to man's will and wisdom, lead either to anarchy or to slavery.

Led by his untiring opposition to necessity, Smyth also saw that Thiers and Mignet were out to justify every bit of the Revolution, and explain away all parties. He saw what became evident later, that Thiers and Mignet founded a nationalist school in Revolutionary historiography, a school which thought primarily of France as a whole, and was conscious of the revolutionary heritage. They never rejected the Revolution bag and baggage, without some qualifications.

We have seen that Smyth's rationalist qualities influenced his didactic aim and method. On the whole Smyth was unaware of new trends in historiography. At first he saw only the spareness of histories written amidst the confusions of the period,[1] and the novelty of compressed writing. When Smyth began to write history, Napoleon had overrun Europe and historical studies were at a low ebb. Smyth shared the feeling, then common, that, since the European states were no more, their previous histories had lost their interest. Privately he expressed this by quoting Burke, that 'all previous history sinks into parish importance'.[2] In 1810 he emphasized, however, that, though the details of history had lost their importance, the philosophy had gained in significance for contemporary history presented the highly instructive sight of the rise and fall of empires. In English historical thought the Revolution emphasized, at first, the old tendency to value generalization above detail. When ten years later, Smyth wrote on the Revolution, England was in the midst of a historical revival marked by Hallam, Mill, Mitford, and Lingard, who were, like Smyth, affected by the Revolution rather in their political than in their historical attitude. Smyth resembled Hallam in his politics and his history. If Hallam expounded the Whig philosophy in English history, Smyth applied it in a study of the French Revolution. Like Hallam he strove to be fair and honest, pretended to avoid current politics, disliked 'bad' periods of history. But while Hallam was criticized for neglecting historical literature, Smyth was especially aware of the influence of historiography.

It is unfortunate for Smyth that he must be judged as a historian

---

[1] *F.R.* I, 51.
[2] R.P. 4574, 16 Dec. 1805. On this ground, that history was no longer popular, he advised Roscoe to recast *Leo* as a biography.

mainly on the basis of work done in 1810 and in the late 1820s. The last lecture he ever wrote, the summary of European history which he gave in 1837, is perhaps his best piece of historical thinking. It is as if the seed sown by Mackintosh in the letter of 1809 was finally bearing some fruit. Smyth surveys European history from the 'irruption of the northern nations', with an emphasis on the working of the 'principle of human intelligence' and freedom of thought. He says, for instance, that the history of science is the most interesting of historical subjects, that Luther never intended freedom of thought to reign, and that the most difficult and the most important subject is to reconcile religion with freedom of thought.

Smyth also became aware, at last, of new theories of history-writing, but this new awareness found its way only into the new introductory lectures. These lectures show that, though Smyth saw new movements, he did not always understand what he saw. He deplored, for instance, political partisanship, and said that historians now write of the figures of the past as if they were members of their retinue.[1] He did not connect this with the temper bred by the Revolution, nor with the romantic tendency to 'realize' the past. He tended to see things in the light of his old theories. When he discerned, especially among foreign historians like Guizot, a tendency to generalize too much, to discover 'great principles' at work, even without the knowledge of the actors, he did not see in this the beginning of the history of ideas, or the expression of a romantic belief in a national spirit, and did not connect it with Burke's teaching on historical continuity and on national instincts. Instead he claimed that such history-writing was 'a flaunting ambitious mode of writing; little suited to the sober phlegm and cautious good sense of our historians', who were satisfied with narratives and facts.[2] He connected this with his old bugbear of 'necessity' and said that a history which sought 'great principles' tended to breed inevitability and was 'favourable to revolutions'. General principles dispose of vice and virtue and deceive people into thinking that bad government must be followed by revolution. On this ground he also criticized Tocqueville. Because Tocqueville wrote that history shows a tendency towards equality, Smyth at once retorts: 'This is the sort of reasoning always adopted by revolutionists and republican writers; from the "ça ira" of the blood-stained mobs of Paris, to the necessarian dogmas of M. Thiers and Mignet ... a revolution must roll on; one movement necessarily leads to another; the spirit of the times cannot be resisted.'[3]

[1] He was thinking of historians like Grote of whom Saintsbury said that he wrote of Cleon 'as if he had been backing that worthy for a seat in an English Constituency'.

[2] *F.R.* III, 404–5.

[3] Smyth even thought that Tocqueville taught the inevitability of a democracy designed by Providence, and therefore regarded his work on America as a continuation of the 'necessarian' theories of Thiers and Mignet (*F.R.* III, 359).

Smyth's own view was that principles cannot be laid down in history since 'we have to do with human beings'. Even when we observe a general tendency in a social class we must remember that groups are usually under the control of individuals. The philosophy of history, he thought, did mean that historians concluded from an event 'what the tendency of things, in given situations, will be hereafter', but we cannot talk of more than probabilities nor predict history as if fate were in our hands.[1] In the light of these new considerations Smyth made his own historical activities appear more systematic than they had in fact been. Twenty-five years earlier he had opposed abridgements simply on the ground that they left nothing in a memory not already stocked with detail. He now claims that his objection to general histories arose from their tendency to bring out apparently irresistible general principles in history. In the light of new historical research he even claimed that to combat theories he had searched the sources diligently for true facts, and for details of individual characters.[2]

Smyth missed the romantic influence on the attitude to history and on its method. He admired Walter Scott as the greatest genius of the century,[3] but had no idea of his influence on history. When he heard that Scott was writing on Napoleon, he considered this a 'literary calamity',[4] for Scott was turning from that which he could do best to that which others could do better. In this Smyth proved right, but he was blind to the more important issue of Scott's influence on historians. The term 'romantic' Smyth used in the purely literary sense. He said, for instance, that romantics like Byron could make Danton or Desmoulins appear heroic and moving, but the philosopher of history must remember the crimes and perversions of the revolutionaries. It is odd that there is something 'romantic' in Smyth's own treatment of Desmoulins. Smyth had been more obviously touched by the romantic spirit in dealing with the medieval period in the early course. An early Cambridge reviewer pointed out the historical advantage which Smyth derived from his poetical mind 'over the mere reasoning and philosophising historian', for it lent to the past the air which time lends to ruins. The comment is particularly interesting because it was applied to Smyth, and in 1819,[5] before Carlyle was filling the periodicals with talk about the poetry of history. Another thing Smyth had done in the earlier course was to draw long periods with bold strokes. These hints of imaginative insight had gone by the time Smyth wrote on the Revolution. He seems to have laid down his romanticism and directness with his enthusiasms, and to have taken up preaching and moralizing in proportion to his disillusionment.

---

[1] *F.R.* III, 272–3. [2] *F.R.* III, 274–5.
[3] Thomson Corresp. B.M. Add. MS. 35.265, 27 Aug. 1818.
[4] R.P. 4646, 22 Apr. 1827.
[5] *Cambridge Monthly Repository or Literary Miscellany* (Jan. 1819), 16–19.

When romantic history was really awakening, Smyth was immune to its touch. Though he treated the worst of the Terrorists as human beings, this was no more than Croker did. His distribution of justice was rational and there was little in it of the identification and the sympathy, which characterized romantics like Southey or Carlyle and became the fashion after them. Another prominent romantic aim in history was the aim of letting the materials speak for themselves. Mill in the *Westminster Review* of 1837 praised Carlyle for producing his materials and allowing his readers to test the truth of his conclusions. In 1856, the same periodical praised Smyth for the same quality.[1] The important distinction which must be made is that though both historians produced their materials, Smyth's materials were none other than previous historians' opinions, whereas Carlyle's material was the historical 'thing' itself, as far as he could get it.

[1] *Westminster Review* (1856), 616.

CHAPTER 6

REVOLUTION AND REFORM (1830–1832)

In the late 1820s, when Smyth, Scott, Hazlitt and Croker were writing, when the Tories had become so liberal that radical agitation was quiet, when Catholic emancipation and the abolition of slavery were the only reforms widely discussed, Whig and Tory versions of the Revolution are hard to tell apart. Fear of revolution subsided and there was occasion to glorify freedom and to lecture to the despots abroad on the merits of liberalism. Mild sympathy for 1789 could raise its head without being taken for Jacobinism. Disagreements were superficial and half-hearted. The idea that only pent up grievances cause disasters was a commonplace in the writings of the period and an argument for economic more than for political reform. Tories like Southey still pointed out that there were in the England of 1829 more open signs of discontent than in France before the States General, but the stock reply to that was that the danger of discontent lies precisely in what remains hidden in the public mind.[1]

THE EFFECT OF 1830

The Revolution of July 1830 in Paris created a dramatic change in the public temper. The popularity and success of that revolution were so complete that intervention was not contemplated. It is sometimes held that Wellington's fall was a direct result of the fall of Charles X, as a *solidaire* party. It is in any case clear that, after a momentary silence when the downfall of legitimacy in France was taken as a warning, a dormant political debate on the French Revolution suddenly blazed forth. The effect of 1830 was strongly felt in the political interpretation of the Revolution. As soon as fears were calmed, moderate approval of both French Revolutions seemed justified. The apologetic argument that the blame for the violence lay with the example and brutalizing effect of the old régime greatly gained force. It was said that the violence of a revolution is in proportion to the misrule which preceded it; that Burke himself had provided for this argument by comparing 1792 to 1776. The new revolutionaries, it was said, were milder because they had fewer grievances and had grown up under a constitution. It was stressed that Charles X, though he had sinned against his people, was not touched and that property was held sacred. Numerous books, articles and memoirs were written on the 1830 Revolution paying tribute to the self-restraint and

[1] E.g. *E.R.* (Jan. 1830), L. 520.

moderation displayed in it. These views were forcibly expressed in the Whig, Radical and popular press, and expounded by people like Macaulay and Mill. They constituted in fact the most generally accepted opinion on the events of 1830.

In England then the Revolution of 1830 was not by any means taken to mean that revolution had permanently installed itself as a factor in European life. On the contrary, people were saying that just as the Glorious Revolution had put the seal on the great Rebellion, so 1830 was the moderate consummation of 1789. The analogy implied that violent revolution was over and a series of peaceful reforms had been inaugurated. The Whigs felt encouraged to go ahead with reform at home; and later, the mildness and success of their programme confirmed that party in their policy. They stressed that it was possible to rejoice at the French Revolution without wishing for one at home.

The Tories felt the urgent need to fight this interpretation of the 1830 Revolution in France which was so conducive to reform. There were among them those to whom a moderate, reforming revolution was as hateful as a violent, bloody one, but it was difficult to make such illiberal principles popular. The Tory battle over the interpretation of the Revolution of 1830 was therefore fought on the assumption that the 1830 July Revolution was merely another beginning of a prolonged, violent, bloody revolution which would moreover lead to European war; that the success of an English reform programme would lead to exactly the same results. They therefore stressed the dangers which revolution held for rich and poor alike. In French Revolutionary history, they liked to show how undiscriminating the Terror had been. The number of writings of all sorts, in the two years between 1830 and 1832, in which the questions of the 1789 Revolution, of the 1830 Revolution, of the Great Rebellion, of the Glorious Revolution, and, above all, of the proposed reforms are discussed in close conjunction with each other, is enormous and unwieldy, but the examination of some prominent examples gives an insight into the historical thought of the time.

ALISON'S BATTLE AGAINST REFORM

From January 1831 to January 1832 there appears in every month's issue of *Blackwood's Magazine* an instalment of a long series of articles on the French Revolution and the question of English reform, written by Alison. *Blackwood's* prided itself that 'never did a resolute journal attempt to stem a more vehement torrent of public opinion'.[1] Alison had started writing his history of the French Revolution in 1829 and an opportunity now presented itself for using his studies to political and financial advantage. The Tories were never allowed to forget that Alison

---

[1] *Blackwood's* (Dec. 1832), XXXII, 931.

fought reform in *Blackwood's*. The whole series is a perfect example of the political application of the history of the French Revolution by a man who was neither a politician nor a professor but a professional historian. Alison, Macaulay, Croker and Smyth all acted in a similar way on the same occasion. Alison unlike Smyth is unambiguous, clear and definite. He states his aim—to fight reform—and his argument is consistent and logical if also repetitive.

Out of hundreds of pages of historical narrative, political argument, quotations from ancient and modern historians and philosophers, economic analysis, administrative statistics, Irish and Scottish governmental problems and many other subjects included in this series of articles against reform, one can cull a complete theory of the anatomy of revolutions supported by numerous illustrations and authorities. The principle underlying this anatomy would be a series of axioms as, for instance, that illegal violence must inevitably lead to military despotism as Hume said; that all revolutions are always started by the higher classes, as Madame de Staël said; that the early leaders of revolutions are generous and self-sacrificing, like Hampden, Bailly or Roland; that power always passes to the violent democratic leaders; that the early leaders are always the first victims; that the transition is always prepared by agitation; that it is never the reality of grievances that causes revolution but the temper with which they are viewed; that initial and moderate revolutionary success gives an incredible impetus to the factious, turbulent and ambitious elements of society; that the great body of men tend to be passive and swim with the current; that the slightest concession of power to the revolutionary element is fatal and is bound to lead to total revolution; that freedom is never in greater danger than after a successful revolution, as Guizot said; that freedom can never be gained by force of arms; that if bad laws endanger liberty, revolutions always destroy it; that 'freedom has emerged from the collision of different classes in society', but never from 'military insubordination'; that 'it is not lawful to do evil that good may come of it';[1] that representative assemblies deteriorate in proportion to the number of their electors; that no constitution is secure unless it includes the leadership of the natural aristocracy; that (as Frederick the Great and Napoleon had said) the way to ruin a country is to place it in the hands of philosophers or economists; that (as Chateaubriand said) the minority of revolutionaries desire liberty, the majority desire power.

Apart from the anatomy of revolutions which emerges from Alison's arguments, the articles are characterized by the weight and forcefulness of his historical illustrations and detailed comparisons. One of the favourite points is the comparison between the doubling of the *Tiers État* and the proposed Reform Bill, between Necker and Lord Grey.

[1] *Blackwood's* (Apr. 1831), XXIX, 626.

Necker in 1789 had the choice between redressing concrete grievances and conceding power to the revolutionary democracy. His fatal choice brought on the Revolution.[1] One point in the political strategy of Alison's early articles is to dispel the contentment and optimism with which the bloodless 1830 Revolution was met. With great conviction and masses of proof Alison sets out to show that for three whole years after 1789 there was also no real bloodshed though, as is the inevitable course of all revolutions, it came at a later stage.

The Constituent Assembly including Lafayette, Bailly and Mirabeau, true lovers of freedom and order, was, like the Presbyters in the Great Rebellion, followed by the Girondins who were humane and republican (like the Independents of England). It was only after 10 August 1792 when the Jacobins ('Fifth Monarchy Men') assumed power, that the massacres began, to be followed by Napoleon as they had been by Cromwell in England. The same fate awaits France after 1830 and England if the Reform Bill is passed, though in both cases the pace of revolution is faster and violence is therefore to be expected sooner. The mildness of grievances offer no security, for it is the passion for sovereignty and power which stirs up Jacobinism. The Reform Bill if granted (for the same reasons which prompted Necker), will be followed by the same scenes of horror, the disappearance of church and landed property, by blood and terror, 'a Danton and a Robespierre'. In tackling the liberal arguments for reform, Alison stresses the danger of errors which are subtly mixed with truth. The liberals claim that timely concessions prevent disaster; true, but in times of fermentation concessions are fatal. They speak of the progress of freedom; but freedom is not the same as democratic ambition. Freedom must be allowed to grow slowly. Not an inch must be yielded to democratic ambition.

Alison's favourite authorities are Madame de Staël, 'warmest friend of the cause of freedom', and Mignet to whom he always refers as the 'ablest of republican historians'. Mignet provides Alison with many a quotation stressing the irresistibility of the Revolutionary current. It was the strongest argument against reform to point out that it committed England fatally and finally to the whole course of violent revolution. The notion of historical 'fatalism' was thus taken up by conservative politicians to support their rejection of reform.[2] Another unexpected authority chosen by the Tory historian is that of Napoleon whose evidence is called in with absolute reliance on points of statesmanship, government, the suppression of insurrections and revolutions. This was

---

[1] Alison believed that there was in 1831 a way of redressing concrete grievances through 'disfranchisement of such boroughs as are convicted of corruption', and transferring their right to 'considerable manufacturing cities'.

[2] *Blackwood's* continued in the same tone after Alison's articles were finished. In July 1832 it prophesied a long period of national punishment, 'with their own hands they have pulled down the ancient and undecayed fabric which sheltered our fathers'.

common among the Tory enemies of Napoleon. In another *Blackwood's* article Napoleon is quoted to have said to young de Staël that his grandfather Necker was 'a fool, an ideologist, an old maniac', and that he, Napoleon, had to repair the damage he had done. One other authority of Alison's is of some interest. He refers to early *Edinburgh* articles for expositions of the nature of English political development and for criticism of French ways. It is to Brougham (to whom Alison ascribes most expositions) that he thus turns. The fact that, in fighting reform, a Tory could use the liberal interpretation of English and French revolutions which the Whigs had developed in the *Edinburgh*, shows the extent to which that interpretation had become the common basis of English views.

THE DEBATE OVER THE REFORM BILL

Perhaps at no other time in English history was the French Revolution so uppermost in politicians' minds as between 1830 and 1832. Amidst great agitation in and out of parliament, grave threats to public order and painful searching of hearts, many people besides Alison attempted to view the crisis they were facing with the help that historical perspective afforded them. Two prominent men, both politicians and not yet well-known historians, the mouthpieces of the two great English parties, each representing what the other hated most in the world, stood up in parliament for what must have seemed like a fight to the death, over the Reform Bill, over their interpretations of modern history, over notions of French revolutionism and English development.

Macaulay was still a young man earning his fame as a Parliamentarian; Croker was an old hand at both history and politics. He had already started his lifelong study of the French Revolution but his best work was not yet done and of recent years he had somewhat neglected the subject, devoting his historical energy to English memoirs. The years 1830 and 1832 induced Croker to resume writing on the Revolution.[1] In the desperate Tory campaign against the Reform Bill, Croker used his faculties for detailed government business, legal argumentation and historical data. It was Peel's task to attack the principles, and Croker's task to master the details and expose the inconsistencies of the Bill. According to the evidence of the Whigs themselves, he was the more formidable of the two contestants, the one who got their party into scrapes.[2]

The Croker–Macaulay controversy over the Reform Bill from 20 September 1831, fought out in French Revolutionary terms, appears to bring to a head the Whig–Tory controversy over the interpretation of the

[1] Croker wrote a military description of the Revolution of 1830 in *Q.R.* (Jan. 1831), XLIV, 226–61, which was also published separately.
[2] J. R. M. Butler, *The Passing of the Reform Bill* (1914).

French Revolution and at the same time to illustrate the influence of these interpretations on English politics. The argument was about the question of 'the lesson to be learnt by the peers from the fate of their counterpart in the French Revolution'. We see Croker in the popular role of heeding Revolutionary lessons for the purpose of preserving the British Constitution, and, just like Macaulay, mixing his politics with his history.

The political point at issue is clear-cut. On two things Macaulay and Croker agreed, on the historical fact that the Revolution destroyed the French nobility and on the political objective that the English aristocracy should be preserved. They differed in their opinion as to how the peerage could be made secure, and their differences about policy resulted from different understandings of why and how the French aristocracy had been ruined.

Have you ever heard that from those magnificent hotels, from those ancient castles, an aristocracy as splendid, as brave, as proud, as accomplished as ever Europe saw, was driven forth to exile and beggary—to implore the charity of hostile governments and hostile creeds—to cut wood in the back settlements of America—or to teach French in the schoolrooms of London? And why were those haughty nobles destroyed with that utter destruction? . . . Because they had no sympathy with the people— no discernment of the signs of their time, because in the pride and narrowness of their hearts, they called those whose warnings might have saved them, theorists and speculators, because they refused all concession till the time had arrived when no concession would avail.[1]

That there was a parallel to be drawn neither of them at first doubted. 'He drew his weapon from the very armoury to which . . . I should myself have resorted . . . the early lessons of the French Revolution', said Croker when he rose to answer. Macaulay attributed the destruction of the French nobility to their obstinate resistance to reforms and Croker to their 'deplorable pusillanimity' in granting them. Consequently Macaulay recommended to the English nobles concessions in time, Croker, firm resistance. Croker claimed that he did not question Macaulay's analogy, only his inference. What Croker in fact questioned were Macaulay's facts. 'It requires no depth of historical research to be acquainted with the prominent features of those interesting and instructive times.'[2] What books had Macaulay read, asked Croker, horrified; what authorities had he consulted to remain ignorant of 'one of the commonplaces of modern history'. Croker quoted a series of revolutionary actions prompted by nobles and lists the names of the nobles (like Montmorency, Noailles) who struck the first blow at their order. To question Macaulay's facts, and not merely his inferences, was no doubt better political tactics, but Croker's insistence on concrete evidence is also characteristic of his historical mind. As a historian, however,

---

[1] Speech of 20 Sept. 1831 (*Parl. Deb.* 3rd series, vol. vii, p. 297).
[2] *Ibid.* p. 313.

Croker like Macaulay is not seen here at his best. He is primarily a politician playing the game of analogies. 'The abolition of the separate Chambers ... was, in fact, the whole Revolution ... The proposition of the *Tiers État* was a *Reform Bill*.' This mode of thought was not indeed completely alien to him: he often elaborated analogies in detail, illustrating them even by drawing up tables. He tabulated, for instance, a detailed comparison between stages and aspects of the Great Rebellion and the French Revolution. He rejected all theories of progress and had always believed what the Duke of Wellington told him in 1841, that human nature never changes, that interests and passions are always the same and bring about similar results. When Macaulay gave up the French analogy, during the debate of 16 December, retreating no doubt under the heavy fire of Croker's factual knowledge, Croker was only too happy to meet Macaulay's new analogy with the Great Rebellion.

The first of Croker's reform speeches[1] had anticipated some changes which were coming over revolutionary writings and debates. Having begun the speech with a horrible dissection of Lord Jeffrey, which cleared the House of the disgusted Whigs, he charged the Reform Bill with being a new political philosophy 'founded on a consideration of the French Revolution'. This is no longer the conventional warning that 'moderate reforms' are dangerous, but a charge of calculated revolutionism. The Whigs, he implied, were not making the same mistakes as the French, they were purposely working towards the same results. The point is further illustrated in the last speech against Macaulay, that of 19 March, in which the Tory explained to the Whigs that the English Constitution was one of compromises and gradual changes, whereas they were introducing a new principle.

Two articles, in the *Edinburgh* and in the *Quarterly*, one by Macaulay and one by Croker, and both, significantly, reviews of a French Revolutionary book, Dumont's *Mirabeau*, round off this remarkable debate. Croker's article came out in March, the Bill was passed in June and Macaulay's article appeared in July.[2] Croker wrote his article in his purely political mind, as an elaboration of his historical point in the debates. A manuscript note in his collection of his own articles,[3] by himself or by Murray, disclaims for Croker any allusions to himself in the article, but the article is in fact constructed round these allusions to himself (characterized as 'Alternis aptum sermonibus, et populares Vincentem strepitus, et natum rebus agendis') even if the actual name was added by somebody else. The first part describes the debate in

---

[1] On 4 Mar. 1831. Croker, *Speech on the Reform Question* (London, 1831). *Parl. Deb.* 3rd series, vol. III, p. 81. It is on the whole a practical speech with little reference to France.

[2] 'Revolutions of 1640 and 1830', *Q.R.* (Mar. 1832), XLVII. It reviews Dumont's *Mirabeau* as well as a work on *The Progress of the Revolutions of 1640 and 1830* (London, 1832) and other works on English politics in 1830. *E.R.* (July 1832), LV, 552.

[3] Croker's *Contributions to Q.R.* vol. III, Art. 6.

Parliament elaborating Croker's role and pointing out that the 'extempore effusion of the statesman surpassed immeasurably as to style and force of language the elaborate concoctions . . .'. The treatment of Dumont in the *Quarterly* is purely polemical; passages are quoted which support Croker's argument in the Parliamentary debate; because Dumont cannot be suspected of anti-revolutionism, his evidence is taken to be decisive on present day problems. The union of the French orders is described as a 'Reform Bill'; the reviewer brings out the parallel by substituting 'British cabinet of 1831' for 'National Assembly of 1789' in a quotation from Dumont. The article simply amplifies the debate. Croker is not thinking of history. He uses a book to illustrate a political view, in the same way in which, in the same year, Smyth at Cambridge was adding a lecture to his course, in order to show that Dumont's book confirmed his own criticism of the Revolutionaries.

Macaulay's review, written in the satisfaction and calmness of victory, makes up, with his 1844 article on Barère, his most important pronouncement on the Revolution. Both Croker's and Macaulay's reviews of Dumont are primarily political articles, and there is more historical thought in that of Macaulay. Croker's review, written in the anxieties of a losing battle, is one of his poorest; Croker, strangely, was never successful in combining politics and history. Since he was so steeped in both the working of the English political machine and in the history of the French Revolution, the need to fight as he did brought out the worst in both his historical and his political mind, his lack of perspective and his narrow reactionary politics.

Macaulay dismisses the Tory glee over Dumont's anti-revolutionism by referring to the period in which Dumont wrote. In 1799, he said, the first excitement had died down but the benefits of the Revolution could not yet be seen; the price had been paid but the goods not yet delivered. The dying words of Madame Roland, 'Oh Liberty, what crimes are committed in your name', were echoed by the most benevolent of mankind. As Guizot wrote of Lainé, liberals were 'discouraged by the Revolution'. Philosophy had reigned and brought crimes. Freedom bowed before despots. Dumont therefore wrote that Burke had been justified by events. To Macaulay Dumont suggested the conclusion, not that the Revolution was not a blessing, but that its enemies deserved some indulgence, considering their times. This seems to have been a standard Whig way of thinking about Burke and the early 'alarmists', as we have already noticed in Smyth.[1] Macaulay thought circumstances were everything, for he said that Canning was but a Pitt of another age, that the Jacobins made Pitt a Tory and the reactionaries made Canning a Whig.

Dumont's judgment on the Revolution, said Macaulay, was like

[1] R.P. 4620, 13 May 1817.

criticism of the first act of a play. Although the Assembly refused to be taught English parliamentary procedure by Bentham through Dumont, it conferred great benefits on mankind. Macaulay, who, like Mill, grew out of a Whig tradition which began by accepting the French Revolution because it was so 'English', learnt to plead for France's right to have her own style in revolutions.

The interpretative idea which Macaulay introduced owes something perhaps to a cue in Mackintosh. 'The glory of the National Assembly is this,' writes Macaulay, 'that they were in truth what Mr Burke called them in austere irony, the ablest architects of ruin.' Here, as in Croker's accusation in Parliament (that the Whigs knowingly aimed at revolution), we meet a vague awareness of new interpretations and no longer mere variations of how much or how little of the Revolution should be accepted or rejected. A new principle is emerging when Macaulay dares to glorify the very destruction as a vulgar but necessary task. 'It is not in the dark that we learn to distinguish colours.'[1]

Alison, Croker and Macaulay were at home in both politics and history. Smyth was merely a professor but he considered the lectures on the French Revolution which he was delivering in Cambridge at that time as a service to wise and moderate politics. We have seen how his letters and lectures reflected his constantly deepening conservatism under various influences. It was natural that he should be affected by the striking juxtaposition of the question of reform with the history of the French Revolution. That he was not opposed to the Reform Bill we can only indirectly deduce.[2] The question of the lessons which the Revolution held for the British nobility, lessons which had first been debated by Burke and Sheridan, and were now revived with a new poignancy by Croker and Macaulay, Smyth had already discussed in his lectures. He had written that the French nobility had destroyed itself by failing to make concessions in time, and before the Reform Bill debate he wrote, 'They saw not their danger—let others take warning'. The introductory lecture of 1832 was devoted to Dumont's *Mirabeau* and written soon after that book had figured in the Parliamentary debate. Smyth, true to his academic impartiality, combined the Tory and Whig arguments. The theme of his lecture is that although Dumont was a member of the popular party, he still confirmed Smyth's criticisms of that party. This was the Tory argument, but Smyth also insisted that Dumont must not be used in an argument against reform. He explains that Dumont refrained from criticizing the privileged classes only because the object

---

[1] Other arguments Macaulay uses are that people made ferocious by misgovernment must not remain misgoverned, that pure minds must not be reconciled to tyranny at the moment when it is made clear what tyranny has done to human nature.

[2] He put his name to Sedgewick's petition against the decision of Cambridge University to unseat its Members who intended to vote for the Bill.

of his work was not a complete judgment, but a criticism of the mistakes of his own party.

THE HEYDAY OF POLITICAL HISTORY

It is generally accepted that the application of French Revolutionary history to England delayed reform in England for over a generation. The over-simplified view that down to 1830 or 1832 a Burkian and extremely hostile view of the French Revolution reigned in English historical studies must be discarded as untenable. Equally wrong is the contradictory assumption that English studies of the Revolution con-sisted of a constant debate between the friends and enemies of the Revolution. It is true that in times of crisis such as 1794, 1816, 1831, Revolutionary history was indeed enrolled to fight the political battles and it is of course true that politics was continuously aware of the Revo-lutionary experience just as history was aware of the English political scene. In viewing the historical writings, however, we found that other developments seemed to loom larger. Various influences were carrying history forward sometimes with the help of political controversy, some-times in spite of it and, most important of all, along lines detached from it. The development of a unified attitude to the Revolution and of a generally homogeneous interpretation of causes, progress and results; a more critical and discriminating method of studying and judging it, were some of the general features gaining relief against the outline of the story.

The Reform Bill, it is true, seemed to bring to a climax the political application of Revolutionary history. But the Reform Bill was passed. Was it because the horror of revolution had abated under the impact of the moderateness of 1830? Was it because a pro-Revolutionary school of history won? The Whigs who won the day in 1832 were eminently not revolutionary in politics or in history. Croker fully believed the analogies he used and when the Bill was passed he resigned from office under a government he believed to be heading towards revolution,[1] massacres and a republic. We also note that it was after the Reform Bill that Smyth's terror of democracy grew. And Alison in 1833 actually went to France to watch the demonstration of the principle, in which he believed, that the course of all revolutions leads to violence and military despotism (most likely after three years).

The Whigs, on the other hand, rested on their laurels. The hope expressed in 1830 that England's constitutional battles were fought for her on the Continent seemed in 1832 to have come true.[2] The Reform Bill

---

[1] There are numerous statements to show Croker expected massacres and a republic. E.g. Croker to Hertford in 1831, Jennings, II, 140; Croker to Peel, *ibid.* II, 137.

[2] 'We take it to be abundantly manifest, that the battle of English liberties has really been fought and won at Paris' (*E.R.* (Oct. 1830), LII, 1).

did not lead to the massacres which had been the Tory nightmare. Even during the 'hungry forties' insurrections were easily put down. The rapid succession of reforms after 1832 conformed to the lessons which the Whigs had taken from the Revolution—that concessions should be made in time, that reform should come from above, etc. The Whigs modified their tone now, dissociated themselves from French politicians like Lafayette (whose moderateness in 1830 they had praised), and compared themselves to the middle party in France. They attacked Hume and the English Radicals as fiercely as they dared and declared French liberty to be in danger from its extreme friends.

The early 1830s, on the whole, then, present a most unsystematic adherence to the 'lessons of revolution' by historians and politicians. What could historians make of all this? Could present day politics prove to them which interpretation of the past had been proved right and which wrong? 'History' proved the Whigs right in not expecting a violent sequel to reform, but it also proved the Tories right in predicting the advent of democracy. Were not even the tendencies of the 'present' a matter of mere contradictory conjectures? Were the historians perhaps disappointed in history because it failed to give a clear answer in the most crucial moment of perplexion?

The Whig–Tory debate was partly a debate over the 'fatalist' interpretation of history. The opponents of reform like Alison and Croker made use of the 'fatalist' theory which the pro-Revolutionary historian Mignet shared with Burke, the theory, in short, that the first step led inevitably to the bitter end. But the theory was defeated with the opposition to the Reform Bill. English politics as well as historiography rejected it in favour of the empiricist interpretation more common in England, that it is never too late for sensible politics.

It was not then any one political or philosophical view of history which won in 1832. More than anything else it was the separation of history from politics which was beginning to win. The dominance of Revolutionary history in English politics had been undermined for a long time. Now the frantic nature of the very attempts to maintain the analogy between two countries, two periods, two systems, had helped to expose the vanity of such attempts. Under the impact of new and powerful influences the analogy was quickly disappearing both in the world of history and that of politics.

Among the impulses driving historians to a new kind of history was the conscious rebellion against existing history. Carlyle's fiercest reaction in thinking about history was not only against eighteenth-century rationalist historiography from which he had also learnt a great deal, but mainly against present-day political dissertations masquerading as history. This was not entirely new. The demand for more faithful, critical and accurate history was not in England a result of a romantic love for antiquities. The spirit of political warfare in which the debate on the Revolution as well as other historical debates were conducted, led, independently of new theories and historical movements, earlier and more directly to aspirations for better history, and attempts to achieve this. The need for sound history appeared urgent and obvious when the debate in popular and widely read literature manifested the follies and dangers of history-writing which was political propaganda in disguise. This led to better methods and their more conscientious application. In the case of the French Revolution, as of other controversial events, the literary weapons of the combatants and their advocates forced investigation forward.

This process had been evident in Revolutionary historiography since the Revolution itself, but it was given great impetus after 1830 and 1832. It is not perhaps mere chance that Carlyle's determination to write a new history of the French Revolution came in the early 'thirties after the frantic exhibition of political history which those years presented. But before we look at Carlyle's *History* we ought to ask some questions about romantic historiography in England.

CHAPTER 7

THE FRENCH REVOLUTION AND THE ROMANTIC MOVEMENT IN HISTORIOGRAPHY

The Romantic movement in historiography was connected with the French Revolution in various and sometimes contradictory ways. That the French Revolution influenced and shaped the Romantic movement has become a classic notion in the history of historiography. According to this notion the effect wrought by the Revolution was a negative one, through the extreme reaction against itself which the Revolution aroused. The shock which a whole generation had undergone, the bitter disappointment from all that the Revolution had promised and not fulfilled, caused a violent reaction against the principles and aims of the Revolution, and more important still, against its intellectual background, that is, the philosophical, social and political notions of rationalism which were believed to have caused the Revolution. The revulsion from what the Revolution had done to nations and to individuals, in the name of its principles, turned many people to love all that the Revolution hated and wished to destroy.

This psychological explanation purports to cover not only the political and social reaction which, as is well known, spread over Europe after the Restoration, but also the new trends of thought, literature and scholarship. It maintains that because the Revolution had attempted to snap the ties which bound a nation to its past, to its constitutional, cultural and religious 'upbringing', because it attempted to impose alien governments on conquered peoples, therefore the liberated nations turned with re-awakened love to their legitimate rulers, to the laws, customs and institutions which were the national heritage. Because the Revolution rejected history and created a violent interruption in historical continuity, trying to build on the ground of abstract theories, therefore all theories in political life were taboo, history became sacrosanct, invested with divine wisdom, the highest authority in the life of the individual and of society. Because rationalism and the Revolution preached a universalist faith which blurred the differences between man and man, nation and nation, class and class, race and race, and sought to see them all as equal, and because the Revolution had failed in enforcing and spreading this new democratic gospel, therefore all differences and distinctions acquired a new and pronounced emphasis. One can prolong the list of principles and beliefs against which the reaction turned: the optimistic view of man as good and perfectible; the expected reign of reason, etc.

This explanation seems to apply directly to history. In France and in the liberated countries, nations which had been torn from their past by the armies of the Revolution or of Napoleon, and which had already experienced a national movement in revolts against France, turned with great enthusiasm to the Burkian teaching of continuity, of cherishing the gifts of past generations. Men of learning headed the campaign for the salvation of the national culture and tradition. Encouraged by reactionary governments, a frantic search for the treasures of the past was inaugurated. Everywhere the antiquities of the nation, the sources of its culture, and, above all, its particular national spirit which was believed to shape, in its own form, the national character, the language, laws, customs, literature, institutions and all that is peculiar to a nation, became the object of scholarly and popular writings. The spiritual self-abandonment to all that is national, original, peculiar, rooted and ancient, and which fulfils the requirement of unbroken existence, had a fertilizing influence on the thought and scholarship of historians. In science and literature it led to a great fervour in studying the national origins in all aspects of the national civilization. History gained the important basic concepts of development and organic society. Historical studies benefited from the anxiety to discover organic development. Great scholars appeared, who, in the light of these assumptions, investigated processes in philology, law and folklore, and made important contributions to knowledge.

When we speak, therefore, of the Romantic movement in history, we generally mean the all-round expressions of the widespread reaction. In political thinking—a conscious conservatism and a willing self-subjection to history and to the accumulated wisdom of past ages; in historical thinking—the theories of continuity, organicism and the action of mysterious forces expressing the genius of a nation and directing history; and in the writing of history—a reaction against rationalist historiography which tends towards generalizations, abstractions, analogies, the learning of lessons from history, the search for the typical, the repetitive, the universal. Against a historiography which prides itself on being 'philosophy teaching by experience', the Romantic movement aimed at a new history, narrative, live, picturesque, direct, full of particular detail and local colour, alive with the touch and the atmosphere of the past, populated by individual characters, a history which is artistically effective, written through artistic identification and creating a sense of emotional identification in the reader.

The most conspicuous quality of this rather wide definition of Romantic historiography in its different aspects, the political, historiosophical and historiographical, is its apparent unity of purpose, simplicity of design and perfection of logic. It presents a harmonious system of thought which includes a comprehensive explanation for a colourful conglomeration of phenomena and activities of an age. Moreover, it contains useful clues from which we could go on to learn something about the sources of the next stage in historiography whose essence is a revolution in men's attitude to historical sources and to the method of studying them. It would be possible to show that Romantic devotion to that which is original, real, authentic, and immediate, gave rise in history to a deeper search and yearning for historical truth, and for more reliable and conclusive methods of pursuing it.

It is too easy in historiography as in other branches of intellectual history to be attracted by abstract schemata on the way in which one idea begets another. There is hardly a scheme which has no basis in reality and there is certainly not a scheme which explains the whole of reality. Also, the correspondence between ideas and political actions is often exaggerated in the light of such outstanding examples as that of Siéyès who seemed to build a political and institutional structure round a philosophical faith. The study of the history of ideas can be blinding as well as illuminating and the assumptions about Rationalism and Romanticism are an example of its pitfalls. The uses to which ideas can be put in politics are not innate in the ideas. The rationalist belief in the sameness of human nature, and hence in perfectibility, led to enlightened efforts to raise people through education as in Condorcet. But the same belief also gave rise to cruel impatience with any lapses from social and moral virtue. Romantic notions, on the other hand, about deep national differences can lead to a persecuting racialism or to mutual toleration on the same assumptions.

It might therefore be useful to examine some of the phenomena related to the connection between the French Revolution and the Romantic movement in history which seem to be problematical or do not fit in with widely accepted assumptions on this connection.

PHASES IN THE ROMANTIC MOVEMENT

The earliest stage in the Romantic movement in literature preceded the Revolution and was not created by it. In the eighteenth century the Romantic movement derived from similar sources to those of the Revolutionary movement and it shared with it above all an element of revolt against the conventions of society; the belief in the essential reasonableness, natural goodness and natural rights of man, and the aspiration for freer expression and fuller fulfilment of human emotions and desires in society and in individual life.

In analysing the intellectual background of the French Revolution, the emphasis tends to be on Rationalism partly because the earliest enemies of the Revolution singled out this side of the Revolutionary spirit for their attack, and partly because in the light of later political experience and political literature Rationalism did seem the most convincing and clear-cut single explanation for the theory behind the calculated and far-reaching aspirations and policies which the French Revolution adopted in order to change the individual and society. There were also practical reasons. The haters of the Revolution may have suffered more from Napoleon than from the ideas of 1789 but it was better policy to attack the spirit of revolution than the ideas of a strong ruler who embodied so much of centralized, ordered, strong, autocratic and nationalist government which his worst enemies admired.

The nineteenth century has inherited and developed this line of attack, and the balance was not really redressed. Given the modern tendency to approach history with the help of sociology, and given modern experience not only in the way mass revolutions are conducted, but also in the way they are followed, it would seem possible to study the climate of opinion in pre-revolutionary France with greater attention to the popular notions which made the ordinary half-educated people of the *Tiers État* give themselves up to revolution. This might balance our knowledge of the rationalist education of the leading revolutionaries and give Romantic notions a greater share among the causes of the Revolution. The extent to which Rationalist or Romantic elements in the background of the Revolution are emphasized corresponds to the extent to which the responsibility for the Revolution is attributed to the leaders or to 'the people'. In the general climate of opinion in France humanitarian and vaguely mystical feelings, of the kind flowing in the *Discours sur l'inégalité*, were also active beside rationalist patterns of thought in the ruthless spirit of the *Contract Social*, on which some revolutionary leaders were brought up, and which was carried to its utmost logical extremity by Marat. All this is to say that there were in the early literary movement, essentially romantic features like revolt, individualism, love of freedom, the sense of the mystery of the will of the people, all of which pointed in a revolutionary and not in an anti-revolutionary direction; Cowper, a precursor of English literary romanticism who embodied in his poetry the warm love of humanity and nature, celebrated in poetry, several years before it fell, the fall of

> —the Bastille.
> Ye horrid tow'rs, th' abode of broken hearts ...
> There's not an English heart that would not leap
> To hear that ye were fall'n at last, to know
> That ev'n our enemies, so oft employed
> In forging chains for us, themselves were free.[1]

The second, and more complicated phase in the relations between the Romantic and the Revolutionary movements, begins with the stormy

[1] W. Cowper, *The Task* (London, 1785), p. 201. Cowper recanted in 1793.

and spontaneous enthusiasm—short lived, but long remembered—rich with literary fruit with which young romantic writers (especially Wordsworth, Coleridge and Southey) received the Revolution. It continued with the appearance of Burke's *Reflections*, and under their influence, with the spiritual conversion which artists, intellectuals and statesmen all over Europe experienced. The result was the creation of conscious, theoretic opposition to the Revolution based on a system of historical, social and moral ideas raised by Burke. The sequence of these extraordinary events is well known but its essence has been the subject of various interpretations. The study of the transformation of the political consciousness of the romantic movement from revolution to reaction started as early as the process itself by the romantics themselves. Deeply engrossed in the emotional and intellectual processes they experienced, they early investigated in series of introspective analyses and in public recantations their immediate reactions and their later awakening, in the light of a new and transformed kind of Romanticism.

Burke's peculiar part in the Romantic movement is paradoxical in several ways. There was apparently little which he had in common with the literary movement of the eighteenth century and nothing at all with its political leanings. Burke's love for political liberty, even in his passionate plea for the Americans, belonged to a tradition in political and social thinking which rejected individual revolt as a matter of principle, even when it accepted the theory of natural rights. Burke believed himself to be fighting for the ancient privileges of the Americans as Englishmen. What, then, made Burke a romantic force so great that he achieved not merely the conversion of a few poets but the essential transformation of the movement itself which now took up an attitude of great hostility toward revolution in general and seemed therefore opposed to the early Rousseauist movement? The nature and the essence of the transformation was that romanticism acquired the dimension of history, the conscious planting of one's roots in the past. The common link which became the lever of the transformation was dependent not on the political views of the romantics but precisely on their non-political mind and temperament, on their literary, emotional, personal attributes. Being captured by Burke's invocation of history was as organic to the Romantic temperament as revolutionism had been. It fed not on a body of views but on the romantic nature itself: the self-abandonment to the power of imagination, the love of the mysterious and the remote, the attraction to extreme and emotional expression in life and art, to tension and revolt against the conventional, to far-reaching aspirations for the regeneration of society. Those whose gaze would always be fixed beyond their own times could easily look forward to the free and utopian future which the Revolution heralded; later, when the Revolution itself cooled down, gave up its declarations of love to humanity in general, and turned cold-bloodedly to war and compulsion, then they could with equal enthusiasm turn their eyes back to the treasures of the past, whose richness held enough in store for the wildest imagination. It was this Romantic susceptibility above all which could be seized as a lever to transform the literary movement into the historical and political movement which romanticism became and which seems at first sight a strange namesake for anything connected with Rousseau or the Lyrical Ballads. True, there were other points of contact. One might wonder if the later interest in 'Volk' was not after all a direct descendant of the early interest in peasants. One must guard, however, against straining after connections in ideas. In the development of romanticism we must distinguish between traits which were essential and others which were incidental, though confusion is often caused by the nature of the development itself, for instance in writers like Wordsworth or Herder, who in their lives and writings seem to embody the transition from a romantic conception of the mystery of nature to a romantic idealization of the mystery of nation. The attention to the people, the love of local colour, the study of the indigenous, were indeed a feature of both the early literary and the late historical movements but they sprang from different sources and were conducted in different ways. Eichhorn's search for the way local customs became national law was a highly sophisticated process charged with theories about history, the concept of the nation, the individuality of cultures, whereas the early literary interest in the villagers was a simple emotion expressing at the most a new 'democratic' love of common people.

In the third stage, that of the Restoration, the statesmen and the scholars who were mainly Burke's followers in Europe did not come to him from the fields of poetry but from the national and political interests which Burke's ideas were designed to save. Statesmen, however, learn more from statesmen, and scholars learn more from scholars than they do from each other. Movements, moreover, are not embodied in single men. The reaction to the French Revolution gave rise to a series of profound changes in the attitude to history and consequently in the methods of study, changes which were inspired and foreshadowed by Burke's *Reflections* but were not widely adopted until the lesson had been learnt through experience.

The general devotion to history and its rise to the height of intellectual and practical life, especially in Germany, proved at one and the same time to be an inspiration to writers, a useful weapon to conservative statesmen and an impetus to fruitful research of scholars. Statesmen for once accepted professors as allies and the professors in their turn rewarded their encouragement by confirming from history the hypotheses offered them by Burke, discovering the forceful action in history of organic development, continuity of custom and tradition. Extreme nationalism and extreme conservatism thus entered both in France and Germany into a formidable alliance which in Germany was cemented and enriched by an onrush of devoted scholarship and in France was beautified and invested with the awesome wave of a Catholic revival.

If, however, we examine the bulk of historical writings as distinguished from political writings produced during the period after the Restoration for the purpose of finding in it internal uniformity and general adherence to the requirements of 'classical romanticism' if one may use such a term, then we must admit that though there were romantic influences there was no uniform romantic school in the historiography of Europe. England, especially, presents a great exception.

ENGLAND'S BRAND OF ROMANTICISM

England had had, as we have seen, strong connections with certain aspects of romanticism before and during the Revolution. After the Restoration it did not share in the extreme political reaction. There had been no violent break in her historical continuity to give rise to an ideology of hatred towards all revolutions. Even anxiety about the Constitution was not strong enough to induce a totally new approach to national problems. For the same reason England did not share in the revival of history with the same zeal. For her there was no urgent need to patch together the broken pieces of the national tradition; as people said then, 'the ancient fabric of the constitution' had weathered the storm. One of the expressions of this relative equanimity was the absence of any strong awakening of interest in the ancient period. Turner's most original work on Anglo-Saxon history was begun before the Revolution. The distinction between antiquarianism and history continued to exist in England perhaps because the frantic search for national antiquities never became a national and popular duty. There was no need to rebuild 'tradition' in order to defend it. There was less scholarly delving into the past for political purposes than there was, for instance, in Germany. Officialdom remained indifferent to historical documents except those juridically valid. The study of the nation's antiquities continued detached from popular history and unvitiated by political aims. It is true that even historians of Rome and Greece wrote with a political bias made more significant since the Revolution. Grote, Mitford and Hallam all had political prejudices but there was nothing new in their approach to history, its subject-matter or methods. There was no serious attempt to reconstruct the whole of English history with the conservative lesson of the Revolution in mind. Neither Hallam, Lingard nor Scott shared the spirit in which Chateaubriand or Eichhorn approached medieval history.

The most conspicuous feature of the historical activities of the Restoration period in England is the paradox that although it was an early English work on the French Revolution, Burke's *Reflections*, which began new trends in history and gave a great stimulus to Romanticism in history, and eventually helped to revolutionize the writing of history, and although it was English history which seemed at that time as the model worthy of study and emulation, the English historians remained for decades un-affected by new attitudes to history and the Romantic movement in historiography at first hardly touched either England, the home of Burke's theories, or the study of the Revolution which provoked his writings.

Among the early writings on the Revolution, expressions of a purely emotional, revolutionary poetical romanticism, there were Odes, ballads, dramas and epic poems glorifying the Revolution, and hoping to make it immortal. A well-known example is *The Fall of Robespierre* begun by Coleridge and finished by Southey 'as fast as newspapers could be put in blank verse'. Coleridge and Southey did not feel the same about the fall of Robespierre and the poem embodies both views. Though it hails the death of Robespierre it breathes a deep confidence in the Revolution and acclaims the 9th Thermidor as a great victory for liberty.

Of Romantic history proper there is, at first, nothing in England. Burke himself lacked many of the requisites. In spite of flashes of pictorial imagination, his was essentially a work of speculation very much in the tradition of philosophy teaching through experience. English historians showed a marked lack of susceptibility to romanticism. Of the theorists, only Coleridge remained loyal to Burke's political theories, and he wrote no history. Although Romantic history everywhere gained force from an anti-revolutionary sentiment this did not mean that anti-revolutionary history was written as 'romantic history', and that which was favourable to the Revolution as rationalistic. The writings on the Revolution con-tinued at first as if a new attitude to history had not arisen. Whether they wrote for the Revolution or against it the English historians continued to model themselves on the great historians of the eighteenth century, Gibbon, Hume and Robertson who have been called 'standard bearers in the intellectual movement which led up to the Revolution', rejecting all new theories which they often did not understand. Some writers, more affected by the events in one way or another, or better acquainted with the personal details, wrote occasionally in the immediate, urgent style of journalism which to respectable academic historians seemed a travesty of the historians' professional code, but which to us seems like the first signs of a new live history.

All this is connected with a second paradox connected with the different influences which Burke had in England and that which he had in other countries. In spite of attempts, from his own time to this day, to show the consistency of Burke's views, it is a fact that different and some-times contradictory teachings have been learnt from Burke. In France and Germany Burke's pupils were mainly people like Gentz, De Maistre, Chateaubriand and later Taine. They made Burke's extreme writings against the Revolution the basis of a conservative ideology and of a theory which adopted the principle of national development which Burke attributes to England. Burke, by making a system and a philosophy out of a process which he himself describes as that of trial and error and *ad hoc* remedies, in a sense distorted the historical process which he described. In the same way that in the time of the American and French Revolutions the world received a false picture of the English constitution because Montesquieu described it as a system of division of powers, so in the nineteenth century, through the systematization of the conservative attitude, Burke made famous a principle of English development and moreover ignored all phenomena which did not fit his system, such as the influence of the Puritans who developed an abstract and revolutionary theory of politics unrelated to the tradition. Burke thus caused political movements to admire and emulate a model which did not exist. An ideology born of a combination of a false understanding of the French Revolution and a one-sided presentation of the principle of development in England became the source of life for European conservatism in the nineteenth century. In England itself Burke had a different kind of following, including Canning, Mackintosh, Macaulay, Gladstone, Morley, Lecky, Stephen, Acton, all liberals. They rejected Burke's extreme attack on the French Revolution, his dogmatism, his exaggerations, his bursting emotionalism which leads him in the heat of the argument to sophism, dishonesty, and slurring over facts. The apparently strange development we see in England is that the founder of modern conservative ideology was not rejected by the Whigs he seemed to have betrayed in 1790. Very early in the nineteenth century they accepted him back into their ranks, complete with his ideas about the organic nature of society, the continuity of national history, the criticism of excessive unrestrained freedom, but with no axiomatic political doctrine. England understood and forgave Burke's extremities as aberrations caused by deep moral shock at the crimes of the Revolution and profound concern for the safety of England and also as an important intellectual and moral antidote to revolutionism. Without actually debating the question, the English followers of Burke continued to reject doctrinaire conservatism as they had rejected abstract revolutionism. We have seen the development of this liberal and Burkian attitude in the *Edinburgh* and *Quarterly* and also the influence which Madame de Staël, a liberal follower of Burke, had in the formation of this English view, common to Smyth and Alison, to Whigs and Tories.

Madame de Staël was also an illustration of the fact that different elements of the romantic movement in historiography could appear separately. A great romantic author, who not only remained loyal to a rational liberalism but who also wrote her *Considérations* in the analytical, speculative style of rationalist historiography which was becoming anathema to true romantic historians. Similarly in other writers, even outside England, we do not find that the various requirements of romantic historiography, in the philosophy of history, in political views and in the style of writing, occur together except perhaps in Chateaubriand in France. French liberal historians from Madame de Staël onwards, Thierry, Barante and perhaps Guizot, wrote history which was imbued with nationalism and the love of the past. But their writings were of a liberal spirit and they often defended revolutionism, as the English did, on the ground of historical precedents. The French romantic historiography of Thierry, Michelet and Quinet was both nationalist and liberal so that even in France not all romantic historiography was politically reactionary. In Germany the artistic, romantic requirements concerning the style of writing were not heeded and in England the Romantic influence on history starts late and then it appears, so to speak, in bits and pieces, in various writers like Southey, Scott, Carlyle, Macaulay, each of whom represents some other aspect of romanticism without there being much in common between them.

PRESCRIPTION AND PRACTICE OF ROMANTICISM

In the 1820s England became aware of romantic history in theory and Scott attempted it in practice. The subject of Romantic history was studied by Scott, Carlyle, Mill and others. A review of Sismondi's *History of France* in the *Edinburgh* in 1821, written by Mackintosh, who was accepted in his time as a philosopher of history and who was really a pioneer in detecting and expounding new movements of thought, contains in its prescription almost all the romantic elements of history-writing. Emotional effect, lively colours, imaginative insight, accuracy of detail, contemporary documentations, a passionate interest in the past and as extreme a demand for romantic history as was ever to be practised in England, all are prescribed in this article by an eminently discursive historian. He believes France to be much in advance of other countries in the collection of national antiquities, especially in advance of England who has neglected even her Parliamentary records. But French historians, he says, lack habits of research, and in France despotism kills historiography. This English friend of Madame de Staël obviously rejects the association of autocratic government and historical research, but he also says that history can be perverted not only by serving a tyranny but also by indignation against tyranny. This is therefore a plea, not for a militant, but for an independent historiography. It was an early cue for the English brand of a non-political Romanticism by a man we have already seen heralding many typical developments. Another interesting remark is that France's best history was produced neither under autocracy, nor in defiance of it, but rather in times of internal war and strife. The idea seems to have been abroad in England at the time that political stability was not conducive to originality in historical thinking and that France owed the superiority of her historians to her revolutions. In England, he says, although compilers are still augmenting each other's errors, there was a new spirit, for instance, in Lingard. 'The genius of history is nourished by the study of original narrators and by critical examination of the minute circumstances of fact.'

Mackintosh practically connects the demand for authentic documentation with a request from the government for the opening of historical archives for study. He shows clearly the sense in which Romanticism aided scholarship. The authentic sources of history should be consulted not only for accuracy but also for dramatic liveliness. The charm of history can be recovered by a modern historian only by his direct use of original sources. When his imagination has been kindled he becomes for a moment a contemporary. However paradoxical it may seem or be made to appear, the means of amusing the readers are to be found by a historian in original research. Narratives of the past, Mackintosh continues, are also a moral education, but not through the paltry repetition of general truths. Both delight and improvement will be gained only through lively narratives. Documentary history will be more instructive to politicians and philosophers than modern speculations. Modern compilers discolour and change ancient facts by mixing them with modern passions. When events are presented in their true colour, statesmen will not apply their lessons in totally different circumstances.

Some interesting points about the development of English romantic history, or rather about the development of history independently of European romanticism, are illustrated by this early English demand for a new history. In the first place, the theorist does not abandon the old ideas that the use of history is in moral improvement and political instruction. He stresses that through lively, colourful and accurate history, these aims should be better achieved. Liveliness excites the imagination and on this depends any improvement. In England, even those who asked for romantic history-writing did not wish for mere story-telling.

When Scott turned to proper history in his *Life of Napoleon*, there was widespread expectation of the 'real' history by the greatest fiction-history writer. When Smyth heard of it in Cambridge he was very apprehensive because Scott had turned from that which he could do best to that which others could do better. Goethe was expectant and Carlyle somewhat bored. For once Smyth was right. Scott's greatest gift to history was lacking in his own work. Scott did not achieve romantic history. Though he expressed his aim privately, in terms which sound

Carlylean, as that of writing on Napoleon 'the most wonderful book which the world ever read—a book in which every incident shall be incredible, yet strictly true', he seems to have dismissed imagination with fiction. Especially in dealing with the Revolution in his first two volumes, he took up analytical history which he helped to destroy. His model was Southey but *Napoleon* fell short of *Nelson* as a romantic portrayal of a great man. Scott was lacking in admiration or even in sympathy. Napoleon's love-letters to Josephine seem to him indelicate, except for such 'chivalrously expressed' phrases as, 'Wurmser shall buy dearly the tears which he makes you shed'. In this history Scott was more romantic by intention than by execution; he failed to be fired by his characters though he knew some to be worthy of it. 'Marat was a madman, raised into consequence only by circumstances, Robespierre a cold, creeping, calculating hypocrite, whose malignity resembled that of a paltry and second-rate fiend—but Danton was a character for Shakespeare or Schiller to have drawn in all its broad lights and shades.'[1]

The work was disappointing; Hegel spoke of it contemptuously and Mill was blind to Scott's influence on historians. In 1828 Mill dismissed any history of Napoleon as unimportant and uninstructive and Scott's *Life* as merely 'sprightly and entertaining'. In 1837 he wrote that Scott left no trace in the national mind. Carlyle, who owed much to Scott's influence, said there was nothing spiritual in him.

It seemed that in Scott, Romanticism would bridge the gulf between history and antiquarianism. Dryasdust's collections were to be used to make history lively and true. But it was Scott's novels rather than his history that had such an influence especially on Carlyle and Macaulay. The aim of recreating contemporary impressions of events and other romantic notions which became dogmas abroad remained secondary requirements in English history. Live and picturesque history did not replace the habits of analysis and explanation which remained the highest goal of history though it was to be prepared now by a more accurate and colourful narrative as in Macaulay.

When romantic influences finally affected the history of the French Revolution to which they owed so much (after they had inspired new writings on ancient and medieval periods), we do not find that England can show an example of romantic historiography in all its aspects. Scott, who was a perfect romantic in literature and also a Tory, was impervious to the new metaphysical theories about the historical process and his political views on the French Revolution a Whig need not reject. Even when we come to Carlyle who more than any other English writer embodied romantic ideals in history, who had outlined the aims of romantic historiography before he started writing it, and who had written a philosophical essay on the nature of the historical process,

[1] Scott, *Napoleon*, II, 314.

even in Carlyle we do not find that romanticism went with a total rejection of the Revolution. Carlyle was so lacking in an obvious political stand-point that from his day to this critics have attributed to his book all the colours of the political rainbow. He has been called the author of Communism, of Fascism, of the British Labour movement, a Liberal, a Conservative, etc. As for the French historian Michelet, who, like Carlyle, was an eminently romantic historian of the Revolution, his politics are less controversial than Carlyle's. Extreme in the practice of the romantic style of historiography he only adhered to one of the romantic dogmas, that of nationalism. The sayings that his book is a song of praise for the Revolution and that its only hero is the French people have become common-places in the history of historiography.

ROMANTICISM NOT A PHILOSOPHY

How then can we explain the fact that on the one hand there are un-doubtedly great romantic influences on history which appeared some-times *en bloc* and more often separately, and yet on the other hand there are so many examples which prevent a well-rounded definition of a European romantic school in historiography? It may be that a Romantic school in historiography never existed in the same sense in which liberal, idealist or materialist schools existed, that is, schools based on a clear view on the nature of the historical process. It may be that the historians of historiography demand from romanticism more than romanticism can yield; for romanticism is, after all, in the first place an attribute of the process of creativeness; it describes the nature of artists more than it defines a body of thought; it denotes a manner of treating historical material more than a *Weltanschauung* based on a concept of history. It is not the object but the manner of historical thinking. We might almost say that every historical school had its own romantics. The literary influence of Romanticism on historiography was much wider than the influence of the political dogmas which accompanied romanticism. In the transformation of historiography the influence of the poets and novelists was greater than that of the political theorists. Schiller greatly influenced both Scott and Carlyle. Historians as different as Chateau-briand, Thierry, Macaulay, Ranke, all acknowledge their debt to Walter Scott. Historians of various schools and political opinions repeat their aspiration to write live, colourful and exciting history, an authentic story in which every word will be true and yet more exciting, interesting and attractive than a work of fiction. Macaulay wished to replace the latest best-selling novel in the ladies' *boudoirs*, Carlyle aspired to write history which would affect the writer like poetry, and Froude (later) wished to compete with Shakespearean drama. The widest common denominator of romanticism in historiography is the influence of Scott rather than that of Burke. And the most lasting contribution of Romanticism to historiography was the imaginative literary qualities it demanded; identification, dramatization and Shakespearean sympathy in drawing characters. The system of dogmas with which Romanticism burst into history did not remain a homogenic body of ideas in historical writings. Moreover, the very formula of Romantic history reflected the diverse origins from which it sprang and romantic influences often formed the beginnings of different and even contradictory developments. Romanticism, thanks to its very dynamism and richness, reared within it its self-destruction.

It was romantic, for instance, to hero-worship in history and to emphasize the role of individuals, but it was also the Romantic movement that through its devotion to nationalism and to the action of powers like the 'genius of the people', the 'genius of the nation', the 'spirit of the age', gave rise to interpretations of the historical process as one which is moved by superhuman forces acting, if one may say so, in the subconsciousness of history. Both approaches to history, the biographical and the impersonal, are true developments of Romantic dogmas but they reach a point of contradiction and they receive concrete historical presentation in historians so different from each other as the late Carlyle of *Cromwell* and *Frederick* and the early Thiers on the *French Revolution*.

Again, the Romantic dogma that nothing in history can be perfectly seen or understood away from the process by which it was created, did not go well with other Romantic dogmas of artistic history writing, and especially not with the express wish to do away with perspective and to write of a past age as it would write about itself, in its own style, spirit and point of view. Barante and Chateaubriand tried to treat the Middle Ages in writings modelled on the chronicles. This devotion to authentic atmosphere and to the uniqueness of each historical moment worked against the dogma of continuity and traditionalism.

Perhaps the most glaring self-contradiction in the romantic collection of dogmas was the attempt to construct a *Weltanschauung* based on the notion that a peculiar national spirit shapes the history of every people, and to attempt this on the ground of an abstract generalization which an Englishman made from his own national history. If war was being waged by romanticism against abstract doctrines in history and against the intrusion of alien ideas, then for Germany, for instance, the conservative doctrine of Burke was as much anathema as the revolutionary doctrine of the Abbé Siéyès. Concretely this contradiction was shown for instance in the attempt to force on German legal history the same peculiar development from precedent to precedent whose life and soul in England is the principle of the Common Law.

Romanticism stressed the differences between the national histories, as well as the organic continuity within those histories. It ignored the degree of cultural unity that Europe had through the power of mobile ideas, art, literature, philosophy, religion. This isolationism therefore meant shedding layers of common civilization and moving towards a primitivism which was really alien to the sophisticated conservatives.

Again, the powers of reaction against the French Revolution, though their guiding idea was that intellectuals and dreamers must not be allowed near politics again after the damage they had done in France, immediately sought the help of intellectuals in order to acquire an ideological basis. They encouraged the construction of a philosophical system which would support the existing régime, in case the traditions and consecrated customs would not, after all, in themselves, prove sufficient.

Romanticism also reached contradiction in its relations with traditional morality, which it set out to defend against rationalist morality based on utilitarianism, to the negation of instincts—the innate supports of traditional morality. This was a central idea in Burke and in Coleridge. The opposite dogma was expressed by Godwin in his famous example saying that in case of a fire a man should save (if the choice were forced on him) not his useless family relations, but the stranger who was a benefactor of mankind. The example became the symbol of the moral perversion of the revolutionists. Their enemies attacked violently a concept of 'right' which contradicts man's innate instincts as well as the idea that we are allowed to do evil in order that good may come. The enemies of the Revolution barricaded themselves behind traditional morality but they themselves sinned heavily against the same set of moral laws. The consecration of habits, customs and, above all, prejudices, the authority they attributed to natural passions and selfish instincts, led them knowingly to defend falseness and crime in politics and history. Evils that had indeed been tolerated before, were now defiantly and cynically defended as a matter of principle.

The heaviest sin against conventional morality of the new ideological conservatism was their admiration of success. Burke's political position leads to scepticism. The sanctification of history and of the past led them to the idea, not of course new, that whatever is is good. There is no science of politics and there are no values to judge politics by. Burke himself did not become a sceptic. He did not believe in following even his own ideas to their logical end, or he lacked moral courage to do so. He would have contradicted his insistence on morality in politics had he followed his sanctification of the past to its bitter, logical end, the idolization of success. His followers thereby let go of the moral and religious criterion and vowed to accept the judgment of power and success, whereas the liberals of the nineteenth century continued to aim at what is desirable, independently of whatever exists. Through the sanctification of success, conservatism prepared another self-contradiction, for it is a disconcerting fact, that revolutionaries or tyrants who succeeded in maintaining power became worthy and justified. If the English system of government is good because it always has managed to survive, then, by the same principle, the *ancien régime* must have been bad because it managed so easily to crumble.

The more a Romantic succeeded in writing imaginative, lively history, sympathetically portrayed, the less he succeeded in serving any particular party or cause, or in conforming to any political, historical or philosophical set of premises, or even to an innate set of moral values. In fact Romantic technique in history ran away with the Romantics. By fulfilling the Romantic prescriptions of identification with the historical objects, richness of imagination, and by being carried away, some Romantics did, indeed, reach the Shakespearean quality of writing about historical characters as if from within those characters, with a full understanding of their motives. This literary approach led to historical writing in which everything done by a strong and exciting character received its inner justification. Even in the writing of French Revolutionary history, we find Romantic writers like Southey, who had solemnly declared against the Revolution, unable to resist their own admiration for deeds of daring and heroism in which groups or individuals sacrificed feelings and even conscience for the sake of the ultimate aim, human acts to which the Romantic soul remained incurably sensitive even after the acceptance of Burke.

The Romantics were neither renegades nor schizophrenics in their attitude to the Revolution. Brinton says that the Romantic poets' politics were nearest those of the 'average man' because they were not professional statesmen. The opposite is true. It is the profoundest statesmen who share a vision with the poets. It was Burke's imaginative quality which enabled him to see beyond the apparently constitutional struggles in France a battle of ideologies. It was Wordsworth's imaginative faculty which made his pamphlet on the Convention of Cintra such a prophetic document on the doctrine of nationalism;[1] and it was their imaginative quality which enabled the poets to see also beyond Burke what took average men generations of hindsight to understand, that the Revolution cannot, and need not, be either accepted or rejected, that even in its general aspect it is part of history because it is part of human nature, which is both sublime and cruel. History to Coleridge did not end in the present, and the present had no special sanctity. A pessimistic conservatism or a vulgar glory in revenge were perhaps the 'average man's' reactions. The Romantic poets like Coleridge and Southey who also thought about the Revolution looked beyond mere political reaction

---

[1] Wordsworth himself did not fully realize his own services to the idea of the supreme power of the national state and he denounces Napoleon 'who acts avowedly upon the principle that everything which can be done safely by the supreme power of a state may be done'.

towards a harmony between the idealism and the destructiveness. Coleridge's concept of revolution was not a conspiracy but an elemental power whose challenge cannot be answered by mere obedience to the past. In this sense the Romantic vision remained in the future. More concretely it meant that the problems of the Revolution were to the Romantics, human, rather than political problems. Both psychologically and historically it was nonsense to reject the whole phenomenon from human experience.

Romanticism therefore did not make for a dull, unthinking conservatism. The Romantics always insisted that it was natural and honourable for young and benevolent hearts to fall for the French Revolution. It is also significant to remember that the poetic converts to Burkianism later took up from their Tory positions, the attack on the capitalist *laissez-faire* society of the early nineteenth century, thus continuing their revolt against accepted conventions and again contributing an emotional humanitarian strain to the new revolutionary movement of socialism shaping itself at the time.

The examination of some aspects of Romanticism ought at least to have shown that Romantic historiography did not simply mean a reactionary attitude to the Revolution; that English historians were not generally amenable to romantic notions; that rationalist aims in historiography died hard. Though Scott and Hazlitt had already written on the Revolution, the greatest English example of Romantic history is Carlyle's *French Revolution*. It is an illustration of romantic history which consists mainly of the writing of imaginative, dramatic and live history. The demand for such writing had been in the air and it was mainly from notions of Schiller and Scott that Carlyle developed it. In his long historical life, Carlyle abandoned himself to the impact of different influences. The extraordinary contradictions which he embodied, and the long, drawn-out torments of his divided soul, bring out the best and the worst in the Romantic condition.

CHAPTER 8

CARLYLE AND THE FRENCH REVOLUTION

Carlyle entered the field of Revolutionary studies when the Revolution was transforming itself from politics to history, and he himself played an important part in this transition. His older contemporaries belonged to the Revolutionary generation and his younger friends, like John Mill, were products of it. William Smyth was at that time lecturing on the French Revolution in Cambridge and looking out upon it 'as from a College window'. Smyth was extricating himself from the spirit of the pamphleteers through wide reading and a conscious training in academic impartiality. John Wilson Croker, from the midst of the political scene, was fighting the phantom of the Revolution, and at the same time delving deep into the Revolutionary sources. For him the Revolution had become a subject of historical inquiry only in the sense that he was able to investigate it from records. Alison's book came out after Carlyle had begun his studies. It stole Croker's thunder, but left Carlyle unmoved.

Carlyle's *History*, when it came out in 1837,[1] established his fame. It is the best known of the English histories of the event, and belongs with Michelet and Lamartine to the class of books which are not brought up to date in new editions.[2] It is often considered as a piece of literature rather than a history, and this raises a central question in Carlylean studies, that of the standards which should be used in estimating Carlyle as a historian. This question has been raised by a group of students of English and history[3] who have attempted a revaluation of Carlyle on the ground that previous estimates had used irrelevant and anachronistic standards. They say that Carlyle was most underrated at the end of the last century when dry, scientific and purely factual writing

---

[1] The essays on Mirabeau and on the Histories, and the *Diamond Necklace* also appeared in 1837. In this chapter the references to [the] *Fr[ench] Rev[olution]* are to the 1869 edition.

[2] Carlyle expected to be done with the French Revolution for ever, as soon as he finished writing about it. His few corrections related to (1) the sinking of the *Vengeur* (see below, p. 142); (2) his assertion that Frederick the Great was the only king ever to attempt suicide (in 1868 he added a note calling this a calumnious rumour which he had got from the *E.R.* review of the *Mémoires de Bastille*. C. R. L. Fletcher's edition (1902) does not contain the correction); (3) Admiral 'Nesham', not 'Needham', and to the sword he had been given in Paris in 1789 which was not 'long since rusted into nothingness'.

[3] E.g. L. M. Young, [*Thomas*] *Carlyle* [*and the Art of History*] (Philadelphia, 1939); C. F. Harrold, 'Carlyle's General Method in *The French Revolution*', in *Publications of the Modern Language Association of America* (1928), XLIII, 1150–69. Much valuable analysis of Carlyle's mind and work loses by being presented as an argument in such a controversy. These are mainly American scholars. Carlyle has always had a special attraction for Americans. His first earnings came from the U.S., and he left his library to Harvard University (J. A. Froude, *My Relations with Carlyle* (1903), p. 72).

was the fashion in English historiography. They want to judge Carlyle 'in the light of what he endeavoured to do' as a literary and not as a scientific historian, as an heir of Gibbon and not as a contemporary of Ranke.[1] This criticism is directed against narrow professional historians who apply to Carlyle standards which did not exist in his time. It is not, however, clear that such a narrowly professional school exists. Gooch who is mentioned in this connection does criticize Carlyle's errors as well as his interpretations.[2] But Gooch belongs to a different tradition of Carlylean criticism, deriving from Mill and Morley and discoverable in Trevelyan and Aulard. At the same time the conclusions of both Mill and Aulard are favourable to Carlyle's scholarship and historical merit.

Those who seek to save Carlyle from the narrow clutch of the professional critics, defend him by applying standards which he himself would not have acknowledged because they are not the standards of history which he knew and pursued. They argue, roughly, that Carlyle regarded history writing as an art. He must therefore be judged, like a creative artist, by the standards that he set himself. The faults which he knew that he had failed to overcome, they glorify into achieved aims. The 'literary' aims which he indeed professed, he tried to achieve not at the expense of historical accurate and factual truth, but emphatically through it.

What Carlyle's own historical aims and methods were must be shown with reference to his own discussions of them, to the process by which he studied and wrote history, and to the *French Revolution* as it stands. His works abound in theoretical discussions of history writing, because, of all the English historians of his time, he was the most conscious of the problems involved and of the transformations which existing historical conventions were undergoing, especially abroad. In his essays on history, mostly written before the Histories themselves, he discussed the theoretical problems of research and scientific history and foresaw the division of labour that must come in historical work.[3] He discussed the difference between narratives which recreate history and those which discuss aspects of history; and he saw the danger and the limitations of drudgery as well as its necessity and its possible elevation.

EARLY INFLUENCES AND WRITINGS

Carlyle was strongly influenced by German thought and enthusiastic over the translation of Niebuhr into English. He announced it to Goethe

[1] Young, *Carlyle*, pp. 3–4.

[2] G. P. Gooch, *History and Historians* [*in the Nineteenth Century*] (2nd ed. 1952), p. 304.

[3] On the division of historical work see, e.g., the article 'On History', *Fraser's* [*Magazine*] (1830); on the significance of small but true facts see 'Biography', *ibid.* (Apr. 1832).

in 1829, adding that German influence had reached the universities.[1] The German influences which were strongest on him were those of the period preceding the beginning of the historical movement proper. But though his teachers were Herder and Schiller, he knew the work of Niebuhr and Ranke well; and it is not the plea of ignorance that can shield him against the charge that his methods were insufficiently critical.

Carlyle was even more influenced by the Romantic movement in literature[2] and by its element of rebellion. But in him individual and intellectual rebellion were stronger than social. There is little in common between Shelley expressing in poetry Godwin's rationalistic ideas and Carlyle developing in tortuous prose his own subjective way of thought, under the influence of Burke amongst others.

Romanticism influenced Carlyle's historical writing in several ways. An unlearned, intuitive enthusiasm appears in his earliest references to historical subjects. His early letters contain a conventional pattern of sympathies such as are familiar in the young and romantic liberals who were taught by Madame de Staël. He frowns at the cold and cruel Revolution and responds warmly to Napoleon,[3] moved especially by the tragic quality of his fall. 'Since the days of Prometheus Vinctus', he knows of nothing more sublime than this great man's torment. 'Captive, sick, despised, forsaken;—yet arising above it all, by the stern force of his unconquerable spirit, and hurling back on his mean oppressors the ignominy they strove to load him with.'[4] This early romanticism survived many developments and formed the emotional basis for his theory of heroes in history.

Carlyle's starting-points in history were a passionate interest in human facts and an endless quest for the answers to the questions which troubled his soul. The human curiosity may have been shallow at first, but it was a stimulus to investigation and it led to a search for true reality. Only that which 'really happened' was really exciting to Carlyle. At the root of his philosophic restlessness and his devotion to history[5] was the belief

---

[1] To Goethe, 22 Dec. 1829 ([*Correspondence between*] *Goethe and Carlyle*, ed. C. E. Norton (1887), 162). Niebuhr's *History of Rome* had been translated in 1828 by Hare and Thirlwall.

[2] The influence of Scott and Byron was great on Carlyle. From Romanticism he learnt early an idea which was to be fruitful for his history writing, that 'the kind of genius named dramatic may be employed in a thousand ways unconnected with the theatre; it gives life and splendour to the picturesque novels of Sir Walter Scott, and forms in a different shape, the basis of much sublime philosophy in the treatises of Madame de Staël' (to Jane Welsh, 30 Apr. 1822, [*The*] *Love Letters* [*of Thomas Carlyle and Jane Welsh*], ed. A. Carlyle (1909), I, 39).

[3] *Love Letters*, I, 43, 69, 80.

[4] To Jane Welsh, Aug. 1822, *ibid.* I, 68.

[5] In his earliest letters Carlyle showed a preference for history which he always recommended to Jane. E.g. 'I still look upon it as the most instructive and interesting of all studies' (13 July 1822, *Love Letters*, I, 66). In time and bulk most of Carlyle's work (15 out of 23 volumes) was devoted to historical writing.

that history was a bible written by God and that it was the historian's function to interpret Providence[1] and expound the essentially moral nature of the world.[2] As a result of all this he was driven to much hard thinking about the meaning of the Revolution. The inquisitive and the philosophic nature of his interest in history explain the two qualities on which he prides himself in this book—the ability to portray stark reality, and at the same time to reveal profound truth behind it. This also explains the contradictory appreciations of the work, which some have called a mere painting and others a sermon on the text of the Revolution.[3]

The passion for human detail was a romantic interest by which even Alison was touched. The subject of Carlyle's investigations for the *History* was human behaviour. This is why his book appears to some a psychological study or a sociological case book. Human interest was in the air and was, in time, to produce social histories, but Carlyle was the first to write a human history of the French Revolution.

Another important romantic influence on Carlyle was the romantic poets' theory of artistic creation. It shaped his own work, for he actually put into practice a subconscious method of writing history. It is the source of much that is extraordinary in his work and for which explanations are often sought elsewhere. Applied to the history of the Revolution, this notion meant a rejection of thought about the event and also of historical perspective. Distance produced the generalizations which Carlyle did not want. To grasp the Revolution historically he lost himself inside the intricate period, wandered about it aimlessly and unsystematically in the hope that close contact would somehow create the right reaction. The process of creating true history for Carlyle was as subconscious as the process of creating poetry was in Wordsworth's theory. To promote a genuine reaction, a historian makes sure that the picture which gives the stimulus is authentic. Once the right reaction has been brought about, it is this which directs the recreation of reality. Writing history was so painful for Carlyle because, while playing a highly active role, he considered himself a passive factor. All he could do was feverishly to pile on the fuel and wait for the flame to burst out and illuminate a picture in his mind.

This notion did much to produce both the best and the worst in Carlyle's book. It led to its greatest fault, the lack of proportion. Many of the individual faults, the neglect of Europe and the provinces, of the past

---

[1] See, e.g., *History of Frederick the Great* (Chapman and Hall, 1897), I, 168.

[2] Basil Willey, in his essay on Carlyle in *Nineteenth Century Studies* (1950), calls Carlyle's history evidence for the reality of a moral order. Carlyle wrote in 'Count Cagliostro': 'With a nation, . . . where the multitude of the chances covers, in great measure, the uncertainty of Chance, it may be said to hold always that general Suffering is the fruit of general Misbehaviour, general Dishonesty.'

[3] E.g. E. Jenks, *Thomas Carlyle and John Stuart Mill* (1888).

and of the future, of events and of phases, of whole spheres of economic and constitutional development, are connected with this defect. Because Carlyle trusted his reactions, he wrote only of what evoked the strongest reactions. He imagined that as long as he was telling the truth he could not go wrong, and in this he laid himself open to attack from historians who demand the whole truth.

The romantic method of creation also let him down in his use of sources, the second great point of criticism against him. He seems to have believed[1] that the reconstruction of any historical object is the result of a multitude of both objective and subjective processes, some of them unconscious, which create a different picture of the object in the mind of every reader.[2] The extraordinary thing is that his own characterizations are generally accepted as remarkably true. But this method, so successful in the treatment of personalities, often proved inadequate when applied to ordinary historical facts.

An attitude to history was also at the root of the unique impartiality which Carlyle claimed[3] and which was claimed for him by historians like Trevelyan[4] and Aulard.[5] The claim seems strange when it is applied to a man who despised even toleration as 'indifferentism'.[6] And detachment would have been a negation of his basic condition for the writing of history, which required a vision seen as if from inside historical objects. His impartiality could not exclude identification and sympathy. What it meant to him was a resolution to avoid a superstructure of systematic ideas. It meant also a sense of the irrelevance of political judgments in histories of the Revolution. He had passed through the stage of seeing all sides and avoiding extremes, and he must have rejected the contention that the aims of the Revolutionaries can only be seen clearly from a distance. Despair of getting at truth through 'mazes of speculation' drove him to extreme persistence in the attempt to paint reality only. His impartiality was therefore a result, not of a political attitude (though it is true that he stood outside all parties) but of a search for a historical truth which is achieved by an historian who abandons himself to the

---

[1] See, e.g., 'Mirabeau' in *Critical and Miscellaneous Essays*, III (1899), 409–10.

[2] 'Each individual takes up the Phenomenon according to his point of vision . . . gives, consciously, some poor crotchety picture of several things; unconsciously some picture of himself at least. And the Phenomenon, for its part, subsists there, all the while, unaltered; waiting to be pictured as often as you like, its entire meaning not to be compressed into any picture drawn by man' ('Parliamentary History', *Critical and Miscellaneous Essays*, IV (1899), 2).

[3] E.g. 'Cavaignac is angry with me for my treatment of the Sea-green man and *Impartialité* generally. I take no sides in the matter. How very singular!' (J. A. Froude, *Thomas Carlyle, 1834–81* (1884), I, 113).

[4] *Carlyle: an Anthology* (1953), 5–68; 'Bias in History' (*An Autobiography and other Essays*, 1949), 73–4.

[5] 'Impartial . . . mais non calme ni insensible' (Aulard, 'Carlyle', 202).

[6] Carlyle praised Mill's sharpness in reviewing Alison: 'I set little store by this so celebrated virtue of Tolerance' (to Mill, 24 Sept. 1833, *Letters to Mill*, 70).

impact of as much reality as he can find, bringing to it nothing from outside, least of all a pattern of politics.[1]

Carlyle's earliest publication, a series of articles written in 1819–22 for Brewster's *Encyclopaedia*, is often ignored or dismissed as hackwork.[2] Some of the articles are connected with the French Revolution and constitute straight historical writing. He used German works[3] and made historical guesses. The best reading is the article on Chatham, full of hero-worship not yet vitiated by any extremes of opinion or political bitterness. The article on Nelson, based on Southey's *Life*, gives good accounts of the battles, and dramatizes the death scene. Nelson's 'sense of rectitude', writes Carlyle, 'embodied itself in a feeling of loyalty to the King and of hatred to all Frenchmen'. In his article on Moore, Carlyle dismisses this man's Revolutionary writings as no longer interesting.[4] The articles on Pitt and Necker contain the narrative of the Revolutionary period on which Carlyle's subsequent picture rested.

The most conspicuous quality of the historical articles is the conventionality and the caution with which politics are treated. There is no hint of the forthrightness which we expect to find in Carlyle. The writer here balances his judgments so carefully that they sometimes cease to make sense. The question arises whether Carlyle then had any political views which he toned down for the sake of the detachment required in an encyclopaedia, or out of his anxiety to make his first appearance in print, or whether he was as impartial as he was non-committal. The artificiality of his elaborate ambiguities in dealing for instance with the question of war and peace in 1793 or with Pitt's abandonment of reform, when compared with the genuineness of passages in the article on Chatham, indicates that he was keeping himself in check on controversial questions. This need might have fostered his strange bitterness of later years towards hackwork or writing for periodicals.[5]

If the articles contain some 'cant' which later made Carlyle blush, they also hinted at better things to come. The statement, for instance, that

[1] Mill, who expounded Carlyle's views of history-writing in Carlyle's own spirit, dissented from him on this point. He thought Carlyle's mistrust of analysis excessive and believed that past politics offer useful hypotheses to prove from history.

[2] See, e.g., A. Ralli, *Guide to Carlyle* (1920). Carlyle himself called them 'miserable compilations' (*Love Letters*, I, 19).

[3] Carlyle taught himself German in 1819–20.

[4] Dr John Moore's *Journal during a Residence in France* . . . (1793) and *View of the causes and progress of the French Revolution* (1795) are sources of some importance, which Carlyle used for the 10 Aug. (*F.R.* II, 260), for the massacres of Sept. (*ibid.* II, 305), and for the scene in the Convention on 24 Oct. (Carlyle says 25 Sept.), when Marat put a pistol to his head (*ibid.* I, 357). Carlyle thinks Moore may have copied the *Moniteur*, but this is unlikely.

[5] An even more bitter memory must have been his proposal to Fraser, when driven by need in the course of the preparations for the *French Revolution*, of a series of articles 'chiefly to be translated from memoirs'. Fraser made such a low offer that Carlyle abandoned the idea (Carlyle to his brother John, 17 June 1834, *Letters* [*of Thomas Carlyle*], 1826–36 (1881), II, 184).

'the Revolution might be accelerated or retarded, it could not be pre-vented or produced', was not in itself unusual, but it stands out among the historical judgments presented here. It marks Carlyle as an indepen-dent thinker, who could already accept the royalist theories on incitement without believing that incitement caused the Revolution, and who, while hating misrule and violence, blamed no one for either. There is, apart from the forced detachment, the ability to see and express the contra-dictory points of view and to make the most of each case, the anti-revolu-tionary and even the anti-reformist. In all this one discerns a faint foreshadowing of the peculiar kind of impartiality which Carlyle later exercised from the omniscient level of the *History*. The compact, ambigu-ous and problematical rendering of various points of view hints at a characteristic peculiar to Carlyle, that of presenting both situations and questions of judgment in the confused, uncertain way in which they appear to the people concerned. They may be distorted historically, but they are true to the working of human nature and they create, out of a multitude of false and subjective reactions, the atmosphere and psycho-logical background which make history credible.

THE PREPARATIONS FOR THE *FRENCH REVOLUTION*

The process by which Carlyle studied and wrote the *French Revolution*, roughly between 1831 and 1837, is known as a series of unspeakable agonies. Carlyle dramatized the way in which he was consumed by the intensity of his absorption and tormented by the nature of his materials. But the making of the book, when reconstructed from his various writings of the time, reveals more than this. It brings out the close relation between theory and practice in his view of history, his initiation into Revolutionary studies, the influence and help of John Mill, the sources he used, the sort of research he engaged in, his method and his progress. Of the material for this reconstruction, the correspondence with Mill is the most revealing[1] and that with Goethe the most disappointing.[2] Had Carlyle stayed in Edinburgh we should have known more about him, for in London he and Mill met to talk about the Revolution and to exchange books. The letters to Emerson[3] begin roughly where those to Mill end, and are sufficiently

[1] The best general account of Mill's help to Carlyle is in M. St John Packe's *The Life of John Stuart Mill* (1954). E. Neff (*Carlyle and Mill*, 2nd edn. 1926) does not study in detail this side of their relations. E. Jenks (*Thomas Carlyle and John Stuart Mill*, 1888) treats the two men separately. He knew that there was a correspondence, but had no access to it. Froude was wrong when he said that Carlyle's letters to Mill had been destroyed, for they were published later (*Letters to Mill*, ed. A. Carlyle, 1923). Those of Mill to Carlyle are in *Letters of Mill*.
[2] *Goethe and Carlyle*. Apart from a few references to the Saint-Simonians and to Scott's *Napoleon* it has little bearing on politics or history.
[3] [*The Correspondence of Thomas*] *Carlyle and* [*Ralph Waldo*] *Emerson, 1834–72* (ed. C. E. Norton, 2 vols. 1883).

infrequent to combine spontaneity with a conscious effort at self-study. They therefore bring out best the crystallization of Carlyle's view of history through the experience of writing.

Two influences, the events of 1830 and Saint-Simonian literature,[1] gave Carlyle an interest in the Revolution, and made him more aware than before of social and political problems. The next state was meeting Mill in 1831. It is sometimes thought that it was then that Mill, under pressure of other duties, offered Carlyle the materials he had been collecting for a history of the Revolution, and that Carlyle started preparing his own history.[2] All that was arranged, however, was that Mill should send books of all sorts to Carlyle who was cut off from any library. Carlyle continued to ask for 'anything at all' Mill could spare.[3] In the course of the correspondence it long remained uncertain which of them was going to write the history. 'Any tolerable history of the Revolution', wrote Carlyle, 'I could still read with interest. I am very curious about France.'[4] But his curiosity was not yet all-absorbing and his letters are full of plans for a history of the Scottish church.[5]

Carlyle's interest in the Revolution gained precedence over his other interests in 1833, after he had read Thiers. He was one of many who were impressed and challenged by the first long history of the Revolution, and stimulated by both its merits and its defects. It is interesting that he shows something of Smyth's opposition to Thiers's deterministic ideas, which reduced the moral responsibility of men by emphasizing the relentless march of events. He sneers at this and talks of it as 'a wonderful system of ethics ... every hero turns out to be perfectly justified in doing whatsoever he succeeded in doing'. It is interesting also that he vaguely suspected at the time the point that Croker was to elaborate later. He objected to 'his hard mechanical all-for-politics disposition, characteristic, I imagine, of the modern French School generally'.[6]

Carlyle's reaction to Thiers provides the first intimation of his own

---

[1] Carlyle first heard from the Saint-Simonians as a result of his article 'The Signs of the Times', *E.R.* (1829). Goethe asked him to keep aloof from them (17 Oct. 1830, *Goethe and Carlyle*, 226), but Carlyle continued to receive material, e.g. on the Three Days (*ibid.* 258), and thought them 'earnest zealous and nowise ignorant'. To Mill he wrote favourably of them as being good and necessary (16 June 1832, *Letters to Mill*, 8), but later he said of them that 'the enthusiast nowise excludes the quack' (16 Oct. 1832, *ibid.* 16).

[2] Young, *Carlyle*, 96. Miss Young suggested that when the decision to write the *French Revolution* took place, between the writing of the article 'On History' and that on 'Biography', Carlyle by way of preparation 'whipped into shape' his ideas on history-writing with the result that the latter article contains more practicable views. But 'Biography' (Apr. 1832) in fact preceded the decision to write the *French Revolution*, which was made in June 1833. Moreover, Carlyle's most extravagant idea about history-writing, that which requires the extraction of poetry from history, had already emerged fully when he wrote 'The Diamond Necklace'.

[3] To Mill, 28 Aug. 1832 (*Letters to Mill*, 11). Carlyle asks Mill not to mind what he could not find.

[4] 16 Oct. 1832 (*Letters to Mill*, 16). [5] 19 Nov. 1832 (*ibid.* 23).

[6] To Mill, 12 Jan. 1833 (*ibid.* 33–4).

interest in topics on which Thiers 'unfortunately is rather uncommunicative; what I might call the private-biographic phasis; the manner in which individuals demeaned themselves, and social life went on . . .'. Carlyle wanted to read books on the prisons, on 'bon mots uttered on the scaffold',[1] the queues at the bakers' shops, the *assignats*. He also wanted a life of Danton and declared that the three great men of the Revolution were Mirabeau, Danton and Napoleon. The letter which he wrote to Mill on this subject anticipates important features of the final *History*. Thiers is lightly criticized, but Carlyle is really looking through him and past him. His own interest, the human, social, dramatic, and biographical are all there. What Thiers does not supply, Carlyle will look for elsewhere. Even the latent thoroughness is there in the impatience to learn from an expert what the *assignats* really were. And the stray thought about the bakers' queues was to mature later into a section of the *History*, 'In Queue'.[2]

A feature of this early reaction is the intuitive, premature, over-confident judgment in the choice of the great men and the portrayal of these from a passing inner vision, uncertain and subjective. Reading Thiers, Carlyle pities Danton, whom he had been in the habit of describing 'à la Walter Scott, simply as a tiger, and imagine that this explained him'. But some time later Carlyle asked Mill about a folio of Revolutionary portraits.[3] 'Tell me if these heads are reckoned genuine', he wrote, and immediately plunged into his 'physiognomic survey': 'Lafayette, looks puppyish, Camille Desmoulins is full of spirit, talent, half-blackguard gaiety'. The picture of Danton as a tiger, borrowed from Scott, had been dispelled by Thiers, but, looking at the portrait, Carlyle again changes his mind: 'True heroism never dwelt in such a tabernacle. I fear Thiers has quite misled me.' But not even the vision fired by a portrait was to last. Mill's logical mind may have been puzzled by Carlyle's hasty judgments; he made inquiries from the editor of the *National* and learnt that the genuineness of some of the portraits was doubtful, 'and without any hint from me at once instanced Danton . . . Ugly but not ignoble either in mind or in feature.' Carlyle kept Danton in his list of the great, after all.[4]

The relationship with Mill changed with Carlyle's progress. Mill was at first the tutor, supplying books, advising, guiding. After Carlyle began writing, his questions became more specific. He then used Mill much in the same way in which he later used his research assistants.

Sometime in June 1833 it had occurred to him that he himself might

---

[1] Three years later Carlyle was still asking for such a book on *bons mots* (A. Carlyle, *New Letters of Thomas Carlyle* (1904), 3).

[2] Book VI, ch. IV (I, 285).

[3] 22 Feb. 1833 (*Letters to Mill*, 40).

[4] The same list of the three great men reappears in the article 'Mirabeau'.

write about the Revolution. He saw 'a great result in these so intensely interesting Narratives'. To extract it would be 'the highest kind of writing'. The wish to write came together with the realization of what history meant to him. It was 'the only *possible* Poem, that hovers for me in every seen Reality'.[1] The vision of a history of the French Revolution, based partly on ideas of history which Carlyle had expressed earlier, seems to emerge from the depth of his struggle with his materials. We can watch his growing dissatisfaction with historians who offer theories instead of information. The urge to write took precedence over the need to achieve complete understanding. It was as though he needed to recreate the Revolution before he could pretend to grasp its meaning. To its riddle his massive reading had brought no answer by the time he asked himself, 'why might I not, too, prepare for such a task?'. It aroused only 'a tumult of feelings, visions, half visions and darknesses'.

When he finished 'The Diamond Necklace', he was repeating in various places that history must be based on all the accurate information that research could yield, and that it was through this truth that reality is made into a poem. He must have found it much harder to achieve this for *The French Revolution* than for the story of the Diamond Necklace. All through his writing two complaints are repeated. The one related to the chaotic, conflicting, repetitious, useless, treacherous materials and the other to the state of his own mind. It was never in control; he could not understand the Revolution. The recurring words are 'darkness' and 'chaos'.[2] It was while mourning the lost manuscript that Carlyle began to see some worth in it, the significance of truth and of fact. World Fact and ordinary fact now become the central theme. The more he searched for it, the more he knew that it eluded him; the more exasperated he became with the materials, the more he cried out for 'Facts, Facts, no theory'.[3]

THE QUALITY OF THE HISTORICAL WORK

Ever since Carlyle's time people have asked what sort of historian he was, whether he was scholarly, whether he was original and whether the result is of permanent value. The imaginative and poetic quality of his work was widely accepted (though not by Hallam and Wordsworth). His treatment of fact has been debated since Mill first claimed for him the 'quality of the historical day drudge', and asserted, from his own know-

---

[1] To Mill, 13 June 1833 (*Letters to Mill*, 57).

[2] E.g. to Mill, early Sept. 1834: 'The French business grows darker and darker upon me; dark as was Chaos. *Ach Gott!*' (*Letters to Mill*, 101).

[3] To different correspondents Carlyle now wrote that he had come to honour 'facts more and more, theory less and less'. See, e.g., his letter to Emerson of 29 Apr. 1836. A fact is great as a 'Sentence printed if not by God, then, at least by the Devil' (*Carlyle and Emerson*, I, 93).

ledge of the sources, and of the use made of them by others, that a more accurate historian never wrote.[1]

From historians in general we hear either that he engaged in the most minute, meticulous and critical collation of sources, or that he was utterly credulous. A detailed study of Carlyle's use of sources by Professor Harrold in 1928 provided the stimulus for certain works, already mentioned, which defended Carlyle as a historian.[2] In that study the *French Revolution* is treated like a 'cento of fragments', and various passages are compared with those in the sources. The changes which Carlyle introduced in his materials, as 'an artist dealing with reported fact from a confusing number of directions', are pointed out and classified. Excluding paragraphs of reflexion, Professor Harrold claims to have assembled the eighty-three sources (cited in 850 footnotes) in which 'the basis of all Carlyle's statements of fact could be found'. Comparison of passages leads him to an elaborate classification of the literary alterations Carlyle made, but the only historical activity he defines is that 'presumably where writers differed . . . he felt at liberty to conjecture the most probable facts'. Yet this is not generally true. Carlyle tried to verify the truth. When he found, for instance, that the English and French memoirs of Lamotte (the villainess of the Necklace affair) differed on her manner of death, he asked Mill to investigate the coroner's inquest, which he thought was 'doubtless still accessible (for day and date are given) and would throw light on several things. In the British Museum you shall look for it.'[3]

The general objection to Professor Harrold's conclusions is that he attempts to reinstate Carlyle as a historian on unhistorical grounds. In view of the 'treacherous nature of his materials', he writes, 'and considering that he was not attempting a strictly documented and scientific history but a work of art, we are hardly justified in stressing his occasional freedom with the original accounts'.[4] In fact, Carlyle always stressed that

[1] Mill's review, in *Westminster Review* (July, 1837), XXVII, is important as laying down the lines for much ensuing criticism and exposing Carlyle's view of history in the spirit and in the words of Carlyle's own discussions of it. ('This is not so much a history as an epic poem; and notwithstanding this, or even in consequence of this, the truest of histories.')

I have not found any comment on Carlyle's *French Revolution* by Croker. J. G. Alger (*Paris [in 1789–1794]*, 1902, 533) speaks of the review of Carlyle's work in *Q[uarterly] R[eview]* (Sept. 1840), LXVI, 446–503, as being by Croker. Nothing could be less likely, and he gives no evidence. The style, the preoccupation with abstract thought, the moderateness of the criticism and, above all, the absence of attack on historical points (except one or two minor ones), rule out Croker as the author.

[2] E.g. R. A. E. Brooks who, editing Carlyle's *Journey to Germany* (New Haven, 1940) and showing its connection with the battle scenes in *Frederick*, says his aim is to 'push forward the field opened with Professor C. F. Harrold's fine study'. Brooks had the advantage of the fact that Carlyle had done field-work for *Frederick*.

[3] 20 Jan. 1834 (*Letters to Mill*, 90). It was a question whether she fell from a roof flying from a bailiff, or was thrown from a window.

[4] Harrold, 1159.

his aim was accuracy. Without it, he asked, 'what other good is possible?'.[1] He had an incessant struggle with the materials precisely because he knew them to be treacherous and was determined to extract the truth from them.

Professor Harrold examined only cited material from which he proved that Carlyle did not invent facts. This leads nowhere since Carlyle had never been suspected of inventing the facts for which he cited authorities. Moreover, Professor Harrold's method is inadequate because Carlyle used twice as many books as he cited (Thiers and Mignet for instance are not explicitly mentioned). One example will illustrate its limitations. He lists as one of Carlyle's 'fabrications' part of the scene in which, after the flight to Varennes, Robespierre's colleagues tried to impress on him the need for preparing the public mind, through a journal called the *Republican*, for a republic, and Robespierre replied 'What is a republic?'. Carlyle cites Madame Roland as his authority. When Professor Harrold could not find all the facts in her *Memoirs*, he thought Carlyle had invented them. They are, however, in her *Appeal to Posterity*, which Carlyle used without citing it at all in his footnotes. The conclusions drawn from Professor Harrold's comparison of the passage in Carlyle with its supposed source fall through because Madame Roland gives different versions in her *Memoirs* and her *Appeal*, and Carlyle, in fact, used both.[2] Much in Harrold is invalidated in the same way (though it is not always easy to show it), because Carlyle's variations from a particular text which he happens to mention, are based on facts and impressions he received elsewhere in the process of his constant collations.[3]

There is some confusion concerning Carlyle's use or neglect of the

[1] To Emerson, Feb. 1835: 'All is so inaccurate, superficial, vague in the numberless books I consult; and without accuracy at least, what other good is possible?'

[2] Harrold, 1166. In his list of fabrications occurs the statement: 'Robespierre's sarcastic question "A Republic, what is that?" does not occur in Madame Roland's account which Carlyle cites.' The following are the relevant passages:

1. Madame Roland, *Mémoires* (1800), II, 69–70. 'Pétion et Brissot disoit qu'il ... fallait préparer les esprits à la République. Robespierre, ricanant à son ordinaire et se mangeant les ongles, demandoit ce que c'étoit qu'une République.'

2. Carlyle, *F.R.* II, 107. 'They ... would fain have comforted the seagreen man; spake of ... a journal to be called *The Republican* ... "A Republic?" said the seagreen, with one of his dry husky *un*sportful laughs "What is that?"'

3. Madame Roland, *Appel à l'impartiale posterité* (1795). In the English translation (1795), I, 58. 'That afternoon I met him at Pétion's ... Pétion and Brissot ... said that this flight would be the king's ruin and that advantage must be taken of it ... prepare men's minds for a republic. Robespierre, with his usual sneer, and biting his nails, asked what was a republic. The plan of a paper entitled the Republican of which two numbers only were published, was now founded.'

[3] Professor Harrold's article is nevertheless of great value. The massive work done in comparing Carlyle with some of his sources brings out the literary activity in Carlyle's writing, but even there it is not exhaustive. When, for instance, a source says 'Sans bas comme sans souliers', and Carlyle says 'wooden shoes', we cannot assume this to be a misquotation or a literary alteration unless there are no wooden shoes in any other source which Carlyle could have read.

British Museum. His best biographer says that he 'discovered' the Croker collections. We know that for some time Carlyle went to the Museum twice a week to read,[1] but not what he read. We also know that he made great efforts to use the Croker collections. In 1837 we have Croker's own testimony that these were uncatalogued and unusable. This explains both Carlyle's efforts to gain access to the shelves and his despair of being able to use the collection otherwise. It has been said that Carlyle was scared from the Reading Room by an offender who sneezed.[2] Since there was no catalogue by means of which the required title could be found, and there was no one who could fetch a book even when it was named, Carlyle's failure to use the collections cannot be so lightly treated. There was an open quarrel with Panizzi involving other people.[3] Carlyle's biographer thinks that Carlyle quietly got what he wanted. Carlyle himself wrote in 1837 that eighteen months earlier 'the respectable sub-librarian' was working on a catalogue of the Croker collection and that by application one gained access to his room and permission to climb on ladders and read 'the outside titles of books', but that there was not even a list. After days of 'weary waiting, dusty rummaging and sickening of hope deferred', one gave up. Carlyle obviously got as far as looking at some of the items, but this desultory reading left no mark on his book.

Carlyle's investigations for the *French Revolution* must not be exaggerated in the light of his later efforts for *Cromwell's Letters and Speeches* and *Frederick the Great*. For those histories he did field work and read original documents. In the *French Revolution* the contact with the sources is less visible because there is more insistence on 'Faithful Genius at the Top' than on 'Faithful Industry at the Bottom'. His contact with Paris and use of oral information is often exaggerated. Carlyle had been to Paris in 1824 and found it 'vastly entertaining'. He spoke to Legendre and in the *Reminiscences* wrote that he had used his impressions for the *History*. One student of Carlyle speaks of the trip as undertaken in the midst of 'the gathering and sifting of the materials' for the history.[4] Carlyle, of course, had no idea of writing on the Revolution at the time.

Later, in September 1833, when Carlyle had decided to write on the Revolution, he contemplated study in Paris. Mill was asked to investigate

---

[1] Carlyle to his mother, 5 Aug. 1834 (*Letters, 1826–1836*, II, 200).

[2] Acton, [*Lectures on the*] *French Revolution* (1925), 358.

[3] It is possible that the quarrel with Panizzi started earlier and prejudiced Carlyle's case. Panizzi convinced the trustees that there was no case for special privileges. Carlyle made further efforts through Lady Ashburton and Lord Clarendon. See L. A. Fagan, *The Life of Sir Anthony Panizzi* (2 vols. 1880), I, 332; Carlyle, in *Critical and Miscellaneous Essays* (1899), IV, 7–8 note; H M. Stephens, *The French Revolution* (1886), V–VI; Acton, *French Revolution*, 358; J. W. Croker, 'Robespierre' (*Q.R.* Sept. 1835, LIV); L. J. Jennings, *Croker Papers* (1884), II, 285.

[4] A. H. R. Ball in his abridged edition of, Carlyle's *French Revolution* (Cambridge, 1930).

economic conditions and resources in men and libraries.[1] When inspiration came, the trip was beyond hope of execution. It was one of his many great plans, well laid, feasible, and never carried out.[2] He lacked what in Voltaire he called 'adroitness', the power to carry out his aims. Paris was the symbol of his striving after authenticity, but he never went there while he was working on the *French Revolution*. He was a hard worker; but to plan a book which would exhaust living experiences and depend on original research, and to escape into the most exacting book-drudgery, was his kind of indolence.

'The Diamond Necklace' marked a turning point in his attitude to sources. So far he had read anything. He now learned to look to materials for solutions to specific problems raised by the construction of the story. He allotted Mill seven tasks of the kind that require research or luck to answer.[3] Mill came back loaded with information. The answers were written by Baron Darnay, and Carlyle received them enthusiastically, 'What would I not give to have the questioning of him for one solar day.'[4] He wrote hectically of going to Paris before the survivors of the Revolution all died.

Whether or not Carlyle actually moved to London in order to have readier access to materials, he certainly had more of them there, 'a perfect outfit', he thought, 'for this present enterprise'.[5] At one time he wrote that he had 150 Revolutionary books, and at another, 300. He wrote by day and spent the evenings reading for the next day's writing. He read unsystematically whatever seemed relevant. While the chapter on the Bastille was holding out for months,[6] greatly delaying him, Carlyle was reading, for instance, the memoirs of Mirabeau by his adopted son, which he also reviewed.[7] This haphazard reading was brought into the chapter on the Bastille. When the scene is laid on the night of 13 July, Carlyle added a paragraph in which he wrote that it was then that old Mirabeau lay dead and his mourning son was away from public life, while the great scene transacted itself without him. For this he cited *Fils Adoptif*.

[1] Mill replied that there was easy access to men and libraries and that living conditions were easier than in London. He had the economic details from Comte and Duchâtel (*Letters of Mill*, 25 Nov. 1833, I, 71).

[2] For years Carlyle considered going to the U.S.A. where he had numerous invitations to lecture. Emerson made financial arrangements and promised great success.

[3] Who wrote the memoirs of Lamotte (which seemed to him unauthentic)? Was Orleans involved in the affair? In which house in London did Lamotte die? What happened to her Count? Was Oliva heard of again? Is Vilate by 'an oversight of the Devil' alive? Where did the jewellers live and where are they now? (28 Oct. 1833, *Letters to Mill*, 76).

[4] 17 Dec. 1833 (*ibid.* 82).

[5] Carlyle to his mother, 25 Oct. 1834 (*Letters, 1826–1836*, II, 232).

[6] Between Oct. and Dec. 1834 he frequently reported that the Bastille was holding out. See, e.g., *ibid.* II, 244, 247.

[7] Carlyle told Emerson that the review was undertaken at Mill's request, as well as 'for needful lucre'. Carlyle had to revise it (letter to Jane, 24 July 1836) and it finally appeared in 1837.

The story of the burnt manuscript has often been told. Mill and Carlyle each vied with the other in sympathy. Consolations and offers of remuneration (partly accepted) finally gave way to practical plans. Carlyle ordered new shelves and new books, the *Biographie Universelle*, Campan's *Memoirs* and others. He wanted his brother to get a score of *Ça Ira* (he had the *Marseillaise*), to look at the Tree of Liberty, at a 'lanterne' and to find some book on Danton.[1]

Carlyle's contact with Paris was through Mill and through his brother. He had some oral information especially from Cavaignac, whom he befriended and used as a living reference library. Cavaignac elucidated numerous little points and took kindly Carlyle's dissent on larger issues. Talking to this admirer of Robespierre, Carlyle yielded not an inch of his own detestation for Robespierre, nor did he allot to Cavaignac's father's career more than a few lines and a note clearing him from a slander.

This leaves Carlyle with his books, which Acton called 'the usual modest resources of a private collection',[2] Gooch dismissed as 'a few volumes of memoirs',[3] and Aulard attempted to prove constituted the best available collection of materials. The footnotes do not give the bibliography, but they show, for instance, that Carlyle did not use four journals which Aulard considered important and which he claimed Carlyle had used.[4] Carlyle indeed quotes from them and also from *L'Ami du Peuple*, but only as far as extracts were published in Buchez and Roux. This collection is the source of all Carlyle's documentation. The *Moniteur* alone, of the journals, Carlyle used in its bound volumes.[5] He had no direct access to any of the hundred of journals which Croker, for instance, collected and studied. The best that can be said for this neglect is that it saved Carlyle from the fallacy which Croker exposed, that the journals included all historical knowledge. The fact that Carlyle's human interest sent him chiefly to the memoirs, though he knew them to be unreliable, cannot in itself be quoted for him as by Aulard, or against him as by Gooch. The memoirs were and are a source. The question is how he used them. He knew they were lying and waged a losing war against their falsehood. Checking a date in Besenval, perhaps his most frequently used memoirs, he wrote, 'a date one rejoices to verify, for nothing can excel the indolent falsehood of these histories and memoirs'.[6] He knew

---

[1] *Letters, 1826–1836*, II, 330–4. The Tree of Liberty is mentioned in the *History*, Book I, ch. XII. The lantern was that of the Place de Grève.

[2] *F.R.* 358.   [3] *History and Historians*, 303.

[4] *Moniteur, Journal des Débats, Révolutions de Paris, Bulletin de Tribunal Révolutionnaire* (Aulard, 'Carlyle', 196).

[5] Alger's statement (*Paris*, 531) that Carlyle 'virtually wrote his book from the *Moniteur* and from Buchez and Roux' is not true. Had Carlyle done this he would have been spared his greatest difficulty of dealing with contradictory evidence. Moreover, the *Moniteur* did not include much about human behaviour. He used it rather for reference, to verify dates. Buchez and Roux he used for its extracts from contemporary documents.

[6] *F.R.* I, 93.

that Vilate's account of Thermidor was 'at bottom, in spite of its title, not a Narrative but a Pleading'. The suspicion of Vilate is used by Aulard in Carlyle's defence,[1] and there are other instances. Campan and Prudhomme, both of whom he used extensively, Carlyle accused of phantasy and lies.[2] Carlyle was critical in treating the memoirs, but he was unsuccessful in his criticism. He checked them against each other, but not against objective sources. But it is not true, as Professor Harrold says (in Carlyle's defence!), that he chose material, right or wrong, merely for dramatic effect.

Aulard cites for Carlyle his use of the *Choix de Rapports*,[3] but it was there that Carlyle found the fictitious story of the *Vengeur* which Barère had invented for purposes of propaganda. Gooch, on the other hand, quotes the story against Carlyle,[4] but when Carlyle discovered the falsehood, he spent months looking into the matter, published a study of the event and its representations,[5] caused some stir in France where admissions of the falsehood finally came out, and added a paragraph in the appropriate place in the book, correcting the story.[6]

Trevelyan[7] is more lenient towards Carlyle than Gooch. He says scientific history had not begun in the 1830s, as if it were an external event happening outside historians. But Gooch is too severe, both upon Carlyle's failure to use the Croker Collections, and when he says that it did not occur to Carlyle to open the archives.[8] Carlyle could have done nothing about that, and it had in fact occurred to him that the archives would help. He was curious about the marching of the Marseillais. 'You search in all Historical Books, Pamphlets and Newspapers', he wrote, and cannot find what made them march. The journals are vague and 'garrulous history' is silent. The Marseilles Council Books, he feels, would throw light on this 'strangest of Municipal Procedures'.[9]

If the errors enumerated by Gooch were all, Carlyle would stand high in scholarship. The latter made a serious mistake about the distance to Varennes, but Browning's essay on Carlyle's errors is, on the whole, trifling.[10] Carlyle did not, as Gooch said, make the flight to Varennes

---

[1] *F.R.* III, 332; Aulard, 'Carlyle', 197.

[2] *Ibid.* I, 29; III, 277. 'Prudhomme . . . a Jacobin Editor, will become a renegade one, and publish . . . *Crimes of the Revolution*; adding innumerable lies withal.' But Carlyle used in Prudhomme both true stories and lies. The only lie he exposes is the slander of Cavaignac (III, 294).

[3] G. N. Lallement, *Choix de Rapports, Opinions et Discours prononcés à la Tribune Nationale depuis 1789 jusqu'à ce jour* (1815), 20 vols. (Paris, 1815). See Aulard, 'Carlyle', 196.

[4] *History and Historians*, 303.

[5] Carlyle, 'On the sinking of the Vengeur' (*Fraser's*, 1839).

[6] *F.R.* III, 298–9.

[7] E.g. in *Nineteenth Century* (1899), XLVI, 493.

[8] *History and Historians*, 303.

[9] *F.R.* II, 337–8.

[10] O. Browning, *The Flight to Varennes and other Essays* (1892). Browning attacks Carlyle, e.g. for saying that Drouet was in a nightgown when in fact he was wearing a dressing gown.

appear like 'a childish prank',[1] and he was, generally speaking, right in attributing the fiasco to mismanagement.

A serious criticism is that Carlyle avoided disputed facts when he could not establish them. Towards the end of the book, his grim determination to find out what happened, loosened. The resolution, mentioned in a letter, to do no more research but splash down what he knows in 'masses of colours',[2] is often unfairly quoted to describe his method throughout.[3] It is really relevant only to the end of the book, which is full of generalizations and reflections.

It is seldom appreciated how far the character of the book was due to the circumstances of its writing as well as to the form. Carlyle wrote for an insecure living while meditating emigration, education, and 'engineership'. He engaged to publish the book at half-profit[4] by a certain date. The time factor remained important. It made his book one of those which are created to order and distinct from those which grow naturally in a man's mind or notebooks. Had Croker written a history it would have been a slowly growing one. Even his essays reveal some of the characteristics of this type of work. Croker could afford to let his materials accumulate, assimilate new information as it came to light, make hypotheses and watch them wrecked or corroborated by facts perhaps accidentally met. He could always attach his findings to some review or other. Carlyle, under the constrictions of a time-limit and a self-imposed artistic form, had to reach conclusions within a certain time and, more important, from a certain amount of materials. Facts tend to appear more final, when questions are not allowed to remain unanswered. Out of 200 books and his own mind, he had to produce the *French Revolution*. The most painstaking and conscientious collation of a limited amount of material can at best produce a 'relative truth', and relative truth has no place in a dramatic narrative in which the reader is supposed to be watching things happening or failing to happen. The merit and convenience of careful statements, like 'X thinks *this* and Y thinks *that*, but the truth cannot be known', which were part of the virtue of Croker, were denied to Carlyle.[5] A critic, like Croker, did not need to be comprehensive, but the builder, constructing an edifice, cannot leave bricks loose or missing.

If Carlyle's artistic form led him to establish facts on insufficient grounds, it also made him think about large spaces at a time and in this

---

[1] *History and Historians*, 304.

[2] To his wife, 24 July 1836 (A. Carlyle, *New Letters*, 21); cf. to his mother, 27 July 1836 (*ibid.* 24).

[3] E.g. Alger, *Paris*, 531.

[4] To his mother, 12 June 1834 (*Letters, 1826–1836*, II, 172–3, 325).

[5] It is interesting that before Carlyle wrote any serious history, in the review of 'Boswell's Life of Johnson' (*Fraser's* (1832), 379–413), he criticized Croker, who edited Boswell, for constantly noting 'The editor does not know, the editor does not understand'.

respect it gave his work a historical as well as a literary merit. Again, this is best brought out by comparison with Croker. Of all the sound history written at the time, none is more shapeless than Croker's. His eye was so fixed on detail, on 'following the vein of the ore', that he reproduced his tracks in his essays. Even when he rewrote an essay he cut it open, stuffed more facts into it and added to the deformity. There is a sense, therefore, in which Carlyle's preoccupation with form, or rather with effect, made him write more significant history. He had described Schiller's historical method as progressing from eminence to eminence. Goethe had written to Carlyle that what he liked in Scott's *Napoleon* were the 'large homogeneous masses'. This amassing of detail for a total effect was a romantic quality of history writing, common to Schiller, Scott and Carlyle.

THE REACTION AGAINST POLITICAL HISTORY

Carlyle was right when he complained that the public expected writers to range themselves behind some party. He himself refused to do this, but when his *History* came out, readers never tired of guessing his political views, bringing out through their contradictions the book's political independence. Mill, who knew Carlyle best, wrote that he was not a Tory, Whig or democrat, but had in him the best of all parties.[1] The terms did not apply even in the negative. What politics did a book profess which was admired by Mill, Emerson, Jeffrey, Arnold, Kingsley, and Southey, of which Thackeray wrote in *The Times* that it was a warning to democracy,[2] and which Macaulay and Brougham disliked for its sympathy with violence? Carlyle's actual historical statements in the *History* can, of course, be generalized to imply a view, in the way that Mill and Aulard, for instance, generalized the statement that 25 million Frenchmen were never less miserable than under the Terror.[3]

The main views ascribed to Carlyle are, on the one hand, that he wrote the Radical antidote to Burke, and, on the other, that he stood directly behind Burke, expounding the latter's views to a later generation. It is

[1] *Westminster Review* (July 1837), XXVII, 179. Mill interpreted Carlyle in the light of his own view that some good came out of the Revolution. He ends his review by a quotation which implies Carlyle's sympathy with the Revolution and adds that the inference is that rulers must not sit indolent on top of chaos: 'That there be no second sansculotism in our earth for a thousand years, let us understand well what the first was; and let Rich and Poor of us go and do otherwise.'

[2] *The Times*, 3 Aug. 1837. Thackeray praised Carlyle's impartiality compared with Scott's Tory prejudices and with the 'immoral impartiality' of Thiers who ascribed only base and selfish motives and saw the Revolution as a struggle for places.

[3] Aulard ('Carlyle', 198–9) lists the passages in which Carlyle implies sympathy with the Revolution, e.g. where Carlyle asks whether France could be regenerated without revolution, or states that the émigrés made the Revolution violent, that the massacres of September were caused by fear of foreigners and that not a personal enemy of Danton died in them. All the quotations that he gives are out of context.

true that Carlyle shared Burke's condemnation of the 'philosophes' as irreverent and irreligious, and that he saw the springs of human action in deep irrational passions. But he differed radically from Burke's assumptions concerning the old régime, which he saw as fit only for destruction. Unlike Burke, he saw everything in history as mortal and mutable.[1] Of all the English historians of the Revolution, not excepting Morse Stephens, Carlyle alone wrote, not as 'affected' by the Revolution but as related to it. His use of the pronoun 'us' when lost among the *sansculottes*, particularly endeared him to Aulard.[2]

Carlyle's hatred for the Radicals grew in the course of his study.[3] Radicals and Girondins discredited each other for him. At the appropriate place in his *History* he stops to write, in a letter to Mill, that he was sick of the Girondins, who like respectable radical Members were patronizing about the masses, formalistic, narrow and barren. 'The Mountain was perfectly under the necessity of flinging such men to the Devil.' At the same moment Croker and Carlyle were attacking the myth of the virtuous Girondins from different angles, equally determined to reject a formulated set of Revolutionary sympathies adapted to liberal politics.[4]

It is often said against Carlyle that he saw the Revolution as purely destructive and ignored its constructive efforts and results. Carlyle did not intend to give his views on the whole of the period or on the results.[5] Because this is usually assumed, he is also criticized for having presented the Revolution as beginning and ending suddenly and for ignoring its European, constitutional and economic aspects.[6] Carlyle often insisted in letters and in the *History* that he was writing a history of sansculottism.[7] It is possible to hold that sansculottism was a phenomenon which grew independently of the reforming tendencies which preceded and followed the Revolution. Carlyle connected the Revolution with its past and future, in the *Signs* and in *Voltaire* of 1829, but he saw the connection

---

[1] 'Conservatism I cannot attempt to conserve, believing it to be a portentous embodied sham, accursed of God, and doomed to destruction, as all lies are' (Froude, *Thomas Carlyle*, I, 24).

[2] 'Carlyle', 202.

[3] To his mother, 1 Dec. 1834 (*Letters, 1832–1836*, 249); to Emerson, 3 Feb. 1835, 29 Apr. 1836. Most students of Carlyle describe him as a Radical in those years. In the same letter Carlyle describes his amusement at a Radical meeting he attended. D. A. Wilson (*Carlyle to The French Revolution*) quotes the letter and omits from it the remarks which are unfavourable to the Radicals. On 12 May 1835 he wrote home, Radicalism was advancing 'which means revolt against innumerable things . . . Dissolution and confusion . . . and a darkness'.

[4] Gooch, in the 'Study of Modern History', writes that Carlyle, like everyone else before Biré, misconceived the Girondins.

[5] E.g. F. Harrison, *Historians of the Revolution* (1886); Gooch, *History and Historians*, 304.

[6] Much of Gooch's criticism concurs with that expressed earlier by Harrison in an article on the revolutionary historians and in another on 'Carlyle's Place in Literature'.

[7] See, e.g., *F.R.* I, 265. Carlyle discusses the question where the French Revolution is taking place. It is easy, he says, to publish volume after volume recorded from the 'Reporter's Chair' in the Assembly, 'easy but unprofitable. The National Assembly . . . goes its course; making the constitution; but the French Revolution also goes *its* course'.

through ideas and not through institutions. In *Heroes* he said that the Revolution of 1830 destroyed the meteoric quality of the Great Revolution and showed that it was not 'a transitory ebullition of Bedlam, but a genuine product of this earth'.[1] Ever since Mackintosh there had been a tendency in English historiography to separate the constructive from the destructive Revolution. When Macaulay in 1832 glorified the Revolution for its very destructive work he was making a theoretic case for destructive legislation. But Carlyle's eyes were fixed on the destruction which originated from the masses. Though he had infinitely more pity for the passions which move men to violence, and though he allowed the *sansculotte* an inarticulate striving after a lofty idea, he did not give violence either moral or political sanction. The idealist view that moral and not material forces shape history was basic in his interpretation. He said that ideas and not actions leave a mark on history, and that no calculations of profit brought about revolutions. The English Revolution was fought for conscience, and in the French Revolution too there was an idea. Carlyle never lost the balance between material and ideal forces in the Revolution. Such balance generally characterizes the English historians of the Revolution. Bread and a vision both play a part in their versions. There are in Carlyle's *History* general reflections which give rise to theories of social changes. Society is a self-generating organism and revolutions are legitimate forces released to crush decaying institutions.[2] On the other hand there are reflections which see the Revolution as a violent punishment. The Revolution can also be seen in the context of a theory of historical cycles, or it can be said that it provided scope for the action of Carlyle's heroes.[3] The abundant contradictions baffle any attempt to reduce Carlyle's views to a system. The mob is the beast and the mob is the hero, the mob is incited, and the mob is nature itself, genuine and morally authoritative. The Revolution is sansculottism, born with anarchy and dead with Thermidor, but it is also history incarnate, a microcosm of world change, the authentic process designed by God. It is difficult to impose a system, even within a single one, of the sources for Carlyle's view of the Revolution; it is impossible to bring them all into harmony.

It is true that Carlyle went to the Revolution eager to understand it, and, through it, the whole of history. When he had done with it he was no wiser as to a system than before. The authentic feeling of chaos was the reality he achieved and because it covered a conglomeration of

---

[1] *Heroes, Hero-Worship and the Heroic in History* (The Centenary Edition, 1897), Lecture VI, 199–201.

[2] E.g. 'Remark, meanwhile, how from amid the wrecks and dust of this universal Decay new Powers are fashioning themselves, adapted to the new time, and its destinies' (*F.R.* I, Bk. I, Ch. 2).

[3] It has also been said that though these men of 1789 laboured hard to make a stable constitution, 'in Carlyle's eyes they stand condemned for the most terrible of all crimes, want of success' (Fletcher's edn. of *F.R.* I, 266 n.).

phenomena it gave him the satisfaction of truth. He sensed perhaps that the Revolution was producing its own causes and motive forces, when he made sheer mad and destructive forces develop a will and an idea of their own.

The distinctive novelty of Carlyle's book is not in interpretation but in historical form. The ring of truth that brought it success was partly due to the choice of the narrative form. A story will be listened to. Carlyle knew only the dramatic narrative form for history writing. Theory and practice influenced each other with him. He both rationalized his preferences and consciously put theory into practice. The form he chose was best suited to perform the tasks he allotted to history and it best suited the age which was awakening to romance, to the live and human interest in the past which Scott had done so much to foster. In the English historiography of the Revolution, nothing was more wanted. Tired of being told what to think about the Revolution, people were glad to glimpse a painting of it. The pamphleteers, lectures, critics, reviewers and early historians, all sought to say something true about it. Alison, before Carlyle attempted a proper narrative, was moved by the human interest, and he had great success. But his volumes were bulky and dull and his tone was political and conventional, so that his book had the popularity of a duty more than of a delight. Carlyle reclaimed the history of the Revolution from the politicians, the teachers, the critics, and the reviewers by following a different course with a different aim. The English approach to the Revolution had by then developed distinctive lines. The preoccupation with other historians, even in scholars like Croker, went far to limit the serious English interest to an academic discipline, to an analysis of books and writers. Contributions were largely made by correction and criticism rather than by independent reconstruction. Carlyle alone noticed that something was wrong. He said that the history itself lay shrouded while writers worried about what the Whigs said, what the Tories, what the Priests or the Freethinkers, and, above all, what they would 'say of *me* (the historian) for what I say of it'. The historical faculty was directed at the 'Writings and the Writers both of which are quite extraneous'.[1] He therefore wrote a pure narrative, a story told by the traditional omniscient observer. He used books for information but rarely commented on them, unless they were by the actors. The Revolution is his only theme. Carlyle, in premature boldness, did what Croker in learned timidity dared not attempt. The scholar retreated before the vastness of his own knowledge into a study of episodes. The artist, mentally excited, was eager to shape his materials almost before they were gathered. Carlyle set out with little more than a deeply aroused interest and a multitude of conflicting opinions, studying and writing about the event simultaneously.

[1] E.g. 'The Diamond Necklace' (*Critical and Miscellaneous Essays* (1899), II, 326).

CHAPTER 9

BETWEEN 1830 AND 1848

A PHILOSOPHY OF HISTORY—THE MIDDLE CLASSES

Since Burke there had not been in England a basically new approach to history and in writing about the French Revolution historians retained the spirit of contemporaries. The Revolution of 1830 did not suddenly create the demand for new schemes of history but it had an impact on it. In France the Revolution of 1830—partly effected by historians—rewarded them with greater freedom for work and a political atmosphere favourable to new departures in historical thinking. Faced with new romantic, Saint-Simonian, fatalist and socialist interpretations there was in England a feeling of inferiority in history and a quest for new views. A reviewer of Chateaubriand in *Blackwood's Magazine* writes in 1832,

No one will accuse us of undue partiality to the French Revolution . . . we are obliged to confess that in historical and political compositions the French are greatly superior to the writers of this country. We are not insensible to the merits of . . . Turner . . . Lingard . . . Tyler . . . McCrie . . . Mackintosh . . . But still we feel the justice of the French observation that there is something 'English' in all their ideas. Their thoughts seem formed on the even tenor of political events prior to 1789 . . . we can hardly persuade ourselves that they have been ushered into the world since the French Revolution advanced a thousand years the materials of political investigation.

The French ascribe this state of affairs 'to the want of *bouleversement* of ideas, and the extrication of original thought which a revolution produces'.[1]

The Reform Bill did not prove a stimulus to original thought on history. The application of the political lessons of the Revolution to England by Alison, Croker, Smyth and Macaulay, who represented history at the time, was ruled by analogy which characterized rationalist historiography. Smyth and Mackintosh remained unaffected in their history writing by new theories, though Smyth consciously fought them and Mackintosh propagated some of them. Alison and Macaulay were influenced but not shaped by romantic notions on the form and style of history.

The prevalent political manner of writing history belonged to a passing age. Politics and history were being pulled apart. There were inquiries about the aims, methods, spirit and form of history. 'Philosophy teaching by experience', though it survived the trial, was being scoffed at. Mill and Carlyle were affected by the quest for comprehensive historical explanation. Carlyle answered the challenge by his single-handed

---

[1] *Blackwood's* (March 1832), XXXI, 553–4.

romantic revolt. His writings embodied echoes of the current philosophies but in the end he despaired of all theories of history. His *French Revolution* is the only original product of the shaking-up of history in England in the 1830s. It divested the history of the French Revolution of the conventional political approach. This was partly connected also with the loosening of the party boundaries. Old party associations as that of the Whigs with the interests of the people were being questioned. There were alliances between Tory and Chartist against the economic selfishness of the Whigs. The issue of conservatism versus revolutionism was less stereotyped than ever. This was not literally true or fully realized at the time. After 1830, when the terms liberal and conservative were coming into use, many spoke of Whigs and Tories as being naturally and fundamentally antithetical. We find this notion in an 1830 *Edinburgh* review of Jefferson, in a letter from Croker to Brougham and in a *Blackwood* letter which reads, 'The distinction between individual freedom and political power, between Liberty and Democracy is the great point of separation between the Whigs and the Tories.' All these observers were describing a real phenomenon of antithesis coming into being in social and political life but they were using the wrong terms to describe it for it was outside Whiggism and Toryism that the deep chasm was opening.[1] A generation was growing up between 1830 and 1840 used to change and reform as the habitual course. Carlyle influenced this questioning attitude. He detached himself from the old party lines before detachment became the fashion in history.

John Mill, on the other hand, influenced by Comte, had evolved ideas about history which pointed in the direction of 'principles' or fixed laws. The Positivists later acknowledged him as one of the authors of their notions of 'scientific history' which with them applied less to the methods of verifying history (as it does today) than to the discovery of fixed recurring laws. The Positivists' 'science of history' was thus influenced, partly through Mill, by the old rationalist quest for universal truths.

The most typical product of the new quest for comprehensive explanation in history was not Carlyle's romantic rejection of all theory, but rather the widely acceptable social theory which based the happiness of every country on the happiness of the middle classes—the repository of public opinion, wealth and wisdom. James Mill who in the 1820 *Supplement* of the *Encyclopaedia Britannica* had evolved a philosophical and social theory of Benthamite principles, wrote of the 'middle rank, which gives to science, to art, and to legislation itself, their most distinguished ornaments, and is the chief source of all that has exalted and refined human nature'. This view, which became the theme of numerous works such as Mackinnon's *History of Civilization*, fitted perfectly the mood of those who had benefited from the Reform Bill of 1832. They

---

[1] See, e.g., Croker to Brougham, *Blackwood's* (Dec. 1832), XXXII, 931.

were now able to place their political and social views and interests in the context of a respectable theory of history. The nature and profundity of this theory is a measure of the English interest in new theories of history. They said that the Revolution of 1789 had gone wrong because the middle classes were not then strong enough to act without the mob; that the achievement of 1789 was the advancement of the middle classes in France; that by 1830, having been politically and morally improved and strengthened by life under a constitution, the middle classes were able to impose revolution above and restraint below. This was a simplified variant of the view of the Doctrinaires (who were foremost in championing the middle classes in France) that the malady of 1789 had been the inability of the 'people' to identify themselves with the state and to assume responsibility for the whole of it, which is really another way of saying that they were as yet unprepared to rule. The new confidence of the middle classes in themselves was connected with economic growth and with the belief in the power of education. Historians of this period testify to the absorbing trust in the powers of education.[1] It is coming to be true that through education one can become middle class. The middle classes are the bearers of public opinion; public opinion is a powerful influence on politics; it is therefore a grand political object to form public opinion through education. Knowledge became through these chains of inference a highly valued commodity with which the immense success, growth and influence of journalism is connected. 'Revolution would be staved off by education', so the word went. What could be a more relevant and effective education than that which combined in a history of the French Revolution an orderly view of divine and human affairs in religion and in history? Alison's success was largely due to the fact that he supplied this demand, and embodied in a full-sized history of the French Revolution prevailing middle class opinions.

THE STANDARD HISTORY—ALISON

The period between 1815 and 1830 had seen the beginnings of the great collections of Revolutionary materials. Croker purchased widely and wisely even before the battlefield of Waterloo had been stripped of its relics. With less materials another Tory traveller, Alison, was to oust Croker out of the kingdom he was best qualified to rule. Alison knew the sources but not how to use them. His bibliographical prefaces are now the best part of the book. Carlyle had not read Alison's book when Mill asked whether it was worth reviewing. Carlyle glanced at it, saw that the 'margin bears mark of great enquiry', knew that Alison had been to France, and advised Mill to review it but tell his own story, without fear or favour. 'It is a thing utterly unknown to the English and ought to

---

[1] Kellett, 'The Press', *Early Victorian England*, vol. II.

be known.' When Mill read the book himself, he found that Alison was 'inconceivably stupid and twaddling . . . has no research', and that the references were to compilations.[1] The last sentence shows that Carlyle had been too undiscriminating in his respect for Alison's footnotes. Mill reviewed Alison in the *Monthly Repository*,[2] not daring or not being allowed to do so in the *Edinburgh*, because he was also keen, while he was at it, to show up Macaulay's ignorance of the Revolution 'as shown in that review'.[3] Mill was still preoccupied, as he was when he reviewed Scott, with the early stages of the Revolution and with its causes, and his criticism of Alison is severe. Alison's book, pervaded by political principle, and meaning to throw 'true light' on the Revolution, was tremendously successful and is now forgotten. His sort of history when improved on, loses all value. As he modestly knew, his success was due to his being the first.

He is an 'Ultra-Tory, and therefore cannot understand the French Revolution'. Carlyle wrote simply, and in utter prejudice and ignorance.[4] Alison had served the Tory cause in 1831 by a series of articles connecting the French Revolution with the phantom of English reforms.[5] The point on which his argument rested was that of the inevitable progress of revolutions from the mildest concessions of political power. He therefore held that the French Revolution of 1830 would lead to massacres, republics, military despotism and European war. Even before the anti-Reform Bill campaign, Alison, who had had liberal sympathies, had begun writing his history in order to show that 'Providence was on the side of the Tories' and to warn the Whigs what comes of radical changes and the weakening of authority. He was deeply moved by the royal martyrology especially under the effect of writings such as those of Hue and Clèry, and wrote to expose the wickedness of the Revolution and the virtue of its victims. But Alison's actual judgments on the Revolution are no other than any Whig's. Ferociousness, violence, monstrosity, only begin with the Jacobins. For the early leaders, constitutional monarchists and Girondins he has praise and admiration.

Croker had been collecting materials for a long time when Alison's book came out in 1833. It was believed that this caused enmity between the two Tory writers. Having been anticipated, Croker gave up his plan and offered his library to Alison before he disposed of it to the British Museum. We know that Croker continued to study the Revolution and to collect materials about it for the rest of his life. He was prevented

---

[1] Mill to Carlyle, 11–12 Apr. 1833. *The Letters of John S. Mill*, ed. H. S. Elliott (1910), I, 46; 18 May 1833, I, 49. When Carlyle read Mill's review, he wrote, 'there is not a word in it that I do not subscribe to'.

[2] *Monthly Repository* (July, Aug. 1833), VII, 507, 513.

[3] This probably refers to the article on Dumont in *E.R.* (1832).

[4] Carlyle to Mill, 18 Apr. 1833, *Letters to Mill, Sterling and Browning*, ed. A. Carlyle (1923), 5.   [5] See above, pp. 99 *et seq.*

from reviewing Alison by Lockhart, who thought ill of it himself, spoke of Alison's negligence, coxcombical pomposity, preachification and, 'worst of all, his affectation of liberty', but he did not want Alison harmed.[1] Good reviews in those days were difficult to get. The anonymity of most reviewers encouraged the indulgence of personal animosities. Also, favourable reviews were taxed as advertisements which displeased the editors. Lockhart asked Croker to review Alison with civility or else to find another author who had led Alison astray and 'who might be shown up with a long whip, without calling the heavy sheriff by name into the ring'. Croker apparently preferred not to write. Alison was annoyed by the silence of the *Quarterly*, especially after his efforts against the Reform Bill in *Blackwood's*. He never suspected that it was through kindness that he went unnoticed in the *Quarterly*. Though treated better by the *Edinburgh* he had 'no more credit with the Whig enemy than with the Tory friend'. Croker was not prompted by jealousy alone, but was genuinely outraged by Alison's shallow research.

Alison spent the rest of his life writing contemporary history, making collections of revolutionary materials and frequently revising his history.[2] Its success is hardly credible today. It was by far the best-selling history of the French Revolution in England and America almost to the end of the century, and was translated into most European and several oriental languages. As late as 1886 Frederic Harrison, who made a study of histories of the Revolution and had no sympathy with Alison's point of view, recommended Alison's book as the best account of the Revolution and its European setting and said it was 'quite as well known as Mignet'.

Acton, who did not study English historians as thoroughly as he did the French, said, rightly (as Mill had said), that Alison had no idea what is meant by research, but Acton chose badly the example of Waterloo, noting that Alison wrote the narrative of the battle in one day. Alison makes a point in one of his revised prefaces of displaying the care with which he had studied and reconstructed the battle *in situ* with the help of military experts. Acton credits Alison with an important contribution to the study of the Revolution. He thought the novelty of his book was that he explained the combinations of nobility and savagery in Revolutionary characters. 'Alison', he wrote in a note, 'has enabled us to understand one of the mysteries of the Revolution, the occasional enthusiasms and generosity of men who were no [trained?] assassins.'[3] Acton overrated Alison's psychological insight. True, he was touched by the

---

[1] Alison, he wrote to Croker on 6 Dec. 1843, is 'a good old Tory and a good honest admirable man'.

[2] He spent £4000 on a collection by Amyot the bookseller which included 700 vols. collected by Gohier the Director. Alison's work on the Empire is not as comprehensive as that on the Revolution.

[3] C.U.L. Add. MS. 5649.

Romantic passion for human detail and it helped him to see the mixed nature of the revolutionary temperament, though, compared with Carlyle or even with Southey, he did it rather in the cold-blooded manner of a Tory being 'fair' to the other side. Alison was also touched by the philosophic attraction which the Revolution had for Carlyle, through its 'microcosmic' quality, when he said, more simply than Carlyle, that 'during the twenty-five years of its progress, the world has gone through more than 500 years of ordinary existence'.

Alison's real importance is simply that he made the first scholarly attempt at a detailed, complete history of the Revolution, putting it in its European setting. He also mastered and surveyed Revolutionary literature. He was struck by the 'great inferiority' of English historians and studied mainly the French ones. He divided them into those who do justice to the republican side like Toulongeon ('fair and impartial'), Deux Amis ('elaborate and valuable'), Thiers and Mignet ('brilliant'), and those who wrote on the royalist side, Lacretelle, La Baume, Bertrand, Chateaubriand, Beauchamp. Alison always insisted on the absorbing interest of the internal and biographical story. The best record of the time he says is in the sixty-six volumes of memoirs. He adds, however, that they do not supply the main need to be near, to hear, feel, and see the Revolution, because they were written after the event. The immediate details he found in the contemporary journals, 'cheaply purchased for their weight in gold'. These entrancing records showed him that the French, like all other revolutions, was carried through by the incessant application of exaggeration or mendacity; that the real aspect was even more gruesome, and some characters even darker than their description by enemies; that if the guilt of revolutionaries and selfishness of aristocrats cause despair, the heroism of the victims shows the dignity of human nature.

Alison was fortunate not only in being the first. His book lived long enough to enable him to imbibe, and somehow incorporate in it, echoes of changing fashions in revolutionary studies. The predominance of memoirs and then the preference for journals and pamphlets; the naïve compilation and later the critical study of historians; the martyrology of royalty and nobility and then the advent of the middle classes; the abstract anatomy of revolutions and later the lust for biographical detail and sensual awareness of atmosphere; these and other contradictory trends were at some time or another reflected in his numerous editions. When Alison began writing in 1829 and publishing in the early 1830s he made much play with the political analogy between his history and English politics. By 1853, when the ninth edition came out, analogy was out of fashion and political detachment was the historians' vogue. Alison now denied that there had ever been any connection between his work and English politics.

MACAULAY ON THE REVOLUTION

Macaulay, like Alison, expressed in history prevailing middle-class opinions. Though he was influenced by romantic notions, they did not diminish the political element in his writing, and they deepened the boundaries of his national feelings. His joy at the Restoration because it would benefit England contrasted with Carlyle's deep feeling of pathos at the tragic fall of a great man, foreshadowing the essential differences between the two historians. The predominant Romantic quality in Macaulay was his intense and exclusive nationalism. Nationalism distinguished nineteenth-century liberal history from eighteenth-century Rationalist history. The liberals, like the conservative Romantics, admired the English model, but they accepted the advent of the middle classes and they accepted revolution into their notion of history. Guizot, Hallam and Macaulay who were all liberal historians traced the power of certain ideas in history. Macaulay like Thierry was nationalist without being reactionary, believed in ideas without being 'intellectual', wrote lively history in the Romantic style. Liberal history suited the middle classes better than any other. It recognized their gains and justified their national and class interests.

Macaulay was the historian of English liberty, and cared little for France or America. Though he approved of the results of the French Revolution, he neither defended the principles of that Revolution nor showed their connection with England as Acton was to do. He early said that he preferred the venerable nonsense 'which holds prescriptive sway over the ultra Tory, to the upstart dynasty of prejudices and sophisms, by which the Revolutionists of the moral world have suffered themselves to be enslaved'.[1] He also showed great contempt for the French character. 'A people which violently pulls down constitutional government and lives quiet under despotism, must be and ought to be despotically governed',[2] he wrote later. This was a double heresy, against his own idea that only liberty trains for liberty, and against the Tory taboo on revolt.

Macaulay wrote little about the Revolution apart from two long reviews,[3] but he put into these much of his thought on the event as a whole. The article of 1832, already discussed in connection with the Reform Bill debates, shows Macaulay's conviction that the Revolution was on the whole a blessing, that it resulted from misrule and that its glory lay in destruction. It also paradoxically completes the Whig reconciliation with Burke's attitude to the French Revolution. Macaulay emphasized that the contemporary horror at the Revolution was justified,

[1] *E.R.* (Oct. 1829), L, 99.   [2] *Life*, II, 443.
[3] 'Dumont's Mirabeau', *E.R.* (1832), LV, 552; 'Barère's Mémoirs', *E.R.* (Apr. 1844), LXXIX, 275–351.

and he did this by taking the Burkian line of stressing the effect of circumstances on the politics of every age. When the Revolution of 1830 made Macaulay think about the character of English and French revolutions, he agreed that the English revolutions were practical, conducted in the spirit of lawyers and not of philosophers. He adds, however, that it is not that the French wilfully abandoned experience for theory. They ranted about the original contract because they had no charter. In 1830, their rallying cry was the Charter. As long as they had no models in their own history they rhapsodized about Brutus and Cato, forgetting, he adds, that they were haughtier aristocrats than any that went with Artois.

The article on Barère of 1844 is the most forceful condemnation of a revolutionary leader, by a serious historian, and through a minute study of detail, to be found at the time, even in Croker. As a historian's impersonation of God on the Day of Judgment, it is unequalled by anything in Acton. Evidence, reason, psychological analysis are gathered to support the crushing verdict that 'Barère approached nearer than any person mentioned in history or fiction, whether man or devil, to the idea of consummate and universal depravity'.[1] Acton's judgment that Robespierre was 'the most hateful character in the forefront of history' seems mild in comparison.

Macaulay's view of the French Revolution is worth summarizing, for although he belonged to that wide liberal school characterized by vague and sometimes contradictory views, his tendency to 'short, clear and decisive' answers to historical questions helped to crystallize some of the vague views. His view of the causes of the Revolution is the classical English view. Intellectual freedom had long existed together with political servility. Neither philosophy nor grievances alone could have started the Revolution, but the combination of both did. It was the war which ruined the Revolution by necessarily causing deposition. It was a just defensive war for France; her question became one of national independence and Macaulay defends those who fought for their country whoever its rulers. Louis could naturally not be trusted, but he would have been more than human if he had not detested the Revolution. He cannot be blamed for wishing for a German victory, nor can the French be blamed for deposing him. 'If the ship is on her beam-ends, it may be necessary to cut the masts away.'

Macaulay readily subscribed to the legend of the Girondins. 'The genius, courage, patriotism, and humanity of the Girondist statesmen more than atoned for what was culpable in their conduct.' They excelled all other parties except in decision, they were zealous for reform, for national independence and for a republic. They loved liberty, civilization and humanity. Horrified by crimes, they demanded justice and morality. Criminally irresolute, they traced a crooked course. They rejected the

---

[1] *E.R.* (1844), LXXIX, 276.

Mountain plea of public danger, but conceded it in voting for the King's death. The day they fell was the saddest of the Revolution. Young, innocent, brave, eloquent, accomplished, they perished for lack of political courage, choosing to be victims rather than oppressors.

The Mountain, though it included sincere men like Carnot and Cambon, was on the whole unscrupulous. Of Danton he says, 'The author of the reign of terror, the captain of the ruffians of September, died the martyr of mercy and order.' They had determination and subjected France to the Paris mob. They invented against the Girondists a crime called Federalism, and knowing Barère's lack of principle they pledged him by making him murder his friends. It was Barère who recommended the burning of libraries, the destruction of history, the ghastly decree of no quarter which the soldiers refused and Napoleon loathed. 'There is no witness so infamous that a court of justice will not take his word against himself; and even Barère may be believed when he tells us how much he was hated and despised.' Carnot, by attempting to enshrine this Jacobin carrion, has forced Macaulay to gibbet it 'and we venture to say that from the eminence of infamy on which we have placed it, he will not easily take it down'.

Macaulay's views of the Jacobins and especially of Robespierre seem influenced by Croker. He writes that Robespierre has suffered from the propensity of the public to pile the blame of a group on one individual. Robespierre, he said, was disinterested, zealous for his system and, according to Napoleon, he had opposed the death of the Queen. The extremes of the Terror took place while he was away. Southey had written that the Revolution of Thermidor was brought on by fear. Macaulay writes that the three who perished were better than those who survived. But he also speaks of 'that happiest and most genial of revolutions, the revolution of the ninth of Thermidor'. On the Terror too, Macaulay borrowed Croker's judgments and perhaps his statistics. Croker had dismissed 'the hackneyed excuse of the Terror occasioned by the advance of the Prussians'. Macaulay said that no degree of danger can justify the indiscriminate cruelty, and that in any case France was not saved from the foreign enemy by the Terrorists but by the people in spite of the Terror. Macaulay says that the peak of the Terror was reached when there was a lull in the national danger, a fact which Croker had taken a great deal of trouble to prove by drawing up diagrams and counting daily executions. The Terror was conducted, says Macaulay, by six men equally free of justice and of cupidity. The Jacobins were a small group of enthusiasts surrounded by depraved masses.

Macaulay's judgments, though clearly expressed, are typical of the ambiguities still haunting the Whigs. Macaulay's difficulty of pronouncing on Louis XVI recalls to mind similar words half a century earlier. The condemnation of the Jacobins is strictly on account of their blood-shedding. The Whig tone survives also in the admiration of the Girondins (although their treachery, cowardice and dishonesty are all admitted), and in such conventional complaints as that the evils of the Revolution discredited liberty and caused a readiness to succumb to the despotism of Napoleon and the Restoration.

On his general attitude to the Revolution, Macaulay was more revealing when he wrote indirectly. In his essay on Milton he had written that even when liberty takes the form of a hateful reptile, it must not be spurned in disgust. Liberty must be cherished and protected even when sullied by crime. It is a commonplace to say that Macaulay was not a revolutionary but like other Whigs wanted reform to avoid revolution. This is true of course for his politics. The interesting point about his history of revolutions was his approval of revolutions not for their lofty ideals, not in indulgence to their philosophies, but simply for their struggle for ordinary day-to-day liberty. Liberty to Macaulay was not an abstract idea; he was impatient with the notion of liberty as an end, which he said the French had learnt from the blind guides of the ancient world. Liberty, he said, was a means of protecting life and property, and it is for their service to this kind of liberty that he accepted revolutions in history.

SOCIALIST THOUGHT OUTSIDE HISTORY

The 1830s, when England, on the whole, felt saved from revolution at first and threatened by it later, saw the rise of European socialism as a political power. Much weighty thought has been given to the connection between socialism and the French Revolution. For our purpose here it is only relevant to ask whether socialism affected the English historians. In France there was early a socialist interpretation of the French Revolution. No political party was complete without a historical attitude to the Great Revolution. The forces which combined to effect the Revolution of 1830 sought to secure the aims of 1789, and those 'calmists' who compared it to the Glorious Revolution had a point. 1830 established the rule of the middle classes, secured the re-organization of government on more efficient lines and the amount of political equality demanded by the moderate reformers. It rejected the whole of the economic revolution of which there were beginnings in the Great Revolution and which, after 1830, both peasants and middle classes, the chief beneficiaries from the Revolution settlement, feared and hated.

The opposition to the bourgeois government became dangerous only in the middle 'thirties when the disappointed old republicans joined forces with the Socialists who were a product of new economic conditions but who also saw their party as the logical continuation of the social Revolution. Where the English 'alarmists', rather than the 'calmists' of 1830, were therefore proved right was in suspecting that there were no longer *final* revolution settlements. The pessimist Tories, although they hastened to read the new revolution in the light of the old one, were only right in sensing a new social revolution coming into existence in France under their eyes, against middle-class government which was frankly using its position to economic advantage. The period of the Restoration was obviously over. The struggle was no longer one of parties, political interests, revolutionary memories, and feudal privileges. It was a starker conflict between property and poverty, between those who did well out of 1789 and 1830 and those who felt cheated. In this sense the old revolutionary tradition of 1789 now became a conservative force, while the new revolutionaries, even though they rooted themselves in the Great Revolution, were really working toward a new social revolution, in industrialized France. The social democratic movements which arose in France and England in the 'thirties frankly wanted to obtain social reforms and a redistribution of property through political power.

'Accepting the Revolution', therefore, now acquired a new meaning. Earlier it had meant accepting the Revolution of 1789 as a natural product of history. Burke and the European Reaction had rejected it as an aberration. But when Reaction, Romanticism and Religion failed to maintain a united front in politics or in history, the principles of 1789 were gradually accepted by liberals and conservatives alike as part of their heritage. But to accept revolution as a live force, to accept a social revolution now gathering force—on this there was far less agreement for this historical question was truly one of life and death. The earliest anti-Jacobin hysteria had been right in that it recognized that the Revolutionary spirit had a mobile life of its own. The Revolution of 1830 curiously lulled the fear at first. It was the opposition to the settlement of 1830 which made people suspect that a revolutionary streak had come to stay in the life of Europe. Some had seen it earlier, but it was socialism, above all, which made the permanent revolution manifest, even before this notion of the permanent revolution was dialectically thought out. The *Edinburgh* called it simply 'the domestication of revolution'.

One of the roots of French socialism was in a religious revival. Buchez represented in Revolutionary history the marriage of religion and democracy, the movement uniting Catholicism and revolution, the belief that Catholicism in its purity was the religion of the suffering masses, that social and spiritual aspirations will be answered together. Lammenais and Lacordaire had moved in the same direction and Buchez looked upon them as allies. Buchez connected these ideas, apparently so opposed to the anti-religious strain in French Revolutionary thought, with the heritage of 1789. Romanticism and especially Chateaubriand had connected Christianity with all that the Revolution negated and destroyed. Buchez wished to separate Catholicism from absolutism which had degraded it. Under the Restoration the church of Rome was for the first time established in a constitutional country. Though experience pointed the other way there were men who believed this to be a healthy condition of things. They said that the association with power had degraded Catholicism and they expected that association with liberty would undo the evil. Buchez went even further. The theory that France, Catholicism, Revolution and Liberty were created to be in fruitful harmony made Buchez who had been an ardent Jacobin also into an ardent Christian. He made a valuable collection of obvious but important revolutionary materials to illustrate his ideas of democratic Catholicism. The *Parliamentary History* (1834–8) was a convenient selection (made with an eye to the hero and the cause) which made it possible to write second-hand histories of the Revolution without much pain. The forty volumes contain prefaces dedicated to the Saint-Simonian ideas and to the hero-worship of Robespierre.

The English were bewildered by this swarm of new theories all tending, as it appeared, towards spreading discontent and revolutionism. Some like Smyth, in fear and disgust, bundled together Saint-Simonianism, Owenism, Benthamism, Democracy, Republicanism, Chartism, Socialism, as revivals of French Revolutionary visionary and chimerical ideas, unfounded in human nature, contrary to divine revelation, utopian and dangerous. It was common to compare the new Benthamite and pre-Marxian economists with the physiocrats in order to discredit them.

English socialism was not connected with the French movement nor did it grow from the tradition of the French Revolution. In England it was rather the historically minded Whigs and even Tories who went back to their immediate reaction to the Revolution (which took it to be a movement similar to English movements) and who came to accept the principles of 1789 as principles which England itself could either produce or absorb. English socialism, on the other hand, grew out of modes of thought eminently unhistorical. There was in England an indigenous socialism of which the first generation (including Spence, Ogilvie, Paine and Godwin) was, indeed, connected with the French Revolution. Spence, in particular, had ideas similar to those of Babeuf. But this movement had failed and the generation of Gray, Thompson and Hodgskin constructed their scientific systems from different materials. In France the Saint-Simonians and other groups although they had abstract ideas as well as a recent industrial origin always felt the need to strike roots into the French Revolution, as Buchez so prominently did. In England scientific socialism, Philosophical Radicalism, and the working-class movements turned their back on history.

Bentham's contempt for the study of history is well known as is his aversion from the French Revolution, its spirit, ideals, mystical theory of rights. When he became a republican, it was an abstract new republicanism he adopted, just as his earlier conversion to parliamentary reform had been a belated abstract conversion so different in aim or method from the old reforming interests continuously held by the old Radicals of the eighteenth century. Philosophical Radicalism continued and developed the most abstract and anti-historical trends of eighteenth-century thought. Though it was later modified in the hands of Bentham's lieutenants to suit prevailing English attitudes, even to religion, this was done in order to meet the needs of practical Radical politics and did not affect the unhistorical approach to society.[1] Bentham's disciples, like Hodgskin, who prepared the way for Marxian economics, and Thompson, ignored history altogether. We go through their life and work and we find no mention of the French Revolution.[2] 'Benthamite historiography' written by Mill and Grote significantly chose far-off periods and places. These historians did not seek a personal or continuous connection with any past; they simply projected into remote societies the abstractions of utilitarianism. The indigenous social and socialist movements, therefore, which fed on utilitarianism, economics and Owenism, had no real connection with the French Revolution. It was these movements and not reforming Radicalism which formed the real antithesis to Burkianism in nineteenth-century England. Not because they offered an opposite interpretation of history but because they offered none.

There were, of course, in the working class movement, men who were personally affected by the French Revolution and who professed themselves pupils of French Revolutionary leaders and parties. But this was not perhaps their greatest appeal. The readers and audiences of popular political literature and oratory in England were not on the whole to be won through an evocation of French Revolutionary memories but through facts and figures nearer home. Does not perhaps the very failure of the revolutionary working-class movement prove the limited appeal that imported cries of *aux armes* had on the working-class audiences in England?

O'Brien and O'Connor, of the Chartist leaders, did turn to France for inspiration perhaps because Ireland's association with the French Revolution brought that heritage closer to them. In the popular, unstamped and persecuted working-class press of the 'thirties, the voice of extreme revolutionism, which had not yet been heard on the pages of history, was now associated with a historical attitude to the French Revolution. It was perhaps the first English attempt at a socialist historiography and it is therefore worthwhile to see what it amounted to.

In a series of articles in the *Poor Man's Guardian* (the most important of the early workers' newspapers which openly preached class war),[3] we

---

[1] Even the Radicals treated Saint-Simonianism with suspicion as seen from Thompson's article on Saint-Simonianism in *Westminster* (1832), XVI, 279.

[2] See, e.g., E. Halévy, *Thomas Hodgskin* (London, 1956); R. K. P. Pankhurst, *William Thompson* (1775–1833), 1954.

[3] Published by Hetherington and edited by O'Brien. O'Brien also wrote in the *Operative, Destructive, Poor Man's Conservative, Bronterre's National Reporter*, and others.

have some of the features of the new socialist view of the Revolution. Robespierre is eulogized in a spirit combining the Saint-Simonian religious strain and the communistic theories of Babeuf and Owen. Another recurring sentiment is that Robespierre had been calumniated by history which is the result of the union of talent and wealth against equality. On this extreme view the writer rejects the teaching of Paine who, he says, was justly punished by Robespierre, for he remained loyal to the constitution of 1791 and to the middle classes, and fell short of Robespierre's social reform. 'There was nothing radical in Paine, he never saw to the bottom.'

The most serious attempts at history writing on these principles were made by O'Brien and it is interesting that like most other English writers on the subject, the aim 'to shake the *credit* of "history" and the *authority of great names*' stands foremost in his mind. 'If I prove him [Robespierre] to be the opposite of what history has represented, I, at one and the same time, destroy the credit of history.' But this is not O'Brien's only aim. As he says, 'I wish to benefit the living as well as to do justice to the dead.' His aims are to redeem the cause of democracy from obloquy incurred by the excesses '*falsely imputed* by "history" to the leading democrats of the French Revolution'; to protect the English democrats against 'our deadliest foes', the middle classes; to aid social reform.

O'Brien's social philosophy was expressed in prose and in verse in similar terms. At its basis was the socialist attitude to the middle classes as the worst enemy of the working classes.

Such is the inevitable march of all revolutions which begin in the upper regions of society ... till they reach ... the classes who live by buying and selling ... No revolution has even yet descended, in practice, below the profit mongering classes ... It can be of no permanent use to destroy aristocracies unless you destroy the sources of accumulation out of which they spring ... When in times of revolution, the profit-monger has, by the aid of the working classes, reduced all the grades ... to his own political level, he flings off his old auxiliaries, and, to keep them down, unites with their and his former oppressors.

Then, he goes on, commences the counter-revolution which brings things back to the initial position. Therefore, he concludes, 'A revolution to be effective must begin at the bottom ... and the first blow must be struck at the profit-monger'. This, therefore, is not a theory of a fixed and inevitable process of revolution but rather an argument for reversing it.

> These latter knaves, self-styled the Third Estate,
> Professed to represent the Industrial Class:
> As well to wolves might sheep entrust their fate.
> They fleec'd us, and disfranchis'd us in mass.[1]

[1] J. B. O'Brien, *An Elegy on the Death of Robespierre* (London [1857]).

In O'Brien's interpretation the *Tiers État* sought the same changes as the 'Reform Act of 1831 effected for the middle classes of this country'. Up to 1830 the middle classes had kept back because 'their dread of innovation was greater than their ambition to rule'. After 1830 cowardice gave way under two influences, Peel's Currency Act and the Paris Revolution. The boroughmongers, on the other hand, decided that half a loaf was better than no bread and reform was passed through a partnership. O'Brien moves easily between English and French associations. The Girondins, he says, would have kept working-men down just as the Whigs did in 1832. It is the same if you do it by priest, bayonet or money. One interesting thing about the English socialist historiography is that they did not defend the Terror as such. They simply shifted the responsibility for it to people they disliked, and away from Robespierre. It was the anti-Robespierre party, they say, which was responsible for the September murders and the Terror.

The most French Revolutionary figure in the working-class movement, apart from O'Brien, was Julian Harney who early styled himself Marat and always signed *L'Ami du Peuple*. His oratory especially was a conscious attempt to emulate the revolutionary speeches. 'Hail, spirit of Marat! Hail! glorious apostle of Equality!! . . . whose imperishable title I have assumed'[1] is a typical example. Harney was also personally connected with Marx and Engels; he was the first man to publish the Communist manifesto in England. His recent biographer[2] writes that Harney could not have been more imbued with French Revolutionary ideas had he been French. Like O'Brien, who influenced him much, Harney parted from Owen's utopian socialism and adopted as his aim the conquest through revolution of political power for the purpose of social revolution. O'Brien learnt from history the simple analogy that in England of 1832 as in France of 1791 the middle classes betrayed the working classes, starting a counter-revolution against equality. Robespierre embodied working-class aims and O'Brien hoped to be the English Robespierre.

Harney went further than O'Brien. Starting from Babeuvian communism in the 'thirties he consistently represented within Chartism the extreme revolutionary party which agitated for physical force, for an international outlook, and for imitating the French Revolution. These trends Harney wished to embody in the Democratic Association which was to be a sort of Jacobin Club watching over the activities of the English 'Convention'. Its meetings were accompanied by French Revolutionary allusions and symbols (caps, tricolors). Harney's line was more successful in Scotland which had had a Convention in 1793, and never became typical of Chartism as a whole.

Harney wrote in the *London Democrat*, which started its life on 13

[1] *London Democrat*, 13 Apr. 1839, p. 5.
[2] A. R. Schoyen, *The Chartist Challenge: a portrait of G. J. Harney* (London, 1958).

April 1839, a series of articles called, 'Scenes and Sketches from the French Revolution', in order that the English Revolution, 'which will speedily take place', should avoid the errors and imitate the heroism of Republican France. The articles quote from O'Brien and others but derive mainly from the 'liberal, stock-jobbing, mountebank Thiers'.[1] The first instalment is on the causes of the Revolution and its summary runs thus: 'The great predispossessing causes of the Revolution were:—the Oppression and Misery of the Peasantry:—The Corruption and profligacy of the Court and Aristocracy:—The Abuses in the Army:—The Writings of the "Philosophers":—The Influence of the American Revolution:—And lastly the Discontent an[d] Selfish Ambitions of the Middle Classes.'[2] Obviously there is nothing narrow or limited in this view of the causes. It merely repeats the stock list, in a tone conveying the condemnation of the middle classes. For this is the one novelty of the English 'socialist' interpretation. The awareness of the economic interests of the French *bourgeoisie* during the Revolution, the greater attention to the social legislation attempted against them and hence their admiration for Robespierre. The revolutionary process described by the socialists is exactly the same as in Whig or Tory historiography. The difference lies in interests and in sympathies. Where the Whig and Tory saw the economically strong and intellectually developed middle classes rightly advancing to share in political and economic power, the working-class historians identified the same historical process, only they called it worse names. Harney sees history as simply a continuous process of exploitation of the working classes. Although Harney was an associate of Marx and Engels in revolutionary activity, he never became a theoretic disciple. His only philosophy was 'Babeuvian égalitarianism based on natural right'. He was empirical and as remote from German philosophical communism as he was from the 'Feudal' Young-England movement. Neither he nor O'Brien ever accepted historical determinism and to them French history since 1794 was simply a continuous reaction to be struck at, but not a necessary historical stage.

Harney in the end went the way of all Chartist and working-class movements in England, which soon took a constitutional form. The Anti-Corn-Law League and the changing attitude to Parliament as representative of the nation rather than of certain classes were the channels into which English revolutionism flowed. Harney, whose life almost spanned the whole century, came to believe in the gradual passage into law of the Chartist aims. He symbolized the 'bourgeoisation' of the working classes, abandoned the class struggle, accepted the alliance of middle-class radicals against which he had fought, and let revolutionary Socialism die with resignation, disillusionment and pessimism.

[1] *The London Democrat*, No. 4, 4 May 1839, p. 25.
[2] *Ibid.* p. 6.

Harney was neither a historian nor a historically minded thinker. He was one of those would be 'professional revolutionists' who looked to history for models of flesh and blood revolutionists to prove inspiration and moving examples. O'Brien (though he was no real socialist and in 1848 opposed the use of force) and Harney emulated the line of revolutionists Marat, Robespierre, Babeuf, Buonarroti, whom they treated apart from the history of revolutionary events as embodying the spirit and practice of social revolution, as human models of no time and place. In their writings, extreme revolutionism was represented in isolated and unscholarly works. Proper history was not affected by them. Especially since they did not introduce a different interpretation of the Revolution, only still another more extreme set of sympathies. It was the 'conservative' tradition of the French Revolution, that based on liberty and not on equality, which was typical of most English historical writings. Whigs, Tories and Radicals were writing on the basis of more or less common assumptions, especially with regard to property.

CHAPTER 10

STUDIES OF ROBESPIERRE

FIRST STUDENT OF ROBESPIERRE—CROKER

Towards the middle of the century, English historians, always attracted to the biographical side in the Revolution, were becoming especially interested in Robespierre. This was part of a general tendency induced perhaps by the socialist interest in Robespierre, by the publication of personal memoirs connected with him and by the first attempts to comprehend the meaning of the Terror and of the social legislation attempted then. The early historians of the Revolution, agreeing on little else, were united in presenting an inhumanly monstrous picture of Robespierre. Adolphus had early questioned the accepted view recognizing the need for deeper probing. Mignet laid down the basis of a popular explanation. Robespierre, he said, had 'l'avantage d'une seule passion, les dehors du patriotisme, une réputation méritée d'incorruptibilité, une vie austère et nulle aversion pour le sang'.[1] In England, two studies of Robespierre written from different political angles, in 1835 and in 1844, afford an illustration of the development towards more serious scholarship in the English historiography of the Revolution which was taking place in the 'thirties and 'forties of the last century.

Croker's article of September 1835 represents the first valuable contribution to the subject. Though to some it seemed 'written from the *Quarterly* point of view', it is not disfigured by political prejudice. The author's enemies and political antagonists paid tribute to its historical merit.[2] Though it later became Croker's best essay, its first version was written, Croker tells us, on a holiday 'at the sea-side without a single book but the *Liste of Condamnés*'.[3] When he returned he spent 'a couple of days' verifying his recollections. He thought the article miserably short of what it would have been, 'if I had written it at leisure and amidst my books'. As it appeared in 1835, the essay was a review of the *Mémoires* of Robespierre and those of his sister,[4] both of which Croker declared to be useless fabrications. 'The only evidence of its approach to truth', he says, 'is its unimportance.' Croker always believed, as he noted down in his interleaved offprint, that 'if it had not been for this exposure they

---

[1] Mignet, *Rév. Fr.* (1826), I, 412–13.
[2] E.g. Lewes describes it as written by a man 'celebrated for his minute and ample knowledge of the period'.
[3] Croker to Peel, 7 Oct. 1835 (Jennings, II, 283). Peel had written to congratulate Croker.
[4] *Mémoires authentiques de Maximilien Robespierre.* 2 vols. (Paris, 1830); *Mémoires de Charlotte Robespierre sur ses deux Frères* (Paris, 1835).

might have still passed for authentic'. Croker's proof is not crushing. One interesting point is that Charlotte complains that LeVasseur in his *Mémoires* garbled and altered a letter of hers. Croker knows that LeVasseur's so-called memoirs were a fabrication and that the letter alluded to had been printed thirty-six years before LeVasseur in Courtois's *Rapport sur les Papiers trouvés chez Robespierre*. The main achievement of the essay is its attempt to give the devil his due. On the ground of a careful and minute study of his career, Croker saw Robespierre as the most prominent and mysterious of the revolutionaries hitherto only inadequately studied.[1] The main questions of the '*real objects* and *extent* of this ambition—his *motives* and actual *share*' had been left obscure mainly because of 'his being made a scapegoat of all the surviving villains', who 'had loaded his memory with their crimes', and who stifled 'any inquiries which might lead to the separation of his real from his imputed offences'. Croker insists on Robespierre's ability and unimpeached integrity. He had distinguished himself as a lawyer and he lost no time in becoming an eloquent speaker. He rose to power through avoiding direct responsibility and he fell when he assumed it. He was disinterested and incorruptible in spite of calumniators. Croker even considered, as not entirely unlikely, the story that Robespierre had negotiations with the court, because Robespierre himself said, 'It was I who opposed the Court and disdained its presents.'[2]

Of special interest is Croker's discussion of the problems which Robespierre presents to the historian. He believed that Robespierre could never be thoroughly known, and he points out problems which to him seem unanswered and in the present state of research as yet unanswerable. Robespierre's charges against Danton, for instance, are so vague that one surmises either that Danton was conspiring against Robespierre or that Robespierre had to sacrifice Danton to his friends. 'We must leave the question as obscure as we have found it with the difference only, that other writers have evaded it and that our doubt may perhaps have the effect of suggesting some deeper researches into this enigmatical point of the history of the Revolution.' Croker believed, however, that much could still be found out by consulting survivors, contemporary publications and the archives. He gives many examples to vindicate his contention that a more minute attention to chronology, and greater accuracy in general, were essential for understanding the truth about the man's character and career. One example, for instance, shows that 'no two writers seem to agree' on the simple question of the date of Robespierre's accession to responsible authority. Croker himself

---

[1] Gérard Walter's *Répertoire de l'Histoire de la Révolution Française* (Paris, 1941), which lists works published between 1800–1940, according to subject-matter, has Croker's 'Robespierre' as the first item in a chronological list of studies of Robespierre.

[2] *Moniteur* (25 Sept. 1792).

established the date, and, though the discovery is not extraordinary, he is right in saying, that 'with the *Moniteur* open before them, we cannot imagine why all these writers should have stated so vaguely and discordantly', a fact of some importance.[1] Another example relates to an undated note found among Robespierre's papers, which Courtois and others had quoted to prove Robespierre's dictatorial aims, because it says 'Il faut une volonté une'. Croker dates the note by internal evidence (a reference to Custine), as written before July 1793, that is, before Robespierre was in power, and concludes that it referred to the republican will and not to 'the will of one', and that it proved nothing about the designs of the next year.

Another point of interest in the article on Robespierre is the revaluation of the Girondins. Croker's minute scholarship enabled him to disentangle the actions and the motives of the 'minor' characters of the Revolution concerning which the world was still so ignorant; and he discovered many details which distributed the responsibilities more widely so as to include also revolutionaries such as the Girondins. All this chimed in with Croker's political prejudices but did not come out of them. It resulted rather from his care for detail. It was then fashionable except among extreme revolutionaries to think of the Girondins as martyrs and to grant them heroic virtue, if nothing else. Macaulay accepted this legend.[2] Croker did not simply hate those whom others loved, but he reconstructed a case against them, by measuring their share of guilt, and exposing their weakness and hypocrisy. They were only meaner and more contemptible villains, selfish, cruel, and cowardly, with the chance, but not the energy or humanity, to save their country.

Against such a timid flock of praters and intriguers, weathercocks and trimmers, who were base enough to arrogate the merits of crimes which they had not committed, and who skulked and cowered under the storm they had raised, it is not surprising that the insane audacity of Marat, the ferocious energy of Danton, and the cold blooded calculation and inflexible consistency of Robespierre, should have prevailed.[3]

How far more penetrating this judgment than the similarly iconoclastic blast against the Girondins from the revolutionary O'Brien, who in his *Life of Robespierre* wrote, 'The Girondists consisted of lawyers, bankers and babbling literati who, jealous of the nobility and privileged orders, sought to swindle the Government . . . into their own hands.'

In the English historiography about the middle of the century, the political attitude is favourable to the Girondins on the part of Tories

[1] Croker, *Essays*, 367.
[2] Alison the Tory also spoke of the 'illustrious leaders of the Gironde' with no less admiration than the Radicals in the *Westminster*, when, e.g., reviewing Brissot's *Memoirs* (1830).
[3] Croker, *Essays*, 352.

like Alison, liberals like Macaulay and Radicals like Mill. Those who questioned this attitude were either the working-class writers denouncing the middle classes, like O'Brien or historians like Croker and Carlyle, of any or no political camp, who had made a scholarly effort to study and evaluate the actual part the Girondins played in the Revolution. In the struggle with Robespierre and the Jacobins, according to Croker, they were the aggressors. They accused them of intending to establish a dictatorship when the sober Jacobins knew there was no escape from anarchy except in the concentration of power. Their imputations against Robespierre were vague, ridiculous and not in any way 'grounds for a formal criminal charge'. They would have treated Robespierre as he treated them, and their conduct at the trial of the King was baser. The evidence of Thiers against them, wrote Croker, had 'almost the weight of a confession', and he admitted that they voted for death out of fear.

Written without a library, the main part of the article has the advantage of freely summing-up much thought and reading about Robespierre and his times, but, for the same reason, it also indulges in excessive scrutiny of the spurious memoirs it reviews. There are in fact more collations of other historians' works than could easily be done in a 'couple of days'.[1] We know from the correspondence of Croker and Murray that the last stages of writing were done in a hurry, that books passed to and fro while the proofs were coming out. Some of the evidence is irrelevant or not integrated. One of the minute tasks later improved on at leisure was an interesting piece of statistics based on the various lists of victims and minutes of the Revolutionary Tribunals, and showing that the number of executions was highest when Robespierre was strongest and safest. This approach to such questions as the necessity for the Terror was to become common later, but Croker was perhaps the first to tackle them in this practical manner and to attempt to answer them through laborious research. Croker considers, for example, the opinion, held among others by Napoleon, that Robespierre was inclined to moderate the Terror and fell victim to these attempts. Croker believes that Robespierre had such intentions but—and nowhere is Croker's legal and chronologically approach better exemplified—'the . . . facts . . . chronologically considered, form . . . irresistible evidence that the Reigns of Robespierre and of Terror cannot be distinguished in fact, or separated in reason'.[2] He arrived at this judgment by examining the measures adopted by the Committe since it was joined by Robespierre, and by counting executions. Though aware of the fallacy of *propter, quia post*, Croker admits that 'the steps of Robespierre were followed so exactly and so invariably by the

---

[1] Croker's model of a book-drawing room held 3000 volumes and he worked in another room which held 1000.

[2] Croker, *Essays*, 373.

streams of blood' that the casual connection is forced on us. He had, says Croker elsewhere, absolute mastery and might have shown some tendency to moderation had he had it, 'but instead of any such symptom, the march of legal massacre became more rapid and bloody'. This contradicts Croker's statement elsewhere that, once Robespierre was alone, he 'stood on an eminence so narrow that he could not turn, and so high that he could not descend'.

From the *Liste Générale des condamnés* Croker extracted some results to 'astonish the reader and prove that the executions grew gradually with the personal influence of Robespierre'. Croker sums up the figures of victims for the period between 17 August, when the Revolutionary Tribunal was first instituted, to 27 July, Robespierre's fall. The numbers rise from 3 to 835, gradually at first and by leaps and bounds later. To maintain his thesis Croker should have explained why the only retrogressions after Robespierre's election to the Committee occur in November, after the execution of the Girondins, when Robespierre's power was rising. Also, the number of victims during Robespierre's last fifty days of attendance of the Committee was 577 and that for the forty-five days of his absence 1286. Croker's explanation is that St Just, Couthon and Fouquier Tinville were receiving daily directions.

The real work began after the article had first been published in 1835. The article itself, the materials for it in the Croker Collection, and Croker's manuscript notes enable us to estimate the care which went into its production. Murray continued to send books, and Croker made journeys to the Museum. He had an interleaved offprint in which he made additions and corrections for twenty years. This copy reached Morse Stephens who offered it to the Museum, in a letter now bound with it. When the article 'Robespierre' was reprinted in 1857, it had swelled to double its size,[1] and incorporated many of the alterations. The result was not only the most critical study of the existing Robespierre materials, but also an astonishingly fair estimate of the man himself. The new essay was based on a more thorough and extensive study of the materials. It reduced the earlier preoccupation with the worthless memoirs it reviewed,[2] modified the tone, elaborated detail, considered new publications, notably Lamartine and Michelet, went deeper into contemporary publications and added information of a technical kind.[3]

Croker's appreciation of Robespierre's powers had grown since 1835. A sentence which had treated lightly Robespierre's legal reputation in

---

[1] From 63 to 130 pages.

[2] Croker deletes, for instance, the discussion of the series in which Charlotte's memoirs appeared, from the list of proofs that they were a fabrication. He leaves out also the elaborate examination of Laponneraye's motives. See *Essays*, 301–2.

[3] Croker's materials are mainly in a collection he made and called *Recueil des oeuvres de Maximilien Robespierre et de pièces pour servir à son histoire*, par J. W. Croker, 11 vols. (1819).

Arras, was replaced by a long argument proving that 'as early as 1783 we find him distinguishing himself . . . in a great cause'. The cause is that of Robespierre's defence of a paratonnere, 'not mentioned by any of his historians or biographers', which Croker found in the *Mémoires de Bachaumont*. Croker had known of it in 1835 but had dismissed it with contempt. He now used pre-revolutionary materials and insisted that their high praise of Robespierre, uninfluenced by prejudice or interest, proved Robespierre's talents which had so often been underestimated.[1] In the light of his greater appreciation of Robespierre's powers, Croker also assembled proof of his scholarship[2] and denied that he could have met Rousseau or written the nonsensical dedication attributed to him, in which 'the perilous career which an unheard of revolution opens to us' was an obvious anachronism.[3] He refused to believe Thiers and his source, Madame Roland, that Robespierre was a heavy and pedantic speaker, partly because this criticism was written in prison where Robespierre had thrown his critic. The legend of Robespierre's political insignificance had been started early by the widely used *Deux Amis*. Carlyle and Michelet characteristically fell for it. It was through the contemporary journals that this could be disproved and Croker was therefore on the right track.

A new point of interpretation in the revised essay concerns the party politics of the year 1792, which, in Croker's opinion, held the key to the understanding of the period and also offered many puzzles. In this connection Croker adds eight pages on Robespierre's life and on his political relations with Madame Roland who offered him asylum in the days of the Champs de Mars.[4] When he reaches the last phase of Robespierre's career, Croker narrates more than analyses. Like most English historians including even Smyth he is carried away by the tragic quality of the human interest and his narrative for once becomes dramatic. He admires Robespierre's last words, 'Cowards, why did you not defend him then?', referring to Danton. Like Acton, later, he conducted endless research into the details of Robespierre's death and disbelieved all the popular accounts of it.

---

[1] *Q.R.* (1835), LXXV, 525; Croker, *Essays*, 308. See also *Q.R.* (1835), LXXV, 528; Croker, *Essays*, 312, where Thiers's view that Robespierre was a bad speaker is traced to the prejudiced evidence of Madame Roland in her prison. See also *Q.R.* (1835), LXXV, 529; Croker, *Essays*, 313; where a footnote adds statistical proof for Robespierre's eloquence, based on the frequency of attacks on him in the royalist press.

[2] *Q.R.* (1835), LXXV, 524; Croker, *Essays*, 306.

[3] *Q.R.* (1835), LXXV, 525; Croker, *Essays*, 308.

[4] Croker adds 8 pages of data on Robespierre's life, a study of Madame Roland, a defence of her moral character against Lamartine and Thiers, numerous changes in detail and in argumentation. E.g. Robespierre's figure of 6000 spectators in the galleries which Croker had disbelieved was later corroborated by Rivarol. There are more interesting changes of interpretation regarding, e.g., the decree that members of the Assembly could not be re-elected.

ATTEMPTS AT EXPLANATION

In 1843, Lord Brougham, who knew Lakanal, Mignet and Carnot well and who was a diligent but superficial student of the Revolution, published some of his series of *Historical Sketches* which contained articles on some outstanding revolutionaries as well as a long study of the Revolution as a whole. He later corrected the severity of his judgment on Danton but the article on Robespierre, which relies on the unreliable Courtois, illustrates the evils of Whig historiography at the time. To protect their liberalism at home, they still tended to make unhistorical pronouncements on the Revolution. They were anxious to condemn anything which might cast a shadow over their English liberalism so that they needed a villain like Robespierre who had violated liberty. Brougham's article leaves us with an accumulation of adjectives describing the revolutionary but with no real Robespierre. It was answered in a remarkable review in the July 1844 issue of the *British and Foreign Review*. This review shows a profound understanding of two major points: the question of what made Robespierre so powerful and the question of what makes him so hateful. It says, 'When a human selfishness, fierce and ravenous, as that of the most ferocious wild beast, regards its own gratification as a duty and a virtue, we have the degree of fanaticism whether religious or political which has raised so many scaffolds and lighted so many fires. And this must be viewed as the master key to Robespierre's character.'

The article is full of examples of the collation of evidence on factual questions; it is impartial, laboriously establishing the ability of Robespierre which had been greatly doubted, while showing with prophetic assurance how the man's conviction of virtue and duty became an actual curse. As a piece of characterization and in its exposure of an underlying idea which acts as a historical force, the essay stands above other contemporary work on the subject. In its overall understanding of Robespierre's personality, including his early humanitarianism, it is in advance of Croker. The interpretation of Robespierre through the convictions which the man had of his own virtue and righteousness would be developed further nowadays, but there is the beginning of an approach which leaves behind mere recriminations or purely political explanations and embarks on thought in the direction of the psychological basis of the total tyranny of virtue. The reviewer wrote that Robespierre's tyranny would have been 'the most intolerable ever known upon earth, being at once a religious, moral and political tyranny'. This approach to the man would now be widely recognized as correct.[1]

This review and the article by Croker are amongst the most important writings on the Revolution in that period. Croker hated Robespierre

[1] See M. Beloff, *The Age of Absolutism* (1954), p. 177.

and all he stood for; while the writer of the other article was taken to be writing in the man's defence. The latter was, in point of fact, writing against Brougham who had dismissed Robespierre (as Carlyle had done) as a contemptible mediocrity; and he relied partly on the findings of the arch-Tory Croker, of whom he says that he was one of the few who had read Robespierre's speeches and that 'he consequently does more justice to him than those who have taken their opinions at second hand'. The political distinctions in the English historiography of the Revolution had never been clear. Now the blurring of the party line was carried further. The principle of division was changing. It was moving, on the one hand, into conformity with the distinctions which came in with the new philosophic interpretations of history, such as idealism or materialism though this never became a common test in England; and on the other hand towards the direct distinctions between professional historical scholarship and the mere use of history for the airing of views.

SOCIALIST AND POSITIVIST—O'BRIEN AND LEWES

O'Brien's *Life of Robespierre*[1] is the only attempt at the time to defend Robespierre's political and social aims. It is important, however, to note that unlike later socialists O'Brien did not defend the policy of terror itself. On the contrary he attempted to reduce Robespierre's responsibility for it. O'Brien's *Robespierre* was undertaken after his translation of Buonarroti's history of the Babeuf conspiracy. As all his work, it was done for the political purpose of extolling his hero. O'Brien does not hope to convince all his readers. 'The more godlike I prove Robespierre's conduct to have been—the greater will be the horror in which his memory will be held by the upper and middle classes.' The purpose of his efforts is to discredit what he always refers to as 'history', and which he consciously thought of as an enemy to be destroyed. He surveys previous writings and is vaguely aware of a recent change towards greater understanding of the revolutionary. He knew Croker's article, but not its value. 'If I prove that all the crimes imputed to Robespierre . . . were, in reality, committed by his assassins, . . . I perform a signal service to my country, in as much as I release radicalism from a load of obliquy . . . and destroy, by anticipation, the credit of similar calumnies which may be levelled against the would-be-Robespierre of my own country'. Like all English historians O'Brien distrusted Thiers and Mignet who, 'crafty fellows' that they are, know that 'extravagance went to destroy their credit' and they therefore chose to portray Robespierre as a 'political bigot of mediocre intellect', who had 'neither the force nor the genius of ambition'. O'Brien's comment is, 'The sole ambition

---

[1] J. B. O'Brien, *The Life and Character of Maximilian Robespierre* (London, 1837). See also above, pp. 160–62.

of Robespierre's life was to establish the reign of virtue ... to establish a reformed organization of society, based on the political and social equality of all its members.'

The *Life of Robespierre* by Lewes reflects the revival of interest in the Revolution as a result of the upheaval of 1848.[1] That upheaval, said Lewes, had brought 'Robespierre's name and doctrines into alarming prominence',[2] and its effects entered into the composition of the biography. Lewes often paused to make comparisons between the Great Revolution and 1848 though some of these are very trivial. He stops, for example, to quote from a current newpaper the report that a women's club in France had voted in favour of the existence of God.[3] Lewes represents the strong interest in biography and in the detailed narration of the events, typical of the period, as well as the new preoccupation with the social ideas at work in Revolutionary times. This latter was taking the place of the old kind of 'speculation' on the lessons of the Revolution. Lewes exaggerates when he says that his book contains 'everything known' about Robespierre, though he had a wide knowledge of previous works on the subject. He used and reproduced some unpublished letters of Robespierre lent him by Louis Blanc. He is really a compiler, however, using the new French histories while taking no pains to be accurate, critical or systematic. As the narrative progresses it seems that his sources narrow down to almost a single book—the Lamartine whom he admired and whom he followed on questions of fact and of interpretation.

Though Lewes belonged to the positivist school which included several revolutionary students, his political views were less extreme than those of Harrison for instance, so that his work on Robespierre was acceptable to ordinary radicals like Stephens. It is mentioned by the *Encyclopaedia Britannica* of 1856 as 'probably the most unbiased account'.[4] It seems that he set out with a general approval of Robespierre's achievements but that, in the course of studying the man's character, he acquired a disgust which outweighed his initial political understanding and aim of a human picture of Robespierre. This made him turn against Robespierre but his analysis of the fanatic's character (though based on a notion he learnt from Lamartine that to suffer for truth is a virtue but to make others suffer for it is not) is unconvincing. He stresses the dogmatism, the pride masked as love of truth and sees Rousseau's influence in every revolutionary act.

The revival of studies of Robespierre in England signified a more

[1] Lewes expressed the hope that recent events had not provoked him into producing the book with 'unseemly haste', but all his critics accuse him of just that.

[2] Lewes, *Robespierre*, p. iv.   [3] *Daily News* (10 June 1848); Lewes, 337 n.

[4] The *E.B.* was not at this stage a judge of historical scholarship. The article on French Revolutionary history had been reprinted without changes in the 1856 8th edition, from the earlier editions. The accounts in the *E.B.* right through the century are favourable to the Revolution and France. 'Even in her most violent moods, her principles have been right, her theories humane and noble.'

scholarly approach to revolutionary history. From different political camps historians and publicists attacked the enigmatic Robespierre. Understanding, as is human, brought sympathy from unexpected quarters. We find, for instance, in the *Athenaeum* review of Lewes's work that, 'Whatever opinion may be entertained of Robespierre's revolutionary career, there can be no dispute as to the purity of his life and character.'[1]

[1] 'Lewes's Life of Robespierre', *The Athenaeum* (March 1949), p. 248. Robespierre is described as one of the great men of history (like Socrates, Mohammed, Luther) who represent an idea. He represents the sovereignty of the masses.

CHAPTER II

JOHN WILSON CROKER

REPUTATION

Croker was a well-known and widely hated man.[1] His fierceness in political controversy, his malignity in personal quarrels, and his heartlessness in literary criticism,[2] gave him the reputation of a 'human deathwatch beetle'.[3] His friends used him for his powers and in his enemies he inspired some of the vilest character-sketches in literature.[4] All this for his own and for later generations obscured his sound merits as a historian. Though his interest in the Revolution and his familiarity with its details have always been known, Croker's work as a historian has not been fully appreciated. Stephens in 1886 mentioned Croker's writings with Smyth's as 'the most valuable English works upon the subject',[5] and Thompson today lists Croker's book as one of the best fifty books on the subject. Gooch did not include him in his chapter on the historiography of the Revolution, and Acton, though he devoted a page of his bibliographical essay to Croker as collector, and interested himself in the Croker–Alison rivalry, did not own a copy of Croker's *Essays*. In French bibliographies, his collections are highly prized, but his own work is often ignored.[6]

Croker the historian was a less interesting figure to his friends than Croker the critic and political adviser. His politics were a visible force and his criticism a deadly weapon, while his historical interests were called upon rather in after-dinner conversations. On such occasions, however, they were in great demand. Louis Philippe in English exile must have shared the general expectation of a Revolutionary history from Croker, for he used to talk to him on Revolutionary scenes and figures. In Tory circles, Croker was the undoubted authority. The Duke of Wellington and others told him their reminiscences, Peel corresponded with him on

[1] There is a defence of Croker's character in J. A. Strahan, 'The Founder of the Athenaeum' [J. W. Croker], *National Review* (Nov. 1923), LXXXII, 414.

[2] A review of Keats's *Endymion* attributed to Croker, in *Q.R.* (May 1818), XIX, was alleged by Byron and by Shelley to have killed Keats. See, e.g., Shelley's Preface to *Adonis*. Earlier a satire of Croker was said to have killed an Irish actor Edwin Young.

[3] Keith Feiling, *Sketches in Nineteenth Century Biography* (1930).

[4] Croker was the model for Rigby in Disraeli's novel *Conningsby* (1844).

[5] H. M. Stephens, *A History of the French Revolution*, vol. I (London, 1886), p. iv. Stephens studied both Croker's collections and his writings.

[6] Fortescue, who published the first catalogue of Croker's Collections in 1899, had a great admiration for Croker. Croker's volumes of materials, he declared, 'the most interesting and the most suggestive book in the English language, on the Revolution'. See below, pp. 300–2, for a note on the bibliography of Croker.

Revolutionary as well as on other matters and urged him to write a history,[1] Southey admitted that Croker was the only man who knew more about the subject than he did;[2] revolutionary students like Alison and even some anonymous reviewers paid tribute to his scholarship.

The only contemporary attempt to define Croker's historical talent was made by Carlyle who was more interested in the art and craft of history than most of his contemporaries. Croker, wrote Carlyle, had 'a certain anecdotico-biographic turn of mind, natural or acquired; we mean a love for the minuter events of History, and talent for investigating these'. He said that Croker was diligent, 'made inquiries perseveringly far and near' and contributed much knowledge that he had to dig for. This was written in connection with Croker's edition of Boswell's *Johnson*,[3] for which Croker had conducted extensive research. Boswell's recent editor confirms that Croker did 'systematic unveiling' and had access to valuable manuscript material.[4]

Carlyle not only understood something of the nature of Croker's talent, he also made the discovery that Croker, though a politician, was perfectly impartial in his historical annotations. Carlyle was also the first historian who attempted, without success, to use Croker's collections of revolutionary materials in the British Museum. When, after the middle of the century, the fame of the collections began to spread, through Louis Blanc and others, their unique value, though it reflected on the collector, did not enhance the appreciation of his work. The anonymity of the book reviews,[5] in which all Croker's historical work appeared,

[1] Peel to Croker, n.d. (1835?): 'I wish you would think seriously of the History of the Reign of Terror. I do not mean a pompous, philosophical history, but a mixture of biography, facts, and gossip' (Jennings, II, p. 276).

[2] 'You are much better acquainted with the history of the French Revolution than I am. Perhaps you are the only person of whom I could say that' (Southey to Croker, 26 Sept. 1832). An unpublished letter quoted by M. F. Brightfield, *John Wilson Croker* (London, 1951), p. 321.

[3] T. Carlyle, 'Boswell's Life of Johnson', *Fraser's* (May 1832). *Critical and Misc. Essays*, vol. III (1899), p. 63.

[4] The merit of Croker's edition has been much debated and it was the subject, though not the cause, of Macaulay's bitterest attack. Macaulay made known his intentions with regard to the edition before it came out (G. O. Trevelyan, *Life and Letters of Lord Macaulay* (1876), I, 218). Birkbeck Hill, though contemptuous of Croker's mind, acknowledges the value of Croker's findings, which 'but for his care would have been lost for ever'. L. F. Powell who revised Birkbeck Hill's edition in 1934 considered Croker's systematic unveiling 'as the most important feature of his edition'.

[5] The secrets of authorship in the *Q.R.* were jealously preserved. Gifford, the first editor, instructed his executor, Dr Ireland, to destroy all his papers 'especially those relating to the *Quarterly Review*' (Sir John Barrow, *Autobiographical Memoir* (London, 1837), p. 513). (Barrow was a contributor to the foundation of that review.) T. Martin, in the *D.N.B.*, writes that no list of Croker's reviews 'has ever been made public', but his estimate of 260 articles is not too wide of the mark. An instance of the uncertainty about authorship is the review of Tennyson in *Q.R.* (Apr. 1833), XLIX. The review had been ascribed to Lockhart by Murray, Saintsbury and others. Croker's authorship was finally established in 1937 by Grierson in *T.L.S.* (24 Apr. 1937). The letters which settle the matter are in Michigan. It should be noted, however, that the review was included, presumably by Murray, in the bound collection of Croker's *Contributions* in the C.U.L.

hindered any wide recognition of Croker. While his essays were making their first appearances in the *Quarterly*, scholarly appreciation could hardly gather round a series of desultory, non-academic, unsigned and widely scattered reviews, which seemed moreover to be pervaded by political purposes. The 1857 publication of Croker's *Essays* included the better half, in quality and quantity, of Croker's work, but by that date the procession of the great French Revolutionary histories, down to Tocqueville and von-Sybel, was absorbing all attention, and Croker's work, which was of unusual merit in the first half of the century, failed, when it wandered into a new age, to excite any admiration.

Nothing has so far been done to redress the balance and focus attention on Croker's rightful place in the historiography of the Revolution. Croker's recent biographer, who says that Croker devoted to the study of the Revolution 'a substantial portion of his life', devotes three pages to an account of it.[1] He extracts Croker's political views on the event and some of its personages, thus misrepresenting the nature of Croker's work and the essence of his achievement.[2] Because Croker was a notorious 'ultra-Tory', it is assumed that he was politically prejudiced in his work on the Revolution. The paradox of Croker's 'political prejudice' was that though of all the English historians he most shared Burke's extreme feelings against the Revolution, he adopted a practical method of studying the event which could only serve to refute the unhistorical basis for Burke's *Reflections*, or any sweeping philosophical generalizations about the essential nature of the French Revolution.

THE NATURE OF PREJUDICE

The colour of Croker's politics is unmistakable, but the nature of his prejudice is not as obvious. He himself declared that he had a strong antirevolutionary bias, in full agreement with Burke's, and added that he had not let it affect his judgment.[3] His claim can only be justified by an examination of his method, but something about the nature of his prejudice must be seen in the context of his views on political attitudes. He believed that men were born Whig or Tory, that political principles were inherent and not a matter of theory, that there are two antagonistic principles, stability and change, at the root of all government. 'The former is Tory and the latter Whig; and the human mind divides into these classes as naturally . . . as it does into indolence and activity, obstinacy and indecision . . . Burke's intellect was Tory, Lord Chatham's

---

[1] M. F. Brightfield, *John Wilson Croker* (Berkeley, 1940), pp. 317–19.
[2] Brightfield quoted, for instance, passages expressing hatred of the Revolution and said, 'against this background, Croker sketched the characters'. He said that Croker applied the lessons of the Revolution to his own times and combated the Whig interpretation of the French Revolution as a salutary movement.
[3] Croker, *Essays*, v–vi.

Whig.'[1] Political development or inconsistency is impossible on this view. Croker held, for instance, that Burke changed not his principles but only his opponents.[2] Croker's own 'Conservatism' (he coined the term in 1830)[3] was as consistent and immovable as he believed all men's politics were.

Since political principles were inherent, Croker neither questioned nor expounded them. He fought his political battles to conquer and not to convert, and he fought them on practical issues. Because he regarded a political bias as natural, he was able to leave it out of his historical writings, which are not political arguments in purpose, plan or achievement. Almost all Revolutionary historians then and thereafter claimed impartiality, but it was chiefly those whose bias was most decided, who did not need to look for 'proof', or were above looking for justification, who could leave political argumentation out of their histories. Smyth was fair and impartial, more moderate than Croker, and he wrote for an educational purpose. His politics are, after all, the theme of his lectures. His 'unbiased' approach—his way of viewing every question from every political angle in order to arrive at a fair judgment—is in fact political history writing *par excellence*. Croker never doubted his own political beliefs, nor did he regard history as a means of persuasion. He therefore left his politics out of his historical investigations even though he did not leave his historical knowledge out of his political battles. In Revolutionary history Croker did not distort fact for the sake of political principle. He simply separated the two, thus at least ensuring good faith. He was not detached, for he had a strong bias and expressed it clearly but it was not for the sake of this that he studied the history of the Revolution.

This is true of Croker's best work but it does not represent the spirit in which he started writing on Revolutionary subjects. His first publication of 1801 was a satirical letter to *The Times* on the visit of Tallien to London and his entertainment by the Whigs of Holland House.[4] Though Croker himself called it 'pert and pedantic', typical of an Irishman just

---

[1] Croker to Brougham, 14 Mar. 1839 (Jennings, II, 351).

[2] Memorandum of 1830 (Jennings, II, 83). Croker had held less extreme views earlier. 'I agreed with his Royal Highness that Whigs in power soon assimilate themselves to Tories and that Tories in opposition would soon become Whigs, but that I still thought there were two marked and distinct parties ... which might for brevity be fairly called Whig and Tory' (Croker's note in his diary, on 6 Jan. 1828, of a conversation with the Duke of Clarence, Jennings, I, 401).

[3] 'The word was first used in this sense by J. Wilson Croker in an article published on 1 Jan. 1830; and almost immediately largely took the place of the term Tory' (Murray's *New English Dictionary*, vol. II (1893)). Croker's phrase is: 'Attached to what is called the Tory, and which might with more propriety be called the Conservative party' (*Q.R.* (Jan. 1830), XLII, 276). Brightfield does not list this article on 'Internal Policy' as written by Croker. Macaulay in *E.R.* (July 1832), p. 557, calls it 'the new cant word'.

[4] *The Times* (6 Apr. 1801). Croker came to London in 1801, entered as a student of Lincoln's Inn. He wrote several satirical letters, addressed to Tallien, for *The Times*.

out of College, its manner of dwelling on the ferociousness of the Revolution and the constant attempt to associate the Whigs with the horror, is characteristic of Croker's early writings.[1] In these he expressed general views, drew outlines which read like a *précis* of Burke,[2] and, above all, baited the Whigs. The review of Morellet in 1821[3] is also an example of this polemical style. The party line is strong and Croker misses no opening for a dig at the Whigs. Repentance, he says, mends nothing except reputations; Oxford and Cambridge would be as 'nationalized' as Morellet found the Sorbonne, if the Whigs had their way. Croker's predominant feeling was horror, his object was political. His method was to discredit 'moderate reforms'. This sort of writing Croker was later to use in politics, but not so much in history.[4]

Croker's early writings on Napoleon stand also in marked contrast to his later work. He was a fighting enemy of Napoleon and his essays on him, though loaded with first-hand information, are shaped by a personal, political and patriotic hatred. 'He is the representative of the Revolution—the lineal descendant and heir of all the Neckers and Rolands, the Marats and Robespierres, the Tom Paynes and Anacharsis Cloots.'[5] The polemical tone used by Croker against the Emperor in his greatness pursues the fallen enemy to his grave and survives into the post-mortem examinations. The fairness one would expect is conspicuously absent; information is gathered and brandished even when the battle is over.

In his mature work on the Revolution, Croker genuinely attempted to be just. He exposed Thiers's 'disgusting affectation of humane impartiality' and knew, therefore, that even by doing justice to an opponent, a historian lays himself open to suspicions of subtle deceit. His own fairness was genuine. His treatment of Drouet, for instance, the man who recognized, pursued and stopped the fugitive royal family at Varennes, amounts to a reversal of judgment on a minor character, for whom liberals had nothing but abuse. Drouet impressed Croker, as he

---

[1] See also the review of Madam Dessand in *Q.R.* (May 1811), v, written by Charles Gran', with the help of Croker.

[2] See, for instance, the review of 'Faber's France', *Q.R.* (Aug. 1811), vi, 235. To this book, Wellington told Croker, he owed knowledge which helped him against Napoleon (Jennings, I, 341). Croker's view at that time was that under mob-rule power was bound to go to the most audacious, that later 'the struggle for power became a struggle for life', the vanquished fled and the malignant remained to exercise under various pretexts, the function of 'the people'.

[3] *Mémoires de l'Abbé Morellet de l'Académie Française sur le 18me siècle et sur la Révolution* . . . 2 vols. (Paris, 1821). Reviewed by Croker in *Q.R.* (Oct. 1821), xxvi, 229–42.

[4] Another example is the review of 'Lady Morgan's France', *Q.R.* (Apr. 1817), xvii. It shows Croker's capacity for marshalling a formidable array of facts to prove other writers' errors. It also indulges in calling the revolutionaries abusive names.

[5] Croker wrote that the Jacobins centred their hopes round Napoleon. This he held in spite of information which he got in Paris from Castlereagh, who had it from Fouché. (See Jennings, I, 66.)

later did Acton,[1] by his coolness, efficiency and 'sagacity that would have done him honour in a better cause'. Allowing for his principles, Croker thought that Drouet's conduct at Varennes was 'not as discreditable as it is generally thought. He performed cleverly what he thought a duty.' In the same spirit Croker revalued Robespierre, admired Madame Roland, and even defended warmly the character of Sanson the executioner.[2]

It has been said that the 'booming gong in Croker's conventicle was the French Revolution'.[3] It is true that Croker used the Revolutionary situation as a key to the interpretation of other times and places, though he did not, as is also said, see only black and white. His flair for analogy resulted from his preoccupation with fixed political patterns. His favourite parallel, between revolutions in France and in England, he expounded in detail, drawing up tables and comparing the separate stages and features of the revolutions.[4] The belief in 'like causes producing like effects as true in the moral as in the physical world' makes history abstract, but Croker combined with this belief an unending search for detail and for minute knowledge, the very means which lend individuality to ages and men. He used analogies but he reserved them mainly for his political writings; the essays, which he himself considered historical contributions are governed by his other quality, the search for detail.

VIEW OF THE REVOLUTION

Croker's political view of the Revolution can be found in the article on the causes (attributed to Croker but written partly by Mahon and touched up by Croker),[5] in the general outlines he supplied in 1857 to bridge the gaps between the collected essays, and in scattered remarks elsewhere. They make it clear that his historical studies modified the blind hostility to the Revolution of his earlier years. Croker was born in 1780, and even if he was, as he says, impressed by the event, he did not in childhood undergo the process so common at the time—the transformation of sympathy to hostility. He was educated by French émigrés and grew up in a period of war and disillusionment. From an undiscriminating hatred for the Revolution, he moved to a more historical judgment. He later said that no one could deny the great social, legal and moral grievances of the French nation and 'that a large and deep reform was desirable and inevitable'; that the States General was justly welcomed and could have effected a restoration of the old constitution of France and not a revolution. Earlier he had spoken in defence of the constitution

---

[1] And much earlier, Goethe.
[2] Croker, *Essays*, 534–6, 570–1.
[3] Keith Feiling, *Sketches in Nineteenth-Century Biography*.
[4] See, e.g., Croker, *Essays*, 10.
[5] *Q.R.* (Apr. 1833), XLIX, 152. See Croker's *Contributions*, vol. III, MS. note.

existing in 1789. He said that the course of reform was interrupted by seduction, bribery and the organization of a small but rich Orleanist party. Croker never lost his belief in the all importance of the Orleans conspiracy, a favourite English view which in 1802 had been shared by Tories like Adolphus and Whigs like Jeffery.

Croker even allowed some time to the 'good' revolution, saw it take a wrong turning in October 1789,[1] and found the roots of the evil in the amalgamation of the Orders. But he is not consistent on the general points. In 1811 he spoke of the 'literary machine' which overthrew France, and in 1835 he said that the 'Literary Societies' merely corrupted taste and morals. He never saw the Revolution as a gigantic conspiracy, nor the whole body of deputies as guilty. On the complicity of the nation as a whole, he also held contradictory views. Sometimes he sees the French nation as united in a good cause until the fall of the Bastille, and sometimes he says that the nation went mad with the proclamation of the States General. A more important contradiction is that on the one hand he held that after October 1789 a minority ruled and 'the people of France . . . had little . . . to do with the revolutionary movement',[2] and, on the other, that the whole nation constituted Robespierre's power. His 'force was the *People* itself'.[3] Earlier he had said that the nation was neither 'the Septembrisers', nor the Jacobins. It was a typically Burkian view, shared with the contemporary counter-revolution and inspiring actions like the Brunswick manifesto which hoped to separate the nation from the Jacobins and found that they were one. Croker at first took it over, but later developed out of it one of his best general points, that few historians had recognized the 'regular systematic organized power, never concealed, never intermitted, rarely resisted and always predominant' which was the power of the mob. In different places Croker expressed different views: that terror and corruption were used together, and that the documents show the recurrence of the same rioters; that the irresistible democratic current caused the fall of all the ablest leaders of the Assembly from Lafayette to Danton who attempted to check it; that the Revolution, from the Bastille to the Empire, from the *lanterne* to the military executions, was one long reign of terror.

THE HISTORIAN: PRACTICE AND THEORY

We have said that Croker declared his political views only to leave them in order to write history. It remains to show what his history writing was.

[1] The days of October are the 'real pivot on which the Revolution turned from good to irretrievable evil' (Croker, *Essays*, 14).

[2] Essay on Roederer (Croker, *Essays*, 167). The days of October were directed against the Assembly as much as against the King, he wrote.

[3] The French, says Croker, cannot exculpate themselves (Croker, *Essays*, 399). The bloody extravagances of the times 'outran his predisposition'.

His distinction was that he was the first English historian of the Revolution who was a real student of it, a researcher, with a method, with aspirations for discovery and with results. His merit lies in his attitude of mind as well as in his achievement. It characterizes him more truly than his political prejudice. His treatment of the Revolutionary sources is his chief claim to importance and it connects his writings with his contribution as a collector.

Little merit can be claimed for Croker's early writings before 1832, which were really political ones and gave but little indication of his future development. The search for detail is hinted at, and the interest in the exposure of memoirs is strong by 1823, when Croker studied the open scandal of Lauzun's memoirs, though he discovered nothing himself. The year 1823 seems to be a turning point in Croker's historical work. While reviewing Madame Capman as any partisan of the royal family would, his studies were producing a different kind of crop in the edition of the *Royal Memoirs*[1] and the review of his own edition. In the notes to the edition he intended to preserve details which posterity might forget, and the study of Varennes, in particular, is for Croker the beginning of history for its own sake. Croker simply says it would be interesting to trace an event so important, and, for the rest, he confines himself to detection. Thirty years later, when Croker really wrote the history of the flight to Varennes, this initial study was to seem very much of a beginning. In 1823 he pointed out inconsistencies but declared them unimportant. This was later replaced by a comprehensive study meant to solve all the little mysteries of the narrative. The study of the flight was also the beginning of Croker's consciousness of the problems of historical certainty. It showed him the difficulty of ascertaining fact;[2] it was 'the strongest encouragement to historical scepticism'. It taught Croker how to become a historian by the process of criticizing previous narrators. He also added the same kind of 'anecdotico-biographical' details as in his editions of English works. But he was still collating the evidences of books and made hardly any references to the materials in his collections.

The parallel reviews of the *Royal Memoirs* in the *Edinburgh*[3] and *Quarterly* provide an insight into the contemporary misunderstanding of Croker's method as well as into the parallel developments of Whig and Tory historiography. The Whig charge against Croker of being 'romantic' about the Revolution; the reluctant praise for his historical

---

[1] *Royal Memoirs on the French Revolution.* With historical and biographical illustrations by the translator [J. W. Croker] (London, 1823). Croker reviewed his own edition in *Q.R.* (Jan. 1823), xxviii, 464–74. In it are phrases like 'we must agree with the English Editor...'. There is special praise for the translator for having translated the memoirs of Mme Royale 'with singular attention to the simplicity of naiveté of the diction and that some very interesting biographical and explanatory notes are added'.

[2] Croker points out the contradictions even between the Queen's evidence in her trial and her daughter's narrative.

[3] *E.R.* (Oct. 1832), xxxix, 84. See above, pp. 54–6.

accuracy; the determination to disapprove and the inability to disagree; all these we have noted as typical of the Whigs at the time. They indirectly paid tribute to Croker by bringing out what they considered his non-party views. It was Croker's achievement to be decried as anecdote-monger, rectifier of dates, collator of accounts. The plodding Tory was well on his way to becoming a scholarly historian, leaving his Whig critics behind in the mazes of political debate.

It is after 1823 that Croker, busy with politics, became more occupied than before with the problem of writing history in order to provide truth for posterity. He even contemplated editing Walpole's letters in order to prevent their 'poisoning the sources of history'; he felt compelled to preserve information about his own age, and we often find him, pen in hand, writing to the dictation of the King or others. This is of interest for us here because Croker had not yet criticized French memoirs well, and it seems that he learnt his trade in an English apprenticeship, through observing how different the history of his own time would appear to posterity from what he knew it to be.

All Croker's writings appeared in the *Quarterly*. The list of about 270 articles compiled by Croker's recent biographer contains about thirty connected with the Revolution.[1] The eight essays in the publication of 1857 are based on ten reviews written between 1823 and 1853. When Murray suggested to Croker the reprinting of some of his reviews, Croker could name only a few. 'Four or five papers on the early French Revolution contain much fact and truth that is not elsewhere to be found, for I gleaned them from multitudes of contemporary and now rare and recondite materials.'[2] His principle of selection was the degree of scholarship and originality. Material was chosen which 'may be of use to the future historian'.[3] The ten reviews were rewritten and amalgamated to meet the requirements of the new form and to reflect the study of new materials. One set of changes which Croker introduced was literary. Repetitions were eliminated and gaps were filled by brief summaries. A collection of reviews written over a period of thirty years was thus shown to constitute an almost consecutive history. It supports the view that Croker conducted his own systematic investigations and merely used the publications he reviewed as starting points from which to produce the results of his own work. In one case he writes clearly that the books he reviews are very imperfect but they 'afford us an opportunity of bringing into one view all that we have been able to collect on a subject so neglected'. The first essay, on Thiers, in fact takes us to October 1789

---

[1] Brightfield, *Croker*, p. 453. This list, the best we have, is not absolutely complete.

[2] Croker to Murray, 24 Oct. 1851; Jennings, I, 248.

[3] He longed to reprint the article on 'Macaulay's romance' to supply an antidote to that 'elaborate compound of falsehood and poison'. In that article he said Macaulay would never be referred to by future historians.

and the second treats the Days of October. The study of the flight to Varennes also contains a summary of the preceding period and is followed by an essay on the transition from monarchy to republic and takes us to August 1792. The fifth essay sees the royal family to the grave. The longest is the essay on Robespierre, followed by a study of the Terror through its central machine, the Revolutionary Tribunals. In the preface, Croker speaks of only half a dozen essays and it is unlikely that he changed his mind without changing the preface. The editors may have added two essays after Croker died in the course of the preparations. The study of the 'Guillotine', though full of original research,[1] might not have been included by Croker in a volume which, though based on scattered writings, was recast to form a consecutive narrative covering the period of the revolution down to the 9th Thermidor.

With Adolphus, Alison, Smyth and Scott, Croker belonged to the first generation of revolutionary historians. His distinction, however, is not dependent on the point of time, for he remained, for long, unrivalled in both the nature and the quality of his work, which he described as being conducted with 'something of the accuracy of contemporaries, the diligence of inquirers and the impartiality of historians'.[2] He brought to his studies aims and methods whose future development he alone foresaw. He engaged in systematic research when this was not deemed a necessary preliminary to history writing. Croker's technical asset was a legal training. It supplied him with methods for the discovery of truth, the identification of the guilty, and the reconstruction of a case on the ground of individual and proven facts. His legal approach to history made him a pioneer because it meant that he began the emancipation of history from previous narratives so badly needed at that stage of Revolutionary historiography—the period of the domination of the memoirs. This resulted in a hitherto unknown historical independence. He did not borrow even true narratives; he dealt with single facts, accumulated, examined and arranged. This does not mean that Croker used no authorities, or that he did not ratify some as reliable. We have seen that even with memoirs he was occasionally not critical enough. He often dealt with them in a way usual for that period, that is, he examined their politics and their motives and conjectured the amount of trust they commanded. Croker did not effect a sudden revolution in history writing and his works vary a great deal in quality, but they contain passages in which episodes are reconstructed from individually examined facts and they are full of corrections of other historians' facts. Nor did he achieve the emancipation of Revolutionary history from the memoirs. The quality

[1] Croker made minute and elaborate inquiries into the origin of the Guillotine, and into all the problems connected with it, as, for instance, its exact location at different times. The most interesting parts of the article are the descriptions of 'guillotines' before the French Revolution.

[2] Croker, *Essays*, 562.

which contributes most to make Croker important is his knowledge of the sources. His own hopes to live as a historian were based on this knowledge. It was at the root of the qualities as an independent reconstructor of narrative, as a critic of memoirs and also of his other mark of power, his criticism of historians. Croker's knowledge of the sources meant an absorbed scholarship aiming at the complete mastery of a period and leading to the formation of tried methods of studying that period. His ideas on method appear, along with his criticisms and his reconstructions, in his reviews. They bring out the fact that, in spite of his devotion to the collection and study of sources, Croker had no illusion as to the finality of his resources. He thought wisely and realistically on what is now called the problem of historical certainty—and which, as he saw, has particular significance in the case of revolutions.[1] He thought that on the most important historical issues, especially in revolutions, governments (that is, the state papers) had little to communicate. The important measures would have been adopted after merely verbal consultations. Croker doubted whether a full history of the Revolution could ever be written when 'many of the main springs of action, are, we fear, irrevocably lost'. 'Can we ever hope to know', asks Croker, 'the real history of the immolation of the Hébertistes, or of the Dantonistes, or of the secret counsels of Robespierre, Couthon and Saint Just . . .?' Croker's knowledge of the insufficiency of retrievable sources had influence in preventing him from ever attempting a complete history of the Revolution, though it did not prevent him from studying thoroughly the sources he could find.

In Revolutionary historiography, the age of the memoirs was closely followed by that of the journals which to many (like Alison) seemed to be a source of primary importance. A great Revolutionary collection, that of Deschiens, was based on the principle that Revolutionary journals supply 'all sufficient sources of historical information'. In 1841, Croker criticized this notion.[2] He recognized the partial use of journals for facts and dates, and (as he says elsewhere) for short summaries of debates, but not for causes or motives 'which after all are the soul of history while the naked facts are, as it were, but the skeleton'. Croker's view of the journals was not based merely on theory, for he found that they often failed to supply even the facts and dates. He collected and produced proof that during the important revolutionary years, 1792–5, the journals, paralysed by fear, were directed by the Jacobin Club.[3] He quotes

[1] See E. L. Woodward, *War and Peace in Europe 1815–1870 and Other Essays* (London, 1931).

[2] 'The correspondence of the Committee of Public Safety', *Q.R.* (Mar. 1841), LXVII, 481–500. This is a review of *La Révolution Telle qu'elle est, ou Correspondance inédite du Comité de Salut Public . . . Mise en ordre par M. Legros* (Paris, 1837). The first volume is on the army of the west, and the second on that of the north, both in 1793.

[3] See the essay on the 'Guillotine', Croker, *Essays*, 519–21. Croker points out that among Robespierre's papers was found a letter in which Grandville, the editor of the *Moniteur*, reminded Robespierre that his paper had always been favourable to the Mountain and

important omissions by the leading journals on points of fact. The *Journal de Paris* of 7 October 1789, for instance, ignored the events of the 5th and 6th. The *Moniteur* of 22 January 1793 was silent on the King's execution.[1]

The criticism of the journals leads Croker to one of his most interesting theses on Revolutionary sources, that of the importance of the contemporary ephemeral publications. Something of the same kind had been said by Adolphus, who in many ways was Croker's precursor. Croker developed his idea in the 'thirties and when he maintains it in 1855 he naturally expects criticism. By then, the study of a different kind of contemporary document had already begun, namely, that of 'unconscious records'—those which are left over from an age but which were not intended to become historical sources. Croker did not entirely go over to this new kind of study except perhaps in his independent use of such records as the minutes of the Tribunals and scraps of materials from archives. His own sources were mostly 'conscious', and often turned out to be consciously deceitful. He knew their limitations and dangers and yet made out a case for them. He said that the contemporary publications, 'however ephemeral in interest or apocryphal as authorities, are still valuable and important as contemporaneous evidence, both positive and negative, for what they tell and for what they do not, [and] are often as instructive in their falsehood as in their truth'. In another context he admitted that they were party controversy, mere 'personal attack and apology, crimination and recrimination'. But he claimed that though they must not be believed, their collation reveals information 'on individual characters and even public events'. In another context again, there is an example which might serve to illustrate what Croker means. On the controversial question of 10 August the contemporary publications all give the lie to each other, but Croker traces a principle in them. The immediate publications all blame the King and the counter-revolution for organizing the attack. The charge was included in the King's trial and condemnation, but after his execution, when the struggle between the Girondins and Jacobins began, both parties enter into a squabble for responsibility for this 'patriotic conspiracy'. In this quarrel they reveal facts and motives that would not otherwise have come out, and which help to fix the blame. Croker notes that this aspect of

reported the other side 'just as much as was absolutely necessary to show some appearance of impartiality'. This was not published in Courtois's report to the Convention, but only after the Restoration (Courtois, *Papiers de Robespierre*, p. 131; Croker, *Essays*, 521).

[1] Marat's assassination happened on 13 July 1793. The *Moniteur* mentions it only on the 15th in a report of a debate. Charlotte Corday was tried and executed on the 17th. No journal mentions this before the 23rd, and the *Moniteur* only on the 29th. In the period of the Convention the *Moniteur* is merely a summary of debates and an unreliable one (Croker, *Essays*, 520).

the question escaped Lacretelle, Pagès,[1] and Alison and is only alluded to by Mignet. Adolphus alone of the early historians noted it and published some of the incriminating documents of the case, a letter from Pétion to the Jacobins of November 1792, and Robespierre's reply to it.

Along with contemporary printed material, Croker classed as being also of first rate importance, the unprinted and official papers which had not begun to be studied. He was alert to developments in this line, although he himself did not do more than acquire, 'almost as waste paper', many thousands of official papers, of which, he conjectured, many thousands more must exist in private hands and official archives. He was also aware of the two opposite tendencies of the time, 'the passion for collecting autographs [which] has brought and is daily bringing to light many portions of private correspondence',[2] and the wilful and negligent destruction of incriminating documents. He hoped that unprinted materials would find collectors as printed material had done, but he realized that the main work must wait for the opening of 'the treasures of the archives'. This, he said, could not happen as long as the government of France was in the hands of descendants of revolutionaries. From the King downward, they must all fear the publication of their fathers' correspondence, and they therefore smother all disagreeable truth.[3] Croker must have thought that the government not only concealed, but also destroyed, documents, for in 1835 he refers to the archives which contain, 'or at least did lately, contain a great deal of curious and unpublished matter'.[4] Croker was right in estimating both the value and the inevitable delay of the opening of the archives. They were in fact opened under Napoleon III, who had less to fear from Revolutionary disclosures than any ruler of France down to 1852.

In speaking of the examination of state papers, Croker does not (like Smyth, for instance) mean odd papers that might come to light, but always insists on the systematic investigation of the archives themselves. It is this insistence on systematic investigation which Croker recommended for unpublished materials and practised for published, which is important. When he admits that Thiers alone had examined contemporary publications, he points out that Thiers had not done so systematically, and failed to work 'the veins of the ore thus accidentally opened to him'—a perfect description of what he himself was doing. His unpublished correspondence with Murray shows that he was always searching

[1] F. X. Pagès, *Secret History of the French Revolution*. Translated, 2 vols. (London, 1797); F. X. Pagès, *Anti-revolutionary Thoughts of a Revolutionary Writer: from the Secret History etc.* (London, 1800).

[2] *Q.R.* (1840), LXVII, 485.

[3] Croker was studying the case in which the King of France prosecuted some publishers who had brought out letters by himself.

[4] 'Robespierre', *Q.R.* (Sept. 1835), LIV, 522.

for particular facts at specific points in his studies and the principle on which he had arranged his collections, which is still maintained in the Museum, brings out a method based on the organization of facts round specific events and characters.[1] When part of the military correspondence of the *Committee of Public Safety* came out, the first thing Croker noted is that it could not be official, nor could it originate from a public office, because it was unsystematic. It was not a complete or consecutive collection of even one department. It must, he concluded, be a publication of odd papers which happened to fall into individual hands.

In judging the authenticity of newly published documents Croker was at a disadvantage. When editors attempted to establish the authenticity of their documents, he could pick holes in their arguments; otherwise he could do little. In the case of the Committee's correspondence, he compared some of the letters with a publication of 1793 and found them identical, but for the rest he had to conjecture. On the whole he had little interest in the dry military reports even of Tallien and Fouché. The only new light he found was that thrown on Custine's trial. It had been represented as resulting from public exasperation at defeats; Thiers, and Croker, independently of Thiers, had believed it was an act of public vengeance against Dumourier and an unsubtle hint to Generals. Croker now learnt it was an act of private vengeance.[2]

Croker's absorption in the problems of the sources limited his production. When he learnt the extent of the materials available and the importance of those unavailable, he did not think that anyone could write a perfect history of the Revolution and he never attempted anything beyond throwing light on 'isolated but important episodes by a critical reference to contemporary documents'. When at the Restoration, Croker began to assemble materials, he thought of a Revolutionary history and must have suggested it to Murray, who in 1816 offered him 2,500 guineas, for three volumes of *Annals of the French Revolution* with an appendix of rare materials. He wanted 'a lively, entertaining, interesting and authentic book, for the instructive amusement of the general reader'. The notion that Croker never wrote a book because Alison did,[3] needs to be qualified by the fact that Alison's book only came out seventeen years later. It is more likely that when Croker began to find interesting materials, it occurred to him to write, but then he became too engrossed in the process of collecting and found so much that he postponed writing until it was too late. Croker early became one of

---

[1] See J. W. Fortescue, *List of the Contents of the three Collections of Books, Pamphlets and Journals in the British Museum Relating to the French Revolution* (London, 1899).

[2] *Q.R.* (Sept. 1835), LIV, 556; (March 1841), LXVII, 494–8.

[3] Acton seems to have thought so. 'Croker was against Alison—angry that he was anticipated' (C.U.L. Add. MS. 5433). 'But Alison stopped the way. Croker gave up his plan, offered his rev. library to Alison and ended by disposing of it to the B.M.' (Add. MS. 5649).

those late-century figures of whom it has been said that the greatest investigators of documents never wrote a book. Only a student thoroughly acquainted with the subject and its problems could refrain from writing on it, although he well knew that he was better informed than anybody else. It was a mark of the high standard he set for history that he never wrote one, but it is also a mark of his narrowness and unimaginativeness. He exaggerated the all-importance of detail until it made the task of writing history seem impossible.

Croker realized that a great co-operative endeavour was needed in Revolutionary studies. Caron dates the beginning of collective work and the organization of Revolutionary studies in 1880, due to the approach of the centenary. But the spirit resulting in co-operative history was growing with the accumulation of materials. Blanc showed it when he wished to make known in France for the benefit of others the treasures he had found in the British Museum; Croker, earlier, when he complained that his collections were inaccessible to anyone but himself, and when he sought to encourage the research of others. Croker thought that the great fault of all previous writings on Robespierre was that they did not face the problems. His own intention was to indicate the problems and difficulties of study 'in the hope of directing . . . the attention of those who may have more leisure and better opportunities of investigation'.

Croker also anticipated a tendency which became more general after his time, when the knowledge of sources which made him unique had become wider, namely, the movement towards specialization for the sake of achieving an original contribution. There was a businesslike quality in his writings which was very distinct from the sort of rambling which frequently went on in Revolutionary writings. Subject-matter is dominant with him, and he does not allow his mental associations to intrude and to lead him aside to general reflections.[1] The specializing tendency was helped by circumstances and by the security he had of being heard. If we compare him with Smyth, his direct opposite in this respect, we must remember how Smyth was limited by the lecturer's time-table. His educational aims fostered his tendency to thin out material by hammering on it with general principles, and stretching it to cover more lessons and morals. With the lecture room as his only platform, Smyth felt it his duty to offer from it the sum total of his knowledge and experience. Croker had as many platforms as he needed and therefore wrote on history, politics, literature, etc., separately, neither afraid of detail, and narrowness, nor in a hurry to make the most of an opportunity.

---

[1] One of the few exceptions to this is in the short introduction to the Essay on the Guillotine in which Croker quotes Shakespeare's grave-digger in connection with 'unequal' means of execution for rich and poor.

Circumstances intensified the basic differences between the contemporary historians, which resulted from different views of history. To Smyth history meant tracing great principles at work, to Croker, accumulating and examining facts. A politician and a hard-working administrator, a harsh, unsparing but honest critic, he believed in detail and hated any tampering with truth. A historian like Smyth, who has general principles as his starting points, chooses to present the historical figures which embody these principles and become types. Croker's familiarity with detail meant that he gave even to minor characters separate identities. In this he stands with Carlyle, far apart from Smyth and even Alison. Croker himself was aware of this. He noted that minor figures, who constantly recurred in his studies of the contemporary materials, are hardly ever mentioned by other historians.[1] It is noteworthy that of all nineteenth-century historians who, as Rudé says, tended to answer the questions concerning the nature of the Revolutionary crowds 'according to their own social ideals, political sympathies',[2] Croker alone in England attempted through minute and painstaking research to follow up the names and careers of obscure men who figured in insurrections, trials, delegations, public meetings. Carlyle had been anxious for a similar familiarity with the motivation of the men and women of the crowds, but what he achieved was rather a personification of a spirit of revolutionism whereas Croker attempted to apply microscopic analysis to sections of the scene. His method was interesting even though it mostly strengthened his belief in the planned bribery of the leaders of the mob.

ORAL INFORMATION

Croker wrote when oral information was still available and he recommended that investigators should consult survivors. His own connections with government circles, with Wellington, Peel and Canning, and his position in the Admiralty gave him ample opportunity for collecting first-hand information. His naval connections were more important for the Napoleonic period, and many reports by officers reached him before anyone else. But he was also thrown against Revolutionary figures like Tallyrand, Dumouriez and Fouché, and he corresponded with Guizot on history, politics and literature. His connections with émigrés, begun at school, continued throughout his life, as new revolutions brought new exiles, whose reminiscences Croker heard and noted. 'I knew him well in his later years', Croker says of Dumouriez, 'and liked the man, and

---

[1] On one of these minor characters Croker based a claim of originality. It was one Desnot whom Croker noticed recurring in all the early insurrections. Croker quotes at length from Desnot's trial at the Chatelet and affirms that no other historian had used this revealing document (*Q.R.* (Sept. 1845), LXXVI, 578; *Essays*, 65–71).

[2] G. Rudé, *The Crowd in the French Revolution* (Oxford, 1959).

loved to talk with him of those revolutionary scenes.'[1] But Dumouriez could not clarify the contradictions in his ministerial career, which troubled Croker's mind. Another informant was Louis Philippe, who, a few months before his death, gave Croker 'with wonderful volubility and graphic power a compendious history of the Revolution, from the selfish profligacy of Louis XV to the well meaning imbecility of Louis XVI— . . . —the anarchy of the Republic—the despotism of Bonaparte . . .'. The lecture lasted forty minutes and impressed Croker so well that he wished for a stenographer. But Croker was no Boswell (except perhaps to his hero Wellington), and did not accept the ex-King's statements as quickly as he wished them recorded. He detected Louis Philippe's aim 'to derive his legitimacy direct from Henry IV', and blame the four Louis for the Revolution, caused by their bowing to public opinion, 'which was opposed to whatever government there was'. Croker also saw 'a sly defence' of the share of his father in forming the National Assembly, in the claim that double representation was copied from the Dauphiné precedent. Croker never accepted these theories, nor Louis Philippe's views on Robespierre's dullness of talent. In his own work he had taken pains to prove Robespierre's natural and later perfected eloquence, a view he held unchanged.[2]

THE CRITIC OF HISTORIANS: MAINLY OF THIERS

Other historians' works have a peculiar place in Croker's own work. They are his excuse for writing. They appear in the reviews like elaborate screens whose art and craft is studied thoroughly before they are removed to reveal the real life behind. Although Croker was anxious to present his own results he never lost his interest in other historians. The scholarly side of his interest was based on his knowledge of the sources and of the use made of them. On this ground he stated as late as 1855, that no one had yet exhausted available materials or investigated them in the right way. He applied his gift of detection to historians as well as to history and was as fond of passing judgment on the living as on the dead. He did not read authors backward through their references, for in most cases he could identify their materials. He often noted in a notebook or in a review, 'This I have read before'. In time he might find the exact place and point it out. He was well equipped for exposing plagiarism, falsehood, dishonest use of sources and the worst crime of all, 'bookmaking'.

[1] Croker, *Essays*, 174.
[2] Croker's 'Robespierre' first came out in Sept. 1835. On 18 Mar. 1850, Croker recorded Louis Philippe's words, 'I heard him in the Tribune; he was exceedingly tedious and confused' (Jennings, III, 209). The case for Robespierre's eloquence is not modified in the manuscript notes on the offprint, nor in the revised essay of 1857. Croker's article on Robespierre is treated in the preceeding chapter.

His other weapon against historians was political exposure. He was not in the position to object to the use of history for political purposes, but he must have thought that he could draw the line between use and misuse, and expose falsifications of history. Croker was at his best when he was able to use both his weapons, the scholarly and the political, in conjunction. This he did in his two most important writings against historians, that on Macaulay[1] and that on Thiers.[2]

Others were aware of the influence of politics on history writing, but Croker was the first to make the charge concrete in his detailed criticism of Thiers. He studied Thiers's historical statements in close relationship with the interests and the movements of the 1820s in France, as parts of an actual plot. Croker represented Thiers's success as historian as being the result of his political elevation. This puts the cart before the horse, in any case with regard to Thiers's early histories.[3] When he reprinted his essays in 1857 he stressed the importance of the essay on Thiers because it exposed views so unjust and yet so popular, and he claimed some credit for himself for exposing the dangerous influence of false historiography. Croker saw himself as a judge of historians. His article on Thiers begins with the declared aim of demolishing 'utterly and irretrievably M. Thiers's credit as an historian' and ends with the judgment, that 'we might close our case against M. Thiers as a historian'.

Croker did not write against Thiers until 1845, and he is not to be believed when he explains this delay as due to the fact that Thiers's *History* had not before been considered as a history but rather as a 'bookseller's speculation on the state of the political parties', or as a conspiracy against the Bourbons, a 'paradoxical apology for the old Revolution', and a provocation to a new one.[4] Croker knew only too well, that Thiers's was *the* revolutionary history of the time. His own friend Peel, having urged him (Croker) to write on the Terror, later wrote to say that having looked at Thiers again, he did not think another history necessary for some time. Croker's firm belief in the political objectives of Thiers's history, far from preventing a review, was a chief cause of the necessity for having one.

The review which professes to deal with all of Thiers's works[5] deals, in fact, with a small portion of one. It attempts to do two things, to demolish Thiers's credit as historian and to expose his political aims, on the one hand, and to reconstruct a narrative of the early stage of the Revolution, other than that offered by Thiers. The real interest of the

---

[1] 'Macaulay's History of England', *Q.R.* (Mar. 1849), LXXXIV, 549–630.

[2] 'Thiers's Histories', *Q.R.* (Sept. 1845), LXXVI, 521–83.

[3] Croker, *Essays*, vii; see also *ibid.* 25, 'The success of the writer [Thiers] has made the reputation of the book.'

[4] Croker claims the same reason caused delay in *R.2.M*'s review of Thiers by St Beuve.

[5] A footnote added in 1855 says 'they now amount to twenty-four', where the text (of 1845) says 14.

article is that it shows Thiers's writings in the context of the activities of the opposition to the Bourbons.[1]

These activities, as Croker saw them, were aimed at enthroning Louis Philippe. Lafitte had already in 1818 spoken of the necessity for another revolution analogous to that of 1688. The leaders of the opposition, especially Lafitte and Manuel, had much to expect from him personally and there was also a wider wish for a revolutionary monarch to ensure revolutionary titles and gains. In order to bring his son to the throne, the opposition needed to have the Duke of Orleans whitewashed and the horrors of the Revolution palliated. History had to be enlisted and Thiers and Mignet were employed to perform this task. They were employed both as journalists (on the *Constitutionnel* and *Courrier* whose subscriptions soon rose), and as historians. To avert the charge of a plot, their histories which were written in concert were planned differently, the one as a post mortem on a skeleton, the other as a theatrical performance. The extraordinary thing about this elaborate charge was that Croker invented it. He could not have had a jot of evidence other than the 'internal evidence' in the works themselves,[2] and the vague boastings of the Kingmakers after 1830, or he would never have qualified his case by saying, 'It is at least certain that if the works had been undertaken with that special object they could hardly have fulfilled it better.' His concrete proof against Mignet is that Mignet only mentions Orleans three times, and then only to minimize his role in the events. Croker followed Thiers's life in detail. His journalistic efforts, especially in the *National*, his conduct during the July Revolution when, Croker says, Thiers kept away

---

[1] The unpublished correspondence with Murray shows the great encouragement Croker received in reviewing Thiers. Murray wrote to Lockhart that Thiers's history 'calls loudly for retribution at the hand of Mr Croker' (B.M. Add. MS. 41.125, f. 136). To Croker himself he wrote that his review of Thiers was 'almost a national affair' (Add. MS. 41. 125, f.142) and many times repeated how very important he thought Croker's discovery 'which has followed your very sagacious conjecture regarding Thiers . . . I hope to get the 1st ed[itio]n from Paris' (B.M. Add. MS. 41, 125, f. 160). See also B.M. Add. MSS. 41, 125, ff. 142, 157, 159, 161, 163, 164. In the last mentioned letter of 26 Sept. (1845) Murray writes: 'I hope you will give his Consulate such a smashing as his Republic has received.'

[2] Croker alone, as far as I know, took the trouble to compare Thiers's editions and to point out some small but possibly significant changes. Thiers always asserted that he had never changed a line of his History (*Discours*, II, 167). This was generally believed, even by Acton, who doubted Thiers's honesty. In the first ed. Thiers had written that the emigration had been 'chassée'. This he changed to 'éloignée'. Another example is:

1st ed:	Other eds:
there were instigators who excited this multitude, and who often directed its blows and its pillage. It is, certainly, not with money and secret manœuvres that one can set in movement an entire nation, but once excited, it is often by this means that it is directed and led astray (égarée).	there were instigators who sometimes excited, that multitude and directed perhaps some of its blows. In other respects this influence is not to be reckoned among the causes of the Revolution; for it is *not* with a little money and with secret manœuvres that you can convulse a nation of twenty-five millions of men.

just as he had himself described Robespierre doing on 10 August 1792. He traces Thiers's prudent changes of alliances and principles in practical politics and quotes Thiers's own boasting as to his revolutionary activity before 1830. The proof Croker is able to assemble against Thiers from his writings is not always plausible and often depends on an assumption of guilt, as when he asserts that Thiers knew and therefore concealed, or rather that Thiers does not mention, and therefore must have known and concealed, the connection between the massacres of September and the impending elections, a connection which Croker spared no trouble in attempting to establish. Some of Croker's assumptions turn out to be strangely out of date. He denied any distinction between the King and the court, and he says that it 'may be most confidently denied' that there was ever an anti-revolutionary plan with the King's or the Queen's approval. For this he makes a long but futile case—perhaps his worst piece of argument. For this he also quotes Dumouriez's authority and he believes Thiers to be perfectly cynical in inventing such a charge for the sake of his revolutionary panegyric.[1] Thiers, he says, invented a treacherous court in order to be able—*faux fuyant*—to admit the benevolence of the King and Queen and thus assume a pretence of impartiality!

Croker's case against Thiers was concretely, though not conclusively, supported. It was based on the vague suspicions which other people felt but which he himself seemed to feel more vividly. In 1845, having expounded Thiers's warlike policy against Guizot's peacefulness, Croker explains why all this was relevant when he had said that he 'should only deal with M. Thiers's political life as it affected his authorship'. The *Consulate*, he said, fruit of involuntary leisure, was written not out of love for Napoleon but in order to overthrow the King Thiers had helped to make, 'to electrify France with false glory . . . renounce Louis Philippe as quasi-legitimate' and to adopt the recollections of Napoleon 'as a stalking horse of faction'. As Brougham said, it was a 'monstrous pamphlet'. In 1855 Croker, in a footnote, boasted of this prophecy, but the odd thing was that he never turned the charge of misusing history for politics, on any of the great historians except Thiers and Mignet, and he ignored the point entirely in Lamartine, Blanc, Michelet or Villaumé. He was particularly violent about Thiers. There may have been envy of a successful historian, political jealousy of one who represented the growing power of the middle classes or hatred for a man who loved Napoleon. Croker mentioned everything he could think of against Thiers; he said that he was a coward, that he came of a poor family, that like Napoleon he never became a gentleman; that he was always 'un peu gamin'; but his main criticism is of Thiers as historian. When he rewrote the article,

[1] Croker also quotes a note Roederer made in his copy of Maton de Varennes, attesting to the King's attachment to the Constitution. 'Eh! le pauvre Sire; il la portait toujours en poche, et la produisait quelquefois avec une naïveté pitoyable.'

he made it less abusive,[1] but he even strengthened the charges against Thiers's good faith as a historian, and added the new evidence of Thiers's policy towards Napoleon III. Incidentally, he also omitted some of the worst names he had called the Duke of Orleans[2] (perhaps for the sake of the son whom he came to know), but he never changed his basic view that Thiers slurred over 'the despicable cowardice and apostasy of the Duke for political purposes'.

In Revolutionary historiography it was not uncommon to write volumes devoted to the errors of others. Croker was perfectly fitted for such a task. The political and personal abuse which Croker heaped on Thiers went with the more interesting and thorough work of supplementing or refuting Thiers's narrative with facts from contemporary materials, as for instance, the *Procès* against Lambesc which 'either the most unpardonable negligence of the most reprehensive bad faith' made Thiers ignore.[3] There is no subject Croker leaves uninterrupted by references to other historians' errors. Thiers is treated in this way even outside the article devoted to him. Mignet is usually damned with Thiers. His trenchant style had gained him a reputation for 'accuracy and impartiality' which Croker denied. Croker said that although Thiers seemed 'too brilliant to be trusted' and Mignet 'too dry to be doubted', they were equally false, the one falsifying detail, the other outline. Michelet and Lamartine figure in the revised essay on Robespierre. Croker's criticism of Lamartine is purely historical and he hit on the main point that Lamartine embroidered facts with unauthenticated anecdotes, whose falsehood Croker could prove (as he does), with 'abundant and indisputable evidence'.[4] If Croker erred in the case of Lamartine, it was for once in the direction of clemency. Was it because Lamartine treated so fully the personality of Robespierre? He treated Michelet more harshly, and in order to pick quarrels with him fell into ardent defences of Robespierre. He denied hotly that Robespierre was ever Madame Roland's protégé, or that Chapelier had any more claims on Robespierre's mercy than any other outlawed Girondin.[5]

Croker found the English historians ignorant and too 'apt, instead of going back to the original and contemporaneous sources of information to content themselves with compiling from the compilations of the French'.[6] He often exposed these faults in Alison. Of the early sources he claimed Moore to be indispensable and he quoted Miss Williams for

---

[1] E.g. from *Q.R.* (1835), LXXV, 539 Croker omits the insinuation that Thiers (after 1830) imitated Polignac's methods.

[2] Especially in connection with the massacres of September.

[3] Croker, *Essays*, 59.

[4] He shows, for instance, that Duplay did not suffer with Robespierre but lived to be implicated in the Babeuf conspiracy.

[5] *Q.R.* (Sept. 1835), LXXV, 525; Croker, *Essays*, 307.

[6] Croker, *Essays*, 399.

a point of fact. Adolphus gains high praise for his spirit and method. In different places Croker names Adolphus, Bertrand and Moore, respectively, as 'the best history of the period'. For Adolphus he finds a special place in the historiography of Robespierre, as being the only one (by 1835) who at least appreciated the difficulties of writing on a man shrouded by so many mysteries.[1] Subsequent writers, Croker complained, 'instead of endeavouring to clear up the obscurities . . . have taken the easier course of finding nothing to doubt'.[2]

TOWARD MATURE INVESTIGATION

Croker's historical writings between 1823, when the first products of his serious work began to appear, and 1857, when the best crop of thirty years was collected, corrected, revised and republished, have so far been treated as a unit and their historical merit judged by their highest points. Certain developments of these years, however, ought to be treated with references to the age and circumstances. The most striking of these is the Croker–Macaulay Parliamentary debate on the Reform Bill conducted in terms of French Revolutionary history, which has been treated above.[3] After the debates and the Tory defeat, Croker, who believed his own historical analogies, resigned from service under a government which he believed to have started on the road to revolution. His literary productiveness rose. Of the five articles written in what remained of 1832, one predicted a restoration to follow the 'English Revolution' of 1832 and three were connected with the French Revolution. That which tore to pieces the so-called *Memoirs of Louis XVIII* was the first of Croker's studies to contain minute detection based on wide materials.[4] Of the thirteen articles of the next year, three are about the Revolution. The one on the causes, written mainly by Mahon, was directed against Lord John Russell's *Causes of the French Revolution* and Macaulay's recent review of Dumont, and was an aftermath of the debates. 'We, let it be observed, are but now in the second month of our States General; we are approaching the night of sacrifices, and by just the same steps which the French trod before us.' Mahon and Croker rightly criticize Russell for not studying the causes at all but merely describing the grievances of *ancien régime*. They quarrel with the principle 'Propter quia post', which he uses, and claim that new theories, and not old grievances, had caused the upheaval.

When the storm of the Reform Bill finally died away, even for Croker, he settled down to steady historical work. A review of 1834 gives the impression that he regarded his articles as a kind of 'Revolutionary

---

[1] Thompson dismisses Adolphus on Robespierre, with contempt (J. M. Thompson, *Robespierre*).　　[2] Croker, *Essays*, 367 n.

[3] See above, pp. 102 *et seq.*　　[4] See above. pp. 68 *et seq.*

column'.[1] He sums up the Paris reactions to a previous review; inserts a completely irrelevant essay on Madame de Staël's 'bon mots' (he thought them not spontaneous) based on his recollections and on his notebooks;[2] he voices an idea on Robespierre, already hovering in his mind, and which he was to develop next year; and even has one of his periodic outbursts against Napoleon whom he now makes out to be illiterate. Very little of what he wrote so far was considered, by Croker, fit to live, but by 1835 he was ready to write *Robespierre*, and in the next year, *Roederer*. Even reviews which were later passed by for reprinting[3] were of a high critical standard. His interests were becoming more purely historical and the article on Versailles is a critical study of a technical kind. Croker's best article was that on Robespierre, begun in the 1830s and continued over many years.[4]

The 1840s were the period of Croker's highest production in sound historical work on the Revolution, though he was also writing contemporary history, with the help of Guizot and others. The essay on the guillotine is a thorough and valuable study of the history of that machine, and is full of surprises. The unpublished correspondence with Murray is particularly revealing in connection with this essay, for it shows how much Murray helped by procuring and even by contributing information.[5]

The correspondence with Murray on the subject of rewriting started in 1851, Croker died in 1856 and the volume came out in 1857. Croker rewrote his essays on the ground of new publications, and even more on that of a more thorough study of the old materials. Though we only have the annotated offprint for 'Robespierre', the other articles, too, bear marks of a long accumulation of detail, and a process of developing judgment, which added many new facts, but also some inconsistencies. Personal abuse was mostly cut down and historical investigation extended. Croker explained, in the case of Roederer, that the review of 1836 had been addressed 'controversially ad hominem', and that this was no longer suitable. In fact he never dismissed a charge against the writers he attacked though he moderated his tone.

The one essay which is almost entirely new is that on Varennes. The original review had three pages on the actual flight while the revised

---

[1] 'Arnault's Souvenirs d'un Sexagenaire', *Q.R.* (Mar. 1834), LI, 1–18.

[2] On 24 Oct. 1825 Croker recalled in a notebook his first meeting with Mme de Staël. His point is that her 'bon mots' were not spontaneous but prepared. It was then that she said 'Les étrangers sont la postérité contemporaine', and Croker adds that he has since found this extraordinary expression in the journal of Camille Desmoulins (Jennings, I, 326).

[3] E.g. those on the 'Correspondence of Louis XVIII' (1836) and on the 'Correspondence of the Committee of Public Safety' (1841).

[4] Croker to Peel 7 Oct. 1835 (Jennings, II, 283). Peel had written to congratulate Croker. He had put Croker on the subject. See above Chapter 10.

[5] B.M. Add. MS. 41,125, f. 108 of 28 October on the 'Edinburgh Maiden' and the 'Halifax Gibbet' both described in Croker's article. B.M. Add. MS. 41,125, f. 109 of 4 November: 'I have discovered that the guillotine with the mallet occurs on a fresco in a Ch[urch] near Mantua.'

study has forty-seven. It incorporated some of the notes of Croker's edition of the *Royal Memoirs*, and collated the evidence on the flight in the collection of memoirs on the subject which had been out but not used by Croker in 1823. The essay is a new and complete reconstruction of the flight, based on a multitude of individual facts critically examined; its results are the more astonishing since it only used materials which had come out by 1823.[1] Croker was as sure as ever that Varennes proved the 'difficulty of ascertaining historical truth'.[2] When he had finished with Varennes, we have an account very near those we have today, but only of the actual journey. He knew nothing about the work of preparation, which could only be studied when the royal correspondences were published. From the materials he used, his conclusions could hardly have been more accurate, both with regard to what actually happened, and to the evaluation of the participants' shares in the execution of the plan. All the complicated technical data, the distances, speed, carriages, causes of delay, various dangers, as well as the most crucial points which caused failure, the presence of troops,[3] Choiseul's premature despair of the King's arrival, the unknown location of the relays, which baffled many historians, are accurately estimated. As far as there is individual blame, it is given to Choiseul and the case against him is reconstructed from evidence, calculation and reasoning, and from Choiseul's subsequent attempts to clear himself.

There was not another historian in England to the end of the century who conducted the kind of original and minute research into the history of the Revolution as Croker did. No one else had the tools for it.

THE CROKER COLLECTIONS

Croker had started his collections of Revolutionary materials before 1814 with whatever journals, tracts, broadsides and other documents he could find. As soon as peace came in 1814 he went to France, traced and observed revolutionary scenes and made more purchases. Immediately after Waterloo, in July 1815, he went again with Mr Peel and Mr Vesey Fitzgerald, and the letters he wrote to his wife on this occasion give his impressions from the midst of the political scene. He knew all the important people and took part in the discussions held in Paris. Naturally he was 'rather glad to see all those heroes and rogues' and with his usual care took copious notes of all he saw and heard. He met Fouché, Talleyrand and others, to discuss the capture of Napoleon, and did business with Castlereagh whom he had to convince that Fouché occasionally

---

[1] It includes a map and a history of the Tuileries from the strategical point of view.

[2] Croker, *Essays*, 122.

[3] Croker's narrative is more accurate than Carlyle's. But he believed Bouillé's *Memoirs* that he had opposed the use of troops. This was later disproved by Bouillé's letters.

lied. Some of his visits were purely historical or inquisitive as when he called on Denon, who, almost in tears, described to him his last parting scenes from Napoleon. Most of the oral information Croker collected then was about Napoleon and some of it is traceable in his later *Quarterly* articles, as for instance his jeering reaction to the letter (of which General Becker showed him a copy) in which Napoleon threw himself on British mercy.[1] He visited the battlefield of Waterloo while it was still being stripped of its souvenirs by the peasants, and found, bought and was given some of these.[2] But mainly he collected a variety of curious stories about the battle. In 1819 Croker was again in Paris, this time spending most of his time in bookshops.[3]

The collections which Croker started in those years are all in the British Museum now. They were acquired from Croker in three batches, in 1817, 1831 and 1856.[4] The first complete catalogue came out in 1899, prepared by Fortescue. In his preface he says that the first collection was 'purchased from a collector in Paris through the late Rt Hon. J. W. Croker'. Croker in 1849 had given evidence before a Royal Commission in which he described his collections in very general terms.[5] In 1854 the Museum authorities wrote to ask him for a history of his collections. Louis Blanc had been using them and wanted to make their origin public since 'in France they doubt his statement that he had found such a collection in England'.[6] In his reply Croker described the collection as consisting of two parts, the first he assembled from different sources, chiefly Colin, Marat's bookseller, who parted with thousands of publications of which he had single copies, but had none of Marat's own publications which were too dangerous to possess. Croker is carried away by his Paris memories and never specifies the origin of the second collection.[7]

In 1855 Croker declared himself the best English collector. Earlier he was probably the best collector of any country. The most famous of early French collections was that of Deschiens, who published his catalogue

[1] Jennings, II, p. 68: 'I called the whole letter a base flattery, and said Buonaparte should have died rather than have written such a one.'
[2] The Duchess of Richmond gave him an orderly book of a French Regiment.
[3] Jennings, I, 150.
[4] They are marked 'F', 'F.R.', and 'R' tracts.
[5] 'The first collection I bought in France between the first fall and the return of Bonaparte. I bought it for the express purpose of offering it to the Trustees of the Museum, if they chose to pay for it; the amount I think was 250 l. or thereabouts. I afterwards got the offer of another library, which I bought for myself—it was a very extensive one, about between 20,000 and 30,000 items,—and which I had at my house in the Admiralty. When I left the admiralty . . . I offered them to the British Museum at the expense they cost me . . . about 250 l. . . . you will perhaps smile at me when I tell you that I have now formed, and have catalogued, a third collection which contains a considerable number of things not in either of the former collections.'
[6] Jennings, III, 318.
[7] Through Colin, Croker met and visited Marat's sister, very like Marat, he wrote, ugly, sharp, and living on watchmaking and charity.

in 1829. Croker early criticized Deschiens's principle of valuing above all the journals, but his own collection exceeded that of Deschiens even in journals. He owned a copy of Deschiens's catalogue, which is now in the Museum and contains his manuscript notes and corrections.[1] It shows that Croker, with more than professional jealousy, studied the catalogue carefully and noted points of interest, correcting Deschiens or describing what he himself possessed.[2] Croker continuously complained of the inaccessibility of his collection. His noble collection of 50,000 pieces, in 4,000 volumes, was uncatalogued and inaccessible, he wrote to Peel, a trustee. Panizzi had been cataloguing it, but had soon been taken away from this work. Croker was able to find a certain book in the collection only because he knew his own arrangement of the materials. 'Neither the librarian, nor any one else alive would have found it', he wrote in 1835.[3] Not one of the trustees, except Peel and Aberdeen, ever used the library or knew its requirements. Writing for the public two years later, Croker was even more indignant. 'They might as well be sold to a cheesemonger', as kept in the state in which they stood.[4]

The lack of a catalogue explains the late recognition of the collections. In 1884, however, the editor of the *Croker Papers* was wrong in saying that the value of the collection (then being catalogued) was but little known. Historians knew it from J. Hermann who had spent a decade locating Revolutionary sources and described those of the British Museum in the *Historische Zeitschrift* of 1878.[5] He said that Croker had made the British Museum the home of French Revolutionary studies, and admired his success in the impossible project of accumulating vast materials in the period of the Restoration when they were hard to come by and dangerous to hold.

It is an interesting tribute to Croker that Hermann deals with him in the context of an historical development which took place long after Croker's time. He says it has become more important to contribute to the knowledge of the sources than to write new histories. Hermann classifies Revolutionary sources in general and describes briefly other libraries in Europe. He noted that the Berlin library was poor, that the Paris library was being catalogued since Napoleon III's time and that the prize-piece of the London library was the Croker collection, so far used

---

[1] It was sold to the Museum by H. M. Stephens. His letter of 9 Feb. 1886 is now bound with the book.

[2] E.g. 'My copy of the Bulletin de Tribunal Revolutionaire par Clements consists of 6 volumes all in contemporary bindings.'

[3] Croker to Peel, 7 Oct. 1835 (Jennings, II, 283).

[4] See also A. Esdaile, *The British Museum Library* (London, 1846). Carlyle testified before the commission in 1848: 'for all practical purposes they might as well have been locked up in water-tight chests and sunk.' Croker was alert to other needs of the Museum and its Library and it was on his suggestion that the movable slips method was adopted.

[5] 'Die Sogenannte Croker-Kolektion im British Museum' (1878), Bd. 40. Hermann describes Croker as 'emsiger, eifriger Forscher auf dem Gebiete der Geschichte'.

only by Louis Blanc. Hermann seems to be confused about the extent of the Croker collections within the Museum collection as a whole. Only part was already catalogued and he studied that part well.[1] Towards the end of his stay he discovered another collection but he was not actually able to see it. He speaks of it as 'the other' (that is, not the Croker) collection and does not know it was Croker's third collection. Acton knew this in 1896 and three years later Fortescue's complete catalogue appeared.[2] Fortescue, who made himself a great expert on French Revolutionary materials, especially in the British Museum, was a great admirer of Croker as a collector whose mastery through 'prolonged research', he goes so far as to say, 'was unsurpassed by Aulard or Lenôtre'.

Louis Blanc in the 'fifties, Hermann in the 'seventies, Morse Stephens in the 'eighties, and Acton in the 'nineties, voiced only few of the many praises the collections earned. In our century their importance is well known through bibliographies. Caron in 1947 points out that periodicals are best represented in it,[3] Tourneux studied it carefully and reproduced Fortescue's index in his *Bibliographie*,[4] and Braesch discovered unique pieces which had escaped Tourneux.[5]

MERIT AND LIMITATION

Reading Croker for the first time, one is struck by the unexpected scholarship and the soundness of the ideas on how the history of the Revolution ought to be studied. Above all, in the problems presented by the vast and growing amount of material, Croker was far ahead of his times. His excellent historical qualities make it appear that the neglect of his work has been unjustified. With his collections, his methodical investigations, and special aptitudes, he could have produced an unusually well-documented and accurate history for the time. The fact remains, however, that he did not write it. The collection of essays shows that he covered the early period of the Revolution systematically. His sharp criticism of other historians' facts was a valuable contribution in a period preceding that of critical history; but such work kept him more busy disproving other historians' points and errors than making his own overall constructions. Criticism and analysis of other historians' writings would have characterized anything Croker might have written.

[1] He lists, for instance, 174 journals and points out those which are unobtainable elsewhere.

[2] J. K. Fortescue, *Lists of the Contents of the Three Collections of Books Pamphlets and Journals in the British Museum Relating to the French Revolution.* (London, 1899.)

[3] P. Caron, *Manuel Pratique pour l'Étude de la Révolution Française* (Paris, 1947), pp. 190–1, 218.

[4] M. Tourneux, *Les Sources Bibliographique de l'Histoire de la Révolution Française*, vol. I, pp. xxvi, xxvii, xli; Fortescue's Index is in vol. 44 (1909), pp. 443–60.

[5] Braesch, *Nouvelles Archives des Missions scientifiques* t. xv (1907), pp. 60 *et seq.*

The personal element which was prominent in his writings did not represent a biographical interest in the Revolution, because it was chiefly the political man which interested Croker. His history would have been, as are his essays, purely political. If we take out of the essays the criticism of historians, and the discussion of sources, and look for the historical compositions, we find them centred on the political behaviour of the prominent figures and the criminal behaviour of the unnamed. Croker looked into the daily working of the Revolutionary machine. He examined the episodes and tried to put his finger, through the knowledge of details, on the points of contact between the policies of the men in power and the actual happenings in the streets. In all his investigations Croker did not see and did not look beyond the personalities, intentions and actions of men. He complained that historians treated the Revolution too much as a tale of blood and fire and neglected the problems of politics, of the personal rivalries and of the institutions.

Although it was Croker who used the new word 'phantasmagoria',[1] to describe the Revolution, no idea could be further from his mind than that there was any unfathomable mystery about it. The only mysteries Croker admitted were those for which sources were not obtainable, as, for instance, the oral discussions that preceded important actions. He thought he could explain everything if only he could look into the hearts and minds of certain people. Croker was not mystified by anything which might appear fatalistic, nor by mass movements, nor by the strange phenomena of human behaviour. Human nature he believed was always the same. All a historian had to do was to apply the usual standard of motives and passions that he knew to exist. For such a task Croker was eminently fitted; he was a master detective with the useful tool of an over-suspicious and uncharitable mind. He was therefore at his best about people whom he disliked. His great shortcoming, even from the point of view of his own method, was his extraordinary limited view of human nature.

---

[1] 'A name invented for an exhibition of optical illusions produced chiefly by means of the magic lantern, first exhibited in London in 1802' (*New English Dictionary*. Ed. by Sir J. A. H. Murray, vol. VII (1909)). Mignet also uses this word.

PART II
THE WANING OF A TRADITION

CHAPTER 12

THE REVOLUTION OF 1848

LIBERAL OPTIMISM

The effect of the 1848 revolutions on England was at first sight strikingly clear. After the height of Chartist revolutionary activity around 1840 the working classes were appeased with economic reform while the Whigs had no desire to extend the gains of 1832 in Parliamentary reform. Political agitation and revolutionism were therefore dormant until the European revolutions threatened to wake them up. Chartism woke up with a dramatic show of force only to fall back more feeble than ever. Some Whigs, like John Russell, blindly followed the example of 1830 and proceeded unsuccessfully to plan further reform.

The new Revolution was bound to open people's minds to new aspects of the Revolution of 1789; and just as the events of 1830 had created a reaction in its favour, the year 1848 provoked a reaction against it. If the year 1830 seemed at first to indicate the end of violent revolutions and the transmutations of those into a policy of peaceful reform, 1848 seemed to be the effect of new revolutionary forces, parties and ideas especially active since 1830. To some people, it thus brought out forcibly the idea of the 'permanent revolution' which had started in 1789 and was still developing, still moving to some unpredictable end.

One general reaction, however, in England to the events of 1848 is, curiously, that of unshaken liberal optimism. Because liberals were so anxious to tone down any excitement against their own reforming ways and because English revolutionism did in fact confirm their confidence by not flaring up into any formidable blaze, many men in England continued to adhere to their optimistic view which refused to regard the democratic spirit as leading to certain doom, the descent starting in 1789 and now become more precipitous. They even determined to read the European events of 1848 in the light of their home-bred optimism. Guizot's revolutionary studies though favourably received in England, which found his historical temperament and his politics congenial, incorporated gloomy views which seemed excessive to many of the liberals. In 1849, for example, the *Edinburgh Review*, while agreeing with Guizot that the monster of 1789 had reappeared in the world, insisted that it had also been vanquished.[1] The *Edinburgh* had always striven for fairness and moderation, but its views, though often accepted as true and therefore acted on for a time, had often been wrong, so that repeatedly since 1802

[1] *E.R.* (Apr. 1849), LXXXIX, 554.

(when it ridiculed the *Reflections* of a writer who predicted that Bonaparte would conquer all Europe), it had had to retract its former opinions. It still saw the new Revolution with spectacles that had been fitted for 1830, and still, therefore, sought to draw anti-alarmist conclusions from the new upheavals. The Revolution of 1848, the *Edinburgh* said, again confirmed that the forbearance of 1830 had been due not to accident but to the improvement which had taken place in morals and politics since 1789. The real evil, in any case, was not 'democracy' as Guizot said, but the 'domestication of revolution', the continued readiness to make appeal to popular force. A democratic monarchy might be the salvation of France, but a spirit of insurrection, a resentment against any authority, was the thing which was proving her ruin. Things would have been just the same if the recent Revolution had been directed to a Legitimist or Bonapartist end. It was the consistent policy of the *Edinburgh*, therefore, to localize the apprehensions aroused by the Revolutions of 1848, and to show that the evils were peculiar to French conditions, and to the French character as had been alleged to be the case in respect of the first Revolution. It pointed out that though in England there were parties which might roughly be analogous to the French parties, nevertheless, the Tories, the Whigs and the Radicals had certain underlying principles which they held in common so that all of them scouted the idea of revolution in England. This whole liberal approach in spite of its caution and sanity had the effect of distorting the historical view which was made to conform to the needs of English politics at the time. It refused to recognize the wide and ideological background to the Revolutions of 1848 because of the danger latent in that background. The *Edinburgh* was perhaps more clear-sighted than Guizot when it made the distinction between the spirit of democracy and the spirit of revolution, a distinction taught and confirmed by both American and English conditions; but it was blind in its refusal to recognize the existence of universal socialism and in imagining that the Revolution of 1848 in France had rid the world for ever of this bugbear. France, it was said, had completed its instructive task by teaching Europe to unlearn the lessons it had taught it in 1789. On this extraordinary view it could describe Louis Blanc as the exponent of a theory that was as obsolete as the *ancien régime*.

This mode of thinking continued in spite of the development of Socialism. It had appeared much earlier when the Whigs had begun to be aware of the nascent socialist movements of Saint-Simonianism, Owenism, etc. We have seen how readily they compared them with the philosophy of pre-revolutionary France and had bundled all socialistic and utopian theories together as 'sanguine' and chimerical. The Whigs had consistently maintained a sane attitude to liberty in spite of the French Revolutions; their mundane treatment of events, and their refusal to be disgraced by enthusiasm again, made them the chief exponents of a cool, fair and moderate attitude conducive to detached historical understanding. But their actual contributions to the interpretation and to the historiography of the 1789 Revolution were therefore on the whole poor. Even when their pronouncements might be politically useful, they would be utterly unhistorical, and distorted by the preoccupation with home politics. They were anxious to condemn anything which might cast a shadow over their English liberalism, so that they needed villains like Robespierre and Barère who had violated liberty, or present-day socialists, to dissociate themselves from. When after the French Revolution of 1848 France again surrendered to military despotism, many Englishmen finally lost all hope either for the regeneration of France or for new discoveries in history. The old analogies and anatomies of revolutions again came into prominence. Some homely truths were crystallizing into their old, hard shapes, but with new shades of meaning borrowed from current thought. That the French were hopelessly incapable of liberty; that national characteristics were everything; that revolution and reaction were happily alien to England ('Thank God! we are Saxons') and any signs of them must be kept down; that only the English brand of moderate liberalism afforded safety; that all sympathies with parallel parties abroad are dangerous delusions; that foreigners on the whole are a sorry lot. 'What is communism in France, becomes highway robbery and burglary in Ireland.'[1]

HISTORIANS MOVE APART

The Revolution of 1848 thus checked and perhaps even reversed the process by which general opinion in England on the subject of French revolutions had come to be moderated and the divergencies levelled down. Each of the continental outbursts at this time reminded Englishmen of the living power and influence of the original French Revolution. The events of 1848 as they had such wide repercussions, and were connected with the widely growing socialism, divided historians and theorists more clearly than before on the questions of the interpretation of the events of 1789. Some English historians became aware that it was no longer the 'lessons' of the Revolution but the theoretical explanations of the whole which decided the significance of this chapter of history. Varieties of opinion on the French Revolution no longer represented merely varying shades of approval or disapproval but sprang from varieties of diagnosis and analysis. England was not given to fanatical systems and simple consistent interpretations, and it remained a characteristic of English historiography that general theories were treated

[1] *The Economist* (29 Apr. 1848), VI, 477: 'Thank God! we are Saxons . . . we feel deeply grateful . . . that we belong to a race, which . . . has an ample compensation in the solid, slow reflective phlegmatic temperament . . .'

with suspicion. The appearance of the great French histories, of Michelet, Blanc and Lamartine, each complete with a view of history, and the reaction against their *a priori* views, brings out a certain continuity in the English view on these points, and the special interest of the early denunciations of general theories of history and of 'sweeping generalizations' about forces which work without the agency of men. Even Blanc's admirers found fault with his thesis that the Revolution was the consummation of the trend towards individualism started by the Reformation, and with his socialist interpretation of history. If Lamartine and Michelet were at first simply received as history which was either more or less favourable to revolution than was expected or approved, in Louis Blanc the link between the interpretation of 1789 and the active revolutionism of 1848 could not be missed. After the Republican stage, control of events in the 1848 Revolution was taken over by a new revolutionary force and it was Blanc's socialism that was considered as being put to the test in Paris. It was naturally the Tories who were better aware of the new ideological forces at work. If the Whigs insisted that socialism was dead, the Tories recognized its force. On 11 March 1848, Murray writes to Croker, 'I sent you Louis Blanc—'Tis the key to all that has just occurred in France.' The new Revolution in France embodied of course different movements. The well-known impatience with the commercial system, and the vulgarity of life, raised against it people as different as Merlin the old Jacobin, Michelet the nationalist and Lamartine, whom England, in 1848, was surprised to find not 'sentimental about the *ancien régime*', since he was a Catholic and a Romantic. And even after 1848 the Christian Socialists praised Lamartine for having practised in the Revolution the moderation he had preached in his *History of the Girondins*. But the new revolution was mainly a socialist revolution against the industrial system, against the middle classes who were the heirs of 1789, by those who had been left out. The July monarchy under Guizot had known the brewing danger to property and Guizot had urged a perpetual war against the spirit of revolution. In England these new realities of French politics and the new resulting interpretations of history were rejected by liberal opinion. It was the Tory friends of Guizot, like Croker on the one extreme end, and the working-class leaders like Harney, on the other extreme end, who were prepared to admit the actual existence of the class war.

This was not an entirely new phenomenon. Even before the Restoration it was Southey who was especially interested in the Babeuf plot and appreciative of its economic aims. And when Buonarroti's history of the conspiracy was translated by O'Brien in 1836, it was met by a very favourable review in the *Quarterly*, which called it the most curious and most important of Revolutionary writings. 'There never was a book more trustworthy in all its statements.' The *Quarterly* reviewer at that point took over Buonarroti's theory of the Revolution in which the principles of equality and of economic revolution are shown to have been strong from the beginning, in which Robespierre and St Just are shown to have had those principles in mind, the same principles towards which present-day revolutionism was also tending. Buonarroti himself supplied the comparison with Owen and present-day socialists. When in 1848 at the age of seventy-eight Owen was in France distributing leaflets of his system with Blanc's blessing, and Doherty was in Paris, writing proclamations inside the Tuileries as soon as Louis Philippe vacated them, the comparison gained force in interested circles. (Owen, of course, was remote from politically revolutionary activity then as before. His attempt to propagate his ideas in Paris of 1848 was not unlike that of Bentham during the Great Revolution which he equally disliked.) Those who were keenest to denounce revolutionary socialism were the readiest to promote the theories connecting the tradition of the French Revolution with revolutionary phenomena most menacing to economic liberalism.

UNHISTORICAL CHRISTIAN SOCIALISM

The appearance of Christian socialism in England, born on the morrow of the death of revolutionary Chartism in 1848, is significant for English political, social and historical attitudes. It was the nearest English equivalent of Saint-Simonianism and the moderate heir of several 'fanatic' trends of thought. The French cult of Christian socialism, as preached, for instance, by Buchez, could not be transplanted to England, not only because it was revolutionary. It was too deeply embedded in the idea of France and in Catholicism. That the French people were chosen to fulfil the gospel through social revolution was the basis of the cult. English Christian socialism was not revolutionary. It was one thing to connect Christianity with an idealist socialism and it was quite another thing to treat socialism as a religion as was done later by Bax.

In England, the influence of religion over the people was used to reject rather than to aid revolution. The Christian socialist attempt to heal great human suffering by directing the currents of religion and socialism to flow together failed in an age intoxicated with science. Acton said that socialism was the worst enemy of mankind because if successful it would have the highest claim on man's gratitude. Socialism, in fact, soberly judged political economy to be a more useful ally than religion long before it became successful. The terms 'socialist' and 'irreligious' continued to be used synonymously in England as in Owen's time. If Christian socialism failed as a political force it was nevertheless a typical product. Religion and economics may have proved to be incompatible occupations for the systematic mind but they both drew the workers and the middle classes to a quasi-socialist attitude as they had earlier drawn them to philanthropy.

Christian socialism was unhistorical except in the sense that it upheld the socialist elements in the teaching of Christ and the practice of the early Fathers. The concrete revolutionary experiences of modern Europe had as little meaning in Kingsley's system as in English pre-Marxian economic theories. The English roots of socialist tendencies in either religion or economics were, unlike the French, detached from the actual history of revolutions; and, unlike the German, free from a pervading philosophy of history centred round concepts of constant strife. Marxists like Bax did try to inculcate a historical determinism as the only basis for socialism later in the century, but for most English socialists no historical background was deemed necessary other than that of revelation and day-to-day facts. If working-class socialism had partly derived from the Revolutionary tradition through Spence and Paine (though it left Paine behind), Christian socialism derived rather from the anti-Jacobins, like Coleridge and Southey, who with Oastler and Sadler conducted a Tory philanthropists' war against *laissez-faire*. These Tory thinkers who inherited Burke's devotion to the state added to his prescriptions state control over economic activity and church and state intervention to overcome poverty. Though it was also influenced by Carlyle's ideas of aristocratic socialism it did not inherit from either Coleridge or Carlyle a sense of history. It was the abstract social ethics of Christianity detached from time or place which influenced Kingsley, Maurice and Ludlow.

The volume of *Politics for the People* shows the Christian socialists to be free of any political doctrine and moved by fear of imminent revolution.[1] 'There is leisure for deliberation now—a year or two hence there may not be.' This fear prompted them to compete with Chartism for the workers' hearts. They wished to purify Chartism of revolution and democracy and to develop its weakest strain, that of idealist socialism. Religion would weld the workers together and make politics more truly a part of life. It would at the same time ward off the danger of violence. God's government of the world is a rich man's warning, a poor man's comfort. When Kinglsey started the *People's Friend* and was writing street placards he saw himself as replacing Chartism by a higher creed. Chartism had not gone far enough, he said.

Kingsley's later conservatism was latent in his beginnings. He had always accepted Carlyle's distinction between aristocratic socialism and a levelling democracy, a notion which had been influenced by the Saint-Simonian idea of the regimentation of industry. In later life he said that the House of Lords represented 'every silver fork in Great Britain', and the hereditary principle, that is, all that is good and honourable. If the

[1] C. Kingsley, *Politics for the People* (1848); see also Tracts by Christian Socialists (1850); J. M. Ludlow, *Christian Socialist* (1850); Ludlow, *Progress of the Working Class 1832–37* (1867).

Commons had the power, they would tax the rich for the poor, with 'ugly results for civilization'. For French philosophy Kingsley had deep contempt and like Smyth, a previous Regius Professor, he traced democracy, the revolutionary doctrine of 1792–1848, as he saw it, to the belief in perfectibility and in natural equality. Both beliefs he disputed as a religious man and as an experienced father and educator.[1] Kingsley came to believe in racial differences and argued against Tocqueville that it was the warping influence of Catholicism and not lack of municipal self-government which made the French incapable of liberty.

One of the popular lecturers of the period who had influence with his generation was A. J. Scott, later Principal of Owen's College. His life's work was devoted to religion and he also lectured on Chartism and Socialism.[2] His faith and his aptitude for social analysis made him an interesting model for a prevalent mode of thought. The Christian socialists sought help from his vigorous attempt to defeat the 'secular creed' and to show that science itself led to faith. An admirer of Scott wrote in 1866 that had Scott been in the pulpit in 1790 instead of Price he would have preached liberty without provoking Burke. His interest at this point is that in a lucid historical sketch of socialism he shows it to be the product of industrialism and capitalism and therefore primarily English. He traced the socialist ideas to the Essenes and the early Christian sects as well as to reformers like Owen. The French Revolution, he said, clearly had purely political aims, even though it increased social suffering. French socialism, a new phenomenon, though possessing an aim, was not at first a political party until it joined forces with the old Republican party, heir of the Revolution, which had power but no clear aim.

English Christian socialism interests us here because it disliked revolution and had no historical attitude to the French Revolution. It therefore helps to explain why there was no English socialist historiography of the Revolution for a long time. It was revolution and not socialism which was defeated by the effect of 1848 on England. With it were silenced the few expressions of an extreme revolutionist historiography as that of O'Brien. The working-class movements now shook themselves free of whatever extravagant influence they had felt of the French Revolutions of 1789, 1830 and 1848. The Chartists, O'Brien and O'Connor, ever in disagreement, now both opposed revolution and socialism. In this sense was the optimism of the Whigs justified. After 1848 socialism became more pacific and entered the arena of politics in a new practical spirit bowing to the conventional rules. The pessimistic Tories, on the other hand, were nevertheless right in hearing the footsteps of democracy. Christian

---

[1] Kingsley felt himself to have more authority on such points than J. S. Mill.
[2] E.g. A. J. Scott, *The Social Systems of the Present Day compared with Christianity* (London, 1841); *Discourses* (1866).

socialism had attempted through the religious element to elevate the conscience of poor and rich alike to a level where they would voluntarily discard both violence and economic oppression. It succeeded at least in enhancing in latter-day English socialism a revulsion from violence and a respectable moral tone, thereby helping to dispel the horror of socialism and indirectly to clear the way for it to spread. They made the economic prospects of socialism, however, appear formidable to orthodox liberals who began to fear that economic socialism was to be realized through the sentimental patronage of the Tory clergy. If, therefore, the working-class movement became less revolutionary, and Radicals like Hume became more conservative and more emphatic in dissociating themselves from revolutionism,[1] it was nevertheless obvious that Radical doctrine was becoming more favourable to economic intervention and Mill, under the influence of 1848, altered the later editions of his *Principles of Political Economy* toward a more favourable attitude to socialist doctrines of labour legislation.

CONTEMPORARY CRITICISM OF FRENCH HISTORIANS

Apart from the direct political effect which the Revolution of 1848 had on policies and theories there was also an effect on historiography as seen, for instance, in Lewes's *Robespierre*. An article by E. Edwards in the *British Quarterly Review* of 1848 shows an interesting contemporary reaction to the great French histories usually connected with the events of 1848. It also shows the preoccupation with the analysis of previous works, characteristic of the English approach to the study of the Revolution. This had sometimes been due to the aim of defeating political propaganda or to the method of discrediting opponents. Many of the writings which mark important stages in the development of English history writing in this field were, in fact, book reviews.

Edwards was a librarian and a scholar[2] experienced in detailed documentary work. This article was ostensibly a review of Lamartine, Michelet, Blanc, Mignet, Thiers, Carlyle and Gallois; and it represents an early attempt to sketch a history of revolutionary studies. Though it deals mainly with individual writers it opens with a survey of the field. Edwards's outline is simple. Until the 1820s all works in France, he says, were governed by their associations with families and with private affairs. Works written outside France added their own national animosities to these personal passions and prejudices. The change began about 1830 and now (i.e. 1849) men were writing histories free from family

---

[1] E.g. *Parl. Deb.* (20 June 1848), XCIX, 881, 'The Radical Reformers . . . improperly called Chartists.'

[2] Edwards had written a life of Raleigh, studies in numismatology, and histories of the British Museum.

prejudice. Outside France, too, men are proclaiming the principles against which they had once sent armies. The rehabilitation of the Revolution started with Mignet though his work was pervaded with an 'undercurrent of fatalism' in his view of the process which led to the Terror, and to the aggression making them both appear as inevitable. Thiers wrote 'at the fittest moment' when the testimony of actors may be gathered without participating in all their prejudices, but Thiers did not take full advantage of this and he himself was not free from passion. 'Success is the God of his idolatry', he atoned for crime and failed to understand (so Edwards thought) that the Rights of Man became the Rights of Money and that thereby they prepared further revolutions. Edwards explains that the Revolution which had given an impetus to social equality failed to provide it with natural outlets in the systems which followed it thus allowing it to 'acquire in darkness an energy only to be manifested by the destructive violence of their ultimate outbreak'. Edwards noticed the recent revival of the debate on the French Revolution and also the revival of extreme anti-revolutionism. He thought that recent polemics justified the writing of new histories, and that of Michelet was important for its own sake as it brought out the unification and the legislative reconstruction of France, which is the great work of the Revolution. He contrasts Michelet's achievement in this respect with the work of Carlyle who brings out nothing but dissolution. In Michelet he rightly stressed the all-important nationalism and the gift for 'vivifying the past'. Edwards gives no indication of seeing the influence which some histories had on the Revolution of 1848 nor of the appearance of new historical theories in the work of Michelet apart from the fact that he recognizes in Michelet the influence of Vico, minimizing the role of individuals and bringing out rather the movements of masses. Edwards disagreed with such a view and said that 'the noblest movements which have ever linked a people in united effort were first ideas in the brain of some solitary thinker'. Michelet's theory of history he regarded therefore as the one objectionable part of the book—'a crude compound of Voltairian skepticism and German mysticism'. In the same way he thought that the theories of Louis Blanc—especially that since the Reformation society had tended to foster individualism—detract from the historical value of his work, though he has the highest praise for the scholarship of Blanc. He thinks that the endeavour to bring history into harmony with a preconceived scheme leads to a torturing of the facts. He rejects not only historiographical theories, therefore, but theories concerning the deep underlying causes of historical events. Both in manner and in method it is Lamartine who suits Edwards's taste. The biographical treatment of the subject; the new information about the private lives of revolutionary leaders; the dramatic theme of the Girondins; Lamartine's patient analysis and picturesque use of detail—are all congenial to the Englishman. At the same time, Edwards, like Lewes, while glad to see Robespierre treated less like a monster, considers Lamartine's judgment of the man too favourable. Edwards, however, chooses to explain this as the result of over-caution on the part of Lamartine against showing his repugnance.

Edwards, therefore, stands typically in line with the traditional English interpretation. He approves of the net achievement of the Revolution while utterly condemning the means employed and the men engaged in the drama. He maintains a belief in progress, and this is unshaken by his repugnance to socialism. He admits that sixty years of convulsions have been the consequences of the Revolution; but he still looks forward with incredible optimism to a fine future promised by both Reason and Revelation. He appends to his survey a study of the lessons of the Revolution and this part of his work indicates the effect which the events of 1848 have had on the English attitude to 1789. Edwards complained that in the revived debate on the Revolution, Burke's extreme anti-revolutionary arguments reappeared and were much the worse for wear; that people again tended to forget the sufferings of France before 1789, and to exaggerate the impatience of the reformers, chronicling only the crimes and not the virtues of the revolutionaries. The future augurs well to those unaffected by the Utopias of Saint-Simon and Owen. France is useful because she serves as the laboratory of Europe.

CHAPTER 13

1848–1870

NEW ATTITUDES TO HISTORY

Though it must not be imagined that there is any distinct dividing line, it would be true to say that in the history of Revolutionary studies in England, the second half of the nineteenth century is of less dramatic interest than the first. Whereas in the earlier part of the century it was possible to trace some general tendencies this has become increasingly difficult to do in the later decades. There appear in the latter half of the century more divergencies between individuals and less between groups. In England historical fashions were studied, absorbed and modified in stages so gradual that a fresh development often represented not a new school of interpretation but something more like a new attempt to fuse previously existing schools. For this reason it is easy to be too definite in one's attempt to fix the moment at which England came under the influence of the nineteenth-century continental movements in historiography. Some awareness of the new movements can be seen in this country since the beginning of the century, but it was not in general currency and it was not even generally noticed at the time. Much that belonged to the older school of historical writing was still visible and was even popular in the middle of the century. Neither would it be true of England that up to 1850 history was written for pleasure like literature and since then for knowledge. Between 1815 and 1848 history was a matter of vital importance even though its study was not professional.

John Stuart Mill was such a keen observer of historical fashions that his widely spaced articles on history serve us as useful indicators of English reactions. In 1826 he had argued with Mignet's sententious generalizations; in 1828 he considered the novelist's story-telling technique as dangerous for the historian because it pushes him to arrange too much of history in patterns of cause and effect; in 1837 he marvelled at Carlyle's achievement. Towards the middle of the century, his review of the early volumes of Michelet's *History of France*[1] is an interesting discussion of history writing by a man who was in other ways ahead of his time. It is a further development of Mill's previous analysis of the best history writing as that in which detail is subservient to a philosophy. It is also an ardent defence of French historical writings against those of Germany and England. In England, writes Mill in 1844, there are no signs of the new history except in Arnold and Carlyle, the latter of whom

[1] *E.R.* (Jan. 1844).

combined laborious accuracy with imagination. The old prejudice against French frivolity and superficiality should be abandoned when Michelet himself acknowledges Christianity at least as an historical factor, and Guizot and Thierry have done more for English history than any Englishman. Mill's complaint about the English contempt for French history was not without some basis. Three years later Lamartine was greeted by *Fraser's* with scorn for attempting 'poetic history' and as exemplifying the general inferiority of the French except in culinary and cosmetic arts. For Mill there are three stages in historical inquiry. The first reads present feelings into the past (as, for instance, when Tory writers on Athens describe Demosthenes as an Anacharsis Clootz). The second stage is to see past ages with their own eyes, either through minute detection such as Niebuhr's, or through imaginative power such as Carlyle's. Thierry, taught by Scott and Chateaubriand, also writes in that manner. The third stage is the construction of a science of history. Mill thought Guizot's speculative mind suited to England, but that his excursions into scientific history were not successful, because in history, 'we must proceed from the ensemble to the details, and not conversely', and great results must be explained by simple laws. Guizot writes the history of France as the history of Europe at its most typical. Michelet, as a poet rather than a philosopher or statesman, tackles what Guizot ignored, individual man.

Mill's ideas about history show the fusion of different current and old theories. Like Mackintosh in reviewing Sismondi in 1821, but from a more advanced vantage point, Mill again exemplifies a tradition of thought about history which refused to succumb to any one strict fashion, be it purely romantic, descriptive, documentary or idealist. Instead it sought to learn from all, adopt something of each, and subject history to the further aim of analysis or, as it was beginning to be called, historical science. In its extreme and logical expression, Mill's science of history would be taken up and developed by Buckle, by the Positivists, and by their political opponent, Sir Henry Maine, but the science of history never became the general tendency.

It was typical of England that in the generation before the death of Macaulay in 1859, historiography became more scholarly in character without any conscious following of historical theories. A development of a more careful scholarship seems to have occurred with the growing conscientiousness of writers, as a result of the stern criticism of the anonymous reviewers, and by the gradual separation of the learned writers from the publicists and the popularizers. Whereas most writings in the first half of the century are reflective, critical or compilatory, there is in the second half a greater awareness of scholarship on the one hand, and of basic interpretations on the other hand. This meant that proper history became more concrete and professional while publicist reflections became more abstract. On the whole, after the middle of the century, a deeper sense of historical responsibility and a greater effort to secure impartiality and even detachment can be discerned. Throughout this period there were outstanding writers like Morley and Browning who wrote of the Revolution with as much intensity as the historians of the previous half-century. Like Tocqueville, however, they would have said that they were trying to write 'without prejudice but not without passion'.

In order that Revolutionary studies could be carried forward, original materials were needed as well as a critical, conscientious and systematic attitude of mind. Frenchmen had been working on primary sources ever since the Revolution, for documents had been slowly released either from private sources or during periods of governmental change. But no Englishmen had gone to France to study original sources though some had gone to collect materials, use the libraries, observe the setting and talk to survivors from the Revolutionary period.

THE OPENING OF THE ARCHIVES

After the influence of ideas associated with Niebuhr and Ranke, the opening of the European archives in the 1860s represents a new stage in the development of historiography generally. Although the French Revolution by destroying the legal relevance of many forms of ancient documents had released these for use of historians, and although, during the Revolution itself, the archives of the *ancien régime* had partly been made accessible, the archives of the Revolutionary period itself only became available under the Second Empire, which is the time when systematic documentary research began. National archives were thrown open one after another and so did municipal, private and other archives. Political revolution, too, favoured historical research. Dynastic archives fell into the hands of people indifferent to the preservation of the secrets of the past, and once archives were being opened no country could afford to lag behind and leave, as Acton put it, its history to its enemies. Since England had no revolution, her archives were less easily available. When the records of the Foreign Office later became accessible they gave a further stimulus to a section of revolutionary studies which had always been favoured in this country—namely, international relations at the time of the Revolution. Tocqueville had opened the documentary study of the Revolution, but the first to study systematically the Paris archives was Mortimer Ternaux with a voluminous work on one year. Compardon and Wallon followed in his footsteps, covering the field of Revolutionary Tribunals and of the *Representatives* in the provinces, and like Ternaux, using faithfully official reports, to display with marked emphasis the revolutionary horrors.[1] In England, people who were most concerned

[1] Social Histories were written by Goncourt and Schmidt who used Police records.

about a fair judgment of the Revolution as a whole treated these works with suspicion at first, as showing one side only. The value of the new materials unearthed, and of the new systematic study was, however, immediately pointed out by people like Acton.

With the beginning of the documentary age in Revolutionary historiography, marked by the opening of the Austrian archives as well as by systematic study of local French archives, English scholarship began conspicuously to lag behind France and Germany.[1] And yet English historians now tended to produce their own technical narratives and became less content with mere commentaries on previous literature. Some of the compilations which cropped up as a result of the greater activity in France were mere abridgments of French works for the English public. Of this kind was the work of Charles Yonge who compiled a *History of the Bourbons* by simplifying a resumé of Sismondi, Michelet and Martin, and had no idea of the use of sources. He made much of the new publications of letters by Conches and Arneth, but he used them in conjunction with such works as Mountjoie, for the purpose of frank adulation, in his *Life of Marie Antoinette* (1867). He exasperated Masson by thinking that the manuscripts had had their last say and was sent by his French critic to the British Museum to learn otherwise. Real scholarship such as that of Croker ceased to be in advance of its age and his *Essays* of 1857 were naturally overshadowed by Tocqueville and von Sybel.

The pioneer work of von Sybel was only taken notice of after its translation in 1867 when some periodicals noted in particular von Sybel's Cassandra-like prophecies for a repeated revolution in France.[2] Because knowledge of von Sybel was delayed till after Sorel had written in a language more easily accessible in England, his work was never fully appreciated and for his pompous conservative style he was later dubbed by Frederic Harrison as a *Franzosenfresser* and, worse still, a 'German Alison'.

Under the second Empire when most of the great historians were working with original materials, under a régime alien to them all, a body of opinion was forming in France with less direct reference to politics. Even Quinet, writing in exile with no research, and believed to be aiming at the Emperor, wrote independently of the known schools of thought on the Revolution. He attacked Jacobinism for its violence, without (as did his friend Michelet) blaming the counter-revolution for having provoked the violence. Like Michelet he was an enemy of the Catholic Church but not of religion. Inconsistently he attacked the

---

[1] The publications in 1864, by Feuillet-de-Conches and by Hunolstein, of the letters of Marie Antoinette led to the opening of the Austrian archives and to the publications of Arneth. The importance of the latter was not immediately seen in England and the *E.R.* greeted them with a frivolous article (Oct. 1876, CXLIV, 319).

[2] E.g. *Christian Observer*.

Revolution both for its violence and for failing to impose Protestantism, thus showing also the limitations of his historical sense. Independently of the diplomatic archives Quinet showed that there were two monarchical policies and that the emigration despised the King and wished him dead.

ENGLAND WELCOMES TOCQUEVILLE

The great French histories were translated and widely read; but those were most admired which had most in common with the traditional comprehensiveness of the English view. Tocqueville, therefore, was the favourite. His earlier work on America, written not without France of 1830 in mind, aroused much interest in England and its reputation had been consistently growing. In spite of its reservations and warnings it seemed too democratic for the Whigs of 1830. In political discussions, Tocqueville's *America* was often taken into account as a book which might encourage revolutions in England. But some of the Whigs had developed their reforming spirit by 1856, while Tocqueville himself had now become more conservative. As in the case of Burke, Tocqueville's reputation was enhanced through the fact that his prophecies had been fulfilled. 'We admire every paragraph and agree with every sentiment', writes the *Edinburgh* on the subject of Tocqueville's French Revolutionary work.[1] Tocqueville's contributions are assessed in much the way they are assessed today; emphasizing the account of the social structure of pre-Revolutionary France, the diagnosis of the origins of the concrete legal and economic grievances, and the tracing of the continuity in the increasing administrative centralization. The book created great surprise. After all that had been written on the causes of the Revolution a new light on this subject, through the examination of unexplored materials, had not been generally expected.

Tocqueville saw that philosophy enhanced the catastrophe of the Revolution and he put much blame on the preference for equality over liberty. The stress he put on the lack of practical experience in the French political writers pleased English readers who despised a Godwin. Tocqueville's insistence on the variety of causes which combined to produce the Revolution was also in conformity with the English tradition, where Burke's diagnosis of 'irreverence' and political atheism as to the root of the evil was combined with a long-established recognition of the nature of the economic and political grievances in pre-Revolutionary France.[2] On this view of the causes, everything could be seen to have paved the way for the Revolution—not only abuses but also the King's efforts to reform them. Tocqueville who had learnt from Burke, for

---

[1] *E.R.* (Oct. 1956), CIV, 531.
[2] That Tocqueville stressed both philosophic and economic causes satisfied for instance the *Westminster* (Oct. 1856), LXVI, 462.

instance, the comparison of the Revolution to a religious movement, the connection between economic and political power, also taught Englishmen the value of their own early writings on the Revolution, especially those of Arthur Young whose *Travels* was declared by Tocqueville to be of the greatest importance. There was much in common between Tocqueville and Arthur Young, especially in that both of them based their views on an acute observation of conditions in pre-revolutionary France—the one directly, and the other through the records of local institutions—and both put great emphasis on the role of the principle of equality and of property in the Revolution.

England was devoted to the ideal of the statesman-historian, and as a practical man Tocqueville was congenial to her through his distrust of theory and his sagacity in observation. (Some conservatives, however, though attracted, could not see how a practical man could be a liberal still.) Tocqueville, moreover, treated the Revolution as having grown out of specifically French conditions so that he supported the English view which sought to localize the evil and which resented Louis Blanc's thesis imputing the Revolution to a natural development in the general European world of ideas. By tracing its ideas to the Reformation and laying stress on the principle of individualism, Blanc seemed to bring the revolutionary ideas too close to England. Tocqueville on the other hand dwelt on the differences between France and England. The biographical interest, however, was strong in England and historians noticed the absence of this in Tocqueville.

The English historians and critics had not been fully aware of the break in revolutionary historiography which the works of Lamartine, Blanc, Michelet and Villiaumé marked. The underlying views of these latter, especially those of Blanc, were criticized, but the significance of the new alliance between history and socialism, and of the break with the tradition of Thiers and Mignet and the middle classes, was not fully appreciated except in the case of Blanc. They were not aware that whereas Thiers and Mignet had tried to explain and justify everything that had happened, thus clearing France as a whole, the new historians marked a tendency to accept and continue certain aspects, or even groups, of the Revolution while rejecting the others. They had no idea of the part Lamartine played in preparing the Republic. They were more aware of the fact that Lamartine, like Mignet, made men neither better nor worse that circumstances made them, creatures of the hatred of tyranny, the bloodshed and the national danger. Some, on the other hand, thought that Lamartine was writing against the 'fatalist' school and that he was too favourable to Robespierre. To say that blood sullied the men but not the Revolution, said a *Fraser's* reviewer, is neither sound history nor common sense.

Tocqueville marked a change they were less likely to misunderstand or to ignore, for he clearly broke with the tendency which had prevailed since Mignet to clear off the infamy. Tocqueville openly condemned his country. His criticism of the French character and his impatience with political metaphysics made him popular in England. It appealed to England that he narrowed the ground, made no effort to connect the Revolution with universal forces, but examined the local administrative facts. They saw him as an antidote to the school of Mignet and the theory of the necessity of the Revolution. Because he was writing like a statesman, they did not mind his writing for the sake of the present and not of history, and they did not see that he failed to distinguish in the Revolution the struggle for liberty from the struggle for power, a distinction often made by English historians. Because he hardly used any authorities except the archives, he seemed the more authoritative and readers were blinded to much that was hollow thinking, pedantry and his basic assumption as to what constitutes historical continuity.

THE PROFESSORS AND THE POSITIVIST

The Professors of History in Cambridge[1] all chose French subjects and all were in that genteel tradition which runs uninterrupted from Smyth to Seeley—using history in order to discourse generally on politics and morals. Stephens and Kingsley did not even come up to the scholarly standard of their predecessor Smyth. When Kingsley was appointed in 1860 his Christian socialism had become a conservative creed indeed. Although he was engaged in historical activity the completely unhistorical quality of his mind never changed. In his lectures on the *ancien régime* he ignored Tocqueville's work.[2] One of his plans for a set of lectures was to show how Carlyle's *French Revolution*, Maurice's *Kingdom of Christ* and Bunsen's *God in History* all disprove Comte who had become to him the embodiment of revolutionism.[3] History to Kingsley was truly a text for a sermon but Acton deemed his lectures sufficiently important to merit an attack. Kingsley's aims and method as a teacher of history are illustrated by his oft-quoted concluding words, 'If I have convinced you that well-doing and ill-doing are rewarded and punished in this world as in the world to come, I shall have done you more good than if I had crammed your mind with many dates and facts.' His predecessor Stephens had also lectured on France. He assumed the students to have read Smyth's *Lectures* which, he said, taught how history should be studied and his own aim was to rescue history from barren detail and barren generalization.

[1] Smyth (1807–49), Stephens (1849–59), Kingsley (1860–9), Seeley (1869–95).
[2] C. Kingsley, *The Ancien Régime* (three lectures given at the Royal Institute in 1867).
[3] The Christian Socialists, esp. Maurice, chose to present Carlyle's *F.R.* as evidence for the reality of a divine and moral order. See Kingsley, 10 Sept. 1868, 23 Oct. 1868.

The three chapters in Buckle, which Acton, forty years later, still declared to be, along with Lecky, the best accounts of the French Revolution in the English language, came out in 1857 and missed all the massive documentary work which was beginning to transform historical studies. These chapters deal with the background to the Revolution, and bring out three points, the influence on eighteenth-century France of English literature and institutions, the intolerable oppression of opinion and writings in the old régime, and the distinct separation between ecclesiastical and political criticism in eighteenth-century literature. Buckle amasses weighty evidence for these points but in citing for instance hundreds of references in French works, he does not work out the actual influence of England on France. When the same subject was taken up later by Stephens, he had more concrete things to say about it. He showed for instance that the different notions of English institutions held by people like Lally, Mirabeau and Marat resulted from their different connections in England, and he explained Mounier's failure on the ground that his notions were theoretic, learnt from books alone.[1] Mounier, said Stephens, illustrated the failure of theory in politics; he stood for 1789 as Mirabeau stood for 1790 and Robespierre for 1794. Buckle's acquaintance with eighteenth-century literature is the only thing that qualifies him to be considered in connection with the Revolution, for he gives no account of it. His importance in historiography lies rather in his conception of history as a natural science in the sense that it conducts minute observation and tries to use them for the purpose of wide generalizations, 'il est moit convaincu qu'il avait été le Bacon des sciences historique'.[2] In this he was a follower of Mill and Comte but he also wished to deepen the empirical system by an actual historical inquiry conducted on 'scientific' lines. In this he anticipated Taine, the realistic school in France, and the Positivist group of historians in England. Acton's criticism of Buckle shows the opposition in England to a 'science of history'. Buckle became popular with socialist historians. It is his views on Burke which are repeated in Kareiev's history of French Revolutionary historiography. The first and most diligent student of theories of history was Flint who rejected all exclusive explanations of history, whether deterministic, optimistic, racial or materialistic.[3] History, he said, must be understood as a joint product of God and sociology. The English point of view was put more simply by an *Edinburgh* reviewer who said that Buckle rejected moral principle in history and that no Englishman could therefore accept his doctrines.[4]

[1] Stephens on Mounier. *E.H.R.* (1888), III, 390.

[2] A. Filon, 'Les Historiens Anglais' *Deux Mondes* (1 Mars 1888), LXXXVI, 59.

[3] Acton made a chapter on historiography in the *C.M.H.* dependent on Flint writing it (D. MacMillan, *Life of Flint*, 212; C.U.L. Add. MS. 7472, Acton to Poole; Acton on Flint, *E.H.R.* (1895), 108).

[4] *E.R.* (1858), CVII, 465.

CHAPTER 14

ENGLISH HISTORY COMES OF AGE

A NEW KIND OF HISTORY?

Towards the end of the century, a great generation of English historians coincided with a great generation of Revolutionary historians in France. By this time the learned periodicals were helping to establish professional ties between the researchers, writers and critics of different nations. The *Revue des Questions Historiques*, for example, had a regular section, '*courrier anglais*', where Gustave Masson reviewed English historical works, showing how far they were behind the researchers in France in the field of Revolutionary studies.[1] The establishment of the *English Historical Review* in 1886 ensured a steady and scholarly contact with the French Revolutionary studies now being organized by Aulard who was appointed to the Revolutionary Chair in 1885. It collected around it professional historians whose judgment was at least as effective in raising the standard as the scurrilous and anonymous reviews had been earlier. There was in that period more thorough study of foreign writings and of documents, published and unpublished. Jervis, Fyffe, Gardiner, Stephens, Browning, Seeley and others were writing their own Revolutionary works and reviewing those of others. They were also the historians called upon to supply the French Revolutionary items for the 9th edition of the *Encyclopaedia Britannica*.

At this period when factual history had become an ideal, and spade work was absorbing the best minds, when French scholars were unearthing unexplored levels of Revolutionary life, English students of the subject gave up pure moral and political reflections and judgments on revolutionaries and historians, and showed aspirations towards original contributions. The more they succeeded in merging with the armies of French researchers, the further they moved from the traditional English school of Revolutionary studies. In order to make contributions they turned mainly to a subject in which interest had always been strong, that of the international aspect of the Revolution. It was connected with English history, and for its study they also had documents of their own. There was a steady trickle of diplomatic information in the published memoirs and papers of English statesmen, diplomats and agents, in the papers of Auckland, Malmesbury, Rigby, Miles, Wickham, Elliot and

---

[1] S. R. Gardiner supplied the *Revue Historique* with bulletins on English historical literature between 1876 and 1881. The British Museum Catalogue was started in 1881.

others, and this was continued from official sources when these became available. Lecky, Browning, Seeley and Fyffe worked with materials from the Public Record Office. Browning's editions of various diplomatic papers in the *Gower Despatches* is still used and his articles make original points. For his study of the flight to Varennes he conducted field work (riding a tricycle along the route of the flight, among other things), and his findings were used by Lenz. Browning assisted Lecky in his work on the Revolution; Lord Acton advised Browning on 'things good to know', helped him with his article on Pitt, and thought of him as a specialist on the foreign relations of the Revolution.[1] From the Public Record Office and the French archives Browning summarized the papers relating to the war of 1793, which he thought was caused by no other reason than the threat to Holland.[2] He used the Auckland papers in 1884 for his study of Pitt before they went to the Museum. Some of these were apparently lost after he had seen them.[3] He had difficulty in finding a publisher for the *Gower Despatches* though Taine and Sorel pronounced them important.[4] One publisher refused them on the ground that, having compared the materials to Carlyle's work, he had found in them nothing new on the flight to Varennes. One wonders how far Browning's determined and absurdly thorough refutation of Carlyle's story of the flight was reinforced by such an outrageous argument. Browning introduced his edition with a disjointed account of the Revolution written from the point of view of the relations between France and England, and including some mistakes. Browning's contributions to Revolutionary studies were the publications of documents and the specialized studies on Varennes, the Triple Alliance, the Treaty of Commerce, and on France and England in 1793.

If Browning's contributions to professional history were specialized, his overall view of history was old-fashioned and narrow. In Cambridge, in Browning's time, the battle was waging in the historical school between history and politics. The debates and reforms had started when Seeley established the historical tripos, were renewed in the 'eighties and again

[1] Acton to Creighton ... 1885. C.U.L. Add. MS. 6871. 'There is another book on the French Revolution by Sorel, of which I have seen only the first volume on the diplomatic history of the Revolution. Surely this would be a job for Browning a specialist in that very department?' Later Acton suggested young Mallet: 'I could imagine him useful for a book like Sorel's—pace Oscar.' But the review was given to Seeley. Browning saw much of Acton in 1879 (Browning, *Memories*, p. 277).

[2] 'France and England in 1793', *Fortnightly* (1883).

[3] Browning, *Memories*, p. 310.

[4] Taine had not read the manuscripts when he wrote to Browning on 15 Nov. 1883 that the publication would be useful. 'Des hommes compétent qui m'ont parlé de ces dépêches m'ont déclaré qu'elles étaient de la plus haute importance ... Je donnerais cinq cent volumes de journaux, pamphlets et brochures pour les lettres qu'un ambassadeur, homme d'Etat, écrit sur place de semaine en semaine, au premier ministre de son pays ou à son souverain.' See also the letters of Taine to Browning of 28 Jan. 1885, 30 Nov. 1885 (*H. Taine, Sa vie et sa Correspondance* (Paris, 1907), IV, 175, 189, 214).

in the 'nineties when Browning headed the camp which fought against a purely historical tripos. Browning always claimed that Seeley had founded the tripos for an educational and political purpose, in the same spirit in which the Chair itself had been founded. He quoted the Royal patent which had established the Regius Professorship in History in 1715 to show that 'there is nothing to suggest research in it'.[1] Against Prothero and others, Seeley and Browning held that history at the University was a training for public life and not for historical research. When he stood for Parliament,[2] Browning explained that as a trainer of politicians he ought to learn the subject from the inside. When in his Inaugural lecture he explains what Political Science is, we find him making a case for an inductive study of political history, and an account of typical political institutions. Political problems are solved in much the same way in different stages of civilization, and in the Africa of today, we may find the best explanations for ancient Roman institutions.[3]

Acton, who in Cambridge opposed Browning's view on the teaching of history, encouraged, both before and after he came to Cambridge, the sort of specialized research to which Browning had in fact contributed. One of the products of his training at the University was Clapham, whom Acton initially launched on French Revolutionary studies. He arranged the publication of Clapham's first piece of research on 'A Royalist Spy during the Reign of Terror', which attempted to prove the unreliability of a series of twenty-eight bulletins from Paris (September 1793–June 1794), published by the Historical Manuscripts Commission (1894), and widely discussed at the time.[4] Clapham, as Acton says, 'disagrees highly with his master Browning'.[5] He also displays an extraordinary amount of minute research to prove the spy a liar. But Clapham also disagrees with his master Acton in minimizing the influence of America on the French Revolution, and when he contemptuously dismisses Siéyès as 'a vain and cowardly political theorist', whose advice Robespierre would not deign to use. To Acton Siéyès was 'the most splendid genius that has appeared on earth'. Clapham later changed his view and

---

[1] O. Browning, The Proposed New Historical Tripos (privately printed 1896); O. Browning, *Political Science*, Introductory Lecture (n.d.); O. Browning, *Memories*, pp. 234, 235.

[2] In 1886 and 1895. Browning, *Memories*, p. 316.

[3] O. Browning, *Political Science*. He explains it is a branch of sociology studying typical institutions. History is too wide and useless. Political science provides instruments useful to historians and to statesmen.

[4] *E.H.R.* (1887), p. 596.

[5] Acton to Poole, 18 Nov. 1896, 24 Nov. 1896 (C.U.L. Add. MS. 7472). Clapham, wrote Acton, 'spent the Vacation at Paris between the library and the archives' and is 'immersed in the French Revolution'. 'I think his conclusions are legitimate and sound.' Acton adds that another friend ('almost adopted pupil') of his has also written on the same question and 'is to appear in Sybel'. See also *E.R.* (Oct. 1896); Browning, *Cosmopolis* (Aug. 1896); *Rév. fr.* (Oct. 1896); *R.Q.H.* (Oct. 1896).

made a thorough study of Siéyès and his political theory. Acton also guided Clapham's researches into the *Causes of the War of 1792*, which won Clapham a prize. This work, unlike the overdone first article, is a perfect example of the new professional research conducted in England. As Clapham says, 'it deals with a subject that has been under discussion almost continually for a century', and the previous work left little room for surprises.

There had been earlier attempts to study isolated aspects of the Revolution, such as Jervis's studies of French ecclesiastical history before and during the Revolution, for which he prepared over many years in French archives. The strong biographical interest produced towards the end of the century some biographies which rank high among the French ones. A new appearance also are works written on a learned level and yet from a socialist point of view, such as the life of Marat by Bax. The rehabilitation of Marat had started with Villiaumé's history of 1848 and was continued by Bougeart[1] and Chevremont. In England the apologists for Marat were F. Bowen-Graves, Bax and to a certain extent H. M. Stephens.[2] Bax learnt much from Bowen-Graves, whose argument he practically reproduces even to the bitter comparison between the massacres of September 1792 and those of May 1871 conducted by the French government. The recurring assumption in the new socialist history is the same as in that of the 1830s, when the first feeble attempts were made in the popular press to reverse historical judgments on the extreme revolutionaries such as Robespierre by stressing their social aims. Again we read that the historians, the 'literary champions of vested interests', control the reputations of the revolutionaries since their rehabilitation would constitute 'the condemnation of the present'. It is opinion governed by a class, says Bax, which has condemned Marat. Bax's treatment of the Revolution is interesting because unlike the previous English admirers of the extreme Jacobins he had in general and philosophical writings openly, if crudely, advanced a Marxian historical determinism as the only intelligible reading of history. 'Either the theory of modern Socialism rests on a solid historical basis, or it is nothing',[3] he said. Apart from producing new socialist writings, there is a striking departure in the way English historical opinion reacted to the new Revolution that had taken place in France. France and England had moved too widely apart in their political histories for any party in England to consider the events of 1871 as relevant to its own fortunes. Halévy in considering the English reaction to the chain of French Revolutions, as moving from sympathy to hostility and indifference, called it the law

---

[1] Bougeart, *Marat Ami du Peuple.*

[2] Bax, *Marat* (1879); Bowen-Graves, *Fortnightly* (Feb. 1874); Bax, *G.M.* (1877), 241, 572; H. M. Stephens, *A History of the French Revolution* (1886–92); *Encyclopaedia Britannica*; *Pall Mall* (1896).

[3] E. B. Bax, *The Religion of Socialism*, p. iv.

of increasing insularity.[1] The Revolution of 1871, when republicans slaughtered socialists, aroused general repugnance in England and even republicans like Harrison were hostile to the Third Republic, while liberal opinion was not unsympathetic to the fallen Emperor. There is therefore after 1871 no great tendency in England to make comparisons or to associate England with French politics, but rather to benefit indirectly through general discussions of revolution, democracy and socialism. The number of individual books and articles is great and there are, especially around 1889 (the year of the centenary), renewed discussions of the principles of the First Revolution. Even these writings, though imbued with political emotion, show how detached on the whole from any party lines the subject had become, except for the few socialist historians. Even Bax in his final estimate of Marat admits his hero's narrowness in failing to recognize the 'synthetic character' of life and to see that intellectual and religious reconstruction must precede the regeneration of society. Marat, he confessed, was no idealist. Not only practical studies but thought about the Revolution had become an individual matter, and the same periodicals often abound in writings from different points of view.[2] One of the writers, for example, who was eminently influenced by Taine was Lilly, whose philosophy was shaped by an antagonism to the French Revolution, and who believed that Gladstone modelled himself on Robespierre. But the political element in Lilly's writings was really abstract, and he ultimately took his stand behind English democracy, against French democracy. Having written a philosophical refutation of the Declaration of the Rights of Man, in 1881, he wrote in 1899 that the Declaration 'impressed deeply, we may hope ineradicably . . . the truth that man does possess certain rights as man-rights which may properly be called natural'.[3]

THE RECEPTION OF TAINE IN ENGLAND

Taine, who introduced into Revolutionary historiography an attack more powerful than any since Burke, had great influence on his generation in France. He had been a materialist who believed that race and environment determine civilizations,[4] and also a radical who had warmly defended the *sansculottes* against Carlyle, as having fought for a higher

[1] E. Halévy, 'English Public Opinion and the French Revolutions of the 19th Century', in A. Colville and H. Temperley, *Studies in Anglo-French History* (1935).

[2] See, e.g., *Contemporary Review* (1881), pp. 944–70, where the principles of 1789 are attacked by Lilly, and that of 1889. 'The principles of the French Revolution have become the common property of the civilised world.'

[3] See, e.g., W. S. Lilly, *First Principles in Politics* (London, 1899), pp. 193–5; 37.

[4] In *Histoire de la littérature Anglaise* (6th ed. 1891), xxii, he says, 'Trois sources différentes contribuent à produire cet état moral élémentaire, la race, la milieu et le moment.'

and more unselfish freedom than the Puritans. His first volume was 'ambiguous' in its politics and pleased even the left through its treatment of the sufferings of the peasants. Taine was changed by the events of 1870 and became an admirer of English conservative principles and of established institutions. He also conceived a passion for scientific history and determined to go to contemporary evidence without paying attention to later controversy. He later claimed that the original documents had changed his view of the Revolution from the delusion fostered by Thiers, but his judgment had been formed before he amassed his illustrative detail. His picture is therefore static, and Aulard exposed the shallowness of his research and the credulous use he made of the contemporary materials.[1]

Taine's lack of positive belief of any kind and his rejection of the *ancien régime*, the Revolution and Napoleon, as well as his formulated analysis of the revolutionary spirit (as deriving from classicism and science), and his 'science of history', gave him an influence in England which could not last. The Catholic and politically reactionary *Dublin Review* credits Taine with 'perfect impartiality'. The influence of foreign thought on France, including that of England, the concrete grievances, the concrete political situation, were by now considered in England as powerful causes of the French Revolution, and the constructive efforts of the Revolution had long been accepted. Taine was an extreme disciple of Burke's anti-revolutionary writings. His work was described by Hanotaux as 'the cry of the vanquished'. 'His Jacobins', wrote Gooch, spring 'fully armed from the brain of Rousseau'. The motive and meaning of the Revolution he also insisted was the transfer of property, and he rejected the distinction between 1789 and the Terror. The French Royalists welcomed Taine as a weapon against the use of the Revolutionary tradition for systematic reform, and since French conservatism was now allied with the *bourgeoisie* against socialism, also for his acquittal of the nation as a whole. England, however, had already made Burke the teacher of liberalism. The leading Revolutionary thinker in England when Taine's work appeared was Morley, who was extreme in his reforming liberalism and (like Leslie Stephen and Lecky) strong in his insistence on Burke's consistency and on his own discipleship to him. Even Buckle, who explained the *Reflections* by saying that French crimes simply drove Burke mad, paid tribute to Burke's foresight.

Taine's method of history writing was criticized as that of 'pouring his notebooks' into a book, but above all, his 'science of history' weighed heavily against him even in Tory scales. In Taine, the late nineteenth-century conception of scientific history reached as pure a form as in Marx. It was the notion that the historian, through minute observa-

---

[1] E.g. of G. Morris, Mallet du Pan and a record of the experiences of an English lady probably fabricated by Gifford.

tion, could discover permanent laws, and thereby foretell the future. Taine observed history as the scientists observed biological life. 'Mon livre, si j'ai assez de force et de santé pour l'achever, sera une consultation du médecin', he wrote.[1] The best historical opinion in England, that of men like Stubbs, Gardiner, Morley, Acton and Lecky, rejected this notion and Morley dismissed as sociology work like Taine's. Non-historical opinion, too, repeated the old argument that history could never be a science since the historian could never be as indifferent to his materials as a zoologist is, being himself a product of history. The old suspicion of 'philosophies of history', as attempts to weave too much into a cause and effect pattern, was loudly raised against Taine, and the reaction against theories like his shaped, for instance, the view of Lecky. Those who were receptive to Taine's science of history, though not always to his view resulting from it (a proper reflection on the finality of his science), were the English Positivists, the old 'political science' school of history (including, for instance, Browning) and, oddly, the jurist Sir Henry Maine who was, at the same time, the most faithful follower that the historical school of Savigny had in England.

ANTI-REVOLUTIONISM—THE *DUBLIN REVIEW*

The one consistent anti-Revolutionary school in England which warmly welcomed Taine is that which can be reconstructed from the pages of the Catholic *Dublin Review*. It had an all-embracing thesis based on ultramontanism. 'Jansenism, Gallicanism and Jacobinism' are identical or mutually generating evils. Protestantism is the source of all these evils. Rationalism resulted from Jansenism and caused Jacobinism. Jacobinism was merely the Gallicanism of the secular people. 'The Revolution was the consummation of a revolt from authority which began in Gallicanism and ended in Jacobinism.'[2] For this recurring variety of formulae, all tracing the Revolution to the Reformation, the writers for the *Dublin Review* quote many authorities. Alison was the most acceptable to this school for his conservative politics but he is corrected on religious points: He traced the Revolution 'to the oppression of Protestantism, we to its influence and diffusion'. Robespierre is quoted to have said of the Encyclopaedists: 'It was they who introduced the frightful doctrine of atheism' and the 'selfish system which reduces egotism to a system.' In an article of 1889 the author rejects the prevailing fashion of treating the Revolution as a beneficiary movement distorted by subsequent developments and claims that 'It was from its initiation an organized attack, captained and led by sworn conspirators, on all pre-existing institutions beginning with religion and the corner stone of

[1] 24 March 1878. Quoted by G. Monod, *Renan, Taine, Michelet* (Paris, 1913), p. 124.
[2] Finlayson, *D.R.* (Sept. 1854), xxxvii, 96–189.

human society.' The doctrines of Jacobinism, anarchy and subversion were formulated before the catastrophe.

The central point for the *Dublin Review* remained the anti-Christian nature of the Revolution and the concomitant view of the Revolution's own character as a religion. For this the writers in the *Dublin Review* quoted Tocqueville who had said that the Revolution resembled a religious movement through its character of universality and through the passions it inspired. They do not repeat any of the qualifications Tocqueville made for this view. They distort Tocqueville's view that the Revolution turned against religion only because of the temporal power of the church, when they say that the hatred of Christianity was the great motive power of the Revolution, imprinting on it what de Maistre called its Satanic character. At the end of an interesting article on the principles of 1789 the writer is carried away so far as to say that the culminating result of those principles was cannibalism. The Catholic *Review* also tried in several articles to minimize the role of the Irish in the Revolutionary movement.

The *Dublin Review* embodied an anti-revolutionary hysteria which was nowhere else to be found among writers of any political party. This is best brought out by the writings of Sir Henry Maine who learnt from the same teachers, but to different purposes. From Burke he learnt historicism, from Taine, a 'science of history', and from Tocqueville methods of administrative research.

CONSERVATISM, HISTORICISM AND SCIENCE IN SIR HENRY MAINE

Maine, like Taine, was a late adherent of historicism, a believer in the 'science of history' and a hater of democracy. He was not a historian of the French Revolution but he has an important place in English historical thought, he studied the *ancien régime* and his ideas bear on the questions asked by English historians. He believed himself to be a true disciple of the school of Eichhorn and Savigny. His historical treatment of jurisprudence was novel in the England of 1861. He saw his work as aimed against *a priori* assumptions in the study of law, man and society and was fierce against Rousseau, natural law and revolution. He attacked Benthamite analytical jurisprudence for deducing from general principles a system of natural equality and for neglecting the concrete elements of custom, politics, ethics, religion, which in fact shape law. He thought that Montesquieu almost founded the historical method though he overrated external conditions and underrated the influence of race and tradition. But Maine differed from his masters in his notion of history as a science in method and in aim, a science ascertaining truth through observation, experimentation and the discovery of recurring laws. In this he came nearer to Bentham than he liked, for if Bentham wished to reform laws according to views, the views would also be the result of observation and not of dogma. History, wrote Maine, is like Astronomy or Physiology, of 'continuous sequence, inflexible order and eternal law'.[1] This important point of departure meant, as Maine actually said, that gaps in historical information could be filled by 'experiments', that is, observing other societies in appropriate circumstances. This is where his system contradicts itself for it presupposes similar and recurring processes of development and thereby impairs the sole historical authority of the national past which was the maxim of Historicism.

Maine was the only English historian who, because of the nature of his own studies, was able to follow closely the researches into the legal, economic and administrative structure of the *ancien régime* which Tocqueville and Taine conducted. Other English historians like Montague continued to study the *cahiers*, not for the economic and legal facts they revealed, but rather for the wishes they expressed. Montague, for instance, derives from them the conclusion that the Revolution for the masses was purely an economic and not an ideological affair. Maine, like many others, accepted and repeated Tocqueville's view that the proper study of the old régime had been delayed due to strong feelings bred by family memories and interests. Both those who suffered from the Revolution and those who based their rights on it were for obvious reasons reluctant to trace the links connecting the Revolution with the *ancien régime*. Hence the view that the Revolution was a sudden catastrophe and hence also the neglect of the old documents especially the *cahiers*.[2] The researchers inspired by Tocqueville revealed the enigmatic and all-important fervour with which the peasants (unlike the provincial cities) rapidly espoused the Revolution, and voluntarily closed France for the escape of royalists more effectively than any police organization could possibly have done. Through the study of peasant landholding in France (which Maine considered to be similar to copyhold tenure in England) Maine arrived at his explanation for the hostility of the peasantry which he denies could have been caused by grievances of land tenure. 'The First Revolution', he claimed, 'took place because a great part of the soil of France was held on copyhold tenures.' Many nobles had no land and lived on the dues from copyhold which were therefore disputed in endless litigation in a defective legal system. The more independent the peasants became, the more they resisted the dues, and a new school of lawyers demanded legal proof for payments before more drastic remedies were found. Seizing the title deeds later became the real object of what Taine called, 'L'Anarchie Spontanée'. The 'sacredness of contract', says

[1] Maine, *Ancient Law* (1861), pp. 73–9; *Village Communities* (1880), pp. 265–6.
[2] Maine, *Early Law and Customs*, p. 392.

Maine, 'was one of the most fundamental ideas of the French philosophical creed', and a tremendous revolutionary movement therefore ran contrary to the philosophical creed. Though in the end the nobles received no compensation for manorial rights, this had not been the intention of the Assembly which distinguished between rights originating from contract and those traced to brute force. 'The distinction', says Maine, 'did some honour to the spirit of justice prevailing in the First Assembly, but no doubt it was founded in historical error.' 'Many causes and among them that personal friction which is the despair of all who would make History a science, had produced among the peasantry such intensity of hatred to their lord.' Once the transfer of property from class to class, through the abolition of feudal dues, was accomplished, the social revolution was over and the personal struggle for power began. It is interesting to note that this idea is also expressed by Acton.

Maine embodied in his own work the separation between research and views which was evident among historians at the time. His compulsive conservatism always seemed to require explanation and justification. Dicey said that it was history that turned him against the amendment of laws; Barker, that it was the lawyer's instinct; Morley, that India convinced Maine of the need for strong authority and of the slow growth of institutions; Pollock put it down to personal temperament; and Vinogradoff to the influence of German Historicism. But Maine's attack on liberalism was neither that of a fiery moralist, nor of a romantic in history. His *Popular Government* (1885), which made him the leader of Conservative opinion, offered a scientific and evolutionist sanction for the rule of the aristocracy. He also broke with the tradition of Burke and Coleridge by despairing of religion as a support for conservatism, and he arrived at an individualism and a distrust of the state which was mostly akin to liberalism, and which was abhorrent to extreme Tories and Socialists alike. Like Taine he had tried and failed to harmonize in one system history, science and politics.

MORLEY—THE LIBERAL TRADITION CONTINUED

Morley had studied the Revolution before he read Taine, and he had written on Burke and the *philosophes*. Carlyle had prejudiced his generation against the *philosophes* and although Buckle, under the influence of Comte, had helped to turn the tide, Morley was still so eager in that cause that he later admitted he had overdone his defence. Although he was steeped in eighteenth-century thought and had made much of Robespierre's Rousseauism, Morley was provoked by Taine's analysis of the destructiveness of pre-revolutionary thought, to deny the influence of this thought and to stress the concrete grievances. It was the evil influence ascribed to eighteenth-century philosophy which Morley resented.[1] He said that the Americans partook of the same literary drug, but being of a sound constitution, were cured by it. In France the philosophers were blamed in proportion to anti-revolutionism, while those who justified the Revolution stressed the concrete causes. Between Michelet and Aulard, for instance, pro-Revolutionary historical opinion was represented mainly in Gambetta's opportunist paper *La République Française* for which people like Avenal wrote. Though they valued the ideas of 1789, they claimed that only concrete grievances caused the outbreak, and only circumstances dictated the changes to Republicanism, Terror, etc. More extreme historians in France, to the right as well as to the left, were less empiric. Even Mathiez was to write, 'The Revolution had been accomplished in the minds of men long before it was translated into fact.' In England it was not quite the same. Jeffrey had asserted the influence on philosophy on the Revolution against Mounier, though he, on the whole, defended some of the Revolution, and Morley, in the same line of political succession, now denied it against Taine. He claims that certain ideas (and those not of eighteenth-century France, but of the Reformation) were seized by the revolutionaries as suitable formulae. Characters and institutions doomed the situation more than books. Dowden later quarrelled with Morley's position. He claimed that whatever grievances there were, were claimed on grounds of metaphysical right. Dowden agrees with Morley that Burke was ignorant of social conditions, but he says that Burke would have opposed the remedy in any case.[2] Macaulay, in mid-century, had represented the balance which was typical of English historiography when he said that neither philosophy nor grievances alone would have availed. Maine, too, rejected as foolish the two extreme views that speculation could have no real effect on the outbreak of the French Revolution, or that real interests had none. He brings out the stereotypes governing thought on this subject when he says that the accepted view was 'that Girondins were Voltairean and the Jacobin Rousseauites, while Danton was of the School of the Encyclopaedia, and Hébert and Chaumette were inspired by Holbach'.[3] Another popular formula was that eighteenth-century philosophy undermined the defences of the old régime but did not cause the Revolution. This view reconciled, especially for historians who believed in the power of ideas, the fact that philosophy had a part to play in the Revolution although it was not in itself a philosophy of revolution. It suited Lecky in England as it did Madelin in France. On the whole the tendency of most English historians (though not of Acton), as the century passed, was to proceed from philosophic to concrete causes.

Morley, unlike Lecky, disbelieved the popular idea that the Revolution

---

[1] Morley reviewed Taine in *Fortnightly* (1876), xxv, 370.
[2] Dowden, *England and the French Revolution*.   [3] Maine, *Popular Government*, p. 75.

checked English reform, though he does not disprove it. He thought that the only disservice it had done to England was to provide it with prejudicial nicknames, as those of Clootz and Babeuf for Cobden and Bright. Morley made light of these analogies though he was personally made a victim of such nicknaming. In 1846, over the Corn Laws, Croker, back in his old role, warned Morley that he was acting like the Noailles and Montmorencies in the French Revolution. Between 1868 and 1888 Morley was constantly attacked as a Jacobin because he was writing on the Revolution, and in connection with his Irish policy. In Dublin he was called 'the Saint Just of our Revolution', and accused of using the methods of the Terror. When Morley spoke of Welsh Disestablishment,[1] a letter to *The Times* said that as a French Revolutionary he was building on 'minor peculiarities of race and dialect', a charge Morley was able to overthrow by pointing rather to the tendency towards centralization of the Revolution. Another letter said that he was in favour of 1793 and the Goddess of Reason. The last charge especially must have rankled, because Morley, though closely connected in the *Fortnightly Review* with the leading Positivists, never went so far as to take seriously the Comtian Religion of Humanity, the ultimate stage of Positivism. As time went on Morley's pain at these accusations grew and he was anxious to dissociate himself from anything violent or abstract in politics. Morley had in the past compared Jefferson and Danton but now he changed his views. He claimed that he had written on De Maistre as well as on Voltaire and Rousseau, that he had never used the term 'Natural Rights' in practical political life. In the course of dissociating himself from the aims and means of the Revolution, Morley opposed the whole system of analogies in history and insisted that historical situations were never the same. His practical experience helped him to form this opinion so opposed to rationalism. He claimed that nothing could serve as a lesson for Irish policy except Irish history. Like Stubbs he said very simply and clearly that no specific lessons can be learnt from history. History influences our judgment indirectly, by making us wiser. Morley had the prized combination of historian and statesman and the breadth of mind which made him the most radical of Burke's disciples, as well as the most 'French' of English thinkers. His 'revolutionary hero' was Turgot to whom he was guided by his two main teachers, Austin and Mill. It was under the influence of Burke and of the empirical utilitarians that he became convinced how limited the power of abstract thought and even statesmen's wills was on politics. He said that *a priori* radicalism never succeeded in England, just as his master, Mill, said that the Reform Bill was not the work of Bentham but of 'interests and instincts'.[2]

---

[1] 'The disestablishment of the Church in Wales . . . is a reform which cannot any longer be kept out of the active objects of the Liberal party' (*The Times* (3 Nov. 1886), p. 6).

[2] Mill, *Dissertations*, I, 332.

Utility and expediency are the final tests for the relative truths of politics. Political problems like the riddles of Clio 'do not admit of mathematical solutions'.

Morley's work on the Revolution was not of the new professional kind as was that of Stephens, but his thought was of greater significance. He wrote no new narratives, but essays in which he expounded the minds of individuals and the ideas of movements. In his study of Robespierre, Morley attempted to revalue the revolutionary who, he said, had suffered from idolators and calumniators alike, and to shift the interest from Robespierre's personality to the constructive side of the Revolution in general. He thought that the subject of history was social progress[1] and that the Revolution, though it was made up of numerous currents and cross currents, led to a definite result in increased happiness. He said that the men engaged in the work of improvement are often wrong, but history traces the torch apart from its bearers. This notion had something in common with Acton but their definitions of the 'torch', that is, of liberty, were widely apart.

Morley's writings on the Revolution were highly admired both for scholarship and for justness of views by Harrison who was also interested in the subject and in its historiography. Both Morley and Harrison were dissatisfied with existing histories and Harrison in his detailed study of Revolutionary historians divided them into dull narratives, egotistical memoirs and unintelligible poems. They both followed the tendency of the age to put the Revolution in a historical context, but they exaggerated the novelty of this tendency when they claimed that all the historians still treated the Revolution as something inflicted, unique and uniform. Harrison's most interesting idea was the wish for a history which would connect the Revolution with the science and the philosophy which preceded it and with the socialism and industrial organization which followed it. Michelet alone hinted at these connections and Harrison lists the materials for such a study. He saw the event as a crisis in a long process, which also continued in 1830, 1848 and 1871, in German Socialism and Russian Nihilism. Harrison, therefore, connects the Revolution with both institutional and ideological history.

Radicals like Morley and a Positivist like Harrison, though widely apart in politics, were, as disciples of Mill, and as holders of a modified eighteenth-century philosophy, in a special position amongst the critics of Carlyle. Because they reacted strongly against Carlyle's scorn for rationalism, they discovered that Carlyle had not written as a Jacobin or as a Radical (as many thought he had), but rather from the height of the reaction against the general ideas which had inspired the revolutionaries. Since they believed that these ideas were largely true and were also governing basic developments in the nineteenth century, they attacked

[1] Morley, 'Review of d'Hericault' (1876).

Carlyle for what they considered to be his interpretation of the Revolution as a purely destructive outbreak. Carlyle's work, wrote Harrison, with the Positivist's contempt for mere literature, was becoming less and less historical every day, as the revolutionary thinkers of France appear less and less like tigers and monkeys and more and more as men 'charged in Europe with the evolution of all our republican and social ideas'. But Harrison also considers Blanc's history ruined by making a hero of a sanguinary tyrant like Robespierre.

PROFESSIONAL HISTORY—MORSE STEPHENS

The historian who first brought to the English public the results of French research was Morse Stephens who wrote the first really detailed and accurate narrative of the Revolution to the end of 1793. He acquired his thorough knowledge from French specialized publications in monographs and periodicals, but he also based one chapter (that on the elections) entirely on materials in the Croker Collection, which he used before it was catalogued. Stephens used some original materials and was the first English historian to use the Croker Collection but his real merit was the summary of the new research of others. Stephens summarized the *cahiers* already published pointing out that they were political, general and therefore uninteresting, whereas the specific local ones were still unprinted. It never occurred to him to study those. Although he knew that many *cahiers* were copied from models he also says that they show 'how completely the ideas of Voltaire and of Rousseau had permeated through every class'. Stephens was therefore often uncritical in collecting results of research, but he opened for England the history of the French provinces, neglected since Arthur Young's times, except by students like Maine. He showed the influence of the provincial assemblies, he summarized much information about the revolutionary press, he presented the Terror as an act of centralization and Thermidor as the revolt of the provinces. It was probably from von Sybel that he learnt the effects of the Civil Constitution and the part played by the soldiers of the *ancien régime* in Revolutionary victories. Stephens assessed French research and pigeon-holed the finds. When he tried to do more, he showed his limitations. He made much, for instance, of an original document, an eye-witness's account of 10 August by one of the Swiss Officers, Durler, which he found in the British Museum[1] and treated as his own discovery. He writes, 'for whom it was drawn up there is no trace'. We know, as Smyth did, that it was drawn up for Mallet-du-Pan and that it was lent to Smyth with two similar documents, by Mallet-du-

[1] Add. MS. 32168. The B.M. acquired it in 1882 from a M. Carter Blake who had obtained it from Dr Westley Gibson who could not explain how his father had obtained it.

Pan's son, and was used by Smyth for his lectures. Stephens also published the manuscript[1] establishing Durler's reliability.[2]

Stephens did not understand the value of letters and said that, unlike other historical documents, they were important only for 'opinions'. He therefore saw nothing new in the correspondence of Miles or Vaudreuil, and quoted from them character sketches, almost ignoring the secret negotiations they reveal.[3] Even less successful were his attempts at interpretation, for his view was behind the times. He justified his revolutionary interest on grounds worn thin by contemporaries, and he even fell back on an analogy between English reforms in the 1880s and French Revolutionary reforms.[4] He relegated the study of the causes of the Revolution not to the historians (who should merely describe) but to the philosophers, though he listed among the causes, the tendency towards centralization of power, taxation, the deficit, the material and intellectual state of the classes. He considered that this kind of analysis and judgment owed a great deal to conjecture. Though he compiled the results of research, Stephens belonged at heart to a school which in England had been called 'speculative'. He wrote a proper narrative and not speculations, but only at the price of avoiding larger questions, for instance, of cause and effect. He did not see recent investigations as a new method for solving historical questions, but merely as affording additional detail. And yet he believed himself to belong to what he himself called the post-Ranke school, in which, he explained, history was based on documents and was not written to prove a theory. It is perhaps typical of the second rank of historians of that period that they understood too literally and narrowly the aims of the new historical research while reserving in their minds a place for incongruous generalizations. This left a great gap between the history they practised and the history they dreamed about. Like Browning, who in his practical work made technical contributions to history, Stephens held that political science was ultimately the richest fruit of history. It comes out in his writings on Mirabeau for whom he had a great admiration (though he later admitted that even he could not have saved the monarchy). His admiration was based on what he considered to be Mirabeau's greatness in political science, the fact that Mirabeau knew that politics should be based on expediency and not on justice. Mirabeau, he said, appears greater the more statecraft is recognized to be divorced from morality. The Revolution, he added, will one day be studied as mere background to the thought of Mirabeau just as Caesar Borgia is studied for the sake of Machiavelli. And the study of the background is needed, he went so

[1] *E.H.R.* (1887), II, 350. See above, p. 91.
[2] The other original documents Stephens used were a letter on Marat's visit to England and the private letters of the Duke of Dorset to the Duke of Leeds.
[3] *E.H.R.* (1892), 184.
[4] Stephens, *French Revolution* (1886), xvii–xviii.

far as to say, in order to identify and discard the prejudices and temporary influences on the pure essence of the political thought. The belief that ethical conceptions were irrelevant to politics, which Stephens ascribed to his three admired political theorists, Machiavelli, De-Retz and Mirabeau, he also incorporated in his history, mainly in dealing with the Terror. He presents an accurate account of the coming of the Terror and also a series of apologetic judgments. The King was treated well in prison; murder is regrettable but common to all revolutions; the Terrorists hoped for a 'stronger and more glorious France'; Robespierre was moral, Marat was wise and Maillard saved many lives. Acton, we learn from his papers, thought highly of Stephens's first volume[1] after Dicey had drawn his attention to it, and when he heard of a second he begged to review it. But it was the rejection of moral principle, the moderation due to a 'rare and remarkable ethical indifference', which finally governs Acton's review of Stephens, as it had governed numerous previous English reviews of revolutionary histories.

Stephens's thought on the Revolution in general seems to have developed after the appearance of his first volume, under the influence of the French historians. A short summary he made in 1892 of the state of Revolutionary studies shows how much he sympathized with the official school in France. Aulard's appointment to the Revolutionary Chair in 1886, the celebration of the centenary year and the organization of research, were events with which he felt closely connected. He speaks like a Frenchman when he says that politicians have no longer to declare their allegiance to some Revolutionary character or other. In England such tests had long been meaningless. In 1886 Stephens spoke of French impartiality to the Revolution as something which could not be achieved for a long time, until 'results of the Revolution cease to be flags, round which parties rally'. In 1892 he writes[2] as if the historians of the Third Republic were well on their way towards 'calm history', absolute impartiality, by putting an end to theoretic disputations, and discovering through critical examination what really happened 'without imputing motives to individuals' or pointing morals. Stephens ascribed great importance to such work and said that only a true narrative can show the true lessons of the period. These had been stock phrases all through the century, and it is of course widely held that the historians of the Third Republic were not objective in their researches. In his own history Stephens did not at all refrain from pointing the lessons, and his edition of Revolutionary speeches which was a real contribution to the publication of documents from the contemporary journals was criticized in England for leaving out the speeches of the political Right (because they

---

[1] Add. MS. 7472. Acton writes (4 Nov. 1891) the book is 'so nearly very good that I gave it to Dick'.

[2] *E.H.R.* (1892), p. 587. This is a review of three lives of Mirabeau.

had no effect, he said); for giving Barère's harangues disproportionate space; for neglecting Cambon's financial reports (because they form an indirect criticism of the Terror); and for a biased commentary. Stephens's French bias leads him to more serious faults in his 1893 volume on Europe in the period of the Revolution. He sees only the one-sided spread of French ideas in Europe to the extent of seeing nationalism purely as a product of the French Revolution and of its national war against Europe and ignoring the origins of nationalism in the counter-revolutionary movement, ignoring also the Romantic revolt and revival, the tyrannical nature of French rule in other countries, and the powers of opposition in general. But Aulard (to whom the volume is dedicated), in reviewing this edition,[1] praises Stephens's accuracy, learning and judgment. His appreciation of Danton is a model of impartiality and he does not follow Macaulay's view of Barère. His edition is a classical work and his method irreproachable.

Stephens remained alone in his detailed and comprehensive study of the internal and provincial history of revolutionary France. English interest in general continued to flow towards the international aspects. The French history most popular in England was that of Sorel and it left a deeper impression than the earlier German studies of the same subject. It was much later still praised as the fairest history of the Revolution by Gooch and by Trevelyan. The professional treatment of diplomatic history, the display of the continuity of the Revolution, and the distinction between 1789 and the Terror had special appeal for England. For a Frenchman to hold that the Terror was caused by the war and yet was unnecessary for victory seemed evidence of a new detachment. The interpretation of Madame de Staël and her friends the Doctrinaires which had always had something in common with the English view, but was not embodied in any great French history, matured in Sorel in a work of the first rank. Sorel, with a diplomatic training more useful for history than Taine's literary criticism, had started his historical work on the Revolution by showing the continuity in foreign relations as Tocqueville had shown that in administrative institutions.

Seeley, however, who first expounded Sorel to England, was unfavourable to his point of view. Though Sorel rejected Taine's idea that the Jacobins acted from abstract principles, Seeley oddly charged him with tracing the war to literary causes, while Ranke showed the concrete diplomatic causes. He thought that Sorel, like Tocqueville and Taine, was writing 'scientific history', which he took to mean, abandoning chronology and tracing the Revolution to inferred causes. Seeley's extraordinary misreading of Sorel seems based on Sorel's first volume in which the international ideas of the eighteenth century are analysed. It is there too that Seeley learnt the ideas which he expounded in his

[1] *Rév. fr.* (1892) xxiii, 382–4.

article on the 'House of Bourbon', that the Bourbon ascendancy was 'an embryo of the Revolutionary and Napoleonic empire', as Anti-Jesuitism rehearsed the anti-spiritualism of the Revolution.[1]

MATURE HISTORY—LECKY ON THE CAUSES OF THE REVOLUTION

If Morley was the last of the traditional English thinkers about the Revolution, and Stephens was the first of the professional historians (the first since Croker to become a serious student and the first since Carlyle to attempt a complete history), Lecky was the historian who combined in a work of stature both trends. Stephens had, ten years before Acton, begun to present the results of new research. But he wrote, as Acton said, without perspective and without reflection. Lecky combined thought and scholarship but at the expense of the latter. Acton criticized him for neglecting the treasures of the archives,[2] and though Acton was thinking of English history, this is even more true of Lecky's treatment of the French Revolution. It was probably due to Browning who helped Lecky with his work on the Revolution, that Lecky read some documents of the kind that Browning knew.[3] But Lecky did nothing for the internal history of the Revolution. Lecky stands closest to Acton in his interest in the political movements of the Revolution, and Acton's judgment, that the best accounts of the Revolution in England are in Buckle and Lecky, reflects his own interests. Lecky did three things with regard to the Revolution in the 500 pages or so devoted to it in his *History of England in the 18th Century*.[4] He examined its literary background, he drew the continuous story of the English reaction, and he studied two international aspects of the Revolution, its relations with Germany and its relations with England. Lecky, like Buckle, gives no full narrative of the internal Revolution.

In the course of his examination of the intellectual antecedents of the Revolution, Lecky raises the question of the philosophic causes. In a chapter entitled 'Causes', which ends with an assertion that the Revolution, 'though undoubtedly prepared by causes which had been in operation for centuries, might, till within a very few years of the catastrophe have been averted', Lecky is mainly concerned with the long-term literary preparations, and when he comes to within fifteen years of the outbreak, he says it is unnecessary for his purpose to examine them in the same detail.[5] All through his work Lecky both emphasizes the influence of the philosophers and asserts that it had been exaggerated. 'The influence

---

[1] *E.H.R.* (1886), I, 86.

[2] Acton to Mary Gladstone, 14 Dec. 1880. 'Neglecting the inexhaustible discoveries before him in the archives, Lecky has to give sentence when he gives too little evidence' (*Letters . . . to Mary . . . Gladstone* (London, 1904), p. 51).

[3] O. Browning, *Memories of Sixty Years* (n.d.), p. 293.

[4] Vols. V, VI (1887).   [5] Lecky, *History*, V, 386.

of Voltaire and his followers in producing the Revolution, though real, has been greatly exaggerated' (p. 319). Of the struggle of the parlements he says, 'The whole conflict I have described was almost unconnected with the philosophical, free-thinking and literary movement to which the Revolution has been too largely attributed.' The problem arises especially with regard to Rousseau and it is there that Lecky's contribution lies. It was left to Lecky to make the important and so obvious distinction to which Burke had blinded numerous historians, between Rousseau's revolutionary teaching and his revolutionary effect. Lecky at first says that Napoleon's statement, that without Rousseau there would have been no revolution, is in a sense, in spite of its exaggeration, plausible. He explains that the French Revolution is distinguished from all other political movements in the fact 'that it was directed by men who had adopted certain speculative *a priori* conceptions of political right, with the fanaticism and proselytising fervour of a religious belief, and the Bible of their creed was the *Contrat Social*'. Lecky thought that 'the political influence of Rousseau appears to me to have been almost wholly evil',[1] and yet he makes the strongest case for the view that the revolutionaries drew from Rousseau a system he did not teach. It would, he said, be doing Rousseau an injustice 'to suppose that he expected, preached or desired any violent revolution'. Although he taught that in periods of extreme danger dictatorship was permissible, he held very strongly (even against Helvetius) that no individual life must be sacrificed 'for the safety of the multitude'. On the notion permitting such sacrifice Rousseau said, 'I hold this maxim to be one of the most execrable that tyranny has invented, the most false that can be promulgated.' Lecky also claims that the revolutionaries drew from Rousseau a 'system of cosmopolitan politics' which 'discarded all national traditions' whereas it had been 'the earnest desire of Rousseau himself to accentuate to the highest degree the spirit of a distinctive and exclusive patriotism'. Lecky showed not only that the Revolution proceeded on principles which Rousseau had explicitly declared abominable but that Burke in opposing the cosmopolitanism of the revolutionary system 'did little more than repeat the arguments of Rousseau'.[2] Lecky also thought the Revolution might have taken a different course if the disciples of Rousseau had not violated his principle by pronouncing their instructions null and void.[3]

In discussing the question of whether the Revolution could have been averted or not Lecky was most in line with his English predecessors and somewhat behind contemporary thought. His statement that when the

[1] Lecky, v, 348. 'The political principles which he [Rousseau] planted so deeply in European society appear to me to have produced an amount of evil which it is not easy to over-estimate' (*Ibid.* p. 365).

[2] *Ibid.* pp. 360–6.

[3] *E.H.R.* (1893), 395. See Lecky, vi, 194.

States General met most benefits of the Revolution could have been attained without difficulty or convulsion and by general consent he supported by the evidence of contemporaries such as Jefferson and by enumerating the vital concessions which could have saved the situation.[1] The prevalent views at Lecky's time were more faithfully represented by Gardiner who wrote:

If there is one thing which is plain to all serious students of the French Revolution it is that the struggle for equality took precedence of the struggle for liberty and that the essence of the movement lay in the controversy of the third estate with the privileged orders; not in the controversy between the three estates and the King. If the French Revolutionists refused to imitate Washington or Lord Somers it was not because they were personally foolish and ill-advised but because the current of feeling bred of the strength of circumstances was sweeping them in quite another direction.

We have seen the question of the inevitability of the Revolution constantly recurring in the context of new stages in Revolutionary historiography and variably connected with current points of interpretation, as, for example, the question whether the Revolution was constructive or destructive, liberal or socialist. Burke's original view of the unity and fatal progress of the Revolution was generally discarded except occasionally for purposes of political polemics, as, for example, in 1832. After the rise of Socialism, the connection of socialism with the French Revolution and the resulting emphasis on the distinction between liberty and equality, the Burkian view seemed, at a superficial glance, again borne out. New studies of the spirit of 1789, as distinct from its institutions or policies, discovered in it ideals from which, by force of popular sentiments or appetites, there was at least an emotional continuity to Equality, or Terror, or Dictatorship, or Socialism. It was, therefore, too readily accepted that the emotional or intellectual continuity need necessarily have affected the machinery of the state. In point of fact, it is not enough to show socialist tendencies in the spirit of 1789 in order to prove the inevitable progress of the Revolution towards socialism. Lecky did not perceive the weakness of the system he opposed but he instinctively, like so many historians before him, fought all deterministic theories. In his resistance to old and new theories of inevitability, as well as in his type of conservatism and his somewhat didactic manner of writing history, Lecky belonged more properly to the middle of the century. In his *Democracy and Liberty* (1896), he laid himself open to the charge of moulding his history to the shape of an indictment against present-day democracy.

For his account of the Revolution, Lecky used a varied range of sources. He relied largely on many recent French histories (chiefly

[1] In *E.H.R.* (1896), 531, Pogson-Smith writes about Lecky that he is not as great a political scientist as Mill and that, as far as his view of the Constitution was concerned, he lived in the period 1832–67.

Sorel and Rocquain) and he had in front of him the English historians. He used Smyth for one of the few important and original manuscripts he printed, Louis XVI's letter to the allies taken by Mallet-du-Pan, and he recommended Smyth's discussions of several points, notably on the constitution of the Legislative Assembly. But he also, oddly, quotes from Smyth an address of the Revolution Society,[1] for which better sources were available; and Lecky's authority for the number of lawyers in the Assembly is Carlyle.[2] In the use of sources, Lecky is at his best in dealing with the foreign relations, for he made use of unpublished documents in the Public Record Office[3] and in the French Foreign Office, in conjunction with many published documents and histories (including Marsh's work of 1799) to reconstruct the diplomatic picture. His studies made Lecky correct the view about the origins of the war which he had held, under the influence of Buckle, when he wrote his *History of Rationalism* in 1865. He admitted he had been wrong and came to hold strongly that Pitt did not want war.

The eighth volume of the *Cambridge Modern History* sums up the English studies of the Revolution at the end of the century, and does not include a word by either of the two best thinkers on the Revolution (apart from Acton), Lecky and Morley. When Acton undertook the editorship, he had special difficulties in finding writers for this volume. More than scholarship had to be counted with. Acton thought of Lecky who was not employed; he was in doubt about Lodge, who contributed several chapters; the Syndics did not wish Morse Stephens to be employed, and though they did not object to Morley, Acton hesitated, fearing that the Bishop of Oxford might.[4] Morley was not employed. The volume embodied the work of a group of professional historians, though not that of Stephens—perhaps the most knowledgeable of them. It is typical of the work of a recent generation. In the bibliographies are listed some of the more prominent figures among the English historians (Alison, Croker, Carlyle, Smyth, Stephens, Lecky, Morley, Seeley, Rose, Ritchie, Higgs). No volume could bring out better the crumbling of the English tradition in Revolutionary studies and the growing divergence between individuals in scholarship and method. Though the editors were unable to unify the variety of approaches and points of view represented in the volume, it is of some significance that the task was considered to be possible. The self-sufficiency of the English historians for building up a complete history was apparently an unquestioned assumption and the divergence of views was not considered to be too wide. 'Views', in any

---

[1] Lecky, p. 498. [2] *Ibid.* p. 432.

[3] Lecky used the Gower despatches before Browning printed them, and also Tallyrand's letters on his mission to England, later printed in Pallain, *Mission de Tallyrand à Londres en 1792* (1889).

[4] Letter to Poole, 26 Nov. 1896. C.U.L. Add MS. 7472. Letters to Creighton 16, 20, 26 Nov. 1896 (C.U.L. Add. MS. 6871).

case, had definitely lost their overall importance in Revolutionary studies. Almost parallel to the volume which signifies the end of the nineteenth-century English school, and the product in a sense of the same mind, we have Lord Acton's own lectures on the French Revolution, uniting in a most peculiar way both the new detached and professional trends which were disrupting the English historical tradition and some of the deepest and most essential characteristics of that tradition.

CHAPTER 15

LORD ACTON

THE AIM OF TEACHING HISTORY

Acton's main work on the French Revolution was the course of lectures he gave in Cambridge as Regius Professor of Modern History. It constitutes his most ambitious attempt to write history on a large scale, as well as the most ambitious attempt in England at the time to write a general history of the Revolution on the ground of all that has emerged since the documentary age began.[1] Acton had criticized Stephens for lack of reflection and praised him for knowledge and for accuracy. He did not compete with Stephens in comprehensiveness, nor did Acton himself go to the archives. His history is essentially second-hand and yet it is original. There was a real need for a general history of the French Revolution in English, and it could not be done from the documents. Acton had complete familiarity with the results of research and with the published sources; the only question is how he used them and what he selected for treatment.

Something about the nature of his lectures should be understood in connection with the Regius Professorship.[2] Acton chose his subject in order to adapt himself to the 'settled curriculum', though he would have preferred to give a general course on European history.[3] This was a period of debates over reforms in history in Cambridge. Oscar Browning who fought for a primarily political tripos particularly objected to '*the* bad subject' of universal history. Acton put his weight on the side of the reformers.[4] He approved of the greater insistence on facts and on scholarship, of the special subjects and outline courses of European history, which were then proposed. Though he helped to secure one of the innovations of 1895, the introduction of three papers on general European history, his actual share in reforming the tripos was not great.

The controversy over the historical tripos is relevant to the nature of Acton's lectures because Acton broke with the tradition of historical

---

[1] 'Our object is to give what is established and acknowledged in the few cases where anything is finally known' (C.U.L. Add. MS. 5467).

[2] Acton was appointed in 1895. G. Himmelfarb writes (*Lord Acton*, 1952, p. 192) that in 1892 Gladstone passed Acton by for the Regius Professorship in favour of Seeley. But Seeley had been Regius Professor since 1869.

[3] Acton to Gladstone, Easter Monday, 1895 (*Selections*, 1 (London, 1917), p. 172). The French Revolution was a set subject for the tripos of 1898. A rival course on the subject was given by O. Browning and in the following year, also by Dr Walker of Peterhouse (*Camb. Univ. Reporter* (1895–6), 350, 616, 974).

[4] In 1885 Prothero had led the reformers. See *Cambridge Review* (Feb. 1885).

lectures which are shaped by a political and by an educational aim. By insisting on both scholarship and outline courses he was pushing history in the apparently opposite directions of specialized research and outlines of universal history. Both occupations, and the compulsion to pursue them simultaneously, were highly typical of Acton's historical mind. In his 'Inaugural', Acton made concessions to the political spirit of the Chair, but the notes in which he prepared his lecture show how troubled his mind was by the need to define the aim of his teaching. He repeatedly asks himself if politics and history are really one, and his answer is that 'the life of mankind which is the subject of history is not confined to government'.[1] He seems unable to reach any other definition of his aim than that of training students to become independent of historians, that is, to become historians themselves.[2]

ACTON'S OBSCURITY

The reviews and articles, which Acton wrote all his life on subjects connected with the Revolution, vary in their character. Earlier in his life, Acton's opinions were more simple and clear and he was more willing to express vigorously and pointedly whatever he thought. Writings which he reviewed helped to crystallize his views on any given subject and they also brought out his minute knowledge through their inaccuracies. By the time Acton wrote his lectures, he had become acutely conscious of his intellectual isolation among historians and statesmen, and revolution was a subject on which next to moral judgments, he was most conspicuously alone. Love of peace often made him hold truth back and this resulted in ambiguities which were not confined to his written work. A friend of his wrote to another in 1889 that Acton irritated him by evading to give a straightforward answer. 'He escapes your question by quoting the wise sayings or the paradoxes of other men which his wonderful memory has always ready.'[3] This was connected with his personal experiences and the religious controversies of the 1860s. The year 1870 was a turning point in his life and the beginning of a period more wholly devoted to historical studies. His disappointments[4] made Acton more reticent, and his absorption in the details of history both resulted from, and strengthened this tendency. His revolutionary writings show that the new documentary research absorbed his interest from its inception. As soon as the results of new study and new materials came out, his manner of reviewing (for instance, the volumes of Mortimer-Ternaux, Feuillet de Conches, Dauban and others), especially after 1870,

[1] C.U.L. Add. MS. 5650.   [2] Add. MS. 5648.
[3] A. Russel to Lady Blennerhasset, 2 Oct. 1889 (C.U.L. Add. MS. 7486, bundle 52). Russel applies his comment only to questions of 'English Politics and H[ome] R[ule]'.
[4] In political and especially Church affairs.

changed, and he limited himself to the examination of new facts. He began to gather his minute information about the authenticity and the significance of individual documents, though he still tended to draw from them general conclusions without the fine scrutiny and the attention to chronology which was to develop later. Judgments and views in his articles are more clear and definite than in his later lectures.[1] Because Acton outgrew some of his earlier views, one must guard against using them to clarify or to supplement the later ideas of the lectures.

In the lectures, Acton's views are rarely as direct, and the historical processes which produced them are not visible. This adds to their fascination but also to what has been called their obscurity.[2] It has been asserted by one authority that Acton's style is difficult only when the ideas were difficult, otherwise perfectly lucid. This is true for readers who are familiar with Acton's subject. To the less informed it is inevitable that Acton's writing should seem excessively subtle. Acton was making his statements from the top of a pile of materials intricately bound together. Once he thought his way to the top, he was content to present his conclusions but not to avoid allusions to the obstacles he had overcome. To those on whom the allusions are lost, this manner must seem devious. True for much 'top-layer' writing, this is particularly apparent in Acton because of the unique disproportion between preparation and output.

METHOD OF WORK

To understand Acton better we must have more of him. We need an insight into the materials through which he waded and the problems he faced.[3] This need can only be supplied by Acton's notes. Those like Bryce, who regretted that Acton had published so little, underrated the notes or even resented them as worthless and repetitive. But the notes connected with the French Revolution represent essential work of preparation for the lectures. Acton got up the latest experts and traced their investigations. He studied contemporary memoirs as well as recent learned articles. He traced the diplomatic and private relations in the sets of correspondence and, like Croker, Carlyle and Browning, he even went into mileage calculations to solve the mysteries of Varennes. His general method seems to have been to jot down in the course of reading quotations specific comments or stray thoughts. Occasionally he tries out a sentence for the text of the lectures or summarizes controversial points, chains of events, lists of sources. This prodigious amount of work would

[1] The preparatory notes for the reviews contain clearer views than the reviews. Cf., e.g., Add. MS. 4862 with the review of May's *Democracy* and 4863 with the review of Seeley's and Roper's books on Napoleon.

[2] E.g. J. Bryce, *Studies in Contemporary Biography*; Gardiner in *E.H.R.* (1896), 112; Bebecke in *E.H.R.* (1908), 538; Montague in *E.H.R.* (1911), 599.

[3] See below, pp. 302 *et seq.*, for a bibliographical note on Acton.

have been impossible without the thorough knowledge of the Revolution which Acton had acquired over many years. He found the task of writing, 'a slow and anxious process',[1] but it was done in a few months in 1895–6 while the series of lectures was being delivered. Acton knew his materials well and could find his places easily. The cards were therefore simply organized. In his notebooks Acton focused his thoughts, made comments, digested information. Rumour has it that Acton composed his final text out of his head, but a collation with the notes indicates a closer connection between the stages of writing. Pollock says that the lectures were written out in finished form, and that the manuscript showed that Acton continuously incorporated new discoveries and 'never ceased to weigh and turn over a statement to which they related'.

The historical character of the lectures is not uniform, and there is a striking difference between the first two chapters, which discuss ideas, and the rest, which narrate events. It is as if Acton drew not only on different materials but also on different parts of his mind. The first two lectures form an essay on the state of the idea of liberty at the outbreak of the Revolution. They belong to the history of liberty in the same way that the two Northbridge lectures do. For these Acton needed to do no new reading or collating. They represent the kind of thought which Acton gave to the subject of revolution and liberty all his life. In the narrative itself the most distinctive historical manner is the organic combination of fact and interpretation. Acton's devotion to minute detail and to bold generalization, helped perhaps to curtail his production, but it marked whatever he wrote with an imprint of a suggested interpretation. This makes his writing, in reality, subjective. His views must be deduced from the tone in which the facts are presented, and the background out of which they have been selected. The full meaning of his heavily charged sentences can best be grasped when the vast amount of reading and thinking behind them is brought out of the notes, and this work would enable us to spot his new ideas as they appear.

Acton was best in dealing with political action and motive, and his history is dominated by outstanding personalities. Whether as cause or effect this is connected with the sort of materials he used. One of his notions about revolutionary historiography was formed by the new publications of revolutionary correspondence. Rewriting revolutionary historiography often meant to Acton, the correction, with the help of a man's letters, of the version bequeathed by his memoirs. Although Acton knew well the value of the official and other records, it was the personal source which came first in his own writings. The preponderant use of certain sets of correspondence often meant that Acton relied on an opinion rather than on a fact. The interest in individuals carried Acton far, and he often indulges in anticipating the future careers of persons he

[1] Acton to Poole, 24 Oct. 1895 (Add. MS. 7472).

mentions, in following to their graves actors who had gone backstage, or nonentities on whom the limelight shone only for a moment.[1]

Acton was not a mere compiler. His notes show that he did not use other historians' results but found his way to the individual facts. His careful building up of detail is shown, for instance, in the notes in which he weighed the evidence concerning Robespierre's last day. He considered the question of who shot Robespierre, one of the mysteries of the Revolution. Acton's method was to follow authorities back to their own sources, which, if printed, he had within easy reach. This can be illustrated, for example, by the manner in which he built up seven lines[2] which show the European monarchs' fear for all 'crowned heads', and the indifference of the émigrés to the fate of their King and Queen. Several notes help us to trace these lines to three sources: a letter from the Swedish King to the Tzarina, a passage in Augeard's *Mémoires* and an entry in Fersen's diary.[3] Although Acton used these sources widely, it is clear[4] that this specific selection was not his own, and that, in an article by Sorel,[5] he found the same illustrations used in the same way. But the notes also show that, having learnt from Sorel, Acton followed the references back to the sources.

With the help of the notes we can compile the list of Acton's sources and also ascertain his authorities for specific points. Acton seems, for instance, to have followed Sybel closely in tracing far-reaching consequences to the effect which the Civil Constitution had on Louis XVI. Both Sybel and Acton begin their chapters on the flight to Varennes by a detailed exposition of the view that it was the ecclesiastical laws which radically changed the King's mind with regard to flight and foreign help.[6] Though the King continued to listen to Mirabeau who advised an appeal to the loyal part of France, he turned more and more to Breteuil who urged flight to the border and the suppression of the Revolution with the help of foreign troops. Acton also differed from Sybel with regard to Mirabeau in a way which is typical of his thought. Sybel thought that Mirabeau's influence had been waning steadily since before the Civil Constitution. Acton, who came to regard the royalist policy of pushing the Revolution to extremes as almost the worst political crime of the Revolution, naturally made much more of Mirabeau's advice to impose the oath on the priests, to encourage them to refuse it, so as to provoke indignation against the Assembly, and enable the King to intervene, a

---

[1] E.g. the father and son of Lally-Tollendal (Acton, *French Revolution*, pp. 90–91).

[2] Acton, *F.R.* p. 178, ll. 23–29.

[3] Augeard, p. 274; Fersen, I, 4; Gustavus to the Tzarina 9 June 1791, Feuillet de Conches III, 399.

[4] Add. MS. 4917.

[5] A. Sorel, 'Varennes et Pillnitz', *Deux Mondes* (1886), III, 334.

[6] Breteuil, writes Sybel, 'drängte auf Flucht in eine Grenzstadt und Erdrückung der Revolution mit Hülfe des Auslandes' (Sybel (1877 ed.), I, 228–9).

policy which even La Marck called Machiavellian,[1] and which Acton (in a note) described as 'profoundly immoral and hopeless'.[2] Acton believed that Mirabeau's influence actually increased when the Civil Constitution was voted but that later the King gave up his counsels when he saw that they held no hopes for the Church.[3]

THE RECONSTRUCTION OF THE FLIGHT TO VARENNES

The story of the flight to Varennes is a test case in historical method. It is often said that it is the Revolutionary episode most written about. Undoubtedly it has an unrivalled combination of attractions. It was a crucial event in the Revolution, romantic, adventurous, and with a strong human interest. For the technical historian it has the additional attraction of a detective problem, for its smallest details were disputed. Acton noted that 'the two parties have their different versions', but the mysteries of Varennes are due to personal as well as to political prejudices, for each of the actors introduced a bias of his own. The reconstruction of the narrative holds the promise of giving the answers to the questions connected with the flight. What were its motives and destination? Who proposed or aided it? Could a rescue have been attempted? Was Drouet authorized to act by the Assembly? Which was the fatal circumstance? Who was the guilty actor? What would have been the result of success? What were the direct results of failure?

The historiography of Varennes has undergone a long process of accumulating materials and sharpening criticism.[4] There were official and unofficial reports by contemporaries; valuable accounts, as that of the Queen, remained long unknown. The evidence of eye-witnesses began with Bouillé's *Memoirs* of 1797, and with the account of Madame Royale printed in the so-called *Memoirs* of Weber in 1804–6. Even the body-guards published narratives in 1815. The wide interest in the affair set in with the controversy between Choiseul and Bouillé's son, over the question of responsibility, in 1822. It resulted in the collection of *Mémoires sur l'affaire de Varennes* (1823), written mainly on Bouillé's side. During the period of recriminations in France, an English historian who was aloof only from the personal squabbles took stock of most of the facts then known. Croker's study of the flight in 1823 was despised in some English circles as pedantic. All through the century the English historians showed a remarkable interest in the flight to Varennes, and gave it disproportionate space in their works. The valuable French reconstructions began in the forties with the advantage of original

---

[1] *Correspondance entre...Mirabeau et...la Marck* (ed. Bacourt). 3 vols. (1851), I, 225. This concerns the advice given in Mirabeau's 47th note.

[2] Acton works the problem out in Add MSS. 4917 and 5452.

[3] But Acton also believed that Mirabeau was unfavourable to the Church because he was for religious liberty.   [4] See below, pp. 305–6, for a list of sources on Varennes.

materials. The important names are Bimbenet and Fournel. The former was the guardian of the documents of the high court of enquiry on the flight, and the latter scanned the municipal archives. Alençon used the unpublished diary of Madame de Tourzel, the governess. In the 'sixties new emphasis and direction were given to the study of the flight by the publication in Austria and elsewhere of many of the letters in which it was planned. These changed our knowledge of the origin of the flight and showed it to have been to a large extent undertaken in opposition to the émigrés. This side of the affair was mainly studied by the Germans and by Sorel.

By the time Acton wrote, the Varennes narrative had reached its authorized version, but his notes show that even in such a technical matter as this, he was not content to summarize the researches of the experts but attempted to cover the whole range of materials himself. The list of books he used covers most of the literature on the subject. He did not go back to the municipal records for instance, but he used the relevant extracts of them printed by historians like Fournel. The correspondence of the period, Acton studied more directly, though there, too, he was often guided by previous historians. Acton's historical method is best illustrated by his manner of dealing with the most strictly factual parts of his narrative. The chapter on Varennes in Acton lends itself to a line-by-line analysis. With the help of Acton's books and notes, almost every statement he makes can be shown to come from somewhere within the literature on Varennes.[1] It is not always easy to judge the degree of independence with which Acton handled his materials. We know, for instance, that Acton studied Bouillé's contradictions.[2] One card which reads: 'Bouillé gave three different accounts in his Memoirs. To Bertrand. To Dutens. Because the King passed all other places safely. But at Varennes young Bouillé did nothing. At St Ménehould and Clermont the troops kept the place quiet. Drouet could do nothing', seems at first like a summary made from wide materials, but there is a letter from Choiseul to Dutens which is undoubtedly the only source for this card.[3] The letter supplied a ready-made summary of Choiseul's case against Bouillé, which Acton could weigh in his own scales for and against the general. There were also the practical questions of the flight. Why was there not an escort in the carriage? Why did they want two carriages? Who suggested the route and the cavalry escort? How did they get out of the Tuileries? Acton believed in the complicity of

---

[1] Add. MS. 4918 contains 286 unnumbered cards on the flight. There are about 100 more in other boxes. About 71 contain clear references to sources, 22 contain clues in the form, e.g., of dates of letters which can be found in publications, 44 contain other clues mostly 'X says that' (X referring to an author or an actor). About 200 cards contain no clues and their sources had to be found in books connected with the flight to Varennes.

[2] Acton, *F.R.* 367; Add. MS. 4917.

[3] Choiseul, 196–7.

Lafayette or at least in his reluctance to pursue the fugitives, and Acton used Fontanges's narrative for things he could not verify elsewhere, such as the Queen's request for three bodyguards who need not be intelligent.

One of the central points in Acton's story of the relations of the court of France with Europe is that of the forgery of Mantua. He learnt the true facts about it at the last moment, after he had made a preliminary outline for his chapter on the flight, and it changed his whole conception of the antecedents of the flight. He attached great importance to this forgery and gathered around it all he had to say about the relations between the royalists in and outside France (which to Acton was a fascinating chapter in the history of the Revolution). These intricate relations Acton worked out in detail, guided by the researches of Sybel, Lenz, Sorel, Ranke, Flammermont and others. The 'treason hatched at Mantua' gave him the key to the urgency of the royal flight, and in telling the story, he followed closely the article in which Lenz printed the proof for the forgery[1] and studied the preparation for the flight.

The story, briefly, is that the King and Queen sent Durfort to the Count d'Artois, warning him as usual against hasty action. D'Artois then had a conference at Mantua with the Emperor, and Durfort was sent back to Paris with the Emperor's comments on certain proposals made by d'Artois. He arrived there with an unsigned and undated document and explained that through excess of prudence he had been ordered to burn the original paper which had been written by Calonne and annotated by the Emperor. The accounts of the document Durfort brought to Paris, as given by the Queen,[2] by Fersen and by Bertrand, are based on a paper later printed by Bertrand. It represented the Emperor as certain of receiving the help of other powers and ready for action, not later than 15 July, on the condition that the King and Queen stayed in Paris where their safety would be ensured by manifestos.

This remained the accepted story for long though neither Acton nor Lenz show how strong the suspicion of the Durfort paper had been, long before the actual discovery of the forgery. Mallet-du-Pan, for example, had declared it false. The forgery was finally exposed with the discovery of the authentic documents written at Mantua, a letter from the Emperor to Kaunitz describing the conference and an attached paper containing

[1] M. Lenz, *H.Z.* (1894), LXXII, 1–43; 213–46. The documents had been discovered by Arneth. The letters between Leopold and Kaunitz had already been printed by A. Beer, *H.Z.* (1872), XXVII, 21, and reprinted in Arneth's collection.

A preliminary outline of the chapter on Varennes shows that Acton learnt the truth about Mantua only at the last moment. In the outline he listed Mirabeau's 47th note as proof that the flight was undertaken against the émigrés. The discovery gave him better proof and he now took over also Lenz's interpretation of the attempt to go to St Cloud on 18 April, that it was an attempt to move the Emperor to action. Like Lenz Acton follows this up by quoting the letters in which the Queen asked for movements of Austrian troops to serve as pretexts.

[2] Fersen, p. 135.

the real articles proposed by d'Artois and the comments on them dictated by the Emperor. Leopold's account shows that the Durfort paper was a forgery. He considered Artois's plans impractical and insisted on a European concert and on flight as the conditions for action. The latter, and more important, paper was printed by Lenz in 1894. The Durfort paper had been forged by Calonne in an attempt to force a foreign intervention. The important practical point was that the Durfort paper required the King and Queen to stay in Paris and thereby showed the indifference of the émigrés to their lives. It was this point which aroused the suspicions of the Queen who knew that her brother always insisted on delaying any action until she and the King were safely out of Paris. She suspected an intrigue by Calonne to secure the domination of the princes in a restored old régime. The intrigues of the émigrés thus drove the King and Queen to hasty flight.

In studying the affair Acton does not quite resolve the question of how much the Queen actually knew. In some place he follows Lenz in saying that they were too well versed in the Emperor's plans to suspect a change of policy on his part, and that they therefore clearly suspected a forgery by Calonne.[1] But in other places Acton also allows for a suspicion in the Queen's mind that the Emperor had changed his mind and had fallen into the hands of the émigrés. Acton not only underrated the degree of certainty the Queen could reach on the ground of letters she had from the Emperor,[2] but he elaborated on her reactions to the Emperor's suspected change of policy, on the ground of a letter she only wrote much later, after the flight,[3] and in which she said that servitude to the émigrés would be worse than to the Jacobins. Acton makes the decision to fly dependent more on the refusal to be saved by the émigrés (who would dictate their own terms), than on the fear of being murdered by the Jacobins.

The story of the Mantua forgery is typical of the sort of investigations Acton engaged in. He collected evidence on various questions, not all of which he later presents. He wanted to know, for instance, whether the Queen was in favour of a Counter-constitution (Acton borrowed the term from von Sybel); whether Breteuil (though he was her adviser) was in favour of a complete reaction. Did Robespierre fall a victim to his wish to remain within the law? How much of his own work would Mirabeau have undone? What caused the failure of the flight? Acton collected evidence for and against the allegation that the crucial loss of time was caused by the King's meal. He decided that it was,[4] apparently on the ground of a footnote in Feuillet to whom the secret was disclosed by Bouillé's son fifty years after he has sworn to keep it for that length of

---

[1] The Queen to Mercy, 1 June 1791 (Arneth, 169), 'Cela furieusement l'air d'une fable forgée.' A letter from Fersen to Taube (Fersen, 135) says the paper contradicts the sentiments of the Emperor.
[2] Leopold (12 June, Arneth, 177) says clearly they must fly.
[3] 16 Aug. 1791.   [4] Acton, *F.R.* 185.

time, 'jour pour jour'. There was also the problem of Louis XVI's frustrated attempt to go to St Cloud on 18 April 1791. Did the King bribe a mob to call him a pig to his face? Most historians say that the King was going to receive communion from a non-juring priest. Acton knew that with the Civil Constitution on his conscience the King was not going to receive communion, and he believed that the affair was staged in order to make known that the King was not a free man. Thiers had said that the King behaved 'according to his old policy of not appearing free'. Croker denied this hotly and could quote Danton's own avowal that he himself had conducted this *émeute*. The words spoken by the King in the Assembly, 'It is important to the nation to prove that I am free', have been quoted for either view.

THE ART OF THE CRITIC-HISTORIAN

Watching Acton's method in writing to the French Revolution, one must conclude that he conducted no original research for it, but studied thoroughly the accounts of others, usually accepting them only on proof. In this way he practised the role of the 'critic-historian' as he had defined it in his inaugural lecture on the study of history. He read books, grew suspicious, checked the sources, examined the authors' positions and motives, weighed their facts, applied the tests of physical and psychological probability, as well as that of new evidence. Though Acton often said that the mastery of printed books did not make a modern historian, he still claimed for the 'critic-historian' the sovereignty in the historical realm. The critic-historian starts his work from the statements of other historians. The activity of investigating truth, as Acton analysed it, does not include raw materials. Acton, without saying so expressly was really making a case for research, conducted not on history, but on historical writings. When he discusses the treasures in manuscripts, he adds that these matters do not concern us, 'for our purpose the main thing is not the art of accumulating material but the sublimer art of investigating it'. Acton apparently did not hold that 'accumulation' already included criticism and investigation. His chief interest was the criticism of historians and not the testing of raw materials. Although his definition of 'criticism' falls short of the best in his own work, it indicates the direction of his historical thinking.

In treating historical literature, Acton was not practising a literary discipline such as the history of poetry for instance. The criticism of historians was to him the way to historical truth itself. Acton often repeats the curious phrase 'to look behind historians'. He seems to have believed that only by mastering all of the literature relating, for instance, to Napoleon can a historian shake off the prejudices and deficiencies of previous writers. It is as if the whole literature on a subject, when thoroughly understood, becomes thoroughly transparent and enables us to look through it at the historical figure itself.

This notion affected Acton's writing. Though his research was conducted on historians, he used it for writing a historical narrative, and this gave an air of unreality to his story of the Revolution. As a picture it does not seem painted from life; as a drama it does not proceed by its own motive force, as does Carlyle's. And yet the lectures were not meant to be detached discussions, and members of the audience testify to the dramatic atmosphere they created. In print, however, the dust of book learning seems to hang over them. Acton's preoccupation with Revolutionary bibliography was not without the danger of leading him round history. He followed the histories of various manuscripts and saw many of them, but, though he inspected, for instance, in a Scottish castle, Marat's own annotated copy of *Ami du Peuple*, we hear nothing of any direct historical point it might have suggested to him.

THE HISTORY OF HISTORY

'The great point is the history of history',[1] wrote Acton in a note, and elsewhere again, 'Besides the history of a subject we require especially to know the history of the study of that subject and the successive growth of knowledge and formation of opinion about it.'[2] Acton's study of the Revolution supports the view that next to the history of liberty, and connected with it, he was interested in studying the development of historical writings. His special contribution was his understanding of the history of historiography as a historical discipline and as a way of thinking. His vast materials seem to be a preparation for the history of history no less than for a history of liberty, and he approaches almost all subjects through the history of the writings about them. The correspondence with Creighton which preceded his famous article on 'German Schools of History' shows that he considered the history of history as his own special line. He pleaded again and again for permission to write a review of Wegele, and 'in such a way so as not to describe all the ...new lights of history'. He would thus say 'all that it was proposed to convey in another manner'. Acton stressed that he would present not a gallery of historians but the growth of a view.[3]

The same approach he adopted for the treatment of Revolutionary historiography, though in print we have only an appendix to his lectures. The editors say that it was compiled from 'such connected fragments' as remain of Acton's discussions of the literature. When Gooch recommends it he is not thinking of its bibliographical value which falls short

---

[1] Add. MS. 5438. [2] Add. MS. 4650.
[3] Letters to Creighton (Add. MS. 6871. 14 Aug., 9 Sept., 2 Dec. 1885). The work is F. X. von Wegele, *Geschichte der deutschen Historiographie* (1885).

of what he had achieved himself.[1] The importance of the essay is that it inaugurated the study of Revolutionary historiography as a body of literature historically connected. He sought to outline this historiography in terms of stages of scholarship and political influences. He studied the pitfalls of the early historians, the partiality, the lack of documents, the apologetic motives, etc. He was able to display the gradual clarification of an episode through the accumulation of knowledge, the exposure of an error or the discovery of a forgery. Acton's manuscripts show that his printed work does not adequately reflect the scope and depth of his investigations of historians. Not only did he conduct his study of the Revolution itself through criticism of its historians, but he often loses sight of the Revolution and looks at the historians, studying their method, background, value, contribution, point of view and the place of their thought in the history of ideas. The connection between their life and work is more closely investigated than a test of reliability alone would require.

There are hints at an unwritten history of history in Acton's notes. By a collation of different sets of manuscripts some parts of his story can be more fully exposed. There is a gap in the beginning of the printed essay where a short introductory section is followed by a discussion of Droz, whose work came out in 1841. Mignet and Thiers do not appear in the printed essay although Acton devoted much thought to them and ascribed great importance to their writings. The review Acton wrote of Thiers's *Napoleon* in 1863 says nothing about Thiers's view of the Revolution except 'M. Thiers began as a fatalist, he is now a believer only in moral causes'. But this was not perhaps Acton's serious opinion. Because Acton is *par excellence* an historian of historiography, and because the reaction to Thiers and Mignet looms so large among the factors affecting the English view of the Revolution, it might be interesting to put together some of the scattered remarks in Acton's unpublished notes on those French historians.[2]

Acton divided Revolutionary historiography into three eras. The first down to 1835 consisted of books written by contemporaries or by men who lived among them. It was followed by the era of the great writers. Thirdly came the documentary period. Contemporaries wrote valuable memoirs but bad histories. Deux Amis, Bertrand, Toulongeon and others, says Acton, have this in common, that we can do without them. The first historians worthy of discussion are Thiers and Mignet. Mignet was an able historian and an explorer in other fields. He introduced the Revolution into European literature in an able compendium requiring

[1] The historians mentioned by Acton are: Droz, Lamartine, Blanc, Michelet, Villiaumé, Genoude, Gabourd, Guizot, Barante, Montalembert, Tocqueville, Duvergier de Haraunne, Laboulaye, Carlyle, Lavalle, Carnot, Martin, Dereste, Lanfrey, Quinet, Ternaux, Sybel, Aulard.

[2] The following comments have been extracted from MS. notes chiefly in Add. MSS. 4917, 4922, 5433, 5649.

no research. He described the logic of events more than the actions of men, and for his views on the persons, we have to go to his later biographical orations. That on Siéyès is important for Siéyès, as the inventor of ideas, was the representative of the Revolution. Mignet writes as if causes produce effects without the wishes of helpless men, who execute, without knowing them, the designs of God. Mignet justified the Revolution not in its men but in its cause. His brevity and vigour, and his way of making thought predominate over fact, stand in contrast to the diffuse style of Thiers, the most widely read of Revolutionary historians. Thiers was an enthusiast for the ideas and the men who opened a way to power and to fortune for people like himself. He owed his career to the destruction of the old régime. He had for Napoleon the prodigious intellectual sympathy of a gifted man for one still more richly gifted than himself. The consciousness of pre-eminent ability determined his attitude to the Revolution and he glorified it for its elevation of middle class, for the ruin of class privilege, and for the reign of talent which it inaugurated. Thiers disliked democracy, and spoke of the vile multitude. He also said that Republics always ended in imbecility and bloodshed. His own leanings were towards constitutional monarchy, but he said that all the kings he had known were insane. Thiers was not a liberal; he hated socialism, nationality, religious liberty, peace, free trade. His only political convictions were protectionism and the old army system, and to the deputies who spoke to him about education, he replied that he wanted an army, and for that he needed brutes. Thiers believed that he represented the national instinct. He loved France because it emancipated Europe and because it subdued it. He believed that constitutional monarchy could only prevail after a long conflict and that it was worth the price it cost, but that the forces promoting the Revolution had not been sufficient for this change. Thiers wrote with a practical and polemical purpose against the conservatives of the Restoration who rested their case on the atrocities of the Jacobins. The more the Jacobins were execrated the more royalism was made to appear as the reign of virtue. Thiers rose against the polemical use of crimes which he neither denied nor denounced with the duplicity of indignant virtue. He did not, like Mignet, merely contemplate the conflict of the elements. He said that because they were regicides and members of the Committee of Public Safety, the men of violence were, none the less, the men who raised the middle classes, and made France the greatest power in the world. For Thiers, conquest redeemed the Revolution. The men of violence were the patriots and they saved France and the world by putting down the traitors, their enemies. Thiers and Mignet do not explicitly praise murder, only its results and the men whom murder made great; and they emphasize the national cause. The atrocities were dreadful necessities. No book was more welcome to modern France than Thiers's, and though poor as a philosophy, it was powerful as politics. It was Thiers's study to present with talent things that were ordinary and vulgar. He had no use for moral codes and believed that you may be a homicide and a liar for your country's good. If Guizot passed by the difference between just and unjust, Thiers saw none, and he did not care for the negative moral qualities which do not make men great and countries powerful. As a history Thiers's work on the Revolution is based on superficial information and insufficient materials. But it does not all come from other books. Thiers learnt so much from survivors that he corrected their recollections, especially on military matters. Dumas testified that Thiers saw the Revolution as it was, especially 10 August.

The analysis of Acton's sources shows that he also read the English historians though this is hardly represented in the historiographical essay. He seems to have assumed that their work did not belong to the main stream and he rightly related them to each other more than to the French historians. He was interested mainly in their views. Perhaps he was put off by his own assumption on English historians, 'Nous aimons moins l'histoire de l'intelligence que l'histoire de la volonté.' Acton did not study the English historians as thoroughly as he did the French. He overrated Smyth's scholarship and Alison's psychological insight. His remarks on Carlyle are usually directed against condoning the crimes of heroes, and this criticism would not apply to Carlyle's history of the French Revolution. Acton detested Carlyle as the most hateful historian, and of Croker he said as Macaulay had done, that he was the most hateful man in politics.[1] He thought him dishonest in not making the strongest case for his political opponents. This, again, would not apply to Croker's best work on the French Revolution which Acton did not study. He never made a single comment on Croker's history writing, and there is only one note from Croker's *Essays*.

CHANGES IN POLITICAL VIEW

Because Acton's thought on the Revolution developed in the course of his life, a collection of his opinions from his published and unpublished writings would present a variety of inconsistencies. It must be borne in mind that Acton gradually changed from a clear and dogmatic, to a highly complicated position, and that we can only understand his view by following the subtle distinctions he made between aspects of the Revolution. When oversimplified views are imputed to Acton on the authority of isolated passages, we get contradictory accounts of his interpretation.

[1] Acton to M. Gladstone 18 Dec. 1884: 'I am conscious of more nearly hating Croker than anybody, except Lord Clare, in English history. It was my one link with a late, highly-lamented statesman and novelist.' Acton means, of course, Disraeli.

Acton's thought on the Revolution developed in three ways, the political, the historical and the scholarly. With regard to the last it has already been said that in proportion to his increasing isolation Acton showed a growing devotion to minute scholarship. He absorbed the results of new research as they came out.[1] In his political ideas Acton, unlike most men, became more revolutionary as he grew older. When he took up periodical writing in his twenties he was at the height of his conservatism, although he kept aloof from politics. He was strongly under the influence of Burke and Tocqueville and he attacked Buckle and Mill.[2] When Acton entered Parliament he kept politics out of the business of the elections, though he wrote to the priest who secured the votes that he would rather oppose Tories than Liberals. When he addressed his constituency his speech contained not a clue as to his politics[3]. The notes to the speech speak vaguely of 'legitimate freedom', of moral influence abroad, of old principles continuously adapted, 'distinguished alike from a revolutionary absolutism which mock (disgrace) the model they profess to imitate'.[4] In 1859 Acton wrote on a Revolutionary subject from an anti-revolutionary point of view.[5] He explained the fall of the monarchy as the result of the revolutionism of its defenders. *Les Actes des Apôtres*, he said, written in the spirit of Voltaire, 'represented that part of the old aristocracy which it was the merit of the Revolution to have exterminated'. On other points in this article Acton was to change his mind. In 1859 he considered as crude the notion that 'the first distinct traces' of the revolutionary theory were in the *Telemachus*, a notion he was later to hold very emphatically himself. Moreover, the writer who is here criticized based this theory on Fénelon's warning that the violation of the contract on the part of the King would render the people exempt; and Acton was to expound in detail the practical use of this very idea, by Marat. At this stage he denied to Fénelon any revolutionism and saw his teaching as conventional for a prelate. He also held that the Revolution transferred to politics what was true in religion, namely, that if a prophet denounced a wicked king, this did not justify men in rebelling.[6] He quoted from Leibnitz a passage he called prophetic, because it detected the signs of revolution, not in irreligion, but in an 'intellectual movement'. In time

[1] Acton at once saw the importance of the first results of systematic research. In reviewing Mortimer Ternaux, Feuillet de Conches, Dauban, he limits himself to the discussion of new facts. In his correspondence with editors of *E.H.R.* Acton often offered to review revolutionary works and he offered criticism of other reviewers. E.g. letters to Poole, 13 May 1890, 4 Sept. 1891, 20 Jan. 1894 (Add. MS. 7472).

[2] Letters of 16 Feb., 6 June 1858.

[3] J. J. Auchmuty, 'Acton's Election', *E.H.R.* (1946).

[4] Add. MS. 4862.

[5] 'Schmidt-Weissenfels's Geschichte', *The Rambler* (Nov. 1859), II, 104–7.

[6] In 1870 Acton criticized the view that 'the doctrine of passive obedience is inculcated by the New Testament' (Review of Portalis).

Acton was to see the danger of the intellectual movement precisely in its irreligion.

Acton retained his hostility to the Revolution in the 'sixties as is shown, for instance, in his review of the *Mémoires* of Carnot, and of the *Political History* of Goldwin Smith whom he called a Jacobin. But he also quoted from Carnot the question, 'Do not kings cause men to be put to death who conspire against them?' And he called it the strongest case for regicide. Acton was much later to put down in a note that Louis XVI was guilty of the crime for which he was tried for he plotted the death of his subjects. By 1867 Acton had changed his view of the nobility. In reviewing Kingsley, he attacked the view he considered Carlylean, that force represents the spiritual power and that the sins of the nobility brought judgment on them. The men whom Acton had condemned for their very self-destruction, he now admired for their self-sacrifice. He spoke of the nobility as distinguished for virtue and reforming zeal, as being of high morality and sound intellect and therefore no less than the *bourgeoisie* at war with a corrupt tradition. It renounced its privileges freely and died nobly, 'as fearless in failure as it had been honest in reform'. Later again Acton put down in a note that when the nobles knew their cause was lost, they stopped Barère from abolishing feudal rights, intending to do so themselves.[1] Acton retained a favourable view of the reforming nobility but of part of the royalist party he later pronounced his severest judgment, calling their policy of pushing the Revolution to extreme, the worst political crime of the Revolution.

Acton's writings in the 'seventies show (perhaps under the impression of Taine's work) a deep sense of the miseries of the people and at the same time a decided antagonism to the principle of equality. In a lecture of 1877, and especially in the notes in which it was prepared, he dwells on the sufferings of the poor. Among the Acton manuscripts there is an incomplete draft of what could have been an opening chapter on the Revolution.[2] It was not used for the Cambridge lectures but a portion of it in a condensed form is to be found at the end of the lecture on 'Freedom in Christianity'. The draft is a connected view on the beginnings of the Revolution which Acton held about 1877. It shows clearly that the distinction between liberty and equality ruled Acton's interpretation at the time. He wrote that the burden of the Declaration of the Rights of Man was equality, and that, having made it, the Assembly went on to satisfy the demands of the middle class and to ignore the needs of the poor who had struck every decisive blow for it. That which had been a struggle between the nobles and the middle class became a struggle between property and labour.[3] The original cause of the Revolution was for-

---

[1] Add. MS. 5444.   [2] Add. MS. 5436.
[3] The idea recurs frequently, e.g. in Add. MSS. 5444, in connection with the formation of the National Guard.

gotten. 'It was amid terror and slaughter that one of the two elements that composed the Revolution neutralized the other and the passion for equality made vain the hope for freedom.'[1]

Acton's emphasis on equality in the 'seventies was affected by contemporary social upheavals. He spoke of equality as having been in the remote past, connected with generous and religious aspirations but as having now revived to constitute 'our most dangerous enemy'. In a note Acton wrote that, having failed in the Revolution, socialism revived in 1836.[2] When, later, Acton accepted the principle of revolution he dissociated it from democracy and equality alike and believed that revolution could be promoted by a love of liberty and not by material hope. In the lectures, Acton retained the distinction between liberty and equality but no longer as the key to his interpretation.

In the 'eighties Acton was forming the views which made the lectures what they are. He wrote of his views to Mary Gladstone and to Lady Blennerhasset whom he considered an authority on the Revolution, and whose conventional views provoked him to attack. Their correspondence shows the growing divergence between their political views, which caused Lady Blennerhasset to pronounce Acton unfit for practical politics. She often criticized Acton and Gladstone together and one of her complaints against Gladstone was that 'he called the 10th Aug. 1792 when 700 Swiss Guards defended those doomed and miserable Bourbons against the mob of Santerre and Danton 40,000 strong "the legitimate defence of the people"'.[3] Acton was now rejecting views he had held, especially under the influence of Burke. In the years round 1860 when Acton was under foreign influences, he had greatly admired Burke's anti-Revolutionary writings as a formulated philosophy. Acton later came to regard Burke as a warning against a philosophy in politics and also as the father of nineteenth-century liberalism. By the time he wrote his lectures his discipleship to Burke had more in common with Morley than with Taine. He came to connect Burke with the English Whigs more than with the continental conservatives and he named among those who lived on 'fragments from Burke's table', Brougham, Lowe, Mackintosh and Macaulay.

Acton rejected Burke's interpretations on the French constitution and on the National Assembly. He enumerated Burke's inconsistencies as well as the limitations in his vision. 'When Burke says that a man has a right to the fruits of his labour, he gets behind the north wind and accepts

---

[1] Add. MS. 5436. In the lecture on 'Freedom' (1877), Acton writes, 'the finest opportunity ever given to the world was thrown away because the passion for equality made vain the passion for liberty.' In reviewing May (1878), Acton again speaks of 'the splendid opportunity' ruined by the 'theory of equality'.

[2] Add. MS. 5487. Note also, 'Socialism not a product of our age'. 'Only Fr. Rev. made it formidable'.

[3] Lady Blennerhasset to A. Russel, 3 Sept. 1886 (Add. MS. 7486).

the Revolution.'[1] Acton, like Burke and Tocqueville, held that equality limited liberty, but he agreed with the latter that revolution was continuous. He did not share Burke's and Tocqueville's preoccupation with aristocracy and he discarded their pessimism which at one time he had thought distinguished the historical thinkers from the narrators.[2]

Acton was growing democratic. He felt close to the tradition of Locke and Adam Smith, though aware of the changes in the minds of those 'who sit in the seat of Adam Smith'. He came to believe in the moral duty of sharing political power with the working classes and he based his conviction on the principle of Adam Smith that contracts between property and labour should be free. This, he thought, required that the making of laws should not be monopolized by the side of property owners.[3] It was to Adam Smith, too, that he traced much of Siéyès. This is important because to Acton the thought of Siéyès was the real revolutionary thought. As Acton was losing ground to revolutionism, he tended to fortify himself more and more behind the idea of conscience, his antidote to growing revolutionism. It kept him from complete surrender to Locke, from basing right on the will of the people. 'We must absolutely disregard and resist popular convictions opposed to our own. The seat of conscience is within.'

HISTORY AS THE HISTORY OF IDEAS

Apart from his growing revolutionism, Acton's writings show a growing inclination towards the history of ideas, as the most significant kind of history. It was this notion which formed the character of his revolutionary history when it came to be written, and it is significant how closely it was connected with Acton's thought about the Revolution. Burckhardt wrote that the French Revolution opened people's minds to spiritual causes, 'their visible transformation into material effects'.[4] In Acton's development we can find this statement illustrated. As early as 1859, in reviewing a history of French Revolutionary writings, Acton said that the novelty of modern history (not yet attained in England) was that the history of ideas was 'now understood in its bearing on the history of events', and he reached this idea through a consideration of the Revolution, which, he said, brought out for the first time within a short period, the impact of ideas on events. This impact had, in previous centuries, been too slow to be noticed, except in a few cases of brisk controversies. Acton immediately carried this idea forward and added that because of this new insight which we have, history must be rewritten as the history

---

[1] Add. MS. 4967.   [2] Add. MS. 5389.

[3] Acton to M. Gladstone 24 Apr. 1881, 27 Oct. 1881. To disprove the notion that the people were unfit to rule he could compile an 'encyclopaedia of error' from the acts of the ablest rulers.

[4] Burckhardt, *Reflections* (1943), p. 25.

of ideas, and that it would not do merely to illustrate events by the ideological background as they do in France, or by the social background as they do in England.[1] The reverse is what is required, namely, a history whose backbone is made of ideas, and from which all the accidental and temporary has been excluded. The fall of the Bastille was merely a great sign whereas Siéyès's pamphlet on the Third Estate was a great fact. This basic notion of Acton's was to develop in various contexts. In one set of notes he asks: why not a history of laws or of institutions? and his answer is that ideas alone show progress and continuity.[2] In connection with Tocqueville's book on the French Revolution, Acton again emphasized the point that the way to connect the Revolution with history is through its ideas. In his letters, where Acton often gives his clearest criticisms of historians, he wrote, for instance, that his quarrel with Seeley was that Seeley saw Whigs where Acton wanted the history of Whiggism. The object of history, he writes in 1880, is 'to get behind men and to grasp ideas', for they have an ancestry and posterity of their own and they push history forward independently of men.[3]

This notion of the history of ideas led to Acton's most general point of interpretation with regard to revolutions. He believed that since Puritanism there was a continuous tradition of revolutionism as a living idea in England. Later he saw America as the heir of this spirit of the English sects, and connected, through their ideas, the Puritan, the American and the French Revolutions in a continuous series. The result was Acton's denial of a basic dividing line between French and Anglo-Saxon revolutions and the rejection of views sanctioned, as he said, by Burke, Mackintosh, Brougham and Macaulay, that the French made new worlds while the English tinkered with the old one. Acton stressed the abstract theories of the Puritans and the Americans, and, on the other hand, 'We must not underrate the force of tradition in the French law of Revolution', he wrote. This had been held by the Romantic-liberal school of Madame de Staël. Acton, because he thought in terms of ideas, went far in ignoring the national boundaries. In reviewing May's *Democracy* Acton said that because May was writing the history of democracies and not of the idea of democracy he left serious gaps. The omission of America left unexplained the connection between the Puritan and the French Revolution.[4] He therefore also rejected the distinction often made between French and English Revolutions as being that of equality on the one hand, liberty and reform on the other.

---

[1] The histories of literature, Acton said, do not meet the case for their selection depends on artistic quality and not on historical significance.

[2] Add. MS. 5438.

[3] Acton to M. Gladstone, 15 March 1880. Acton's complaint against Alison's history is that he does not tell us what we want to know, 'why the old world that had lasted so long went to ruin, and the doctrine of equality sprang to omnipotence'.

[4] See also Add. MS. 4862.

This connection between the great modern revolutions led to their justification on the ground of the idea of liberty for which they fought. Thinking about ideas thus helped to define Acton's growing revolutionism. In the early article on 'Nationality', Acton had explained that the French Revolution was totally new because it rejected authority on principle and was not merely a revolt against particular wrongs. Through the quest for a continuity in ideas, Acton now took his stand one stage earlier and the revolutionary novelty was no longer the rejection of authority on principle, but the fighting for liberty on principle. 'Un terrain sur lequel on pourrait défendre Washington et rejeter Siéyès, condamner George III et excuser Louis XVI n'existe pas', Acton wrote in 1887.[1]

ON THE CAUSES OF THE REVOLUTION

The notion of history as the history of ideas also affected Acton's practical treatment of the Revolution, especially the question of its causes. In a note he enumerates all the usual causes and adds that he does not deny some truth in each of these. But 'they do not explain the intensity of the result. To find the cause of it one must look deeper and wider afield'.[2] Acton saw the Revolution as the product of many causes but allowed preponderance to eighteenth-century philosophy and to the irresistible example of America. Both in the lecture and in his notes he repeats the view that in order to see the Revolution 'as a product of historic influences' we must bind it to the ideas which preceded it.[3] To find the genesis of Revolutionary ideas he ignored national boundaries, traced some of Rousseau to Locke, some of Siéyès to Adam Smith, and law reform to Beccaria. In his survey of pre-revolutionary thought Acton mentions no writer without connecting his thought with some Revolutionary action. In a lecture of 1877 he had already said that he would like to show the practical effect of philosophical ideas in the Revolution, and in a manuscript draft of the same time[4] he worked out in detail Marat's practical application of the theory of the social contract. The principle of Rousseau was applied with implacable logic and fanatic energy by Marat, who taught that 'those to whom society brought nothing but wretchedness were released from the obligations (bonds) of the past', and Acton says that the force of the argument was generally seen. In the Cambridge lectures Acton did the same. Domat, for instance, whose 'principle of higher law signifies revolution' pointed the way to 'the

---

[1] Letter to Lady Blennerhasset May 1887 (*Selections*, p. 280).

[2] Add. MS. 4921.

[3] Acton, *F.R.*, pp. 1–2. See, e.g., Add. MS. 4921 for notes connecting the Revolution with history through ideas. 'It is by the ideas that the Revolution recovers its roots.' See also the review of Stephens who is criticized for omitting 'the philosophy of the Revolution, its causes in the reign of thought'.

[4] Add. MS. 5436.

primitive system which the lawyers of the Assembly, descending from Domat, prefixed to their constitution'.[1] With the immediate procursors Acton was even more precise. He said that Montesquieu's views on taxation and the division of power gave him influence in 1789, that Turgot's idea of progress 'forged a weapon charged with power to abolish the product of history and the existing order', and his influence can be traced in acts of the Assembly. His idea that land is wealth produced the *assignats*, and he was the protagonist in Europe of the single legislature which was France's model.

Thought, said Acton, was not directly responsible for the outbreak. It hung like a cloud and America provided the spark which burst it. The thought of America, said Acton, 'influenced the French next to their own'. When, however, Acton specifies the American lessons he repeats ideas which he had previously attributed to French philosophers, so that the predominance of 'thought' in Acton's view of the causes is not really upset. He says, for instance, that Lafayette learned from America that resistance is a duty, and that authority comes from the governed; but Acton had already attributed these principles to Domat and Jurieu. Jurieu 'taught that sovereignty comes from the people'. Domat learnt from Saint Thomas the duty of resistance. Another 'American' idea, that the past was a warning, he had already ascribed to Turgot. The great discovery which Acton imputed to America, namely the principle that liberty is the ultimate end of politics, was not an idea taught at the time. It represents the essential innovation produced by the American revolt, but one which can only be recognized on a later analysis of long-term results. Acton did not, therefore, replace the influence of French philosophy by the influence of American theory, but rather showed that American boldness, in theory and practice, added force to a revolutionary attitude in France: 'The confluence of French theory with the American example caused the Revolution to break out.'

Acton's view of the causes was not another version of 'Voltaire's fault', and he did not, like Burke or Carlyle, see disease in the very prevalence of philosophy. In his view of history every event was preceded by an idea. Guizot had said that in France policy is prepared by ideas and Acton added the comment, 'The Revolution is the great example.' Many remarks in the notes show that ideal causes for events were for Acton so obvious that he did not feel the need to prove it in his lectures. This is the fundamental difference between Acton's view and that of the *Cambridge Modern History*, and to a certain extent, that of Lecky. Willert, in the *Cambridge Modern History*, posed the question of the philosophic causes and denied their efficacy. His detailed analysis of pre-revolutionary thought and its effects on Revolutionary legislation,

[1] Also Maultrot, Fénelon, etc. Acton even points out when a pre-revolutionary writer did not have an actual influence on the Revolution as, e.g., d'Argenson.

which is so similar to Acton's ends with an opposite conclusion because of this basic difference that Willert did not think ideas are the real makers of history. Theory, he said, was only effective when it offered remedies to concrete, social and economic evils. The difference between the two historians is not in emphasis, but rather in the underlying assumption. Willert relegated the philosophic influences to a spiritual sphere and thereby removed them from 'real' history. For Acton the distinction did not exist.

Acton saw the Revolution as folded up in the intellectual movements which preceded it. Here several of his beliefs meet in a crucial point posing a formidable question. If the Revolution was folded up in its guiding ideas, its failure too was foredoomed. How would Acton explain the failure of the great liberal ideas which both caused the Revolution and caused it to fail? To understand Acton's answer we must understand his notion of religion in history. His answer was that the Revolution was doomed because the religious element was missing from the revolutionary ideal of liberty. When Acton speaks of the religious element in this way he may not be thinking specifically of his own Catholic Church, its dogmas, structure, and theology. His capacity to think separately about the Church and about religious conscience caused, after all, his conflict with the Church. When he says that the revolutionary ideas had been pervaded by irreligion, he means that they lacked the positive faith which holds sacred, Divine laws, moral values and human life. In a note he writes, 'Religion needed for liberty. Because it is often a powerful restraint. Secondly because a religious man has a higher notion of that which liberty is required for. To be free to enjoy his fortune and employ his faculties is well. But that is flea bite compared to saving his soul and the souls of his children. As to that the Rev. was not clear. It might be so; but it was not certain and that basis was not to be found in the liberal classics: Jefferson, Hollbach, Siéyès, Paine.'[1] Because cruelty was associated with religious persecution the campaign for reforming the law became anti-religious, and 'ended in a wild cry of vengeance'. Thus Acton saw even the fire and sword aspect of the Revolution as implicit in its intellectual background. In his notes and in his lectures he goes through pre-revolutionary writings stringing them together by their irreligious, and therefore to him illiberal, element. Of other than intellectual causes Acton says little. He stressed the economic factor as active in the Revolution, but not as an initial cause. His treatment of the social revolution seems based on the study of the idea of equality more than on that of social forces.

Acton's interpretation of the actual course of events was based, like that of most English historians, on the view that that course was directed by 'crimes of men and by errors more inevitably fatal than crime', and on the belief in the importance of the early stages. An especially crucial

[1] Add. MS. 4925.

moment was 23 June. That day decided that 'France, so near the goal in that month of June, should wade to it through streams of blood'.[1] It was then that the King took the road to the scaffold, and it was then, too, that the social revolution had taken the lead, for there was a demand for the privileges of the aristocracy as well as for the prerogatives of the monarch. Another of Acton's 'decisive moments' was the invasion when the instinct of freedom gave way to the instinct of force, 'the liberal movement was definitely reversed'. This, says Acton, was a more important transition than that to a republic. Since Terror alone could save France and since it was an illegitimate power, it could only quell opposition by violence.

Because the question of the ideal causes meant for Acton more than the explanation of the outbreak, it is not confined to the introductory lectures. In the course of the narrative, Acton stops to extract from an event an ideal significance. As a result, some Revolutionary events appear curiously disembodied as a battle of ideas and not of wills. The constitutional struggles are discussed as a debate between Turgot's idea of a king ruling a democracy and Rousseau's idea of a democracy ruling itself through the agency of a king. At times it seems that Acton is really concerned with the history of the idea of liberty and he often stops to point out that some Revolutionary manifestation was not truly liberal. The preoccupation with ideas sometimes interfered with the simple accuracy of the narrative. When Acton says, for instance, 'If the King was right in America, he was wrong at home', he was not really imputing to Louis XVI any sympathy with America, but summarizing the significance of a moment in general terms.[2] Acton knew that historians of ideas tended to formulate too much. 'Il est commode de dire que les Jacobins c'est la democratie directe, les Girondins le Fédéralisme, que Danton représente Diderot, et Robespierre Rousseau.'[3] Though he gave warning against 'cette méthode de précision', Acton himself did not avoid it. Some of his striking statements are achieved through devising a culminating paradox. In this extra jump which may be a blind one, he sometimes brings out an important intuitive truth. At the same time the result may be a rigid simplification.

ACTON'S FORMULAE OF BASIC IDEAS

The view of the Revolution which Acton finally arrived at was closely interwoven with the central trends of his mind, with his movement towards revolutionism and towards the history of ideas; the preoccupation with the idea of liberty and with universal history; the definition of

---

[1] Acton, *F.R.* p. 19; Add. MS. 4865.
[2] Acton had already said this in abstract language, 'Si l'independence d'Amerique est justifiée, la Monarchie française est condamnée' (*Selections*, p.280).
[3] *Selections*, p. 276.

liberty as the freedom of conscience and the insistence on moral judgments in history. In Acton's own writings, and in those about him, these fundamental notions always come to the fore. Acton was always concerned with them directly or indirectly, constantly and inconsistently. Students of Acton have tried to discover the key to his mind by treating as pivotal one or the other of these issues. Acton never worked them out as a unified system. But to understand the essence of his mind and of his work as a historian, it is important to realize how closely this complex of basic interests and beliefs was interconnected in his thought. To examine its inner connections would bring out the peculiar quality of Acton's nature as a historian; the special place of the French Revolution as a focal point in his thought; and perhaps the explanation to the paradoxical quality pervading all aspects of Acton's life, and culminating in the tragic discrepancy between great promise and failure of fulfilment.

The widest background against which Acton's work as a historian should be examined are the nineteenth-century movements in history writing. Acton was shaped by them and experienced them with great intensity all through his life. He did not hesitate to say that what happened to history in the nineteenth century was more revolutionary than the classical Renaissance. The peculiar relationship which Acton had with the historical movements, combining intellectual enthusiasm, conscientious reservations, and strategic aloofness (intended to facilitate an overall view of the whole process), reflects and partly explains the paradoxality of his work in general. This requires clarification. Acton was both the product, the critic and the historian of the historical movement in its romantic, historicist, critical and documentary stages. Its progress was one of his chief interests. When the archives began to open he studied their contents and followed closely the use which was being made of them in new reconstructions, discoveries, directions of research. He was endlessly surveying achievements and failures. His knowledge of what was in the archives and what was missing, of what was important or worthless, genuine or forged, was phenomenal. But Acton never became part of the new documentary scholarship. In a period when research was expanding he attempted to encompass its whole progress. Although this interest curtailed his own historical production he valued it highly as the sovereign role in the realm of history. Acton's failure in output should cease perhaps to mystify us when we realize on the one hand his ambition to embrace the whole of historical research and on the other hand his meticulous care for detail. An architect planning a city cannot afford to inspect the masonwork of individual stones. This *reductio ad absurdum*, however, should not be taken too literally. It would be a mistake to imagine that Acton escaped into petty work for want of daring or imagination, or, on the other hand, that he did not understand or practise documentary work at all. He was always wandering about archives and having transcripts made by overt and secret arrangements. It is true that he was often caught up in searching for the sensational or dramatic, and some of his critics regretted his interest in the kitchens of history. Acton was drawn to famous mysteries, stories of treachery, scandal and, above all, forgery. One could fill pages with Acton's 'petty' researches but it would be a mistake to overrate their place in his work. For in all he wrote, Acton always aspired to the heights from which history could be viewed in its significant outlines, hidden connections and large units.

Where Acton made an original contribution was in the history of historiography, which he treated as part of the history of ideas, and therefore as a factor affecting 'real' history. He felt personally committed to the historical movements of which he considered himself the authoritative historian. But his absorption in the study, criticism and survey of historiography was linked with another ingredient of his basic compound of beliefs, his well-known insistence on moral judgments in history. The sight of historians condoning bloodshed in history and whitewashing the murderers is Acton's obsessive idea of evil incarnate. Nothing else rouses him to the same prophetic wrath. Though he did not deny a certain development in morality he held on to a few absolute tests. 'For the purposes of history, murder is the worst crime.'[1] The objectivity he demanded from the historian did not include moral impartiality. The perfect historian is equipped with a taste for moral judgment. He must in turn fulfil all the tasks required in a court of law. He accumulates the materials, acts as prosecutor and counsel to all parties ('no cause is too odious to be fairly stated'); as the detective, the witness, the expert on handwriting and on bloodstains. Above all, he is the supreme judge, who fearlessly dons the black cap and on the ground of all the evidence and the laws, sentences the culprit to the 'undying penalty which history has the power to inflict on wrong'.

How then does moral judgment connect with Acton's other pursuits and especially with his paramount interest in the historical movement and in criticizing historians? Acton, like many others, connected the beginning of the historical movement with the Romantic revolt against the French Revolution's violation of historical continuity. He never ceased to wonder at 'the unexpected truth stranger than fiction', that the Revolution which sought to destroy history brought on its magnificent revival. 'History issues from the Romantic school. Piecing together what the Revolution snapped. It hails from Burke as Education from Helvetius or Emancipation from the Quakers.' Acton always overrated the threefold influence of the French Revolution, the Romantic movement

---

[1] 'Murder as the conventional low-water mark is invaluable as our basis of measurement' (Review of Stephens *E.H.R.* (1892)).

and Germany on the development of historiography, perhaps because he was so susceptible to dramatic juxtapositions in history between great events and great movements of thought. His enthusiasm was also deepened by the fact that the historical revival came with a Catholic revival, with the development of a scientific school in ecclesiastical history and with attempts to weave together Catholicism and liberty. All these movements were, to Acton, aspects of a great spiritual drama unfolding before his eyes. It is because of his great emotional involvement than an ambivalence in his attitude to the historical movement prevented his wholehearted participation in it. For this was the crucial point, that these great movements, as Acton became deeply aware, also embodied that evil doctrine of withholding moral judgment in history. 'Romantic taught to understand the past. Comprendre c'est pardonner', Acton wrote simply in one of numerous notes on this subject. 'Their tendency was to debase the currency, to bend the standard of morality. They established the theory that every age must be understood and judged on its own terms.' On another card he writes bitterly that the Church is satisfied for it does not want its past actions to be judged by nineteenth-century standards.

THE IDEALIST–HISTORIAN'S PARALYSIS

The moral indifference which Acton ascribed to the Romantic and historical movements deeply repulsed him and he always criticized Ranke for not condemning the inquisition. On this question Acton felt painfully isolated even from friends like Doellinger, Gladstone, Creighton. 'I am absolutely alone in my essentially ethical position and therefore useless', is his often quoted confession. Some critics (like Kochan) think justly that this isolation silenced Acton. But it is not weakness, pliability or the fear of unpopularity which checked Acton, but a more profound kind of paralysis. It was not merely that Acton kept quiet because he held unorthodox beliefs. The absolute and inflexible beliefs which made up his mind and acted on each other made history writing objectively impossible. The crucial point is, that his active participation in the historical movement, which was the centre of his intellectual activity, was rendered impotent by his abhorrence of that school's attitude to moral judgment in history. Again, the olympic interest in the criticism of other historians is not merely a methodological approach, but an exacting moral compulsion always to judge not only the evil doers in history, but also their historians, the false judges. It is in the same light, as another of these mutually stifling urges, that we can now view also Acton's absorption in the history of ideas. We have seen how it affected his understanding of the causes and progress of the French Revolution, how it affected his manner of writing history and his tendency towards ideal revolutionism. It also led by a clear logical step to universal history. Ideas alone do not recognize national boundaries. Ideas are therefore the very substance which gives universal history both unity and continuity. In his plan for the *Cambridge Modern History*, Acton meant to give the separate studies a universal significance. He also meant to open the series with a general chapter on the stock of ideas with which modern history set out. The sovereign among these ideas, whose progress is the life and soul of modern history, is of course the idea of liberty, the most confident, continuous and forceful of ideas operating in history. The emergence of the idea of liberty, through a universal interplay of ideas, affected Acton's treatment of the intellectual antecedents of the French Revolution and modern revolutionism in general.

The French Revolution was thus the focal point for all the main currents in Acton's thought, ideas, liberty, judgment, etc. It is the natural and the ideal test-case for Acton's capacity to write history on the basis of his own intellectual system. What, for instance, can be a better test case or a greater challenge for Acton's system of beliefs than the need to judge crimes committed for the sake of the idea of liberty? Acton may have thought so himself, for the French Revolution is his only attempt at a comprehensive history.

Viewed in this light, Acton's achievement in the history of the Revolution is that he viewed it purely in its connections with history. Though he was primarily concerned with the political side, he did not seek to solve the problems faced by Revolutionary France, or to fix his hopes on any party or phase. Detachment was a recognized aspiration in Revolutionary historiography, but it meant different things to different historians. Acton's achievement of a rare kind of objectivity is often misunderstood. It is the crux of his nature as a historian. 'How could one condemn Siéyès and still keep faith with Liberalism?' asks one student of Acton.[1] In the conventional pattern of Revolutionary historiography it would indeed imply confusion in a historian to admire Siéyès's political writings, to condemn his practical political behaviour, to trace the descent from Siéyès to Robespierre, to damn Robespierre as a murderer, and yet apparently not to have a moral or logical difficulty to resolve. The explanation surely is that within Acton's idealist approach to history, he separated phenomena which in history appear connected. He had no difficulty in recognizing the truth and the force of Siéyès's political ideas as contributing to the progress of the idea of liberty, while utterly condemning the moral man in him and in his disciples. Acton had always done this, for instance, in the case of Macaulay, when he said, 'We must never judge the quality of a teaching by the quality of the teacher.' To say, therefore, that because Acton cursed the democrats and not democracy his judgments were blurred, is to ignore Acton's separation of ideas

[1] Himmelfarb, *Acton*, p. 214.

from men, and his peculiar achievement which was boldly to face truth wherever he found it, and not to impose a system where there was none.[1] What he attempted to do can be illustrated by two manuscript notes he wrote on Mirabeau.

The advice which he gave was unpatriotic and immoral. History has condemned him. He was wrong without the poor consolation (compensation?) of success.

It is otherwise if we apply to him the common and perpetual test of all political characters in civilized history. That is, was he at heart on the side of freedom or of force, of emancipation or of oppression, of individual right or of public authority. On this ground, on the great permanent ideas which he served, M. is superior to his reputation. His true convictions were better than his public utterances or his confidential counsels.[2]

Acton's attempt to write a history of the French Revolution shows how his system of basic ideas forced on him as a historian an impossible complex of tasks. It is wrong to say that Acton 'approved the act of revolution itself which was an implicit—for Acton sometimes even an explicit—condonation of murder'.[3] Acton did come to accept revolution, to deny that laws are sacred, to regard the past as a warning, to value the changes achieved through revolutions. This was not totally new. Macaulay said we must love liberty even in the shape of a reptile, and Lamartine, that the idea remained pure for all the blood with which humanity stained it. The difference in Acton was that he did not attempt to draw practical conclusions through apology or compromise. In practical politics this would undoubtedly have led him to guilt or to inconsistency. As a historian he could still judge conscientiously, approve the revolution and condemn the revolutionaries. Because Acton accepted 'revolution' he did not approve of the French Revolution as a specific event which combined a group of aims and methods, men and movements. He approved of those of its ideas which belonged to the history of liberty, which 'push history forward independently of men'. He traced the operation of such ideas over long periods of time. In dealing historically with specific events, he also had a great interest in the minds which carried the ideas and he felt strongly the moral duty of judging the characters. The attempt to think simultaneously on so many different levels of historical activity, to trace the origin of the Revolutionary ideas and to present their result as gain for liberty, while condemning the spirit of the Revolution as illiberal because it was irreligious, its method as criminal and its men as murderers, became a practical impossibility. A set of standards in history *ipso facto* creates an unhistorical attitude. Moreover, a simultaneous history of ideas and events showing on the one hand their constant interaction, and on the other hand,

[1] Acton to M. Gladstone 9 Apr. 1885: 'Taine fancies that to show the horrors of the Revolution is a good argument against democracy.'
[2] C.U.L. Add. MS. 5430, pp. 17, 18.   [3] Himmelfarb, *Acton*, pp. 216–17.

judging them separately on different grounds, became in Acton a supreme demonstration of the power of objective analysis, but as a historical reconstruction it had to fail; for as Acton said, actions are arbitrary and in ideas alone there is continuity. Acton traced the genealogy of ideas and the rolling of events but the two chains are only occasionally linked. The ideas Acton traced do not in fact sustain the whole of the concrete Revolution.

Having followed the ingredients of Acton's historical mind we seem to be trapped in a vicious circle. The more one admires the scholarship, analysis, objectivity, and moral stamina, the more do his great principles and beliefs appear like a tightening vice stifling his capacity for writing history. The group of axioms, of absolutely perfect ideals in scholarship and in conscience, form a harmonious system, but a system so perfect that it cannot constructively be set in motion among ordinary sinful and erratic men, who are, after all, as Acton himself said, 'the subject of all history'

CHAPTER 16

CONCLUSIONS

The study of the English historians of the French Revolution has brought out some common features they share in method, in political view and in historical interpretation. For the greater part of the century they were chiefly compilers, made relatively few discoveries of fact, and wrote their histories from secondary sources. At the same time their work showed from the beginning a conscious effort at the critical examination of previous accounts, and a marked tendency towards the impartial handling of fact. One of the basic features common to the historical method of the English historians is the unusual interest which they show in the previous historiography of the subject. It even seems true to say that their interest in the subject and their desire to write about it was often provoked by books or by opinions rather than by the events themselves. This may have been caused by the great awareness from the time of the Revolution itself of the great practical influence that historical accounts can have. In the earliest period they were provoked by accounts of the Revolution written with a political motive; and if it is true that they had a political motive too, they directed their attack against books and ideas which sought to promote or to discredit revolution through the agency of words. It is as though they were led to believe that a revolution in England could only break out, or be prevented, as a result of a mental reaction to a historical experience 'properly' understood. Thus, while the French were producing, on the same subject, works which were often like political arguments, the English (even when their own purpose was political in the same way) would try to achieve their effect by employing historical criticism, checking the histories and the memoirs against each other and collecting further evidence, however unsystematically, to check the recorded story. Because they had less materials, they treated them with greater respect. Because they always professed impartiality, they had to a certain extent to learn to practise it. The method was useful even when the results were poor. National animosity, suspicion of all French writers as biased liars, contributed to this critical attitude. The outsider's bias thus became an asset to English historians in the role of critics and interpreters, which they chose to fill for long. Croker's work is an example of the way in which the critical activity transcended the political motive. Not only was the impetus to study given by books which were often assumed to be deceitful, but the presentation of the history often had as its starting point, or its framework, the criticism of other writers. Many of the most interesting English writings on the Revolution

274

have, in fact, been book reviews. Smyth wrote lectures frankly intended
as guides to reading, and they were described in his own time as a 'history
of histories'. The articles of Croker, though they are laden with the result
of original historical investigation, are in the form of book reviews.
Acton not only studied revolutionary history through the criticism of its
historians, but he also betrays a predominating interest in the historiography of any subject with which he may deal. His reading comprised
works which the mere reconstructor of historical narrative would have
disdained to touch; for he held the view that ideas produced both the
Revolution and its historiography, and that it was through ideas that the
Revolution influenced subsequent history. Carlyle alone had only a
secondary interest in the books he used, for he attempted to approach the
Revolution directly, his narrative beginning and ending with the event
itself. Although what we call secondary sources were primary sources
to him, and he showed much contempt for them, he used nothing save
these authors in spite of his early plans of conducting his own research.
Though Acton drew on a far wider field of reading, in his case, too, what is
produced is an apparently straightforward narrative, charged with interpretation and based on secondary sources.

The political side of the English historiography of the Revolution is
different from that of the French historiography. To have a political
attitude to the Revolution was a point of intellectual honesty or even
social responsibility in France. Taine said, 'The essential thing is the idea
we hold of the principles of 1789.' Though Carlyle, too, wrote, 'I should
not have known what to make of this world at all if it had not been for
the French Revolution', Carlyle's quest for an interpretation of world
history in the light of the French Revolution was not the same as Taine's
demand for taking a stand on the problems which the Revolution posed
to France. This demand is often projected to the historians. The students
of French historiography often stress the historians' political views, the
effect of these views on their histories and the subsequent effect of their
histories on current politics. The French Revolution played a part in all
subsequent French political history and had done this partly through the
writings of historians. It is, for example, widely recognized that Mignet
and Thiers prepared the way for the constitutional monarchy; while
Lamartine, Michelet and Blanc did the same for 1848 and the Republic.
The immediate political objectives and effects were not as obvious to
contemporaries as they are now. The more people became aware of this
connection between history and politics the more they developed,
consciously, the art of discussing politics with the help of Revolutionary
terminology. They used it in the political struggles of the Third Republic
even on occasions when there was no question of violent change and no
issue which involved any consistent imitation of a Revolutionary programme. Narratives of the Revolution were overlaid with discussion

concerning their tendency. These thickening layers of revolutionary thought stamped historical patterns on the French political mind and as the century progresses the influence of revolutionary historiography seems actually to have increased. The political use of history worked against the process whereby history became more professional in the course of the nineteenth century. The growing body of socialist thought, for example, had the effect of keeping the Revolution in the forefront, both as a key to a general interpretation, and as a test case in political action. The connection between Revolutionary historiography and French politics has become so obvious that it is often exaggerated. Sometimes this is done in the belief that all history is, and should be, deeply embedded in the problems of the period in which it is written. Attempts have been made to go through the list of French Revolutionary historians and to show that each had his views on philosophy or politics or on the problems of his time, and at worst wrote narratives which were merely weapons in the political struggles of his own day. It is sometimes said that the accumulation of knowledge under the Third Republic and since, has not lessened the conflict over the interpretation of the French Revolution and that this interpretation was in all cases determined by the social background and experience of the historians. Although it is clear that Tocqueville, Taine, Aulard and Sorel were subject to political and social influences, the most important and lasting part of their work is that which narrows the margin of historical disagreement. It is easy enough to show that Buchez was influenced by the Saint-Simonian creed and by the notion that the Revolution was essentially a Christian effort; that Aulard was a loving son of the Revolution as he called himself; that Sorel was a French patriot and Sybel a 'Franzosenfresser' who in his way helped to bring about the mood of Sedan. It is not, however, enough to say that Aulard's interest in the religious tenets of the Revolution reflects the spiritual hankerings of his own age, in order to condemn him as biased. A historian can have a 'philosophy' without writing merely biased history.

The same approach, when applied to the English historiography of the French Revolution, has resulted in the assumption that it is possible to think of the English historiography as containing two warring currents, as a political debate between Burkianism and Revolutionism, recurring in every generation, never decided and never abandoned; that the ideas of Burke had the predominance up to 1830 when the new French Revolution changed people's minds. Carlyle's work, we are told, 'is a document in the democratic and radical movement in England during the thirties'. His success, it is also said, prevented another attempt for fifty years until Stephens, in spite of his conspicuous efforts at impartiality, produced a work which manifested his strong prejudice in favour of England and the British constitution. His bias even affected the structure of his narratives and is shown in his admiration for Mirabeau. His excuse for the Terror is typical of Gladstone's England. This view has to be revised.

The study of the English historians has brought out the fact that there is among them a basic agreement on certain key issues, and that this body of historiography underwent in the course of the century a process of development which was not determined by the party lines. There are no fundamental differences between the party views especially if we regard them as historical interpretations; there is above all no Whig versus Tory interpretation, Revolutionism versus Burkianism warring as two philosophies of history. The fact that the French Revolution was first debated in England between Whigs and Tories misled many people in nineteenth-century England to continue to assume a profounder antagonism between the party views concerning revolution than in fact existed. After 1830 when Radicalism brought out the warring streams within Whiggism, and Socialism was introducing new principles into political and social life, people who were deeply disturbed by these new appearances still thought about them in the old outdated terms. From various political camps, but especially from the conservatives, we hear about the eternal and natural distinctions between Whigs and Tories. Viewed from a distance it is striking that both Whigs and Tories held remarkably close opinions in political and social matters, and similar interpretations of historical phenomena. Certainly Whigs and Tories entertained similar sentiments for the English system and similar views on the French Revolution. Real antagonism in these matters was indeed coming into being, but it arose outside Whig and Tory, and for a long time outside any new view of history. Even the new socialism did not at first introduce a new interpretation of the course of history, but merely a new set of revolutionary sympathies.

Though there were among Tories, Whigs and Radicals variations of opinion on more shallow levels, the general result of their historical thinking is an equivocal attitude to the Revolution which reconciles the extremes of partiality for the Revolution and hostility to it, as these were sometimes found among non-historians. This attitude undergoes no violent changes throughout the century. It is part of the prevailing outlook on history, on political development, on reform, on liberty, on constitutional rights, as well as on what is conventionally and morally the best kind of social order to possess. It is therefore not possible to classify the English historians of the Revolution as purely Whig or Tory, pro-revolutionary or pro-Burke. The distinction would lead to difficulties and self-contradictions even in the case of such a 'simple' Whig as Smyth or such a 'typical' Tory as Alison; and the party test is futile when applied to Carlyle or Acton, who both achieved a remarkable—if highly individual—impartiality, and the test would be irrelevant when applied to the historical work of Croker in spite of his diehard Toryism. The English

277

view of the Revolution in the course of the nineteenth century is comprehensive in the same sense that nineteenth-century liberalism was open to both conservative and radical and even socialist influences without overmuch philosophical consistency. Both Burkianism and the principles of 1789 were among its ingredients.

In England there existed a greater variety of individual views within a more restricted political range. The extreme Jacobin or reactionary views had no following among historians, and there are no clear distinctions between royalist, constitutional and republican schools as in France. When writers try to classify the English historians, they often pick up opposite ends of the stick so that a single author—particularly Carlyle —may find contradictory views imputed to him. A bewildering yet consistent ambiguity in their political attitude to the Revolution characterizes the English historians, none of whom stood directly behind Burke even when it seemed that public opinion did; and Burke himself decided that France would be better off without reforms only when he perceived whither reforms were leading her. To the English historians Burke was an inspiration but not a model. He outlined the topics for historians. From his day the Revolution was discussed on his terms even by those who opposed his views. Aspects which he ignored as for instance the economic aspect only came into their own when his influence waned. In a sense the real 'emancipation' from Burke only came in our century when English historians rejected the set of questions which Burke prescribed for the treatment of the Revolution and which reigned to the end of the nineteenth century.

The political attitude was liberal and Burkian, in favour of reforms and violent against violence. The reaction to the Terror was emotional and moral. The English historians mostly find virtues in the original reformers and in the Girondins who meant well but were still to blame. It is the view which was held by people who had been reformers before the Revolution and for that reason first accepted it and then rejected it. They were slow in discerning the novelty of the Revolution and even when they did discern it they attributed the departures to the whims of individuals rather than to the principles of the Revolution. It was the extreme writers from the days of Burke and Paine who proclaimed that it was a new phenomenon. The liberal, half-sympathetic view was in this sense the most conservative one, and it lasted longest, though it gradually imbibed ideas ascribing various innovations to the French Revolutionists. The alienation of the liberals from the Revolution at various stages of it, 1791, 1793 or as late as 1798, remained the pattern for future historians, who based their interpretations simply on the distinctions between the stages of the Revolution and on their varying degrees of sympathy with them.

In this sense the English attitude was a conservative one. As a general view it was closest to the pattern of practical political development. While the French historians were letting their imagination carry them to daring flights, a practical political tradition was shaping itself round those achievements of the Revolution which were consolidated under the Empire and hardly questioned later. The tenure of land, the centralized administration, the equality of opportunity, for example, from having been the heritage of a revolutionary ideology became a conservative force in politics, in whose interest social revolutions were suppressed. In ranging themselves with conservative middle-class opinion, English historians remained attached to opinions too prosaic for the superior historians of France who were led by intellectual and emotional involvements to evolve striking historical conceptions worthy both of the era in which France shaped the destinies of Europe and of that in which so much was expected of history. But it is the common-sense attitude of the English historians, as that of the French Doctrinaires, which has come into its own in the official school of Revolutionary studies in France.

Throughout the century there also persisted in England a tendency to treat the event in as direct and immediate a way as contemporaries would, and with special attention to the people at the helm. The French and Germans might produce more and more original interpretations in their search for the key which would decipher the enigma. The English insisted on treating the Revolution as a political and social revolt prompted by both grievances and a system of ideal aims, as in all revolutions. Realizing as early as anyone the startling dimensions of the event and predicting its everlasting influence on history, they still applied the normal instruments of analysis applicable to other revolutions. This rational approach managed to survive the more romantic and imaginative, interpretations of the nineteenth century, though not the new economic interpretation.

The unorthodox interpretation in England was not therefore an opposite political view but rather a belief shared only by the extreme haters and the extreme lovers of the Revolution that its course had been inevitable and that it was the necessary climax of one predominant historical process. One of the historical features of the nineteenth century was that of consistent interpretations of history in terms of general ideas or forces underlying the historical process. This tendency which owed something to the consideration of the Revolution—to the way in which it seemed to be produced by certain abstract notions and seemed to follow an irresistible course—was often apparent in French Revolutionary histories. It is a consistent feature of the English historians that they generally rejected any general interpretations. That the Revolution was the climax of a revolt which had started with the Reformation, or that it was ruled by the economic selfishness of the middle classes, or by the rapaciousness of the poor, or that it was a grand conspiracy against religion, that terror and dictatorship were its essence, that 14 July was not what senti-mental liberals made of it but the beginning of open war, such single and simple interpretations were sometimes voiced in England but only by extremists like the socialists or the extreme conservatives of the *Dublin Review*, who express curiously similar interpretations both as to the origin and to the inevitability of the process. It was Burke who through his prophecies bequeathed the notion of the inevitable process. It was De Maistre who hinted at the impersonal forces, the idea so aptly taken up later by the left. 'Ce ne sont point les hommes qui mènent la révolution, c'est le révolution qui emploie les hommes.' 'Ella va toute seule.'

The English historians, on the whole, objected both to the notion of ideas pushing history forward regardless of the wishes and actions of men, and even more to the corollary of such a notion, namely to the tendency to diminish the responsibility of the individual actors, and therefore dispense with moral considerations. The course of the Revolu-tion, they always insisted, was determined by 'error and crime'. Lecky in 1887 attacks the school of 'fatalists' in almost the same words as Smyth had done in 1830, though Lecky, oddly, thinks of it as a new pro-duct of his generation. Acton, of all the English historians, stood closest to the notion that impersonal ideas make history but it was Acton, too, who was the first to try to separate this notion from the moral indifference which was attached to it. Because ideas are the real makers of history, men are not exempt from the moral law.

The question of moral judgment in history, on which Acton believed himself to be alone, has special bearing on the English historiography of the Revolution. It ought not to be treated statically as a question between an eternal code and a sliding scale, but as something which, in the nine-teenth century, grew with romanticism, with the notion of impersonal forces in history, and with the effort to see past ages as they saw them-selves. The more historians understood, the more they justified, and this to Acton was the evil spirit lurking in romanticism, confusing science and morals. Some of Acton's contemporaries in the study of the Revolution like Fisher, Montague, Legg, Rose, were not morally indiffer-ent but they allowed their interests to move away from questions of this kind. Acton, though he shared the new professional attitude to history, also brought to a climax the passionate interest in the moral issues of the Revolution which had prevailed since Burke, and which Carlyle too made prominent through his contempt for the moral degeneration which felled old France. The English historians might agree on nothing else, but they combined to combat any attempt to ignore the moral issue in the Revolution. Burke had taught the ideal significance of the political struggle and Acton went farther when he said that the historian's treatment of the Revolution had something to do with his hopes of heaven. Between them, in every age, historians found 'moral indifference' to rebuke. Thiers and Mignet first presented to Englishmen the sight of an amoral historiography, and Smyth took up the challenge on the ground of the lesson he learnt from Burke. Croker believed Thiers insincere for political purposes but Acton went farther when he probed into the very amoral nature of Thiers's character as a historian. Morse Stephens outraged Acton by his lack of a moral basis for judgment. From the seat of moral judgment it mattered little to Acton that Stephens was a competent historian as it had mattered little to Smyth that Thiers was a fair-minded constitutional monarchist. Acton studied Mignet and Thiers closely, stressing the point of moral indifference, of an impersonal attitude to crime. He quotes the typical opinion of Bulwer that Thiers's 'infernal fatalism' was false because it denied the possibliity of accident, 'horrible because it breaks down all distinctions between crime and virtue'.

The English historians paid for their political independence and ambiguity in historical reputation, but in England their peculiar standpoint gave them influence. Smyth, unknown abroad, had influence on his Cambridge audience which at one time included Macaulay, and English historians went on referring to him to the end of the century. Acton had read Smyth, exaggerated his scholarly merit and made a note to tell his audience that he felt honoured to succeed him. He described Smyth's work as an endeavour to explain 'what was known for certain before the great epoch of revolutionary studies began'. In this he was projecting some of his own spirit into Smyth, who was not concerned with the certain, but tried to make some sense out of anything he happened to read. The real connection between the two Regius Professors was a political interest in the Revolution, a search for true liberty, a religious temperament, and a primarily moral view of history.

Though Acton's knowledge was French and German, his view was unmistakably English perhaps with an unmistakable difference. Like Burke, he transformed the very principles of the English attitude by pushing them too far. When we speak of a nineteenth-century English attitude to the Revolution, it is not enough to point out its moderate politics, its Burkian and liberal spirit. The distinctive feature is the pervading 'moral tone' which is not enlisted to fight the battles of the suffering millions or of the noble victims, but illuminates the whole scene. This aspect of the historiography, Acton brought to a climax and to an end. He went farther than his predecessors. In the chaotic picture of the moral aspect of the Revolution, where the will for absolute good reached the intensity of purpose which made it become evil, in a whirl of contradictions, where other historians were content to point out the perversions—Acton tried to use the moral criterion consistently and systematically.

Burke, Smyth, Carlyle and Acton shared the belief that history was the manifestation of religion. English judgments on the Revolution between Burke and Acton converged on the point of the Revolution's irreligion (though there were those like Lecky or the Christian Socialists who denied the necessary connection between democracy and irreligion). But the extreme view to which Acton brought the English historiography in this respect is not the same as that from which Burke had inspired its beginnings. Burke was offended by irreligious thought and action, he lamented the duty of submission and the shattered symbols of devotion. He knew that irreligion was bound to show also in political behaviour. Acton's view was unlike Burke's or Tocqueville's, which was often misrepresented in England. Tocqueville pointed out that the writings disseminating revolution were anti-religious and that the Revolution acted against Christianity. Yet he claims that this must not blind us to the historical truth that the anti-religious strain was incidental to the Revolution and resulted from the political rather than from the spiritual power which the Church held; that far from being opposed to Christianity, democracy was the system most akin to it. The similarity of the Revolution to a religion, Tocqueville says, lies merely in the universality of its ideas, in its concern with individual man detached from any social structure, in its aspirations for regeneration and in its missionary fervour. But he points out that the lack of a God and of a future life separates the Revolution from the real religions.

Acton, on the other hand, identified the evil of irreligion in the essence of the political ideal itself. The distinction arises from the fact that in Acton's world of ideas politics and religion tended to become one. 'Church history is to universal history as the soul is to the body.'[1] He was always drawing analogies between church and state. 'The supreme lawgiver in the church is public opinion, and in the state nothing is legitimate if it contradicts the general sense of right.' The essence of liberalism, he wrote, is the superiority of divine right over human will of either king or people. The Revolutionary ideals lacked that imprint of divine right which would override mere human will. Burke did not see any innate connection between religion and politics. 'The cause of civil liberty and civil government gains as little as that of religion by this confusion of duties', he wrote. For politics Acton wanted not, like Burke, a religious background but a religious purpose. Freedom of conscience, the only absolute freedom, was the aim towards which both religion and politics pointed. While Burke was offended by the Revolutionary outrages against sanctified authority in church and state, it was the violation of conscience which ultimately damned the Revolution for Acton. He

[1] C.U.L. Add. MS. 4860.

never condemned the Revolution for the political heresy of pursuing abstract principles to their logical end, or for proceeding from a concept of right. On the contrary he condemned it because it did not pursue principles far enough, and because it neglected that very concept of right which he called natural, universal or divine law, and which he believed ensured the basic requirement of liberty. 'Definitions of liberty', he wrote, 'Mine—Liberty of Conscience.'

BIBLIOGRAPHIES

A GENERAL NOTE

The following bibliographies cover the sources used for this study. The development of the historiography has been constructed on the ground of many books, essays, articles, reviews, and other materials, some of which turned out to be worthless, though even those latter indicate, through their collective impression in any given period, where the wind was blowing in English studies of the Revolution. Bibliography A is a chronological list of the English writings on the French Revolution used for this study. It has been compiled from various sources, especially catalogues of libraries, bibliographies, and notices in periodicals. But it is not of course an exhaustive list of all the English writings on the Revolution. The works connected with the Revolution, written by Smyth, Carlyle, Croker, and Acton, especially the separate articles, are not included in the general chronological list but they are collected in separate bibliographies for each of those historians. The separate bibliographies list published and unpublished materials on which the individual studies are based.

A. A LIST OF THE ENGLISH WRITINGS ON THE REVOLUTION

1788

The Annual Register of a View of the History, Politics and Literature. For the years 1788–1795.

1789

R. Price, *A Discourse on the Love of our Country* (London, 1789).

1790

S. Romilly, *Thoughts on the probable influence of the French Revolution on Great Britain* (London, 1790).

J. Courtenay, *Philosophical Reflections on the late Revolution in France* (London, 1790).

E. Burke, *Reflections on the Revolution in France* (London, 1790).

C. Lofft, *Remarks on the letter of the Right Hon. Edmund Burke concerning the Revolution in France* (London, 1790).

Rev. C. Hereford, *The History of France from the first Establishment of that Monarchy to the present Revolution.* 3 vols. (London, 1790). [Only the last few chapters are relevant, by J. Addams?]

M. Wollstonecraft [afterwards Godwin], *A Vindication of the Rights of Men* (London, 1790).

C. Mahon (3rd Earl of Stanhope), *A Letter . . . to the Rt. Hon. E. Burke containing a short answer to his late speech on the French Revolution* (London, 1790).

Tyranny Annihilated . . . Containing a particular account of the rise, progress and various incidents [of the French Revolution] [1790?].

H. M. Williams, *Letters written in France in the Summer of 1790* (London, 1790).

J. T. Dillon, *Historical and Critical Memoirs of the general Revolution in France in the year 1789 . . . Deduced from authentic papers communicated by M. H[ugon] de B[assville]* (London, 1790).

284

Bibliographies

The History of the Bastille, with a concise account of the late Revolution in France (1790).

1791

T. Paine, *Rights of Man. 1st Part* (London, 1791).
Rev. J. Priestley, *Letters to the Rt. Hon. E. Burke* (Birmingham, 1791).
C. Lofft, *Remarks on the Letter of Mr Burke* (London, 1791).
J. Mackintosh, *Vindiciae Gallicae* (Dublin, 1791).
T. Christie, *Letters on the Revolution of France* (London, 1791).
E. Burke, *A Letter from Mr Burke, to a Member of the National Assembly* (London, 1791).
An Abridgment of the History of France (London, 1791).
J. Gifford [i.e. J. R. Green], *The History of France*, 4 vols. (London, 1791–3).

1792

W. Playfair, *A Letter to the People of England on the Revolution in France* (Paris, 1792).
T. Paine, *Rights of Man . . . Part the second. Combining Principles and Practice* (London, 1792).
T. Paine, *Lettre de Thomas Paine au peuple françois* [on the occasion of his being nominated a Member of the National Convention] (Paris, Sept. 1792).
A. Young, *Travels in France* (Bury St Edmunds, 1792).
J. Peltier, *The Late Picture of Paris; or narrative of the Revolution of the Tenth of August etc.* 2 vols. (London, 1792).
H. F. Groenvelt [i.e. P. E. L. Dumont], *Letters comprising an account of the late revolution in France etc.* [to this translation are added several original letters of Sir S. Romilly] (London, 1792).
Discours de MM Cooper et Watt, députés de la Société constitutionelle de Manchester, prononcé à la Société des amis de la constitution, séante à Paris, le 13 avril 1792 [Paris, 1792].
J. Gifford [i.e. J. R. Green], *A Plain Address to the Common Sense of the People of England* (London, 1792).
Ten Minutes reflection on the late events in France.
H. O. Symonds, *The French Senator* (1792).
Major J. Cartwright, *A Letter to the Duke of Newcastle . . . Touching the French Revolution* (London, 1792).
T. Cooper, *A reply to Mr Burke's Invective against Mr Cooper and Mr Watt in the House of Commons on 30th April 1792* (London, 1792).
H. M. Williams, *Letters from France; containing many new Anecdotes relative to the French Revolution* (London, 1792–6).
An Historical Sketch of the French Revolution . . . to the year 1792 (London, 1792).
[Stephen Weston], *Letters from Paris During the summer of 1791* [June to October] (London, 1792).

1793

Rev. J. Priestley, *Letters to the Philosophers and Politicians of France on the Subject of Religion* (London, 1793).
[Editor T. Spence], *Pig's Meat; Or Lessons for the Swinish Multitude*. vols. I–III (1793–5).
W. Playfair, *A general view of the actual forces and resources of France in Jan. 1793* (London, 1793).

Biographical sketches of some of the leading men at present at the head of affairs in France (*Péthion, Orléans, Brissot, Robespierre, Condorcet, Marat, Gorsas, Carra, Chabot, Dumouriez, Merlin*) (Edinburgh, 1793).

A Comprehensive Display of the Different Opinions of the most Distinguished British Writers on the Subject of the French Revolution. 2 vols. (London, 1793).

A Tour through the theatre of war in the months of November and December 1792, and Jan. 1793 etc. (London, 1793).

C. J. Fox, *Two Speeches: on the Execution of Louis XVI; and on the Declaration of War against England by France* (London, 1793).

W. Playfair, *Thoughts on the Present State of French Politics* (London, 1793).

T. Paine, *Reasons for wishing to preserve the Life of Louis Capet, as delivered to the National Assembly* (London, 1793).

Politics for the People (afterwards called *Hog's Wash*). Ed. by D. I. Eaton (London, 1793–4).

[R. C. Dallas], *Thoughts of Marie Antoinette on the Morning of her execution. Oct. 16, 1793. A poem.*

H. More, *Village Politics* (1793).

Biographical Extracts; particularly such as relate to the Revolution in France (London, [1793]).

Flower of the Jacobins; containing biographical sketches (London, 1793).

W. Godwin, *Enquiry Concerning Political Justice* (London, 1793).

Rev. J. Adams, *History of France from the Establishment of the Monarchy till the Revolution.* 3 vols. (London, 1793).

J. Moore, *A Journal During a Residence in France, from the Beginning of August to the Middle of December 1792.* 2 vols. (London, 1793).

A. Young, *The Example of France a Warning to Britain* (London, 1793).

C. James, *Audi Alteram partem; or an extenuation of the Conduct of the French Revolutionists from 1789* (London, 1793).

J. Gifford [i.e. John Gifford Green], *A narrative of the transactions personally relating to Louis the Sixteenth* (London, 1793).

W. A. Miles, *The Conduct of France towards Great Britain Examined*; with an Appendix and Notes (1793). [The Appendix contains letters by Miles, e.g. to Maret.]

1794

The History of Robespierre, political and personal (2nd ed., London, 1794).

J. Gifford [i.e. John Richards Green], *The Reign of Louis XVI; and a complete history of the French Revolution with notes* (London, 1794).

J. Courtenay, *The Present State of the Manners, Arts and Politics of France and Italy, etc.* (London, 1794).

An Impartial History of the Late Revolution in France. 2 vols. (London, 1794).

W. Beckford, *History of France ... to the death of Louis XVI* (London, 1794).

Earl of Lauderdale, *Letters to the Peers of Scotland* (London, 1794).

M. Wollstonecraft [afterwards Godwin], *An Historical and Moral View of the Origin and Progress of the French Revolution etc.* vol. I [and only] (London, 1794).

J. Money, *The History of the Campaign of 1792 ... with an Account of what passed in the Tuileries on the 10th of August* (London, 1794).

[A. Young], *An Idea of the Present State of France, etc.* By the Author of the *Example of France a Warning to Britain* (London, 1794).

A. Young, *Travels during the years 1787–8 etc.* (2nd ed., Bury St Edmunds, 1794).

Bibliographies

A Collection of State Papers, relating to the War against France, now carrying on by Great Britain and several other European Powers (London, 1794).

J. P. Brissot de Warville, *To his Constituents*; translated from the French, with a Preface, and occasional Notes by the Translator [William Burke] (new ed., London, 1794).

1795

W. Playfair, *The History of Jacobinism, its crimes, cruelties and perfidies, etc.* (London, 1795).

Rev. J. Priestley, *An Answer to Mr Paine's Age of Reason etc.* (London, 1795).

J. Moore, *A View of the Causes and Progress of the French Revolution*, 2 vols. (London, 1795).

H. M. Williams, *Letters containing a sketch of the Politics of France from the 31st May 1793 till the 28th July 1794.* 2 vols. (London, 1795).

J. Adams, *View of Universal History . . . including an account of the celebrated Revolutions in France etc.* (London, 1795).

Sir Francis d'Ivernois, *A Short Account of the late Revolution in Geneva and the conduct of France towards that Republic, from Oct. 1792 to Oct. 1794* (London, 1795).

J. Bowles, *Thoughts on the Origin and Formation of Political Constitutions* (1795).

J. Gifford, *A Letter to the Earl of Lauderdale* (London, 1795).

J. Gifford, *The Reign of Louis XVI*, 2nd edition (London, 1795).

A Whig's Apology for his Consistency (London, 1795).

1796

R. Macfarlane, *History of the Reign of George III* (1783–96).

A Chronological Epitome of the most remarkable events that have occurred during the French Revolution (London, [1796?]).

An Historical View of the French Revolution, 2 vols. (Newcastle-upon-Tyne, 1796).

Malmesbury (J. Harris, 1st Earl of), *Official Copies of the Correspondence of Lord Malmesbury* (London, 1796).

H. M. Williams, *Letters containing a Sketch of the Politics of France* (1796).

W. Hunter, *Travels in the year 1792, through France etc.* (London, 1796).

1797

E. Burke, *A Letter for the Duke of Portland* (London, 1797).

E. Burke, *Two Letters on the Conduct of our Domestick Parties with regard to French Politics* (London, 1797).

Biographical Anecdotes of the Founders of the French Republic, 2 vols. (London, 1797) [erroneously ascribed to Adolphus].

T. Erskine, *A View of the Causes and Consequences of the Present War* (London, 1797).

J. Gifford, *A Letter to the Hon. T. Erskine containing some Strictures on his View etc.* (London, 1797).

J. Gifford, *A Second Letter . . . Containing further Strictures* (London, 1797).

J. Bowles, *French Aggression proved from Mr Erskine's View of the Causes of the War etc.* (1797).

J. Gifford, *A Residence in France . . . in a series of letters from an English lady*, 2 vols. (1797).

A. Danican, *The Banditti Unmasked . . .* Translated with a preface by J. Gifford (London, 1797).

John Robison, M.A., *Proofs of a Conspiracy against all the Religions and Governments of Europe.*

1798

The Anti-Jacobin, 20 Nov. 1797–8 July 1798 [Edited by William Gifford].
The Anti-Jacobin Review and Magazine (1798–1812) [Editor J. R. Green].
A Sketch of Modern France, in a series of Letters to a Lady of fashion, written in the years 1796 and 1797, during a tour through France (London, 1798).
Quentin Crauford, *Histoire de la Bastille* (1798).
Sir Francis d'Ivernois, *Tableau Historique . . . or, an Historical and Political View of the losses which the French Nation has suffered by the Revolution and the War* (London, 1798).

1799

J. Adolphus, *Biographical Memoirs of the French Revolution*, 4 vols. (London, 1799). Reviewed: *M.R.* (Jan. 1800), 67.

1800

'Bertrand's Annals', *M.R.* (Oct. 1800), 106.
'The Correspondence of the Duke of Orleans', *M.R.* (1800), 497.
R. Fellows, *Morality United with Policy; or, Reflections on the Old and New Government of France* (London, 1800).
F. X. Pagès, *Anti-revolutionary thoughts of a revolutionary writer: from the secret history of the Revolution in France, by M. F. Pagès.*
R. C. Dallas, *Correspondence between M. Bertrand de Moleville and the Hon. Charles James Fox on his Quotation of the Annals of the French Revolution in the House of Commons* [3 Feb. 1800] (London, 1800). Reviewed: *M.R.* (Oct. 1800), 166.
H. Marsh, *The History of the Politics of Great Britain and France, from the time of the Conference of Pilnitz to the Declaration of War against Great Britain.* 2 vols. (London, 1800). Reviewed: *M.R.* (Feb.–Mar. 1800), 165.

1801

W. Belsham, *Remarks on a late Publication styled the History of the Politics of Great Britain and France* [by H. Marsh] (London, 1801).
H. Marsh, *The History of the Politics of Great Britain and France Vindicated* (London, 1801).
W. Belsham, *Reply to Herbert Marsh's Vindication* ([London], 1801).
J. Bannantine, *A Parliamentary Retrospect; or the opinions of His Majesty's Ministers respecting the French Revolution* (London, 1801).
Rev. A. Ranken, *The History of France, Civil and Military, Ecclesiastical, Political, Literary, Commercial, etc.* 3 vols. (London, 1801–5). Reviewed [by H. Hallam]: *E.R.* (1805), VI, 209–228.

1802

[F. Jeffrey], 'Mounier on the Influence attributed to Philosophers', *E.R.* (1802), I, 1.
Bowles, *Reflections at the Conclusion of the War.* Reviewed: *E.R.* (Oct. 1802).
R. Wilson, *History of the British Expedition to Egypt* (1802).

1803

'Necker's Dernières Vues', *E.R.* (Jan. 1803), I, 382, 395. [F. Jeffrey], 'Gentz's De l'Etat', *E.R.* (Apr. 1803), II, 1–30.

Bibliographies

J. Adolphus, *Reflections on the causes of the Present Rupture with France* (London, 1803).

A. Stephens, *The History of the Wars which arose out of the French Revolution.* 3 vols. (London, 1803). Reviewed [by J. A. Murray], *M.R.* (Jan. 1804), III, 486–93.

J. Adolphus, *The History of France from 1790 till the Peace of 1802.* 2 vols. (London, 1803).

R. Bisset, *The History of the Reign of George III.* 6 vols. (London, 1803).

H. M. Williams, *The Political and Confidential Correspondence of Louis XVI: with Observations on each Letter* (London, 1803). Reviewed [by F. Horner]: *E.R.* (Oct. 1803), III, 211–31.

1804

[A. F. Bertrand de Moleville], *A Refutation of the Libel on the Memory of the late King of France, published by H. M. Williams* (London, 1804).

J. Bigland, *Letters on the Modern History and Political Aspect of Europe* (London, 1804).

'Puisaye's Memoirs', *E.R.* (Apr. 1804), IV, 99–117.

1805

'Lacretelle's Précis Historique', *E.R.* (Jan. 1805), V, 421–37.

[F. Jeffrey], 'Bailly's Memoirs', *E.R.* (Apr. 1805), VI, 137–161.

Stewarton, *Memoirs of C. M. Talleyrand de Périgord* (London, 1805). Reviewed [by F. Horner]: *E.R.* (Oct. 1805), VII, 151–5.

1806

G. Sanon, *The Causes of the French Revolution . . . an epic and philosophical poem* (London, 1806).

[H. Brougham], 'Dutens's Mémoires d'un Voyageur', *E.R.* (July 1806), VIII, 345–57.

J. Bigland, *Letters on the Study and Use of Ancient and Modern History* (1806).

1808

Characters Moral and Political of the Principal Personages throughout the French Revolution (London, 1808).

1809

'Biographie Moderne', *E.R.* (Apr. 1809), XIV, 211–43.

J. Gifford [i.e. John Richards Green], *A History of the Political Life of W. Pitt.* 3 vols. (London, 1809).

[Jeffrey and Brougham], 'Don Cevallos', *E.R.* (1809), XXV.

1810

'The French Government', *Q.R.* (May 1810), III, 320.

Occasional Tracts relative to the War between Great Britain and France . . . from 1793 (London, 1810).

1811

J. Bigland, *A Sketch of the History of Europe from the Peace of 1783 to the present time.* 2 vols. (London, 1811).

1812

[R. Southey?], 'Biographie Moderne', *Q.R.* (June 1812), VII, 412.

Bibliographies

1813

W. Playfair, *Political Portraits*. 2 vols. [+ Supplementary volume, 1816] (London, 1813).

[F. Jeffrey], 'Madame de Staël', *E.R.* (Feb. 1813), XXI, 1–50.

1814

'Lévis's Souvenirs et Portraits', *E.R.* (Jan. 1814), XXII, 281–94.

'Lacretelle's 18th Century', *Q.R.* (Apr. 1814), XI, 138.

[H. Brougham], 'Carnot's Memoir', *E.R.* (Nov. 1814), XXIV, 182–207.

1815

'Carnot's Exposé de la Conduite', *E.R.* (Oct. 1815), XXV, 442–55.

J. Bigland, *A Sketch of the History of Europe, 1783–1814*. 2 vols. (London, 1815).

1816

[F. Jeffrey], 'Madame de Larochejaquelein', *E.R.* (Feb. 1816), XXVI, 1–36.

'Madame de Larochejaquelein', *Q.R.* (Apr. 1816), XV, 1.

E. Baines, *A History of the Wars of the French Revolution*. 2 vols. (1816–18).

1817

R. Southey, *Wat Tyler* (London, 1817).

'Lavallée's History of the Revolution', *M.R.* (1817), LXXXIV, 467.

Authentic Memoirs of the Revolution in France (London, 1817). Reviewed: *M.R.* (1818), LXXXVII, 214.

J. Bigland, *Letters on French History for the use of schools* (1817).

1818

Mrs Moore, *A History of France from its Foundation to the Restoration* (1818). Augmented 3rd ed., 1829.

[F. Jeffrey], 'Madame de Staël's Considerations', *E.R.* (Sept. 1818), XXX, 275.

'Abbé Georgel's Memoirs', *E.R.* (Sept. 1818), XXX, 425–43.

J. Bigland, *Letters on French History . . . For the use of Schools* (London, 1818).

1819

'Madame de Staël's Considerations', *M.R.* (Jan. 1819), LXXXVIII, 1, 138.

'Lanjuinais's Constitutions', *M.R.* (1819), XC, 449.

1820

[Chevenix], 'Mounier on the Causes that hindered France from being free', *E.R.* (Aug. 1820), XXXIV, 1–39.

[Chevenix], 'Chenier's Tableau Historique', *E.R.* (Mar. 1821), XXXV, 158–190.

1821

C. West, *A Ten Years' Residence in France . . . 1787 to 1797* (London, 1821).

[Sir James Mackintosh], 'Sismondi's History of France', *E.R.* (July 1821), XXXV, 488–509.

1822

'Montlosier's Historical Works', *Q.R.* (Apr. 1822), XXVII, 146.

Bibliographies

1823

'Lacretelle's Constituent Assembly', *Q.R.* (Jan. 1823), XXVIII, 271.
'Royal Memoirs', *E.R.* (Oct. 1823), XXXIX, 84–109.

1826

'Mignet's French Revolution', *Eclectic R.* (1826), CLIV, 231.
J. S. Mill, 'Mignet's History', *Westminster* (1826), V, 385–98.
The Reign of Terror; a collection of authentic narratives. 2 vols. (London, 1826).
'Prior's Life of Burke', *Q.R.* (Sept. 1826), XXXIV, 457.
C. H. B. G. Solari (Marchioness), *Secret Memoirs of the Royal Family of France.* 2 vols. (1826). Reviewed: A. F. Pollard, *E.R.H.* (1895), 588.

1827

W. Scott, *The Life of Napoleon.* 9 vols. (London, 1827).
[T. B. Macaulay], 'Burke's Correspondence', *E.R.* (Oct. 1827), XVLI, 269–303.
H. M. Williams, *Souvenirs de la Révolution Française* (Paris, 1827).

1828

W. Hazlitt, *Life of Napoleon Bonaparte.* 4 vols. (London, 1828).
'Thiers's French Revolution', *M.R.* (1828), CXVI, 44.
Markham (Mrs) [i.e. Elizabeth Penrose], *History of France.* 2 vols. (London, 1828).
J. S. Mill, 'Scott's Life of Napoleon', *Westminster* (Apr. 1828), IX, 251–313.

1830

'Jefferson's Memoirs', *E.R.* (July 1830), LI, 496–526.
'The Revolution of 1830', *E.R.* (Oct. 1830), LII, 1.
'On Elections', *E.R.* (Oct. 1830), LII, 261.
E. E. Crowe, *The History of France.* 3 vols. (1830–1).
J. S. Mill, 'Prospects of France', *Examiner* (10, 26 Sept., 3, 10, 17 Oct., 14, 28 Nov. 1830), 594–5, 609–10, 626–7, 641–4, 660–1, 724–5, 756–7.
J. S. Mill, 'The Quarterly Review versus France', *Examiner* (25 Oct. 1830), 674–5.

1831

'Buonarroti's Conspiration', *Q.R.* (Apr.–July 1831), XLV, 167–209.
'Imprisonment during the Reign of Terror', *Blackwood's* (1831), XXX, 920.
'Memoires de Brissot', *Westminster* (Apr. 1831), XIV, 332.
Poor Man's Guardian (1831–2).
J. Bell, *A History of the Revolutions in France.* vol. I [no more published] (London, 1831).
'Revolutions of France', *Westminster* (1831), XV, 406.
'Historians of France', *Blackwood's* (1831), XXX, 230, 731.

1832

'National Convention', *F.Q.* (1832), XIII, 35.
G. Lea, *An Abridged History of France* (Bristol, 1832).
Lord John Russell, *The Causes of the French Revolution* (London, 1832).
Mirabeau's Letters during his Residence in England. 2 vols. (London, 1832).
T. B. Macaulay, 'Dumont's Mirabeau', *E.R.* (July 1832), LX, 552.
'Robespierre', *Poor Man's Guardian* (Nov.–Dec. 1832).

291

Bibliographies

1833

Sir A. Alison, *History of Europe during the French Revolution.* 10 vols. (Edinburgh, 1833–42) [and many other editions]. Reviewed: *E.R.* (1842), LXXVI, 1–60; (1853), XCVII, 135–270; (1860), CXI, 119; *Fraser* (1856), LIII, 297–611; (1859), LX, 211–26; (1859), LX, 603–19; (1860), LXII, 660–78; *N.B.R.* (1857), XXVII, 275–324; *D.R.* (1852), XXXIII, 408–18; *Q.R.* (1843–4), LXXIII, 271, 432; *Blackwood's* (1837), CLII, 715; (1839), CLVI, 272; *M.R.* (1834), CXXXVI, 251; (1842), CLVIII, 420.
'Sarran's Lafayette', *E.R.* (Jan. 1833), LVI, 481.
E. E. Crewe, *Lives of the most Eminent Foreign Statesmen.* vol. I. (London, 1830).
The French History Briefly Told (London, 1833).
C. Buller, 'Mirabeau', *F.Q.R.* (Nov. 1833).
'Roederer's Addresse', *E.R.* (Apr. 1835), LXI, 216.
'Fils Adoptif', *E.R.* (Apr. 1835).

1836

G. P. R. James, *Lives of the most Eminent Foreign Statesmen.* vols. 2, 3, 4, 5 (London, 1836–8).
[J. Bronterre O'Brien], *Buonarroti's history of Babeuf's Conspiracy . . . illustrated by original notes* (London, 1836).

1837

J. Bronterre O'Brien, *The Life and Character of Maximilian Robespierre* (London, 1837).

1840

Sir S. Romilly, Memoirs. 3 vols. (London, 1840).
E. B. Lytton, 'The Reign of Terror', *F.Q.* (1840), XXIX, 275.

1841

'Historical Inquiry in France', *E.R.* (Apr. 1841), LXXIII, 84–120.
D. W. Jobson, *History of the French Revolution* (London, 1841).

1842

'Historical Data of the French Revolution', *Westminster* (1842), XXXVIII, 193–214.

1843

H. Brougham, *Historical Sketches. 3rd Series. With remarks on the French Revolution* (London, 1843).
M. Norris, *Life & Times of Madame de Staël* (London, 1843).

1844

J. S. Mill, 'Michelet's History of France', *E.R.* (Jan. 1844), LXXIX, 1.
T. B. Macaulay, 'Barère', *E.R.* (Apr. 1844), LXXIX, 275–351.
'The Works of Thomas Carlyle', *B.F.R.* (1844), XVI, 262–93.
'State of Historical Science in France', *B.F.R.* (1844), XVI, 72–118.
'Robespierre', *B.F.R.* (1844), XVII, 606–45.
J. H. Malmesbury, *Diaries and Correspondence.* 4 vols. (London, 1844).

1845

J. S. Mill, 'Guizot's Histories', *E.R.* (Oct. 1845), LXXXII, 381–421.

Bibliographies

1847

'Lamartine's History of the Girondins', *Fraser* (Sept. 1847), XXXVI, 253–76.

1848

Politics for the People 1–17 (London, 1848).

J. G. Millingen, *Recollections of Republican France from 1790 to 1801*. vol. I (London, 1848).

Analogies and Contrasts, or Comparative Sketches of France and England. By the author of *Revelations of Russia* (London, 1848) [By C. F. Henningsen].

'France, her Revolutions etc.', *Fraser* (June 1848), XXXVII, 615–29.

'Lamartine's Girondins', *E.R.* (Jan. 1848), LXXXVII, 1–46.

H. Brougham, *Letter . . . on the Late Revolution in France* (1848).

T. W. Redhead, *The French Revolutions from 1789 to 1849*. 3 vols. (1848).

1849

'Tocqueville on Louis XV', *E.R.* (July 1849), XC, 77–106.

P. H. Stanhope (5th Earl), *Historical Essays Contributed to the Q.R.* (London, 1849) [including the review of 1832 of Macaulay and Russell, without the additions which had been made by Croker].

E. Edwards, 'Historians of the French Revolution', *B.Q.R.* (1849), X, 168.

G. H. Lewes, *The Life of Maximilian Robespierre; with Extracts from his Unpublished Correspondence* (London, 1849).

'Guizot's Democracy in France', *E.R.* (Apr. 1849), LXXXIX, 554–81.

A. Alison, *History of Europe from the Commencement of the French Revolution to the Restoration*. New ed., 14 vols. (Edinburgh, 1849–50).

A. Alison, *Essays political, historical and miscellaneous*. 3 vols. (Edinburgh, 1850).

1851

J. S. Stephen, *Lectures on the History of France*. 2 vols. (London, 1851). Reviewed: *Fraser* (1851), XLV, 170, 261; *Christian Observer* (1852), LII, 308; *New Q.R.* (1853), I, 14.

H. Reeve, 'Mirabeau', *Q.R.* (Sept. 1851). [This article was corrected and modified by Croker. Reeve printed his own original text in *Royal and Republican France* (1872).]

1852

'De Maistre', *E.R.* (Oct. 1852), XCVI, 289.

'Mallet du Pan's *Memoirs*', *E.R.* (1852), XCV, 481.

1856

'The Ancien Régime', *E.R.* (1856), CIV, 531.

'The Ancien Régime', *Dublin Univ. Magazine*. (1856), LXVIII, 442.

'Tocqueville's Ancien Régime', *Westminster* (Oct. 1856), LXVI, 462.

'France before and since the Revolution of 1789', *Fraser* (Sept. 1856), LIV, 363.

1857

'The Directoire', *E.R.* (Jan. 1857), CV, 205.

'Blanc's History of the French Revolution', *Colburn's New Monthly Magazine* (1857), CXI, 369.

J. Bronterre O'Brien, *An Elegy on the Death of Robespierre* (London, 1857).

Bibliographies

J. W. Croker, *Essays on the Early Period of the French Revolution* (London, 1857).
H. T. Buckle, *History of Civilization in England* (London, 1857–61). Reviewed: *E.R.* (1858), CVII, 465.

1859

G. D. Elliott (Mrs), *Journal of my Life during the French Revolution* (London, 1859) [also in French translations].
'The Life of Marie Antoinette', *E.R.* (July 1859), CX, 132.
J. Bronterre O'Brien, *A Dissertation and Elegy on the Life . . . of . . . Robespierre* (London, 1859).
Cornwallis (C. C. 1st Marquess), *Correspondence*, ed. C. Ross. 3 vols. (London, 1859).
J. White, *History of France from the Earliest Times to 1848* (Edinburgh and London, 1859).

1860

A. Alison, *The Philosophy and History of Civilization* (1860).

1861

H. Reeve, 'Tocqueville', *E.R.* (Apr. 1861).
P. H. Stanhope (5th Earl), *Life of Pitt*. 4 vols. (London, 1861–2).
Lord Auckland, *Journal and Correspondence*. 4 vols. (London, 1861–2).

1862

W. H. Jervis [formerly Pearson], *The Student's France* (London, 1862).
'The Reign of Terror', *Fraser* (1862), LXV, 753; LXVI, 153.

1863

'Blanc's History of the French Revolution', *E.R.* (1863), CXVIII, 101.
'Blanc's History of the French Revolution', *Westminster* (1863), LXXX, 147.

1865

'The Principles of 1789', *D.R.* (1864), LV, 253; (1865), LV, 279.
H. Reeve, 'Tocqueville', *E.R.* (Oct. 1865).

1866

C. D. Yonge, *The History of France under the Bourbons, 1589–1830*. 4 vols. (London, 1866).
C. Stanhope (3rd Earl), *The English Friends of the French Revolution, January to June 1792* [privately printed correspondence] (London, 1866).
H. Reeve, 'Marie Antoinette', *E.R.* (Apr. 1866) [a review of Arneth, Hunolstein and Feuillet de Conches].

1867

C. Kingsley, *Three Lectures on the Ancien Régime* (London, 1867).
J. R. Green, 'The French Revolution in a Country Town', *C.R.* (1868), VII, 416.
'Quinet on the French Revolution', *L.Q.R.* (1867), XXVIII, 88.

1868

[A. Meves], *The Authentic Historical Memoirs of Louis . . . Dauphin of France* (London, 1868).

Bibliographies

'History of France', *E.R.* (1868), CXXVIII, 289.
'Sybel on the Causes of the French Revolution', *Christian Observer* (June, Sept., Oct. 1868), LXVIII, 456, 672, 784.
Minto (Countess of), *A Memoir of Hugh Elliot* (Edinburgh, 1868).

1869

'Pressensé on the French Revolution and the Church', *Christian Observer* (Nov., Dec. 1869), LXIX, 857, 897.
'Sybel's French Revolution', *Christian Observer* (Oct. 1870), LXX, 770.

1870

Malmesbury (J. Harris, 1st Earl of), *A Series of Letters, 1745–1820.* 2 vols. (London, 1870).
W. Wickham, *The Correspondence of the Rt. Hon. W. W.* Ed. by his grandson. 2 vols. (London, 1870).

1871

H. Reeve, 'Communal France', *E.R.* (July 1871).

1872

'The Reign of Terror', *Q.R.* (1872), CXXXIII, 43.
H. Reeve, *Royal and Republican France.* 2 vols. (London, 1872).
'Decline of the Monarchy', *Westminster* (1872), XCIX, 70.

1873

G. W. Kitchin, *A History of France.* 3 vols. (Oxford, 1873–7).
'Lessons of the French Revolution', *Q.R.* (1873), CXXXV, 265.
A. V. Dicey, 'Lessons of the French Revolution', *Nation* (1873), XVII, 307, 322.

1874

B. Graves, 'Marat', *Fortnightly Review* (Feb. 1874).
Life and Letters of Sir Gilbert Elliot, first Earl of Minto, from 1751 to 1806. Ed. by the Countess of Minto. 3 vols. (1874).
C. K. Adams, *Democracy and Monarchy in France* (New York, 1874).
W. O'c. Morris, *The French Revolution and First Empire: an historical sketch* (London, 1874).

1875

'Malouet's Mémoires', *E.R.* (Apr. 1875), CXLI, 363.
'Tocqueville', *D.R.* (1875), LXXX, 111.
'An Incident of the French Revolution', *Chambers's Journal* (1875), LII, 331.
Life of William, Earl of Shelbourne. By Lord Edmond Fitzmaurice. 3 vols. (1875–6).

1876

'Taine's Origines de la France Contemporaine', *Saturday* (20 May 1876), XLI, 651.
'Marie Antoinette', *E.R.* (Oct. 1876), CXLIV, 319.
A. Besant (Mrs), *History of the Great French Revolution* (London, 1876).
J. C. Morrison, 'Taine on the Ancien Régime', *Macmillan* (1876), XXXIII, 470.
J. Morley, 'Taine on the Ancien Régime', *Fortnightly* (1876), XXV, 370.
'Taine on the Ancien Régime', *Q.R.* (1876), CXLI, 386.

C. D. Yonge, *Life of Marie Antoinette.* 2 vols. (London, 1876).
J. Morley, 'Robespierre', *Fortnightly* (1876), xx, 167–97, 326–63.

1877

E. B. Bax, 'Marat', *G.M.* (Nov. 1877).
'The Ancien Régime', *C.R.* (1877), xxxi, 538.
J. Morley, *Critical Miscellanies,* 2nd series (London, 1877) [including Robespierre, Condorcet].

1878

W. E. H. Lecky, *A History of England in the Eighteenth Century.* 8 vols. (1878–90).
H. Van Laun, *The French Revolutionary Epoch.* 2 vols. (London, 1878).
E. B. Bax, *Jean Paul Marat* (London, 1879).
'The Revolution and the Ancien Régime', *C.R.* (1879), xxxvi, 432.

1880

E. Rigby, *Letters from France in 1789* (London, 1880).
C. A. Fyffe, *A History of Modern Europe* (London, 1880).

1881

C. C. Jackson (Lady), *The French Court and Society. Reign of Louis XVI and First Empire.* 2 vols. (London and Edinburgh, 1881).
A. Stevens, *Madame de Staël* (London, 1881).

1882

W. H. Jervis, *The Gallican Church and the Revolution* (London, 1882).

1883

Cordery [afterwards Gardiner], B.M., *The French Revolution, 1789–1795* (London, 1883). Reviewed: *R.H.* (1883), xxvi, 483; Masson, *R.Q.H.* (1883), xxxiv, 298; Stephens, *Academy* (1883), xxiii, 21.
F. Harrison, 'Histories of the French Revolution', *North American R.* (1883), cxxxvii, 388 (Reprinted in *The Choice of Books,* 1886).
O. Browning, 'France and England in 1793', *Fortnightly* (Feb. 1883).
'Englishmen in the French Revolution', *Spectator* (1883), lxiii, 308.

1884

H. M. Stephens, 'Les Cahiers de 1789, au B.M.', *R.H.* (1884), xxiv, 468–71; xxv, 226–7.

1885

O. Browning, *The Despatches of Earl Gower . . . June 1790 to August 1792* (Cambridge, 1885). Reviewed: B. M. Gardiner, *E.H.R.* (1886), i, 805; G. Masson *R.Q.H.* (1886), xl, 248.
Dorset (J. F. Duke of), *Relations inédites de la prise de la Bastille* (Paris, 1885).

1886

J. R. Seeley, 'Sorel's Europe and the French Revolution', *E.H.R.* (1886), i, 593.
H. M. Stephens, *A History of the French Revolution,* vol. i. (London, 1886); vol. ii. (1892). Reviewed: A. H. Johnson, *E.H.R.* (1887), ii, 387–9; Acton, *E.H.R.* (1892), xii, 382; Bondois, *R.H.* (1891), xlvii, 381; Dicey, *Nation* (1887), xliv, 166.
J. R. Seeley, 'The House of Bourbon', *E.H.R.* (1886), i, 86.

1887

J. R. Seeley, *Napoleon* (1886). Reviewed: Acton, *E.H.R.* (1887), II, 593.

H. M. Stephens, 'M. de Durler's Account of the Defence of the Tuileries on 10th August', *E.H.R.* (1887), II, 350.

'English Actors in the French Revolution', *E.R.* (1887), CLXVI, 445.

'Sorel's Europe and the French Revolution', *E.R.* (1887), CLXVI, 185.

1888

G. Smith, 'The Centenary of the French Revolution', *National Review* (1888), XI, 729.

H. M. Stephens, 'Lanzac's Mounier', *E.H.R.* (1888), III, 390.

J. Morley, 'A Few Words on French Revolutionary Models', *N.C.* (March 1888), XXIII, 468.

'English Eye-Witnesses of the French Revolution', *E.R.* (1888), CLXVIII, 139.

1889

'Lilly on the French Revolution', *Spectator* (1889), LXIII, 368.

J. G. Alger, *Englishmen in the French Revolution* (London, 1889). Reviewed: Chuquet, *R. Critique* (1894), LXLIV, 390–1; *R.H.* (1894), LV, 219–20; Lambelin, *R.Q.H.* (1894), LVI, 611–12.

F. Harrison, *The Centenary of the French Revolution* (London, 1889).

H. Dunckley, 'Two Political Centenaries', *C.R.* (Jan. 1889), LV, 52.

F. Harrison, 'What the Revolution of 1789 did', *Fortnightly* (1889), N.S. XLV, 757–79.

Wolseley, 'The French Revolution and War, *Fortnightly* (1889), N.S. XLV, 780–91.

'Prisons of Paris during the French Revolution', *Saturday* (1889), LXVIII, 644.

'Side Lights on the Fr. Rev.', *Saturday* (1889), LXIX.

'New Lights on the French Revolution', *Blackwood's* (1889), CXLV, 865.

'Madame de Staël and Gouverneur Morris', *Blackwood's* (1889), CXLV, 865.

F. B. Harrison, *The Contemporary History of the French Revolution from the Annual Register* (London, 1889).

'The Centenary of the French Revolution', *E.R.* (1889), CLXIX, 519.

1890

F. Harrison, *Centenary of the Revolution. Celebrated by English and French Positivists* (London, 1890). Transl. from *Revue Occidentale* by J. H. Bridges.

E. Crawford, 'Mute Witnesses of the Revolution', *C.R.* (1890), LXII, 867.

'Men and Women of the French Revolution', *L.Q.R.* (1890), LXXVI, 1.

B. M. Gardiner, 'Sciout's History of the Civil Constitution', *E.H.R.* (1890), V, 390.

E. B. Bax, *The Story of the French Revolution* (1890).

D. Bingham, *The Marriage of the Bourbons*. 2 vols. (London, 1890).

C. P. Miles, *The Correspondence of W. A. Miles on the French Revolution* (1890). Reviewed: H. M. Stephens, *E.H.R.* (1892), VII, 184, 188; *R.Q.H.* (1891), L, 637; *E.R.* (Apr. 1891), 173.

J. H. MacCarthy, *The French Revolution* (1890–97). Reviewed: J. Moyes, *R.Q.H.* (1891), L, 637–8.

W. H. D. Adams, 'Great Talkers of the French Revolution', *G.M.* (1890), XLVII, 478, 606.

W. Pater, 'Lilly on the French Revolution', *N.C.* (1890), XXVII, 992.

Bibliographies

1891

A. Griffith, *French Revolutionary Generals* (London, 1891).

J. E. Symes, *The French Revolution, 1789–1795* (1891). Reviewed: *Spectator* (1892), LXIX, 821.

1892

W. J. Fitzpatrick, *Secret Service under Pitt* (London, 1892).

E. Armstrong, 'Sorel's Madame de Staël', *E.H.R.* (1892), 384.

H. M. Stephens, *The Principal Speeches of the Statesmen and Orators of the French Revolution 1789–1795*. 2 vols. (Oxford, 1892). Reviewed, Gardiner, *E.H.R.* (1892), VII, 796–7; Chuquet, *R. Critique* (1892), 479; Aulard, *Rév. fr.* (1892), XXIII, 382–4; Dicey, *Nation* (1892), LV, 377.

H. M. Stephens, 'Mirabeau', *E.H.R.* (1892), 587.

H. M. Stephens, 'The Correspondence of Vaudreuil and Miles', *E.H.R.* (1892), 184.

E. Lowell, *The End of the French Revolution* (Boston, 1892). Reviewed: Pierre, *R.Q.H.* (1893), LIII, 597–8; Dicey, *Nation* (1892), LVII, 311.

O. Browning, *The Flight to Varennes and other Essays* (London, 1892).

G. Elliot, *Correspondance de Sir Gilbert Elliot* (1892–99).

Lally (Comte de), 'The French Revolution', *New Review* (1892), VII, 197.

W. E. H. Lecky, *A History of England in the Eighteenth Century* (new ed., 1892).

1893

A. D. Vandam, '1793–1893', *Fortnightly* (1893), LX, 377.

C. E. Mallet, *The French Revolution* (London and New York, 1893).

H. M. Stephens, *Periods of European History, 1789–1815* (London, 1893).

A. T. Mahan, *The Influence of Sea-Power on the French Revolution and Empire, 1793–1812*. 2 vols. (London, 1893). Reviewed: Johnson, *E.H.R.* (1893), VIII, 784; Moyes, *R.Q.H.* (1894), LV, 608; *E.R.* (Jan. 1893), 187; *Saturday* (1893), LXXV, 72.

E. Evans, *The Story of Louis XVII of France* (London, 1893).

H. A. L. Fisher, 'Aulard's Culte de la Raison, and Études et Leçons', *E.H.R.* (1893), 798.

Rothschild (Baron F.), 'The Financial Causes of the French Revolution', *N.C.* (1893), XXXIII, 375, 652.

1894

J. Holland-Rose, *The Revolutionary and Napoleonic Era 1789–1815* (1894). Reviewed: Montague, *E.H.R.* (1896), XI, 175–6; *R.H.* (1895), LVIII, 237.

J. G. Alger, *Glimpses of the French Revolution* (London, 1894). Reviewed: Montague, *E.H.R.* (1895), 393.

F. Harrison, *The Meaning of History* (London, 1894).

H. Holst, *The French Revolution tested by Mirabeau's Career*. 2 vols. (London, 1894). Reviewed, *E.H.R.* (1895), 816; *Nation* (1895), LX, 347.

Montague, 'Thiébault's Memoirs', *E.H.R.* (1895), 807; (1895), 809.

H. S. Wilson, 'Carlyle and Taine on the French Revolution', *G.M.* (1894), LIII, 341.

H. A. L. Fisher, 'La Révolution française en Hollande', *E.H.R.* (1895), 591.

A. F. Pollard, 'Secret Memoirs of the Royal Family of France', *E.H.R.* (1895), 588.

H. M. Stephens, 'Recent Memoirs', *A.H.R.* (1895–6), I, 473–89.

R. Hesdin, *The Journal of a Spy in Paris* (London, 1895). Reviewed: Stephens, *A.H.R.* (1895–6), 755; *E.R.* (Oct. 1896); *E.H.R.* (1896), II, 594–7.

A. Hassal, 'Pasquier's Memoirs', *E.H.R.* (1895), 592.

Bibliographies

1896

F. C. Montague, 'Lanzac's La Domination Française en Belgique 1795', *E.H.R.* (1896).

A. Hassal, 'Brettes's Recueil des Documents', *E.H.R.* (1896), 387.

1897

A. Hassal, *A Handbook of European History, 476–1871* (London, 1897).

E. Dowden, *The French Revolution and English Literature* (London, 1897).

G. B. Adams, *The Growth of the French Nation* (London, 1897). Reviewed: *E.H.R.* (1897), 605.

C. D. Hazen, *Contemporary American Opinion of the French Revolution* (London, 1897). Reviewed: Willert, *E.H.R.* (July 1898), 590; Seignobos, *R.H.* (1899), LXXVII, 163–4.

J. H. Clapham, *A Royalist Spy during the Reign of Terror*, *E.H.R.* (1897), XII, 67–84. Reviewed: Aulard, *Rév. fr.* (1897), XXXII, 121–8.

P. F. Willert, 'Pierre's Deportation Ecclesiastique', *E.H.R.* (1897), 179.

A. F. Pollard, 'Isambert's La vie à Paris', *E.H.R.* (1897), 591.

W. H. Jervis, *History of France* (1898).

B. SMYTH

The study of Smyth is based on (I) Smyth's published writings: *Lectures on Modern History*, 2 vols. (Cambridge, 1840); *Lectures on the French Revolution*, 3 vols. (Cambridge, 1840); 3rd ed. 1848; New ed. 2 vols. (Bohn's Standard Library 1855); *Evidences of Christianity* (1845); *English Lyrics*, 5th ed. (1850), with an 'Autobiographical Sketch'; (II) writings printed for private circulation: *Memoir of Mr Sheridan* (1840); 'Lady Morgan's Lecture' (1840); *A List of Books recommended ... on Modern History* (Cambridge, 1815); ed. of 1823, interleaved with MS. notes; (III) manuscript material: Roscoe Papers. The Correspondence between William Smyth and William Roscoe (1795–1843). The manuscripts are in the Picton Library, Liverpool. Roscoe Papers, letters 4555–4670, 650 are (except for 4656) the letters written by Smyth to Roscoe or to Roscoe's son. 4656 is from Roscoe to Smyth. Letters 999, 2291, 1836, 2157A, 975, 976, 2157 are other letters in which Smyth is mentioned. Thomson Papers. About seventy letters written by Smyth to the composer Thomson (1810–30). They are in the British Museum. Add. MS. 35.263 f. 315, Add. MS. 35.264 ff. 108–324 *passim*, Add. MS. 35.265 ff. 2–218 *passim*. Mallet Papers. Letters from Smyth to Mallet (1812–40). British Museum. Add. MS. 39.809 ff. 1, 14, 18. Extracts from Smyth's *Memoir of Mr Sheridan*, 1849–50. British Museum, Add. MS. 32.568 f. 258. (IV) Other books and articles. Smyth's private papers are lost. It is unlikely that he destroyed them for he regrets that his predecessor Dr Symond destroyed his own papers and we know that an unpublished paper of Smyth was found after his death among his papers and was first published in 1855. I have seen books in the library of Peterhouse which bear manuscript notes in Smyth's writing, but there are, it seems, no papers. The best collection of materials on Smyth is assembled in a file which Miss K. T. B. Butler, late Mistress of Girton, collected over many years and partly used for an article. I am grateful to the Picton Library, Liverpool, for the loan of the letters of Smyth to William Roscoe, and to Miss McMorran, former Vice-Mistress and Librarian of Girton, for going through Miss Butler's papers and letting me have the use of Miss Butler's file on Smyth.

Bibliographies

C. CARLYLE

I. Carlyle's Writings Mainly Used.

The Edinburgh Encyclopaedia. Ed. D. Brewster. 18 vols. (1808–30). The articles by Carlyle are, Lady Mary Wortley Montague, Montaigne, Montesquieu, Montfaucon, Dr Moore, Sir John Moore, Necker, Nelson, Netherlands, Newfoundland, Norfolk, Northamptonshire, Northumberland, Mungo Park, Pitt, Lord Chatham, William Pitt; 'Schiller's Life and Writings', *London Magazine* (1823–4); 'State of German Literature', *E.R.* (Oct. 1827), XLVI; 'Voltaire', *Foreign Review* (Apr. 1829), III; 'Signs of the Times', *E.R.* (June 1829), XLIX; 'Thoughts on History', *Fraser* (Nov. 1830), II; 'Schiller', *Fraser* (Mar. 1831), III; 'Characteristics', *E.R.* (Dec. 1831), LIV; 'Biography', *Fraser* (Apr. 1832), V; 'Boswell's Life of Johnson', *Fraser* (May 1832), V; 'Sir Walter Scott', *Westminster* (Jan. 1833), XXVIII; 'Diderot', *F.Q.R.* (Apr. 1833), XI; 'On History Again', *Fraser* (May 1833), VII; 'Count Cagliostro', *Fraser* (July, Aug. 1833), VIII; 'Mirabeau', *Westminster* (Jan. 1837), XXVI; 'The Diamond Necklace', *Fraser* (Jan., Feb. 1837), XV; 'Parliamentary History of the French Revolution', *Westminster* (Apr. 1837), XXVII; *The French Revolution. A History.* 3 vols. (London, 1837); 'The Sinking of the Vengeur', *Fraser* (July 1839), XX.

II. Some Nineteenth-Century Reactions to Carlyle

J. S. Mill, *Westminster* (July 1837), XXVI, 179; *Fraser* (July 1837), XVI, 85; Thackeray, *The Times* (3 Aug. 1837); *M.R.* (1837), CXLIII, 543; *Athenaeum* (20.5.37); *The Literary Gazette* (27.5.37); *Literary Examiner* (17.9.37); *Monthly Repository* (Sept. 1837); *D.R.* (1838), V, 349; Chasles, *Deux Mondes* (Oct. 1840), XXIV; Mazzini, *Morning Chronicle* (1840), V, 71; [Sewell?], *Q.R.* (1840), LXVI, 446; *L.Q.R.* (Sept. 1840); *E.R.* (1840), LXXI, 411; É. Montégut, *Deux Mondes* (15 Apr. 1849), 270; *B.Q.R.* (1849), X, 1; J. Milsand, *Deux Mondes* (15 June 1850); J. Milsand, *Deux Mondes* (1 Sept. 1850); *D.R.* (1850), XXIX, 169; Lamartine, *Le Civilisateur* (1853); G. H. Lewes, 'Carlyle's Frederick', *Fraser* (1858), LVIII, 631; *E.R.* (1859), CX, 377; *D.R.* (1860), XLVII, 132; L. Stephen, *Saturday Review* (4 June 1864), XVII; *Fraser* (1864), LXIX, 539; *Q.R.* (1865), CXVIII, 225; *N.B.R.* (1865), XLV, 79; L. Stephen, *Fraser* (Dec. 1865); *The Rambler* (Dec. 1868), 429; Valbert, *Deux Mondes* (1 Mar. 1881); *E.R.* (1881), CLIII, 479; *Blackwood's* (1882), CXXXII, 18–35; *Fortnightly* (1883), XXXIX, 622–42; *D.R.* (1885), XCVI, 63; *Q.R.* (1885), CLXI, 142; *L.Q.R.* (1885), 1; *B.Q.R.* (1885), LXXXI, 143–59; *D.R.* (1885), XIII, 63–90; *National Review* (1886–7); A Filon, *Deux Mondes* (1887), 5, 101; O. Browning, *The Flight to Varennes and other Essays* [containing an essay on Carlyle's errors in his story of the flight, read before the R.H.S. in 1886] (London, 1892); F. Harrison, *The Forum* (1894), 546; J. G. Alger, *Paris in 1789–94*, Appendix D, Corrigenda in Carlyle's *French Revolution* (London, 1902).

D. CROKER

A Note on Bibliography

Croker has found few biographers. The account in the *D.N.B.* by T. Martin, who had information from Murray and others, mainly reproduces what is said in the two *Quarterly Review* articles on Croker of 1876 and 1884. A well-known selection from the *Croker Papers* was edited in 1884 and again in 1885 by Jennings. Its materials are of great value, but it does not bring out Croker's life, character or work. The numerous Croker papers surveyed by Jennings were later scattered in many libraries and a great number of them are in the British Museum. The first *Life of Croker*, by M. F. Brightfield, came out in America in 1940 and was reprinted in England in 1951.

Bibliographies

It is based on an extensive collection of facts from published and unpublished materials and is written from the point of view of the student of literature. It is a study of the influence of politics on literature, and it also aims to rehabilitate a Tory who is alleged to have been maligned by Whig historians. But Brightfield has not studied Croker's work as a historian.

There is, in the Cambridge University Library, a bound but incomplete collection called, *Croker's Contributions to the Quarterly Review, 1817–50*, 9 vols. (Lib.6.81.30). It was probably bound for Croker by Murray as was done for other regular contributors. John Barlow, for instance, writes in his *Autobiography* (1847, p. 513) that one evening he found 'a parcel from Mr Murray enclosing 11 thick octavo volumes, neatly bound in red Russia and containing the whole of the articles I had supplied up to that time'. The Guildford bookseller (Thorpe) who had sold the volumes to the University Library, and of whom I made enquiries, was unable to trace the previous owners of this collection. It contains, throughout, manuscript notes of which some are clearly by Croker, and indicate that he was in possession of the volumes. One note, for instance, reads, 'very little of this article on education was by me', and is signed, 'J.W.C.'. Another material correction in an article on Napoleon is obviously in Croker's hand. A footnote in an early article, alleging that Napoleon was really born on 5 February 1768 and not on 15 August 1769, is later corrected by the words, 'see post a correction of this—he was really born 15 August 1769. I suspect now that the attempt to appear a year older was that he might become sooner qualified for office'. See Bounell, i, 299 where it is said that he aspired to be one of the directory 'malgré ses 28 ans'.

I. *A List of Croker's Articles in the Quarterly Review, used for this study.*

'Letters of Madame du Dessand', (May 1811), v, 498–528; 'Faber's Internal State of France', (Aug. 1811), vi, 235–64; 'Intercepted letters of Napoleon', (Jan. 1814), x, 481–94; 'Memoirs of Buonaparte's Deposition', (Oct. 1814), xii, 238–70; 'Buonaparte', (Oct. 1815), xiv, 53–96; 'Chateaubriand's Monarchy', (July 1816), xv, 219–440; 'Buonaparte's Appeal to the British Nation', (Jan. 1817), xvi, 480–511; 'Morellet's Mémoires of the French Revolution', (Oct.1821), xxvi, 229–43; 'Mémoires du Duc de Lauzun', (Jan. 1822), xxvi, 405–9; 'O'Meara's Napoleon in Exile', (Oct. 1822), xxviii, 219–65); 'Madame Campan's Memoirs', (Jan. 1823), xxviii, 449–64; 'Royal Memoirs', (Jan. 1823), xxviii, 464–74; 'Military Events of the late French Revolution', (Jan. 1831), xliv, 226–61; 'Revolutions of 1640 and 1830', (Mar. 1832), xlvii, 261–300; 'Stages of the Reform Revolution', (July 1832), xlvii, 559–89; 'Mémoires de Louis XVIII', (Dec. 1832), xlviii, 455–80; 'La Fayette et la Révolution de 1830', (Dec. 1832), xlviii, 523–42; 'Mémoires de René Le Vasseur', (Apr. 1833), xlix, 29–47; 'Lord John Russell on the Causes of the French Revolution', (Apr. 1833), xlix, 152–74; 'Duchess of Berri in la Vendée', (Oct. 1833), l, 189–205; 'Souvenirs d'un Sexagénaire', (Mar. 1834), li, 1–18; 'Mackintosh's Revolutions of 1688 and 1831', (June 1834), li, 492–535; 'Personal History of Louis Philippe', (Nov. 1834), lii, 519–71; 'Robespierre', (Sept. 1835), liv, 514–79; 'The Tenth of August—Roederer's Chronique', (Feb. 1836), lv, 329–54; 'Private Correspondence of Louis XVIII', (July 1836), lvi, 301–8; 'Versailles', (Jan. 1838), lxi, 1–37; 'Correspondence of the Committee of Public Safety', (Mar. 1841), lxvii, 481–500; 'The Guillotine', (Dec. 1843), lxxiii, 235–80; 'The Revolutionary Tribunals', (Mar. 1844), lxxiii, 375–438; 'Thiers's Histories', (Sept. 1845), lxxvi, 521–83; 'The French Revolution of 1848', (Mar. 1848), lxxxii, 541–93; 'Macaulay's History of England', (Mar. 1849), lxxxiv, 549–630; 'Lamartine's Refutation of the *Q.R.*', (June 1850),

LXXXVII, 276–88; 'Lord Holland's Foreign Reminiscences', (Mar. 1851), LXXXVIII, 492–528; 'Revolutionary Literature', (Sept. 1851), LXXXIX, 491–543; 'The British Museum', (Dec. 1852), XCII, 157–82; 'Louis XVII', (Sept. 1853), XCIII, 387–432.

II. *Other writings by Croker*

'Tallien', *The Times* (6 Apr. 1801); *A sketch of the state of Ireland, past and present* (London, 1808); *A second letter from the king to his people*, 7th ed. [a fictitious letter] (London, 1821); J. Boswell, *The Life of Johnson*, ed. by J. W. Croker (London, 1831); *Speech on the reform question, March 4, 1831* (London, 1831); *Speech on the question that 'The Reform Bill do pass' Sept. 22, 1831* (London, 1831); *Six Speeches delivered in the House of Commons at the close of the debate upon the Reform Bill* (London, 1831); *Resolutions moved by Mr Croker, on the report of the Reform Bill, March 14, 1832* (London, 1832); *History of the Guillotine . . . Revised from the Quarterly Review* (London, 1853); *Essays on the Early Period of the French Revolution* (London, 1857); *Royal Memoirs* [translated, edited and annotated by Croker] (London, 1823); *Correspondence with Lord John Russell on some passages of Moore's Diary* (London, 1854).

III. *Printed works bearing manuscript notes by Croker and kept in the British Museum.*

Robespierre. The *Quarterly Review* article of 1835 with copious manuscript notes by Croker; Deschiens (Avocat à la Cour Royale de Paris), *Collection de Matériaux pour l'Histoire de la Révolution de France*, with manuscript notes by Croker; Riquetti (H. G.) *Count de Mirabeau, Oeuvres oratoires* 2 vols. (1819), with manuscript notes by Croker; L. S. Mercier, *New Picture of Paris* (1800), with manuscript notes by Croker.

IV. *Manuscript letters.*

Croker Papers. vol. II. Letters of John Murray (III) 1831–46 B.M. Add. MS. 41. 125 (231 folios); Croker Papers. vol. III. Letters of John Murray (III) 1847–63 B.M. Add. MS. 41.126 (251 folios); Croker Papers. vol. IV. Letters of John Murray (III) 1853–7 B.M. Add. MS. 41.127 (253 folios); Croker Papers. vol. V. Correspondence with Guizot, 1837–56 B.M. Add. MSS. 41.128; Peel Papers. vol. CCX. General Correspondence, 1841. B.M. Add. MS. 40, 490; vol. CCCXIV (1841), B.M. Add. MS. 40, 494; vol. CCCXXXIII (1842), BM. Add. MS. 50.513.

E. LORD ACTON

A Note on Bibliography

The study of Acton is based mainly on his published writings and on about eighty notebooks, wallets and boxes of manuscript notes in the Cambridge University Library. For the development of Acton's thought, his uncollected articles and reviews, as well as his printed correspondence, have also been used. The study of Acton's historical method made it necessary to go, with the help of his notes, through many Revolutionary works and publications of materials, which were his sources for the study of the Revolution and for the preparation of the lectures. Most of the books Acton used are in the 'Acton Library' in the Cambridge University Library. Since Acton's use of sources has here been examined most systematically in a sample study of his reconstruction of the flight to Varennes, a list of the main literature on the subject, which he used, is also given. Studies of Acton have been consulted.

I. *A List of the Acton Manuscripts used.*

Add. MS. 4607, 4651, 4666, 4860, 4861, 4862, 4863, 4865, 4866, 4867, 4869, 4870, 4871, 4893, 4916, 4917, 4918, 4919, 4820, 4921, 4922, 4923, 4924, 4925, 4926, 4927, 4930,

4931, 4967, 5418, 5419, 5420, 5421, 5422, 5423, 5424, 5425, 5426, 5427, 5428, 5428a, 5429, 5430, 5431, 5432, 5433, 5436, 5437, 5438, 5444, 5452, 5453, 5454, 5455, 5456, 5457, 5461, 5462, 5463, 5464, 5465, 5466, 5467, 5468, 5470, 5471, 5472, 5476, 5478, 5484, 5486, 5487, 5489, 5648, 5649, 5650, 6871, 7472, 7486.

II. *Collected Writings.*

Lectures on Modern History, ed. by J. N. Figgis and R. V. Laurence (London, 1906); *Historical Essays and Studies*, ed. by J. N. Figgis and R. V. Laurence (London, 1906); *The History of Freedom and Other Essays*, ed. by J. N. Figgis and R. V. Laurence (London, 1907); *Lectures on the French Revolution*, ed. by J. N. Figgis and R. V. Laurence (London, 1910); *Essays on Freedom and Power*, selected by G. Himmelfarb (Boston, 1949); *Essays on Church and State*, ed. by D. Woodruff (London, 1952).

III. *Reviews, Articles and Essays.*

1858

'Macknight's Life of Burke', *The Rambler* (April 1858), IX, 268–73.
'Mr Buckle's Thesis and Method', *The Rambler* (July 1858), X, 27–42 (Reprinted in *H.E.S.* 305–23).
'Mr Buckle's Philosophy of History', *The Rambler* (Aug. 1858), X, 88–104 (Reprinted in *H.E.S.* 324–43).
'The Count of Montalembert', *The Rambler* (Dec. 1858), X, 421–28.
'Carlyle's Frederick', *The Rambler* (Dec. 1858), X, 429.

1859

'Schmidt-Weissenfels's Geschichte der Französischen Revolutions Literatur', *The Rambler* (Nov. 1859), II, 104–7.

1862

'Mortimer Ternaux's Histoire de la Terreur', *H.F.R.* (Oct. 1862), I, 547–8.
'Carnot's Memoirs', *H.F.R.* (Oct. 1862), I, 548–50.

1863

'Thiers's Consulate and Empire', *H.F.R.* (Jan. 1863), II, 244–8.
'Sorel's Couvent des Carmes pendant la Terreur', *H.F.R.* (July 1863), III, 311–12.
'May's Constitutional History of England' (Oct. 1863), III, 715–18 (Reprinted in *E.C.S.* 397–400).

1867

'Kingsley's Ancien Régime', *The Chronicle* (13 July 1867), 379–80 (Reprinted in *E.C.S.* 411–13).
'Goldwin Smith's Political History of England', *The Chronicle* (31 Aug. 1867), 543–4 (Reprinted in *E.C.S.* 406–10).
'Guizot on Barante', *The Chronicle* (16 Nov. 1867), 810.

1870

'Katschendorf's Archives Judiciares 1792–1840', *N.B.R.* (Jan. 1870), LI, 565–6.
'Lavollée on Portalis', *N.B.R.* (Jan. 1870), LI, 566–7.
'Feuillet de Conches's Louis XVI, Marie Antoinette et Madame Elisabeth', *N.B.R.* (Apr. 1870), LII, 259–62.
'Mortimer Ternaux's Terreur', *N.B.R.* (Oct. 1870), LIII, 259–61.

'Dauban's Paris in 1794 and 1795', *N.B.R.* (Oct. 1870), LIII, 261–63.
'Budinger's Lafayette', *N.B.R.* (Oct. 1870), LIII, 271.
'Malmesbury's Letters', *N.B.R.* (Oct. 1870), LIII, 273.

1877

The History of Freedom in Antiquity, an address delivered 26 Feb. 1877 (Reprinted in *H.F.E.* 1–29) (Bridgenorth, 1877).
The History of Freedom in Christianity, an address delivered 28 May 1877 (Bridgenorth, 1877) (Reprinted in *H.F.E.* 30–60).

1878

'May's Democracy in Europe', *Q.R.* (Jan. 1878), CXLV, 112–42 (Reprinted in *H.F.E.* 61–100).

1886

'German Schools of History', *E.H.R.* (Jan. 1886), I 1 (Reprinted in *H.E.S.* 344–92).

1887

'Seeley's and Ropes's Lives of Napoleon', *E.H.R.* (July 1887), II, 593–603 (Reprinted in *H.E.S.* 442–58).

1890

'Doellinger's Historical Work', *E.H.R.* (Oct. 1890).

1891

'Talleyrand's Memoirs', *N.C.* (Apr. 1891), XXIX, 670–84.

1892

'Stephens's History of the French Revolution', *E.H.R.* (Apr. 1892), VII, 381–4 (Reprinted in *H.E.S.* 491–5).

1893

'Tocqueville's Souvenirs', *N.C.* (May 1893) XXXIII, 883 (Reprinted in *E.C.S.* 419–20).

1895

'Flint's Historical Philosophy in France', *E.H.R.* (1895), X, 108–13.

A Lecture on the Study of History. Delivered in Cambridge 11 June 1895 (London, 1895).

1896

Scheme for the Cambridge Modern History (Cambridge, 1896).

IV. *Acton's Correspondence.*

Letters to Mary daughter of the Rt Hon. W. E. Gladstone, ed. by Herbert Paul (London, 1904); *Lord Acton and his Circle*, ed. by Abbot Gasquet (London, 1906); *Selections from the Correspondence of the first Lord Acton*, ed. by J. N. Figgis and R. V. Laurence. vol. I (London, 1917).

Bibliographies

V. *A List of the Main Sources used by Acton for his Reconstruction of the Flight to Varennes.*

Procès-Verbal de l'Assemblée des Communes et de l'Assemblée Nationale, imprimé par son ordre, 75 vols. (1789–91); P. V. Malouet, *Collection des opinions*, 3 vols. (Paris, 1791–2); F. C. A. Bouillé (marquis de), *Memoirs relating to the French Revolution*, trs. from the French manuscript (London, 1797) [Acton used the 3rd ed. of 1823 and that of 1859]; A. F. Bertrand de Moleville (marquis de), *Mémoires secrets pour servir à l'histoire de la dernière année du règne de Louis XVI*, 3 vols. (London, Paris, 1797); J. Weber, *Mémoires concernant Marie Antoinette*, 2 vols. (London, 1804–6). [Acton used the editions of 1821 and 1860.]; L. Dutens, *Mémoires d'un Voyageur qui se repose*, 2 vols.; G. H. R. Montgaillard, *Revue Chronologique de l'histoire de France, 1787–1818* (Paris, 1820); J.-S. Bailly, *Mémoires*, 3 vols. (Paris, 1821); Choiseul-Stainville (Le duc Claude A. G. de), *Relation du départ de Louis XVI, le 20 Juin 1791* (Paris, 1822); J. L. H. G. Campan, *Mémoires* (Paris, 1822) [Acton used the edition of 1823 and 1867]; Angoulême (M.-T.C. duchesse d'), *A narrative of the journey of Louis XVI and his family to Varennes* (London, 1823); Ferrières (Charles Elie, Marquis de), *Memoirs*, 2nd ed. 3 vols. (Paris, 1822); *Mémoires sur l'affaire de Varennes* (Paris, 1823) [including the accounts of L. de Bouillé, Raigecourt, Damas, Deslon, Valory]; F. Goguelat, *Mémoire sur les évenéments relatifs au voyage de Louis XVI à Varennes* (Paris, 1823); E. Dumont, *Souvenirs sur Mirabeau et sur les deux premières Assemblées Législatives* (Paris, 1832); Lafayette (M. J. P. R. Y. G. M. Marquis de), *Mémoires, correspondance et manuscrits du général Lafayette*, 6 vols. (1837–8); M. Dumas, *Souvenirs de 1770 à 1836*, 3 vols. (Paris, 1839); F. X. J. Droz, *Histoire de règne de Louis XVI* (Paris, 1839–42); L. Blanc, *Histoire de la Révolution française*, 12 vols. (1847–62); A. M. R. La Marck, *Correspondance entre le Comte de Mirabeau et le Comte de La Marck pendant les années 1789, 1790 et 1791* recueillie, mise en ordre et publiée par Ad. de Bacourt, 3 vols. (Paris, 1851); Cornwallis (C. C. 1st Marquis), *Correspondence*, ed. by C. Ross, 2nd ed. 3 vols. (London, 1859); P. Thiebault, *Souvenirs de vingt ans*, 2 vols. (Paris, 1860); Auckland (W. E. 1st Baron), *The journal and correspondence of William, Lord Auckland*, 4 vols. (London, 1861–2); Feuillet de Conches (F. S. Baron), *Louis XVI, Marie Antoinette, et Madame Elisabeth*, 5 vols. (Paris, 1864–9); Lescure (M. F. A. de), *Correspondance secrète inédite sur Louis XVI, Marie Antoinette*, 2 vols. (1866); Ancelon (E.-A.), *La Verité sur la fuite et l'arrestation de Louis XVI à Varennes* (Paris, 1866); A. R. von Arneth, *Marie Antoinette, Joseph II und Leopold II, ihr Briefwechsel* (Leipzig, 1866); A. Geffroy, *Gustav III et la cour de France*, 2nd ed., 2 vols. (Paris, 1867); P.V. Malouet, *Mémoires publiés par son petit-fils*, 2 vols. (Paris, 1868); J. E. Bimbenet, *Fuite de Louis XVI à Varennes*, 2nd ed. (Paris, 1868); A. Beer, *Joseph II, Leopold II und Kaunitz, ihr Briefwechsel* (Wien, 1873); Sybel (H. von), *Geschichte der Revolutionszeit von 1789 bis 1795* (1853–79); Leopold von Ranke, *Ursprung und Beginn der Revolutionskriege 1791 und 1792* (Leipzig, 1875); G. Avenel, *La Vraie Marie Antoinette d'après la Correspondance secrète* [1876]; Fersen (G. H. A. von), *Le Comte de Fersen et la Cour de France. Extraits... publiés par R. M. de Kinckowström*, 2 vols. (Paris, 1877–8); G. Fishbach, *La Fuite de Louis XVI d'après les archives municipales de Strasbourg* (Paris, 1879); J. Flammermont, *Négociations secrètes de Louis XVI et du baron de Breteuil avec la cour de Berlin, déc. 1791–juillet 1792* (Paris, 1885). *Extrait du Bulletin de la Faculté des lettres de Poitiers*, 1884; Tourzel (L. E., Duchesse de), *Mémoires 1789–95*, 2 vols. (London, 1885); A. Sorel, 'La Fuite de Louis XVI et les essais d'intervention en 1791', *Deux Mondes* (1886), III, 314; A. Sorel, *L'Europe et la Révolution française* (Paris, 1885, etc.); M. Pingaud, *La Correspondance du Vaudreuil avec le comte d'Artois* (1889); M. la Rocheterie, *Histoire de Marie Antoinette*, 2 vols. (Paris, 1890); V. Fournel, *L'Evénement de Varennes* (Paris, 1890); Talleyrand-Périgord, *Mémoires publiés par le Duc de Broglie*, 5 vols. (Paris, 1891–2); E. A. C. Stockmar, *Ludwig XVI und Marie Antoinette auf der Flucht nach Montmédy* (1890); J. Flammermont, *Correspondance Secrète du comte de Mercy-Argenteau avec l'empereur Joseph II et le prince de Kaunitz* (Arneth and Flammermont. Paris, 1889–91); Max Lenz, 'Die Vorbereitung der Flucht Ludwig XVI (Oktober 1790 bis Juni 1791). Ein Beitrag zur Kritik der französischen Memoirenliteratur', *Historische Zeitschrift* (1894), LXXII, LXXIII, p. 1, 213; Thiébault (P. Ch. F. A. H. D.), *Mémoires*, 5 vols. (Paris, 1895–6); La Rochterie (M. de), *Recueil des lettres authentiques de la reine*, 2 vols. (Paris, 1895–6); J. M. Augeard, *Mémoires secrets* (Paris, 1866).

INDEX

Acton, John (Lord), 170, 175, 201, 218, 224, 229, 275, 281; basic ideas, 267–70; on Carlyle, 34, 141, 258; on the causes of the Revolution, 264–70; critic historian, 254–5; development, 259–62; historical method, 257–60; historiography, 256; influenced by Burke, 118, 259–62, 265, 269; on liberty, 248, 260, 270–1; obscurity, 246–7

Adolphus, J., 35, 181, 184, 196; on the causes of the Revolution, 23; *Memoirs*, 4, 21–3

Alison, Sir A., 57, 65, 89, 127, 130, 148, 152, 175, 184, 195, 277; battle against reform, 99–102; Girondins, 167 n.; importance, 153

American Revolution, 9, 24–5, 264

ancien régime, 19, 54, 57, 82, 98, 101, 206, 208

Angoulême, Duchesse d', 66; *Memoirs*, 250

Annual Register, 3–5, 7, 20–1

Anti-Jacobinism, 17, 35, 43, 48; *see* Jacobinism

Aquinas, St. Thomas, 265

archives, opening of, 217–19

aristocracy, 40, 78, 80, 103, 106

Auckland, Lord, 223–4

Aulard, A., 64, 88, 128, 131, 141–2, 223, 228, 238–9, 276

Babeuf plot, 44, 159, 162–3, 172, 208, 234

Bachaumont, F de, 69

Bailly, J-S., 60, 100–101; *Mémoires*, 35, 37

Barante, G. P. B., 119, 123

Barbauld, Mrs A. L., 83

Barère, B., 105, 155, 207, 239

Barnave, A., 44

Barras, P. F., 64

Barruel, Abbé, 35

Bartholomew, massacre of St, 54

Bastille, 7, 82, 140, 263

Bax, E. B., 210, 226–7

Beauchamp, 64, 153

Beaulieu, J. P., 35

Beccaria, C., 264

Belsham, W., 28, 39

Bentham, Jeremy, 14, 41, 50, 76, 149, 159, 230

Bertrand de Moleville, 21, 30–1, 52, 63, 92, 153, 252; Louis XVI, 32

Berville, A. D., 54

Bezenval, 69, 141

Bigland, 24–5, 47

Blackwood's Magazine, 56, 99, 102, 149, 152

Blake, W., 12

Blanc, Louis, 54, 173, 176, 194, 199, 201, 208–9, 212–13, 220, 275

Blennerhasset, Lady, 261

Bouillé, Marquis, de, 28, 52; *Mémoires*, 21, 63–4, 250

Bourbons, 46, 87, 93, 240

Bowen-Graves, F., 226

Bowles, J., 28

Breteuil, Baron de, 33, 249, 253

Brissot de Warville, 5, 60; Burke on, 22; Jacobins, 31; *Letter*, 12; *Memoirs*, 167 n.

Briton, 6

British and Foreign Review, 171

Brougham, Henry (Lord), 30, 36; Carlyle on, 144; Carnot friend of, 47; Don Cevallos, 40; *Historical Sketches*, 171; on Robespierre, 171–2; on St Just, 44; opposed to Southey, 49

Browning, O., 142, 217, 223–5, 229, 245

Brunswick manifesto, 15, 25, 90, 181

Buchez and Roux, 52, 141, 258–9, 209, 276

Buckle, H., T., 216, 232, 240, 259; Acton on, 222

Bunsen: *God in History*, 221

Buonarroti, P-M., 164, 172, 208–9

Burckhardt, J., 262

Burke, Edmund, 3, 158, 242, 278–82; Acton, influence on, 118, 259–62, 265, 269; on Brissot, 22; Buckle on, 222; Carlyle on, 129, compared to, 144–5; Croker on, 177; *Edinburgh Review*, 34, 42; and Fox, 8, 123; historiography, 15–18, 148; Lecky a follower of, 118;

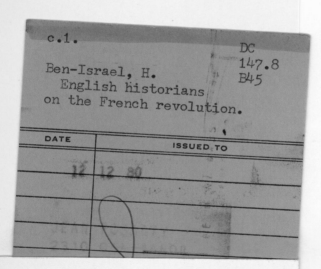